Optimization Techniques for Problem Solving in Uncertainty

Surafel Luleseged Tilahun
University of Zululand, South Africa

Jean Medard T. Ngnotchouye
University of KwaZulu-Natal, South Africa

A volume in the Advances in Data
Mining and Database Management
(ADMDM) Book Series

Published in the United States of America by
    IGI Global
    Engineering Science Reference (an imprint of IGI Global)
    701 E. Chocolate Avenue
    Hershey PA, USA 17033
    Tel: 717-533-8845
    Fax: 717-533-8661
    E-mail: cust@igi-global.com
    Web site: http://www.igi-global.com

Library of Congress Cataloging-in-Publication Data

Names: Tilahun, Surafel Luleseged, 1979- editor. | Ngnotchouye, Jean Medard
    T., 1980- editor.
Title: Optimization techniques for problem solving in uncertainty / Surafel
    Luleseged Tilahun and Jean Medard T. Ngnotchouye, editors.
Description: Hershey : Engineering Science Reference, 2018. | Includes
    bibliographical references and index.
Identifiers: LCCN 2017035104| ISBN 9781522550914 (hardcover) | ISBN
    9781522550921 (ebook)
Subjects: LCSH: Decision making. | Problem solving. | Mathematical
    optimization. | Soft computing. | Uncertainty.
Classification: LCC T57.95 .O68 2018 | DDC 658.4/033--dc23 LC record available at https://lccn.
loc.gov/2017035104

This book is published in the IGI Global book series Advances in Data Mining and Database Management (ADMDM) (ISSN: 2327-1981; eISSN: 2327-199X)

British Cataloguing in Publication Data
A Cataloguing in Publication record for this book is available from the British Library.

For electronic access to this publication, please contact: eresources@igi-global.com.

Advances in Data Mining and Database Management (ADMDM) Book Series

ISSN:2327-1981
EISSN:2327-199X

Editor-in-Chief: David Taniar, Monash University, Australia

MISSION

With the large amounts of information available to organizations in today's digital world, there is a need for continual research surrounding emerging methods and tools for collecting, analyzing, and storing data.

The **Advances in Data Mining & Database Management (ADMDM)** series aims to bring together research in information retrieval, data analysis, data warehousing, and related areas in order to become an ideal resource for those working and studying in these fields. IT professionals, software engineers, academicians and upper-level students will find titles within the ADMDM book series particularly useful for staying up-to-date on emerging research, theories, and applications in the fields of data mining and database management.

COVERAGE

- Data Mining
- Decision Support Systems
- Enterprise Systems
- Quantitative Structure–Activity Relationship
- Cluster Analysis
- Data quality
- Factor Analysis
- Predictive analysis
- Data Analysis
- Profiling Practices

IGI Global is currently accepting manuscripts for publication within this series. To submit a proposal for a volume in this series, please contact our Acquisition Editors at Acquisitions@igi-global.com or visit: http://www.igi-global.com/publish/.

Titles in this Series

701 East Chocolate Avenue, Hershey, PA 17033, USA
Tel: 717-533-8845 x100 • Fax: 717-533-8661
E-Mail: cust@igi-global.com • www.igi-global.com

Table of Contents

Detailed Table of Contents

    Adem Guluma Negewo, Addis Ababa Science and Technology
       University, Ethiopia

This chapter provides a literature review of optimization problems in the context of grey system theory, as proposed by various authors. The chapter explains the binary interactive algorithm approach as a problem-solving method for linear programming and quadratic programming problems with uncertainty and a genetic-algorithm-based approach as a second problem-solving scheme for linear programming, quadratic programming, and general nonlinear programming problems with uncertainty. In the chapter, details on the computation procedures involved for solving the aforementioned optimization problems with uncertainty are presented and results from these two approaches are compared and contrasted. Finally, possible future work area in the subject is suggested.

    Nawaf N. Hamadneh, Saudi Electronic University, Saudi Arabia

The optimization problems are the problem of finding the best parameter values which optimize the objective functions. The optimization methods are divided into two types: deterministic and non-deterministic methods. Metaheuristic algorithms fall in the non-deterministic solution methods. Prey-predator algorithm is one of the well-known metaheuristic algorithms developed for optimization problems. It has gained popularity within a short time and is used in different applications, and it is an easy algorithm to understand and also to implement. The grey systems theory was initialized as uncertain systems. Each grey system is described with grey numbers, grey equations, and grey matrices. A grey number has uncertain value, but there is an interval or a general set of numbers, within that the value lies is known. In this chapter, the author will review and show that grey system modeling is very useful to use with prey-predator algorithm. The benchmark functions, grey linear programming, and grey model GM (1,1) are used as examples of grey system.

Chapter 3

This chapter considers the extension of the calculus of variations to the optimization of a class of fuzzy systems where the uncertainty of variables and parameters is represented by symmetrical triangular membership functions. The concept of fuzzy dual numbers is introduced, and the consideration of the necessary differentiability conditions for functions of dual variables leads to the definition of fuzzy dual functions. It is shown that when this formalism is adopted to represent performance indexes for uncertain optimization problems, the calculus of variations can be used to establish necessary optimality conditions as an extension to this case of the Euler-Lagrange equation. Then the chapter discusses the propagation of uncertainty when the fuzzy dual formalism is adopted for the state representation of a time continuous system. This leads to the formulation of a fuzzy dual optimization problem for which necessary optimality conditions, corresponding to an extension of Pontryagine's optimality principle, are established.

Chapter 4

The aim of this chapter is to study fully fuzzy linear fractional programming (FFLFP) problems where all coefficients of the decision variables and parameters are characterized by triangular fuzzy numbers. To deal with this, the authors have first to transform FFLFP problems to fuzzy linear programming (FLP) problems by using Charnes and Cooper method and then use signed distance ranking to convert fuzzy linear programming (FLP) problems to crisp linear programming (LP) problems. The proposed method is solved by using the simplex method to find the optimal solution of the problem. The authors have studied sensitivity analysis to determine changes in the optimal solution of the fully fuzzy linear fractional programming (FFLFP) problems resulting from changes in the parameters. To demonstrate the proposed method, one numerical example is solved.

This chapter considers the use of fuzzy dual numbers to model and solve through dynamic programming process mathematical programming problems where uncertainty is present in the parameters of the objective function or of the associated constraints. It is only supposed that the values of the uncertain parameters remain in known real intervals and can be modelled with fuzzy dual numbers. The interest of adopting the fuzzy dual formalism to implement the sequential decision-making process of dynamic programming is discussed and compared with early fuzzy dynamic programming. Here, the comparison between two alternatives is made considering not only the cumulative performance but also the cumulative risk associated with previous steps in the dynamic process, displaying the traceability of the solution under construction as it is effectively the case with the classical deterministic dynamic programming process. The proposed approach is illustrated in the case of a long-term airport investment planning problem.

In this chapter, the authors give a brief introduction to important concepts of RO paradigm. The remainder of the chapter is organized as follows: Section 2 gives an introduction on optimization under uncertainty, and presents brief comparisons among the well-known sub-fields of optimization under uncertainty such as RO, stochastic programming (SP), and fuzzy optimization (FO). Section 3 presents important methodologies of RO paradigm. Section 4 gives insights about alternative ways of choosing the uncertainty set. Section 5 shows alternative methods of assessing the quality of a robust solution and presents miscellaneous topics. Finally, Section 6 summarizes conclusions and gives future research directions.

In a vehicle routing problem (VRP) with time windows, the start of service needs to take place within the customer time window. Due to uncertainty on travel times, vehicles might arrive late at a customer's site. A VRP is mostly solved to minimize a total cost criterion (travel time, travel distance, fixed and variable vehicle costs). But the dispatcher might also take into consideration the risk of non-conformance with the service agreement to start service within the time window. Therefore, a measure of risk, called "vulnerability of a solution," is developed to serve as a second criterion. This chapter develops such a measure based on a distance metric and investigates its strengths and weaknesses.

Chapter 8

The objective of this analysis is to determine optimum parameters for maximum performance and minimum emission for biodiesel-fueled diesel engine. The experiments were designed using Taguchi L25 orthogonal array. Five parameters—fuel blend, load, speed, injection timing, and injection pressure—each with five levels were selected. Cylinder pressure, exhaust temperature, brake thermal efficiency, brake specific fuel consumption, carbon monoxide, unburned hydrocarbons, nitric oxide, and smoke were response parameters. Optimum combination of parameters was determined by grey relational analysis. The confirmatory test was performed at optimum combination. The grey relational grade and signal-to-noise ratio was determined. The contribution of individual parameter was determined by ANOVA analysis. Optimum performance was obtained at 80% load and 1900 rpm speed with B50 fuel at injection timing of 15.50 BTDC with 225 bar injection pressure. Finally, grey relational grade was improved by 3.7%.

Texture feature is a decisive factor in pattern classification problems because texture features are not deduced from the intensity of current pixel but from the grey level intensity variations of current pixel with its neighbors. In this chapter, a new texture model called multivariate binary threshold pattern (MBTP) has been proposed with five discrete levels such as -9, -1, 0, 1, and 9 characterizing the grey level intensity variations of the center pixel with its neighbors in the local neighborhood of each band in a multispectral image. Texture-based classification has been performed with the proposed model using fuzzy k-nearest neighbor (fuzzy k-NN) algorithm on IRS-P6, LISS-IV data, and the results have been evaluated based on confusion matrix, classification accuracy, and Kappa statistics. From the experiments, it is found that the proposed model outperforms other chosen existing texture models.

Dynamic environment imposes such conditions that make it necessary for companies to consider sources of uncertainty in designing core business processes and optimizing supply chain operations. Efficient management of a supply system requires an integrated approach towards various operational functions and related source of uncertainties. Uncertain conditions in supply network design problem such as market demands, delivery time, and facility capacity are considered and incorporated by many studies at the mathematical programming formulations as well. In this chapter, extensive review of existing SCND literature, brief overview and classification on uncertainty sources, useful strategies to deal uncertainties, model formulation with uncertain/stochastic parameters, efficient developed solution methodologies, and improvement adjustment mechanisms are discussed. Lastly, some directions for further research in this area are suggested.

Preface

Optimization refers to the analysis and searching for a solution for problems in which a single choice must be made from a range of feasible ones in order to optimize an objective function. Feasible choices are modeled as the elements of some set—the feasible set. The goal is to find a "best" choice (not necessarily unique), or at least a "better" one than might readily be detected. Choices are compared according to the values they give to the objective function in the problem. The goal may be maximization or minimization of such values. Problems of optimization under uncertainty are characterized by the necessity of making decisions without knowing what their full effects will be, which refers to solving problems with incomplete information. Such problems appear in many areas of application and it present many interesting challenges both conceptually and in computation. In fuzzy theory, the uncertainties in a problem have to be represented in such a manner that their effects on present decision-making can properly be taken into account. This is an interesting and challenging subject for which this book aims to contribute. There are a number of ways to deal with uncertainty including stochastic, fuzzy and grey theory. In stochastic modeling, the uncertain elements in a problem can often be modeled as random variables with a given probability density function to which the theory of probability can be applied. In deterministic modeling, the optimization problem is formulated in a way that uncertainty plays no role. Fuzzy theory is another concept widely used in this context. The uncertain quantities can be formulated as an interval with appropriate membership function. In some case the level of available information may not be enough to construct either the probability density function or the membership function. In such cases, a grey or interval model can be used. Grey optimization is then optimization under very limited available information.

This book deals with recent advances in the domain of decision making under uncertainty including survey papers, solution methods of optimization problems under uncertainty along with some applications.

The first two chapters are focused on grey optimization. In the first chapter the author present a comprehensive survey on recent advances in grey optimization whereas in the second chapter a metaheuristic based algorithm for grey optimization is proposed. The approach uses a uniform distribution for the grey numbers and randomly generates values in each of the iterations while using the prey predator algorithm.

The next three chapters are devoted to recent advances on fuzzy optimization. Chapter 3 defines optimal control problems for fuzzy dual numbers and solves them using the fuzzy-dual optimality condition and the fuzzy dual Hamilton-Jacobi-Bellman equation. The fourth chapter is a study of fuzzy linear fractional programming by sensitivity analysis. The fuzzy triangular numbers are used to define a linear programming problem which is solved using a fuzzy simplex algorithm. The changes in the solution of the problem are investigated when the constraints are changed or a new variable is added. The fifth chapter is concerned with some advances in fuzzy dynamic programming. The authors define fuzzy numbers as in Chapter 3 and the dynamic programming problem is defined as a natural generalization of dynamic programing for real numbers. The problem is solved using the principle of optimality and it is applied for the solution of an airport planning case study.

Chapter 6 discusses basic advances and applications of robust optimization. Basic similarity and differences between stochastic and robust optimization is highlighted along with recent advances in the field of robust optimization.

The last four chapters focus on applications involving uncertainty. The seventh chapter discusses a vehicle routing problem. The problem deals with finding optimum routes for multiple fleets to serve multiple customers under uncertain travel times. The authors of Chapter 8 propose a way to determine the optimum parameters for maximum performance and minimum emission for biodiesel fueled diesel engine. They used the robust method, called Taguchi methods, along with grey relation analysis for this purpose. Chapter 9 discusses land cover classification. The problem is identifying the various land cover types including land, vegetation, and water. Multivariate Binary Threshold Pattern along with fuzzy k-Nearest Neighbor classifier is used in the chapter. The last chapter is devoted to the supply chain network design optimization under different uncertainty sources. The authors surveyed different models along with the corresponding solution approaches.

The results included in the book chapter reflect some recent trend in research and outline new ideas for future studies of optimization problems with uncertainty.

Surafel Luleseged Tilahun
Jean Medard T. Ngnotchouye

Acknowledgment

We would like to express our sincere gratitude to the authors who have submitted papers for consideration in this book. We also thank the reviewers of these papers for their thorough and timely comments which were important for us when making editorial decisions. May thanks are also given to the publishing house IGI for their great support and help in making this book chapter possible. We hope that this book will be of help for researchers working in optimization with uncertainty and that it will provide some motivation to stimulate future research in this fascinating area of research.

Surafel Luleseged Tilahun
Jean Medard T. Ngnotchouye

Chapter 1
A Survey on Grey Optimization

Adem Guluma Negewo
Addis Ababa Science and Technology University, Ethiopia

ABSTRACT

This chapter provides a literature review of optimization problems in the context of grey system theory, as proposed by various authors. The chapter explains the binary interactive algorithm approach as a problem-solving method for linear programming and quadratic programming problems with uncertainty and a genetic-algorithm-based approach as a second problem-solving scheme for linear programming, quadratic programming, and general nonlinear programming problems with uncertainty. In the chapter, details on the computation procedures involved for solving the aforementioned optimization problems with uncertainty are presented and results from these two approaches are compared and contrasted. Finally, possible future work area in the subject is suggested.

INTRODUCTION

In traditional deterministic optimization problems, it is assumed that all the relevant data to the problem are known. However, this assumption is not always realistic. In many practical situations, it is required to deal with optimization problems in which the relevant data to the problem are not fully available and decisions have to be made in the face of uncertainty.

Several methods for dealing with uncertainty in optimization problems have been thoroughly studied so far. These methods mainly relate to stochastic optimization and fuzzy optimization.

Stochastic optimization methods are based on probability theory; and they are useful to deal with the uncertainty in input parameters when their probability distributions are known. The major problems of these methods are the difficulty in

DOI: 10.4018/978-1-5225-5091-4.ch001

the availability of probability distributions of model parameters and the computational difficulty in implementation, since the methods may lead to large or complicated intermediate models (Huang, 1994).

Fuzzy optimization methods, derived from fuzzy set theory, contain two major categories: fuzzy possibilistic programming (FPP) and fuzzy flexible programming (FFP) (Inuiguchi et. al. 1990 as cited in Huang, 1994). In FPP methods, fuzzy parameters are introduced into the modelling frameworks, which represent the fuzzy regions where the parameters possibly lay (Zadeh 1978 as cited in Huang, 1994). The major problems with the FPP methods are the difficulty in obtaining the possibility information and the computational difficulty when applied to practical problems. In FFP methods, the flexibilities in the constraints and fuzziness in the system objective are expressed as fuzzy sets with their membership grades corresponding to the degrees of satisfaction of the constraints/objective (Tanaka et al. 1974; Zimmermann 1985 as cited in Huang, 1994). The major problem with the FFP methods is that only the stipulation uncertainties are reflected. In addition, the methods are indirect approaches containing intermediate control parameters which may be difficult to determine by certain criteria (Inuiguchi et. al. 1990 as cited in Huang, 1994).

The concept of grey systems and grey decisions are introduced into the existing optimization approaches and grey optimization models (Huang et al. 1992) are developed in order to address the aforementioned limitations.

This chapter presents a literature review of the most significant results on grey optimization. In order to facilitate the discussion of these methods, the chapter is structured into different sections. A brief introduction to the grey system theory is provided first. In this introduction, some useful terminologies and basic concepts of the system are highlighted. Next, optimization problems in the context of grey system theory are discussed. In this section, various formulations of optimization problems (namely grey linear programming, grey quadratic programming and grey nonlinear programming problems) together with methods of solutions, previously suggested, to solve these problems are reviewed. A discussion and summary of the methods presented is provided next. Potential future areas of research are also indicated in this section. In the final section, some concluding remarks about the grey optimization techniques discussed in the chapter are provided.

Basic Concepts in Grey System Theory

In this section, some useful terminologies related to grey system theory are introduced. The section also introduces the concept of grey decisions.

Definition 1: Let x denote a closed and bounded set of real numbers. A grey number $x^{\pm}$ is defined as an interval with known upper and lower bounds but unknown distribution information for x (Huang et al. 1992):

$$x^{\pm} = [x^- \ x^+] = \{t \in x : x^- \leq t \leq x^+\}$$

where x^- and x^+ are the lower and upper bounds of $x^{\pm}$, respectively. When $x^- = x^+$, $x^{\pm}$ becomes a deterministic number, and $x^{\pm} = x^- = x^+$.

Definition 2: A grey system is defined as a system containing information presented as grey numbers (Deng 1985; Huang et al. 1992).

Definition 3: A grey decision is defined as a decision made within a grey system (Deng 1985 and 1986; Huang et al. 1992; Huang and Moore 1993).

Definition 4: Let $\Re^{\pm}$ denote a set of grey numbers. A grey vector $x^{\pm}$ is a tuple of grey numbers, and a grey matrix $A^{\pm}$ is a matrix whose elements are grey numbers (Huang et al. 1992 and 1993e):

$$x^{\pm} = \{x_i^{\pm} = [x_i^- \ x_i^+] : \forall i\}, x^{\pm} \in (\Re^{\pm})^{1 \times n}$$

$$A^{\pm} = \{a_{ij}^{\pm} = [a_{ij}^- \ a_{ij}^+] : \forall i, j\}, A^{\pm} \in (\Re^{\pm})^{m \times n}$$

The operations for grey vectors and matrices are defined to be analogous to those for real vectors and matrices.

Definition 5: Let $* \in \{+, -, \times, \div\}$ be a binary operation on grey numbers. Then for grey numbers $x^{\pm}$ and $y^{\pm}$, $*$ is defined as (Ishibuchi and Tanaka 1990):

$$x^{\pm} * y^{\pm} = \left[\min\{x * y\}, \max\{x * y\}\right], x^- \leq x \leq x^+, y^- \leq y \leq y^+$$

Thus,

$$x^{\pm} + y^{\pm} = [x^- + y^-, x^+ + y^+]$$

$$x^{\pm} - y^{\pm} = [x^- - y^+, x^+ - y^-]$$

3

$$x^{\pm} \times y^{\pm} = \left[\min\left\{x \times y\right\}, \max\left\{x \times y\right\}\right]$$

$$x^{\pm} \div y^{\pm} = \left[\min\left\{x \div y\right\}, \max\left\{x \div y\right\}\right], y^{\pm} \neq 0$$

Definition 6: For a grey number $x^{\pm}$, we have,

$$x^{\pm} \geq 0 \ iff \ x^{-} \geq 0 \ and \ x^{+} \geq 0$$

$$x^{\pm} \leq 0 \ iff \ x^{-} \leq 0 \ and \ x^{+} \leq 0$$

Definition 7: For grey vectors and matrices

$$x^{\pm} \geq 0 \ iff \ x_{ij}^{\pm} \geq 0 \forall i, j, x^{\pm} \in (\Re^{\pm})^{m \times n}, m \geq 1$$

$$x^{\pm} \leq 0 \ iff \ x_{ij}^{\pm} \leq 0 \forall i, j, x^{\pm} \in (\Re^{\pm})^{m \times n}, m \geq 1$$

Definition 8: For grey numbers $x^{\pm} = [x^{-}x^{+}]$ and $y^{\pm} = [y^{-}y^{+}]$:

$$x^{\pm} \leq y^{\pm} \ iff \ x^{-} \leq y^{-} \ and \ x^{+} \leq y^{+}$$

$$x^{\pm} < y^{\pm} \ iff \ x^{\pm} \leq y^{\pm} \ and \ x^{+} \neq y^{+}$$

Definition 9: The whitened value of a grey number $x^{\pm}$ is defined as a deterministic number, $x_{v}^{\pm}$, whose value lies between the upper and lower bound of $x^{\pm}$, i.e. $x^{-} \leq x_{v}^{\pm} \leq x^{+}$.

Definition 10: The whitened mid-value, $x_{m}^{\pm}$, and width, $x_{w}^{\pm}$, of a grey number $x^{\pm} = [x^{-}x^{+}]$ are defined as (Huang et al. 1992; Huang and Moore 1993):

$$x_{m}^{\pm} = \frac{1}{2}\left(x^{-} + x^{+}\right)$$

$$x_{w}^{\pm} = x^{+} - x^{-}$$

4

Definition 11: The grey degree of a grey number $x^{\pm}$, denoted by $Gd\left(x^{\pm}\right)$, is defined and is expressed in percentage as follows (Huang et al. 1992; Huang and Moore 1993):

$$Gd\left(x^{\pm}\right) = x_w^{\pm}\Big/x_m^{\pm} \times 100\% .$$

Definition 12: The sign of a grey number $x^{\pm}$, denoted by $sign\left(x^{\pm}\right)$, is defined as

$$sign\left(x^{\pm}\right) = \begin{cases} -1, & if \ x^{\pm} < 0 \\ 1, & if \ x^{\pm} \geq 0 \end{cases}$$

Definition 13: The grey absolute value of a grey number $x^{\pm}$, denoted by $\left|x^{\pm}\right|$, is defined as:

$$\left|x^{\pm}\right| = \begin{cases} x^{\pm} & if \ x^{\pm} \geq 0 \\ -x^{\pm} & if \ x^{\pm} < 0 \end{cases}$$

$$\text{Thus, } \left|x^{-}\right| = \begin{cases} x^{-} & if \ x^{\pm} \geq 0 \\ -x^{+} & if \ x^{\pm} < 0 \end{cases} \text{ and } \left|x^{+}\right| = \begin{cases} x^{+} & if \ x^{\pm} \geq 0 \\ -x^{-} & if \ x^{\pm} < 0 \end{cases}.$$

Grey Optimization

Grey optimization or grey mathematical programming (GMP)(Huang et al1992) of grey systems theory (Deng, 1982) consists of methods which incorporate uncertainties in model parameters directly into an optimization framework. The grey uncertainty of model parameters can be addressed by representing them as grey numbers, instead of deterministic real numbers. Thus, the optimization problem of a grey system can be written in the following general form

Max $f^{\pm}\left(x^{\pm}\right)$

subject to: $g_i^{\pm}\left(x^{\pm}\right) \leq b_i^{\pm}, \forall i$

$x^{\pm} \geq 0$

where $f^{\pm}\left(x^{\pm}\right)$ is a grey objective function, $x^{\pm}$ is a grey decision variable vector and inequalities $g_i^{\pm}\left(x^{\pm}\right) \leq b_i^{\pm}, \forall i$ are grey constraints.

The GMP improves upon existing optimization methods by allowing uncertain information to be directly communicated into the optimization processes and solutions such that decision alternatives can be generated through adjusting the grey decision variables with in their stable solution intervals and making relevant tradeoffs between different system objectives/restrictions according to projected applicable conditions (Huang et al. 1992).

GREY LINEAR PROGRAMMING

Model Formulation

A grey linear programming model in standard form can be defined as (Huang et al. 1992):

$$\text{Max } f^{\pm} = \sum_{j=1}^{n} c_j^{\pm} x_j^{\pm}$$

$$\text{s.t. } \sum_{j=1}^{n} a_{ij}^{\pm} x_j^{\pm} \leq b_i^{\pm}, i = 1, 2, 3, \cdots, m \tag{1}$$

$$x_j^{\pm} \geq 0, j = 1, 2, 3, \cdots, n$$

where $a_{ij}^{\pm}, b_i^{\pm}$ and $c_j^{\pm}$ are grey parameters and $x_j^{\pm}$ is a grey decision variable.

The parameters $a_{ij}^{\pm}, b_i^{\pm}$ and $c_j^{\pm}$ consist of the following grey numbers:

$$a_{ij}^{\pm} = [a_{ij}^{-}, a_{ij}^{+}], i = 1, 2, 3, \cdots, m \text{ and } j = 1, 2, 3, \cdots, n$$

$$b_i^{\pm} = [b_i^{-}, b_i^{+}], i = 1, 2, 3, \cdots, m$$

$$c_j^{\pm} = [c_j^{-}, c_j^{+}], j = 1, 2, 3, \cdots, n$$

The use of the grey parameters $a_{ij}^{\pm}$, $b_i^{\pm}$ and $c_j^{\pm}$ in the model results in grey objectivefunction $f^{\pm}$ and grey decision variables $x_j^{\pm} = [\,x_j^-, x_j^+\,], j = 1, 2, 3, \cdots, n$.

Since the objective function and the constraints involve grey parameters, the GLP model can have optimal grey solutions which can be expressed as follows (Huang et al. 1992):

$$\left(x_j^{\pm}\right)_{opt} = \left[\left(x_j^-\right)_{opt}, \left(x_j^+\right)_{opt}\right], \left(x_j^+\right)_{opt} \geq \left(x_j^-\right)_{opt}, j = 1, 2, 3, \cdots, n$$

$$f_{opt}^{\pm} = \left[f_{opt}^-, f_{opt}^+\right], f_{opt}^+ \geq f_{opt}^-$$

SOLUTION METHODS

Binary Interactive Algorithm Approach

Huang et al. (1992) proposed a solution technique for solving grey linear programming models based on interactive relationships between model parameters and decision variables in the objective function and in the constraints. The method assumes that an optimal solution to the problem exists. According to Huang et al.(1992), the grey linear programming model can be converted into two whitened (deterministic) sub-models which can then be solved using the standard linear optimization techniques. The two sub-models correspond to the upper and lower bounds of the grey objective-function. The procedure of the method is outlined below.

Step 1: Group the coefficients $c_j^{\pm}$ based on their signs

If k_1 of the n grey coefficients $c_j^{\pm}, j = 1, 2, 3, \cdots, n$ in the objective function are positive and the remaining k_2 coefficients are negative, it can be assumed that the former k_1 coefficients are positive and the latter k_2 are negative.

i.e. $c_j^{\pm} \geq 0 \left(j = 1, 2, 3, \cdots, k_1\right)$

and

$c_j^{\pm} < 0 \left(j = k_1 + 1, k_1 + 2, k_1 + 3, \cdots, n\right),$

where $k_1 + k_2 = n$.

Step 2: Define the upper and lower bounds f^+ and f^- respectively of the objective function $f^\pm$

    If

$$c_j^\pm \geq 0 \left(j = 1, 2, 3, \cdots, k_1\right)$$

and

$$c_j^\pm < 0 \left(j = k_1 + 1, k_1 + 2, k_1 + 3, \cdots, n\right),$$

where $k_1 + k_2 = n$., then the upper and lower bounds of the objective function $f^\pm$ can be formulated as:

$$
\begin{aligned}
f^+ &= \sum_{j=1}^{k_1}\left[c_j^+ x_j^+\right] + \sum_{j=k_1+1}^{n}\left[c_j^+ x_j^-\right] \\
f^- &= \sum_{j=1}^{k_1}\left[c_j^- x_j^-\right] + \sum_{j=k_1+1}^{n}\left[c_j^- x_j^+\right]
\end{aligned}
\tag{2}
$$

Step 3: Define the relationships between decision variables and coefficients of the constraints

Step 4: From steps 2 and 3, formulate constraints corresponding to upper and lower f^+ and f^- respectively of objective function $f^\pm$

    The relevant constraints corresponding f^+ to f^- of step two and can be given as

$$\sum_{j=1}^{k_1}\left[\left|a_{ij}^-\right| sign\left(a_{ij}^-\right) x_j^+\right] + \sum_{j=k_1+1}^{n}\left[\left|a_{ij}^+\right| sign\left(a_{ij}^+\right) x_j^-\right] \leq b_i^\pm, \forall i$$

and

$$\sum_{j=1}^{k_1}\left[\left|a_{ij}^+\right|sign\left(a_{ij}^+\right)x_j^-\right]+\sum_{j=k_1+1}^{n}\left[\left|a_{ij}^-\right|sign\left(a_{ij}^-\right)x_j^+\right]\leq b_i^\pm,\forall i$$

respectively.

When $b_i^\pm = b_i$ is a deterministic number, these constraints will take the following form:

$$\sum_{j=1}^{k_1}\left[\left|a_{ij}^-\right|sign\left(a_{ij}^-\right)x_j^+\right]+\sum_{j=k_1+1}^{n}\left[\left|a_{ij}^+\right|sign\left(a_{ij}^+\right)x_j^-\right]\leq b_i,\forall i$$

$$\sum_{j=1}^{k_1}\left[\left|a_{ij}^+\right|sign\left(a_{ij}^+\right)x_j^-\right]+\sum_{j=k_1+1}^{n}\left[\left|a_{ij}^-\right|sign\left(a_{ij}^-\right)x_j^+\right]\leq b_i,\forall i$$

Step 5: Based on Steps 2-4, formulate two whitened sub-models corresponding to the upper and lower bounds of the objective-function value.

When the problem is to maximize the objective function, the whitened sub-model corresponding to the upper bound of the objective function value should be formulated and solved first. The whitened sub-model corresponding to the lower bound of the objective function value should be formulated based on the upper bound solution obtained for the first sub-model.

For a maximization problem the whitened sub-model corresponding to f^+ (assuming that $b_i^\pm = b_i$ is a deterministic number) is:

$$\text{Max } f^+ = \sum_{j=1}^{k_1}\left[c_j^+ x_j^+\right]+\sum_{j=k_1+1}^{n}\left[c_j^+ x_j^-\right]$$

$$\text{s.t. } \sum_{j=1}^{k_1}\left[\left|a_{ij}^-\right|sign\left(a_{ij}^-\right)x_j^+\right]+\sum_{j=k_1+1}^{n}\left[\left|a_{ij}^+\right|sign\left(a_{ij}^+\right)x_j^-\right]\leq b_i,\forall i \tag{3}$$

$$x_j^\pm \geq 0 \forall j$$

The grey decision variables $\left(x_j^+\right)_{opt}$ $j = 1, 2, \cdots, k_1$ and

$\left(x_j^-\right)_{opt}$, $j = k_1+1, k_1+2, \cdots, n$

can be obtained from the whitened sub-model corresponding to f^+; and

$$\left(x_j^-\right)_{opt} j = 1, 2, \cdots, k_1 \text{ and}$$

$$\left(x_j^+\right)_{opt}, j = k_1 + 1, k_1 + 2, \cdots, n$$

can be obtained from the sub-model corresponding to f^-.

The whitened sub-model corresponding to f^- (assuming that $b_i^\pm = b_i$ is a deterministic number) is:

$$\text{Max } f^- = \sum_{j=1}^{k_1} \left[c_j^- x_j^-\right] + \sum_{j=k_1+1}^{n} \left[c_j^- x_j^+\right]$$

$$\text{s.t. } \sum_{j=1}^{k_1} \left[\left|a_{ij}^+\right| sign\left(a_{ij}^+\right) x_j^-\right] + \sum_{j=k_1+1}^{n} \left[\left|a_{ij}^-\right| sign\left(a_{ij}^-\right) x_j^+\right] \leq b_i, \forall i \qquad (4)$$

$$x_j^+ \geq \left(x_j^-\right)_{opt}, j = k_1 + 1, k_1 + 2, \cdots, n$$

$$x_j^- \leq \left(x_j^+\right)_{opt} j = 1, 2, \cdots, k_1$$

$$x_j^\pm \geq 0 \forall j.$$

The whitened sub-models given above are deterministic LP models. Therefore,

$$\left(f^+\right)_{opt}, \left(x_j^+\right)_{opt} j = 1, 2, \cdots, k_1$$

and

$$\left(x_j^-\right)_{opt}, j = k_1 + 1, k_1 + 2, \cdots, n$$

can be solved from the first model; and

$$\left(f^-\right)_{opt}, \left(x_j^+\right)_{opt}, j = k_1 + 1, k_1 + 2, \cdots, n$$

and $\left(x_j^-\right)_{opt}$ $j = 1, 2, \cdots, k_1$ can be solved from the second sub-model. Thus, the solutions of the GLP model become:

$$f_{opt}^{\pm} = \left[f_{opt}^-, \; f_{opt}^+\right], f_{opt}^+ \geq f_{opt}^-$$

$$\left(x_j^{\pm}\right)_{opt} = \left[\left(x_j^-\right)_{opt}, \left(x_j^+\right)_{opt}\right], \left(x_j^+\right)_{opt} \geq \left(x_j^-\right)_{opt}, j = 1, 2, 3, \cdots, n$$

When the problem is to minimize the objective function, the whitened sub-model corresponding to the lower bound of the objective function value should be formulated and solved first.

Step 6: When the constraints' right-hand side constants are also grey numbers, determine the relationships between decision variables and coefficients of the constraints to formulate the relevant constraints

When $b_i^{\pm}$ is also a grey number, various possible relationships can be analyzed to establish the constraints corresponding to f^+ and f^- (detailed discussion of this is given in Huang, 1994).

Huang et al. (1994) further provided detailed explanations and examples to illustrate the modeling and the solution processes. The modelling approach is also applied to a hypothetical problem of waste flow allocation planning within a municipal solid waste management system.

Generally, the interactive binary algorithm proposed by Huang et al. (1992) can be used for solving grey linear programming problems reliably and relatively quickly for many real-life decision-making scenarios in the engineering field. However, this binary algorithm has some limitations. One of them, for example, is that the method does not include the situation where the upper and lower bounds of the grey coefficients have different signs. In order to address this limitation, Chan et al. (2013) proposed a genetic-algorithms-based approach for linear optimization problems with uncertainty.

Genetic Algorithms (GA) Based Approach

The genetic-algorithms-based approach for solving the grey linear programming problem under consideration also assumes that an optimal solution exists; and it also consists of converting the grey linear programming model into two whitened sub-models which can be easily solved using standard linear optimization techniques. The method is outlined as follows.

Step 1: Find an initial suboptimal decision variable x_j^s

A suboptimal solution f^s and the corresponding decision variable x_j^s can be obtained from the following problem, which is a problem transformed from the original GLP problem:

$$\text{Max } f^s = \sum_{j=1}^{n} c_j^r x_j^s$$

$$\text{s.t. } \sum_{j=1}^{n} a_{ij}^r x_j^s \leq b_i^r \text{ for } i = 1, 2, 3, \cdots, m \tag{5}$$

$$x_j^s \geq 0 \text{ for } j = 1, 2, 3, \cdots, n.$$

where a_{ij}^r, b_i^r, c_j^r are random numbers which satisfy the continuous uniform distribution in the intervals $[a_{ij}^-, a_{ij}^+], [b_i^-, b_i^+]$ and $[c_j^-, c_j^+]$ respectively.

The problem is solved by the GA linear program solving engine of GASGOT, which uses the objective function in Eq. (5) as the positive term of the fitness function and the constraints of Eq. (1) as the negative punishment terms (Chan et al., 2013).

Step 2: Whiten the grey coefficients $a_{ij}^{\pm}, b_i^{\pm}, c_j^{\pm}$

If $a_{ij}^{\pm+}, b_i^{\pm+}, c_j^{\pm+}$ and $a_{ij}^{\pm-}, b_i^{\pm-}, c_j^{\pm-}$ denote the whitened coefficients corresponding to f^+ and f^- respectively, then these values can be found as follows.

Assuming that $a_{ij}^{\pm}, b_i^{\pm}, c_j^{\pm}$ are variables, the objective function of the following problem can be constructed to find $c_j^{\pm+}$:

$$\text{Max} f^{\pm} = \sum_{j=1}^{n} c_j^{\pm} x_j^s$$

$$\text{s.t.} \sum_{j=1}^{n} a_{ij}^{\pm} x_j^s \leq b_i^{\pm}, i = 1, 2, 3, \cdots, m \tag{6}$$

Similarly, the objective function of the following problem can be constructed to find $c_j^{\pm-}$:

$$\mathrm{Min} f^{\pm} = \sum_{j=1}^{n} c_j^{\pm} x_j^s$$
$$\mathrm{s.t.} \sum_{j=1}^{n} a_{ij}^{\pm} x_j^s \leq b_i^{\pm}, i = 1, 2, 3, \cdots, m \tag{7}$$

There are two kinds of decision schemes for inexact programming problems, which are the conservative schemes and optimistic schemes (Huang et al., 1992). The former assumes less risk than the latter, so that, for a maximization objective function, planning for the lower bound of an objective value represents the conservative scheme, and planning for the upper bound of an objective value represents the optimistic scheme (Huang et al., 1992). In terms of constraints, the conservative scheme involves more rigorous or stringent constraints, and the optimistic scheme adopts more tolerant ones.

Thus $a_{ij}^{\pm+}$ and $b_i^{\pm+}$ of the optimistic scheme, and corresponding to f^+ can be obtained from:

$$\mathrm{Max} \sum_{j=1}^{n} (a_{ij}^{\pm} x_j^s - b_i^{\pm})$$
$$\mathrm{s.t.} \sum_{j=1}^{n} a_{ij}^{\pm} x_j^s \leq b_i^{\pm}, i = 1, 2, 3, \cdots, m \tag{8}$$

and $a_{ij}^{\pm-}$ and $b_i^{\pm-}$ of the conservative scheme, and corresponding to f^- can be obtained from:

$$\mathrm{Min} \sum_{j=1}^{n} (a_{ij}^{\pm} x_j^s - b_i^{\pm})$$
$$\mathrm{s.t.} \sum_{j=1}^{n} a_{ij}^{\pm} x_j^s \leq b_i^{\pm}, i = 1, 2, 3, \cdots, m \tag{9}$$

Step 3: Formulate the two whitened sub-models corresponding to the upper and lower bounds of the objective-function value

The two whitened sub-models corresponding to f^+ and f^- become

$$\text{Max } f^+ = \sum_{j=1}^{n} c_j^{\pm+} x_j^{\pm}$$

$$\text{s.t } \sum_{j=1}^{n} a_{ij}^{\pm+} x_j^{\pm} \le b_i^{\pm+}, i = 1, 2, 3, \cdots, m \tag{10}$$

$$x_j^{\pm} \ge 0, j = 1, 2, 3, \cdots, n.$$

and

$$\text{Max } f^- = \sum_{j=1}^{n} c_j^{\pm-} x_j^{\pm}$$

$$\text{s.t } \sum_{j=1}^{n} a_{ij}^{\pm-} x_j^{\pm} \le b_i^{\pm-}, i = 1, 2, 3, \cdots, m \tag{11}$$

$$x_j^{\pm} \ge 0, j = 1, 2, 3, \cdots, n.$$

respectively.

GREY QUADRATIC PROGRAMMING

Model Formulation

Grey quadratic programming (GQP) is an extension of conventional quadratic programming for handling both nonlinearities in objective functions and uncertainties in input parameters.

A general grey quadratic programing model is formulated by introducing the concepts of grey systems and grey decisions in to an ordinary quadratic programming framework as(Huang, 1994):

$$\text{Max } f^{\pm} = \sum_{j=1}^{n} c_j^{\pm} x_j^{\pm} - \sum_{j=1}^{n} \sum_{k=1}^{n} q_{jk}^{\pm} x_j^{\pm} x_k^{\pm} / 2$$

s.t. $\displaystyle\sum_{j=1}^{n} a_{ij}^{\pm} x_j^{\pm} \le b_i^{\pm}, i = 1,2,3,\cdots,m$ \hfill (12)

$x_j^{\pm} \ge 0 \text{ for } j = 1,2,3,\cdots,n$

where $x_j^{\pm}$ and $x_k^{\pm}$ are grey decision variables; and $c_j^{\pm}, q_{jk}^{\pm}, a_{ij}^{\pm}$, and $b_j^{\pm}$ are grey parameters.

Since the objective function and the constraints of the GQP model may involve grey numbers, it can have grey optimal solutions of the following form (Huang, 1994):

$f_{opt}^{\pm} = [\, f_{opt}^{-}, f_{opt}^{+}\,], f_{opt}^{+} \ge f_{opt}^{-}$

$\left(x_j^{\pm}\right)_{opt} = \left[\left(x_j^{-}\right)_{opt}, \left(x_j^{+}\right)_{opt}\right], \left(x_j^{+}\right)_{opt} \ge \left(x_j^{-}\right)_{opt}, j = 1,2,3,\cdots,n$

SOLUTION METHODS

Interactive Binary Algorithms Approach

Huang (1994) provided a solution method, which depends on the interactive relationships between model parameters and decision variables in the objective function and in the constraints, for a typical grey quadratic programming model of the form:

$\displaystyle \text{Max } f^{\pm} = \sum_{j=1}^{n}\left[c_j^{\pm}x_j^{\pm} + d_j^{\pm}\left(x_j^{\pm}\right)^2\right]$

s.t $\displaystyle\sum_{j=1}^{n} a_{ij}^{\pm} x_j^{\pm} \le b_i^{\pm}, i = 1,2,3,\cdots,m$ \hfill (13)

$x_j^{\pm} \ge 0, j = 1,2,3,\cdots,n$.

The method assumes that an optimal solution exists; and it consists of transforming the model into two whitened sub-models which correspond to the upper and lower bounds of the desired objective-function value. The solution procedure is outlined below.

Step 1: Group the coefficients $c_j^{\pm}$ and $d_j^{\pm}$ based on their signs

When $c_j^{\pm}$ and $d_j^{\pm}$ have the same sign, let the former k_1 pairs $\left\{ c_j^{\pm}, d_j^{\pm} \right\}$ be positive and the latter k_2 pairs be negative, i.e.

$$c_j^{\pm}, d_j^{\pm} \geq 0 \left(j = 1, 2, 3, \cdots, k_1 \right)$$

and

$$c_j^{\pm}, d_j^{\pm} < 0 \left(j = k_1 + 1, k_1 + 2, k_1 + 3, \cdots, n \right),$$

where $k_1 + k_2 = n$.

Step 2: Define the upper and lower bounds f^+ and f^- respectively of the objective function $f^{\pm}$

If the first k_1 pairs of the n coefficients $\left\{ c_j^{\pm}, d_j^{\pm} \right\}$ are positive and the last k_2 pairs are negative, then, theupper and lower bounds of the objective function $f^{\pm}$ can be formulated as:

$$
\begin{aligned}
f^+ &= \sum_{j=1}^{k_1} \left[c_j^+ x_j^+ + d_j^+ \left(x_j^+ \right)^2 \right] + \sum_{j=k_1+1}^{n} \left[c_j^+ x_j^- + d_j^+ \left(x_j^- \right)^2 \right] \\
f^- &= \sum_{j=1}^{k_1} \left[c_j^- x_j^- + d_j^- \left(x_j^- \right)^2 \right] + \sum_{j=k_1+1}^{n} \left[c_j^- x_j^+ + d_j^- \left(x_j^+ \right)^2 \right]
\end{aligned}
\tag{14}
$$

Step 3: Define the relationships between decision variables and coefficients of the constraints

Step 4: From steps 2 and 3, formulate constraints corresponding to lower and upper bounds f^- and f^+ respectively of objective function $f^{\pm}$

For a combination of different bounds of decision variables corresponding to f^+, let the former k_1 decision variables have the upper bound values and the latter k_2 variables have the lower bound values. i.e.

$$x_j^\pm = x_j^+ \left(j = 1, 2, 3, \cdots, k_1 \right)$$

and

$$x_j^\pm = x_j^- \left(j = k_1 + 1, k_1 + 2, k_1 + 3, \cdots, n \right),$$

where $k_1 + k_2 = n$. The relevant constraints corresponding to f^+ can be specified as (Huang et al., 1994):

$$\sum_{j=1}^{k_1} \left[\left| a_{ij}^- \right| sign \left(a_{ij}^- \right) x_j^+ \right] + \sum_{j=k_1+1}^{n} \left[\left| a_{ij}^+ \right| sign \left(a_{ij}^+ \right) x_j^- \right] \le b_i^\pm, \forall i$$

and the constraints corresponding to f^- are:

$$\sum_{j=1}^{k_1} \left[\left| a_{ij}^+ \right| sign \left(a_{ij}^+ \right) x_j^- \right] + \sum_{j=k_1+1}^{n} \left[\left| a_{ij}^- \right| sign \left(a_{ij}^- \right) x_j^+ \right] \le b_i^\pm, \forall i$$

When $b_i^\pm = b_i$ is a deterministic number, these constraints will take the following form:

$$\sum_{j=1}^{k_1} \left[\left| a_{ij}^- \right| sign \left(a_{ij}^- \right) x_j^+ \right] + \sum_{j=k_1+1}^{n} \left[\left| a_{ij}^+ \right| sign \left(a_{ij}^+ \right) x_j^- \right] \le b_i, \forall i$$

$$\sum_{j=1}^{k_1} \left[\left| a_{ij}^+ \right| sign \left(a_{ij}^+ \right) x_j^- \right] + \sum_{j=k_1+1}^{n} \left[\left| a_{ij}^- \right| sign \left(a_{ij}^- \right) x_j^+ \right] \le b_i, \forall i$$

Step 5: Based on Steps 2-4, formulate the two whitened sub-models corresponding to the upper and lower bounds of the objective-function value

When the problem is to maximize the objective function, the whitened sub-model corresponding to the upper bound of the objective function value should be formulated and solved first. The whitened sub-model corresponding to the lower bound of the objective function value should be formulated based on the upper bound solution obtained for the first sub-model.

When the problem is to minimize the objective function, the whitened sub-model corresponding to the lower bound of the objective function value should be formulated and solved first.

Step 6: When the constraints' right-hand side constants are also grey numbers, determine the relationships between decision variables and coefficients of the constraints to formulate the relevant constraints

When $b_i^\pm$ is a grey number, various possible relationships between decision variables and the coefficients of the constraints can be analyzed to formulate the relevant constraints (detailed discussion of this is given in Huang, 1994).

Huang(1994) further provided detailed explanations and examples to illustrate the modeling and the solution processes.

Generally, the method provides grey solutions that are stable in the given decision space and flexible in reflecting potential variations in the condition of the system caused by uncertainties in input parameters. The algorithm also has fairly low computational requirements, since it leads to only two sub-models.

The main challenge for solving a GQP model through Huang's approach is the difficulty in defining bounds for decision variables corresponding to the upper and lower bounds of the objective function value when $c_j^\pm$ and $d_j^\pm$ have different signs. According to Huang (1994), when $c_j^\pm$ and $d_j^\pm$ have different signs, various combinations of the upper and lower bounds of $x_j^\pm$, $\forall j$ could be examined for formulating a number of objective functions. The relevant quadratic programming sub-models should then be solved. Consequently, the optimal bound distribution for $x_j^\pm$ (i.e., the choice of the upper or lower bound for each $x_j^\pm$) corresponding to f_{opt}^+ and f_{opt}^- could be identified through series of comparisons of the generated solutions.

For example, for

$$f^\pm = c_1^\pm x_1^\pm + d_1^\pm \left(x_1^\pm\right)^2 + c_2^\pm x_2^\pm + d_2^\pm \left(x_2^\pm\right)^2,$$

if different signs exist between $c_1^{\pm}$ and $d_1^{\pm}$ and between $c_2^{\pm}$ and $d_2^{\pm}$, we can formulate four objective functions from the four possible combinations of the upper and lower bounds of $x_j^{\pm}$ according to the principle of factorial design (Box et al., 1978), namely:

$$f_1^+ = c_1^+ x_1^- + d_1^+ \left(x_1^-\right)^2 + c_2^+ x_2^- + d_2^+ \left(x_2^-\right)^2$$

$$f_2^+ = c_1^+ x_1^- + d_1^+ \left(x_1^-\right)^2 + c_2^+ x_2^+ + d_2^+ \left(x_2^+\right)^2$$

$$f_3^+ = c_1^+ x_1^+ + d_1^+ \left(x_1^+\right)^2 + c_2^+ x_2^- + d_2^+ \left(x_2^-\right)^2$$

$$f_4^+ = c_1^+ x_1^+ + d_1^+ \left(x_1^+\right)^2 + c_2^+ x_2^+ + d_2^+ \left(x_2^+\right)^2$$

Then we formulate and solve four quadratic programming sub-models, whose objective functions are as given above, and the corresponding constraints are specified according to Huang (1994).

For example, for f_2^+, we can formulate a sub-model as follows (Huang, 1994):

$$\text{Max } f_2^+ = c_1^+ x_1^- + d_1^+ \left(x_1^-\right)^2 + c_2^+ x_2^+ + d_2^+ \left(x_2^+\right)^2$$

$$\text{s.t } a_{i1}^{\pm} x_1^- + a_{i2}^{\pm} x_2^+ \le b_1^+, i = 1, 2, 3, \cdots, m$$

$$x_1^- \ge 0.$$

$$x_2^+ \ge 0$$

After a series of comparisons of the optimal solutions of the four sub-models, the optimal bound distribution for $x_1^{\pm}$ and $x_2^{\pm}$ that leads to the highest f^+ (and f^-) value can then be identified.

Obviously, when many pairs $\left\{c_j^{\pm}, d_j^{\pm}\right\}$ of coefficients have different signs, the number of combinations could become great (2^n for n pairs (Box et al., 1978)).

Thus, a large amount of computation will be required for identifying the optimal bound distribution of $x_j^{\pm}$ that leads to the f_{opt}^{+} value (when the objective is to maximize). Since the method is based on an interactive process, the solution process can become less efficient and more error prone when intensive interaction is necessary.

Derivative Algorithm

As an improvement of the algorithm presented in Huang et al. (1994), Chen et al. (2001) introduced a derivative algorithm(DAM) which simplifies the problem solving process by providing a quantitative expression for uncertain relationships between the objective function and the decision variables. The method from Chen et al. (2001) reduces the amount of computation necessary compared to the method proposed by Huang et al. (1995). The modelling procedure can be outlined as follows:

Step 1: Formulate and solve the whitened mean value sub-model

$$\text{Max } f_m = \sum_{j=1}^{n} \left[\left(c_j\right)_m \left(x_j\right)_m + \left(d_j\right)_m \left(x_j\right)_m^2 \right]$$

$$\text{s.t. } \sum_{j=1}^{n} \left(a_{ij}\right)_m \left(x_j\right)_m \le \left(b_i\right)_m \text{ for } i = 1, 2, 3, \cdots, m \tag{15}$$

$$\left(x_j\right)_m \ge 0 \text{ for } j = 1, 2, 3, \cdots, n .$$

where $\left(a_{ij}\right)_m, \left(b_i\right)_m, \left(c_j\right)_m$ and $\left(d_j\right)_m$ are the whitened mean values of $a_{ij}^{\pm}, b_i^{\pm}, c_j^{\pm}$ and $d_j^{\pm}$.

If $x_{mopt} = \left\{ \left(x_j\right)_{mopt} \forall j \right\}$ is the optimal solution of this model, then according to Huang et al.(1995), it can be contained in the grey solution set for the GQP model,i.e., $\left(x_j^{+}\right)_{mopt} \in \left[x_{jopt}^{-}, x_{jopt}^{+}\right] \forall j$.

Step 2: Identify the optimal bound distribution for $x_j^{\pm}$ that leads to the highest f^{+} value

According to ..., if $c_j^{\pm}$ and $d_j^{\pm}$ have different signs, the optimal bound distribution for $x_j^{\pm}$ that leads to the highest f^+ value can then be identified through the following criterion:

1. $f_j^+\left(x_{jopt}^+\right) \geq f_j^+\left(x_{jopt}^-\right)$ when $2d_j^+(x_j)_{m\;opt} + c_j^+ > 0$
2. $f_j^+\left(x_{jopt}^+\right) \leq f_j^+\left(x_{jopt}^-\right)$ when $2d_j^+(x_j)_{mopt} + c_j^+ < 0$

where $f_j^+\left(x\right) = c_j^+ x + 2d_j^+ x^2$ and $f_j^-\left(x\right) = c_j^- x + 2d_j^- x^2$.

Step 3: Formulate two sub-models corresponding to the upper and lower bounds of the objective-function value.

The derivative algorithm was derived from the interactive binary algorithm and reduced the degree of complexity in the modeling process; it also decreases the computational complexity. However, the method still involves formulating sub-models and depends on judgments on how to combine different signed coefficients. Thus proposed method cannot be automated and directly generated.

Genetic Algorithms Based Approaches

Chan et al. (2013) extended the genetic-algorithms-based approach for solving grey linear programming problems to solve grey quadratic programming problems. In the GA approach, the upper and lower bounds of the inexact numbers of coefficients $a_{ij}^{\pm}, b_i^{\pm}, c_j^{\pm}$ and $d_j^{\pm}$ can be determined by substituting the initial suboptimal decision variables into the objective function. f^+ and f^- can be calculated directly without any uncertainty in the coefficients. The procedure for solving the problem is briefly outlined in the following three steps.

Step 1: Find an initial suboptimal decision variable x_j^s

A suboptimal solution f^s and the corresponding decision variable x_j^s can be obtained from the following problem, which is a problem transformed from the original GQP problem:

$$\text{Max } f = \sum_{j=1}^{n}\left[c_j^r x_j + d_j^r (x_j)^2\right]$$

$$\text{s.t. } \sum_{j=1}^{n} a_{ij}^{r} x_{j} \le b_{i}^{r} \text{ for } i = 1, 2, 3, \cdots, m \tag{16}$$

$x_{j} \ge 0$ for $j = 1, 2, 3, \cdots, n$.

where $a_{ij}^{r}, b_{i}^{r}, c_{j}^{r}, d_{j}^{r}$ are random numbers which satisfy the continuous uniform distribution in the intervals $[a_{ij}^{-}, a_{ij}^{+})], [b_{i}^{-}, b_{i}^{+}], [c_{j}^{-}, c_{j}^{+}]$ and $[d_{j}^{-}, d_{j}^{+}]$ respectively.

Step 2: Whiten the grey coefficients $a_{ij}^{\pm}, b_{i}^{\pm}, c_{j}^{\pm}, d_{j}^{\pm}$

If $a_{ij}^{\pm+}, b_{i}^{\pm+}, c_{j}^{\pm+}, d_{j}^{\pm+}$ and $a_{ij}^{\pm-}, b_{i}^{\pm-}, c_{j}^{\pm-}, d_{j}^{\pm-}$ denote the whitened coefficientscorresponding to f^{+} and f^{-} respectively, then these values can be found as follows.

Assuming that $a_{ij}^{\pm}, b_{i}^{\pm}, c_{j}^{\pm}, d_{j}^{\pm}$ are variables, $c_{j}^{\pm}, d_{j}^{\pm}$ are obtained from the optimization problems

$$\text{Max } f^{\pm} = \sum_{j=1}^{n} \left[c_{j}^{\pm} x_{j}^{s} + d_{j}^{\pm} \left(x_{j}^{s} \right)^{2} \right]$$
$$\text{s.t.} \sum_{j=1}^{n} a_{ij}^{\pm} x_{j}^{s} \le b_{i}^{\pm}, i = 1, 2, 3, \cdots, m \tag{17}$$

and

$$\text{Min } f^{\pm} = \sum_{j=1}^{n} \left[c_{j}^{\pm} x_{j}^{s} + d_{j}^{\pm} \left(x_{j}^{s} \right)^{2} \right]$$
$$\text{s.t.} \sum_{j=1}^{n} a_{ij}^{\pm} x_{j}^{s} \le b_{i}^{\pm}, i = 1, 2, 3, \cdots, m \tag{18}$$

$a_{ij}^{\pm+}, b_{i}^{\pm+}$ of the optimistic scheme and corresponding to the upper limit of the objective value of f^{+} can be determined from the problem

$$\text{Max} \sum_{j=1}^{n} abs \left(a_{ij}^{\pm} x_{j}^{s} - b_{i}^{\pm} \right)$$
$$\text{s.t.} \sum_{j=1}^{n} a_{ij}^{\pm} x_{j}^{s} \le b_{i}^{\pm}, i = 1, 2, 3, \cdots, m \tag{19}$$

and $a_{ij}^{\pm-}, b_i^{\pm-}$ can be determined from

$$\text{Min} \sum_{j=1}^{n} abs\left(a_{ij}^{\pm}x_j^s - b_i^{\pm}\right)$$
$$\text{s.t.} \sum_{j=1}^{n} a_{ij}^{\pm}x_j^s \leq b_i^{\pm}, i = 1, 2, 3, \cdots, m \tag{20}$$

Step 3: Formulate the two whitened sub-models corresponding to the upper and lower bounds of the objective-function value

The two whitened sub-models corresponding to f^+ and f^- become

$$\text{Max } f^+ = \sum_{j=1}^{n}\left[c_j^{\pm+}x_j^{\pm} + d_j^{\pm+}\left(x_j^{\pm}\right)^2\right]$$

$$\text{s.t } \sum_{j=1}^{n} a_{ij}^{\pm+}x_j^{\pm} \leq b_i^{\pm+}, i = 1, 2, 3, \cdots, m \tag{21}$$

$$x_j^{\pm} \geq 0, j = 1, 2, 3, \cdots, n.$$

and

$$\text{Max } f^- = \sum_{j=1}^{n}\left[c_j^{\pm-}x_j^{\pm} + d_j^{\pm-}\left(x_j^{\pm}\right)^2\right]$$

$$\text{s.t } \sum_{j=1}^{n} a_{ij}^{\pm-}x_j^{\pm} \leq b_i^{\pm-}, i = 1, 2, 3, \cdots, m \tag{22}$$

$$x_j^{\pm} \geq 0, j = 1, 2, 3, \cdots, n.$$

respectively.

GREY NON-LINEAR OPTIMIZATION

Model Formulation

The general grey nonlinear programming model can be expressed in the form:

Max $f^{\pm}\left(x^{\pm}\right)$

subject to: $g_i^{\pm}\left(x^{\pm}\right) \leq b_i^{\pm}, \forall i$

$x^{\pm} \geq 0$

where $f^{\pm}\left(x^{\pm}\right)$ is a general nonlinear grey objective function, $x^{\pm}$ is a grey decision variable vector and inequalities $g_i^{\pm}\left(x^{\pm}\right) \leq b_i^{\pm}, \forall i$ are grey constraint conditions.

Solution Methods

In general there are not much generally applicable algorithms proposed for solving generic nonlinear programming problems under uncertainty. In particular, the interactive binary algorithm approach proposed in [5] is not intended for dealing with generic grey nonlinear optimization problems. However, Chan et al. (2017) proposed the genetic algorithms based approach for solving such generic grey non-linear programming problems.

GA Based Approach for Grey Non-Linear Optimization Problems

Chan et al. (2017) proposed an innovative genetic algorithms based approach for solving grey non-linear programming problems. Chan et al. (2017) conducted computation experiment to illustrate the method with the help of the following grey nonlinear optimization problem.

Max $f^{\pm} = c_1^{\pm} x_1^{\pm} - c_2^{\pm}\left(x_1^{\pm}\right)^{0.3} - d_1^{\pm} x_2^{\pm} + d_2^{\pm}\left(x_1^{\pm}x_2^{\pm}\right)$

s.t. $a_{11}^{\pm}\left(x_1^{\pm}\right)^{0.5} + a_{12}^{\pm}x_2^{\pm} \leq b_1^{\pm}$ \hfill (23)

$$x_1^\pm + a_{22}^\pm x_2^\pm \leq b_2^\pm$$

$$x_1^\pm \geq 0, x_1^\pm \geq 0$$

where $a_{ij}^\pm, b_i^\pm, c_j^\pm, d_j^\pm$ are grey parameters and $x_j^\pm$ is grey decision variable.

The procedures for solving the problem are outlined in the following three steps.

Step 1: Find an initial suboptimal decision variable x_j^s from the transformed problem

To obtain the initial suboptimal variable x_j^s, the random numbers $a_{ij}^r, b_i^r, c_j^r, d_j^r$ are selected to transform this NLP problem with grey parameters to a deterministic NLP problem, such $a_{ij}^r, b_i^r, c_j^r, d_j^r$ satisfy the continuous uniform distribution in the intervals of $[a_{ij}^-, a_{ij}^+)], [b_i^-, b_i^+], [c_j^-, c_j^+]$ and $[d_j^-, d_j^+]$

$$\text{Max } f^s = c_1^r x_1^s - c_2^r \left(x_1^s\right)^{0.3} - d_1^r x_2^s + d_2^r \left(x_1^s x_2^s\right)$$

$$\text{s.t. } a_{11}^r \left(x_1^s\right)^{0.5} + a_{12}^r x_2^s \leq b_1^r \qquad (24)$$

$$x_1^s + a_{22}^r x_2^s \leq b_2^r$$

$$x_1^s \geq 0, \ x_2^s \geq 0$$

Then, the GANLP solver engine of GASGOT, can be used to identify a suboptimal solution f^s (Chan et al., 2017), and the corresponding decision variable x_j^s. The objective function in Equation (24) is used as the positive term of the fitness function and the constraints of Equation (23) adopted as the negative punishment terms.

Step 2: Whiten the grey coefficients $a_{ij}^\pm, b_i^\pm, c_j^\pm, d_j^\pm$

Substituting x_1^s, x_2^s into Equation (23), the inexact coefficients of $a_{ij}^\pm, b_i^\pm, c_j^\pm, d_j^\pm$ will be determined.

The x_1^s, x_2^s obtained in step one are used to construct two optimization problems in order to determine the coefficients of $a_{ij}^{\pm+}, b_i^{\pm+}, c_j^{\pm+}, d_j^{\pm+}$ and $a_{ij}^{\pm-}, b_i^{\pm-}, c_j^{\pm-}, d_j^{\pm-}$.

The coefficients from the first group are considered to be corresponding to the optimistic scheme f^+, while the second group correspond to the conservative scheme f^-.

Assuming that $c_j^\pm, d_j^\pm$ are variables, they can be determined from:

$$\text{Max } f^+ = c_1^{\pm+} x_1^s - c_2^{\pm+} \left(x_1^s\right)^{0.3} - d_1^{\pm+} x_2^s + c_2^{\pm+} \left(x_1^s x_2^s\right)$$

$$\text{s.t. } c_1^{\pm+} \in [c_1^-, c_1^+] \tag{25}$$

$$c_2^{\pm+} \in [c_2^-, c_2^+]$$

$$d_1^{\pm+} \in [d_1^-, d_1^+]$$

$$d_2^{\pm+} \in [d_2^-, d_2^+]$$

and

$$\text{Min } f^- = c_1^{\pm-} x_1^s - c_2^{\pm-} \left(x_1^s\right)^{0.3} - d_1^{\pm-} x_2^s + c_2^{\pm-} \left(x_1^s x_2^s\right)$$

$$\text{s.t. } c_1^{\pm+} \in [c_1^-, c_1^+] \tag{26}$$

$$c_2^{\pm+} \in [c_2^-, c_2^+]$$

$$d_1^{\pm+} \in [d_1^-, d_1^+]$$

$$d_2^{\pm+} \in [d_2^-, d_2^+]$$

To determine $a_{ij}^{\pm+}, b_{ij}^{\pm+}$ of the optimistic scheme corresponding to the upper limit of the objective value f^+, the objective function can be constructed as follows:

$$\text{Max } abs\left[a_{11}^{\pm}\left(x_1^s\right)^{0.5} + a_{12}^{\pm}x_2^s - b_1^{\pm} \right]$$
$$\text{s.t. } a_{11}^{\pm}\left(x_1^s\right)^{0.5} + a_{12}^{\pm}x_2^s \le b_1^{\pm} \tag{27}$$

and

$$\text{Max } abs\left(x_1^s + a_{22}^{\pm}x_2^s - b_2^{\pm} \right)$$
$$\text{s.t. } x_1^s + a_{22}^{\pm}x_2^s \le b_2^{\pm} \tag{28}$$

The objective functions to get $a_{ij}^{\pm-}, b_{ij}^{\pm-}$ of the conservative scheme are:

$$\text{Min } abs\left[a_{11}^{\pm}\left(x_1^s\right)^{0.5} + a_{12}^{\pm}x_2^s - b_1^{\pm} \right]$$
$$\text{s.t. } a_{11}^{\pm}\left(x_1^s\right)^{0.5} + a_{12}^{\pm}x_2^s \le b_1^{\pm} \tag{29}$$

and

$$\text{Min } abs\left(x_1^s + a_{22}^{\pm}x_2^s - b_2^{\pm} \right)$$
$$\text{s.t. } x_1^s + a_{22}^{\pm}x_2^s \le b_2^{\pm} \tag{30}$$

Step 3: Formulate the two whitened sub-models corresponding to the upper and lower bounds of the objective-function value

In this step, the objective function presented in Equation (24) is converted into the following two sub-problems:

$$\text{Max } f^+ = c_1^{\pm+}\, x_1^{\pm} - c_2^{\pm+}\left(x_1^{\pm}\right)^{0.3} - d_1^{\pm+}\, x_2^{\pm} + d_2^{\pm+}\left(x_1^{\pm}x_2^{\pm}\right)$$

$$\text{s.t. } a_{11}^{\pm+}\left(x_1^{\pm}\right)^{0.5} + a_{12}^{\pm+}x_2^{\pm} \le b_1^{\pm+} \tag{31}$$

$$x_1^{\pm} + a_{22}^{\pm+}x_2^{\pm} \le b_2^{\pm+}$$

$$x_1^\pm \geq 0, x_1^\pm \geq 0$$

and

$$\text{Max } f^- = c_1^{\pm-} x_1^\pm - c_2^{\pm-} \left(x_1^\pm \right)^{0.3} - d_1^{\pm-} x_2^\pm + d_2^{\pm-} \left(x_1^\pm x_2^\pm \right)$$

$$\text{s.t. } a_{11}^{\pm-} \left(x_1^\pm \right)^{0.5} + a_{12}^{\pm-} x_2^\pm \leq b_1^{\pm-} \tag{32}$$

$$x_1^{\pm-} + a_{22}^{\pm-} x_2^\pm \leq b_2^{\pm-}$$

$$x_1^\pm \geq 0, x_1^\pm \geq 0$$

In this stage, the uncertain parameters in Equation (24) have been eliminated, and two typical non-linear optimization problems have been generated instead.

It has be seen (Chan et al., 2017) that the GA based method can generate the optimal result without any simplification or assumption, and it can be adapted for applications of optimization problems with uncertainty.

DISCUSSION

Both the binary interactive algorithm and genetic algorithms based methods, reviewed in this chapter, were applied to management of a set of case scenarios related to municipality solid waste management.

The binary interactive algorithm problem solving approaches have limitations due to the complexity involved in selecting the upper or lower bounds of decision variables and model parameters when the intermediate sub-models are being constructed. The complexity arises due to the extensive computation and the necessary associated assumptions and simplifications.

In contrast to the binary interactive algorithm approaches, the solution procedures of the GA-based optimization methods do not involve any such assumption or simplification, and the analysis of the results of these methods suggests the practicality and flexibility of the methods for solving more complex grey nonlinear programming problems. The GA based methods were implemented in MATLAB, and they can be integrated with other operation programming software packages (Chan et al., 2013 and 2017).

As far as the author is aware, the genetic algorithms based optimization methods, which have been shown to be superior over the traditional binary interactive methods, are not available for grey multi objective and multilevel optimization problems. Therefore, further consideration of GA based methods will help to broaden applicable ranges of grey optimization models.

CONCLUSION

In the preceding sections of this chapter, commonly used grey optimization methods for solutions of GLP, GQP and GNLP problems have been reviewed. These methods can be put in to two major categories: the binary interactive algorithm approaches and the genetic algorithms based approaches. The binary interactive algorithm methods are available to solve grey linear programming and grey quadratic programming problems; whereas genetic algorithms based approaches are proposed to solve grey linear, grey quadratic and grey general nonlinear programming problems.

As mentioned in the discussion section the GA based optimization methods for solving grey optimization problems have been shown to be superior over the traditional binary interactive methods.

REFERENCES

Chen, M. J., & Huang, G. H. (1999). A derivative algorithm for inexact quadratic program – application to environmental decision-making under uncertainty. *European Journal of Operational Research*, *128*(3), 570–586. doi:10.1016/S0377-2217(99)00374-4

Huang, G., Baetz, B. W., & Patry, G. G. (1992). A Grey Linear Programming Approach for Municipal Solid Waste Management Planning Under Uncertainty. *Civil Engineering Systems*, *9*(4), 319–335. doi:10.1080/02630259208970657

Huang, G., & Dan Moore, R. (1993). Grey linear programming, its solving approach, and its application. *International Journal of Systems Science*, *24*(1), 159–172. doi:10.1080/00207729308949477

Huang, G. H. (1994). *Grey mathematical programming and its application to municipal waste management planning* (Ph.D. Dissertation). McMaster University, Hamilton, Canada.

Huang, G. H., Baetz, B. W., & Patry, G. G. (1995). Grey Quadratic Programming and Its Application to Municipal Solid Waste Management Planning Under Uncertainty. *Engineering Optimization*, *23*(3), 201–223. doi:10.1080/03052159508941354

Jin. (2005). *A Genetic Algorithms Framework for Grey Non-Linear Programming Problems*. Saskatoon: IEEE CCECE/CCGEI.

Jin, W. H., Hu, Z. Y., & Chan, C. (2017). An Innovative Genetic Algorithms-Based Inexact Non-Linear Programming Problem Solving Method. *Journal of Environmental Protection*, *8*(03), 231–249. doi:10.4236/jep.2017.83018

Jin, Hu, & Chan. (2013). *A Genetic-Algorithms-Based Approach for Programming Linear and Quadratic Optimization Problems with Uncertainty*. Hindawi Publishing Corporation Mathematical Problems in Engineering.

Liu, S., & Lin, Y. (2010). *Grey systems Theory and Applications*. Berlin: Springer.

Rosenberg, D. E. (2009). Shades of Grey: A critical review of grey number optimization. *Engineering Optimization*, *41*(6), 573–592. doi:10.1080/03052150902718125

Sifeng, L. J. F. Y. Y. (2012). A brief introduction to grey systems theory", Grey Systems. *Theory and Application*, *2*(2), 89–104.

Chapter 2
Grey Optimization Problems Using Prey–Predator Algorithm

Nawaf N. Hamadneh
Saudi Electronic University, Saudi Arabia

ABSTRACT

The optimization problems are the problem of finding the best parameter values which optimize the objective functions. The optimization methods are divided into two types: deterministic and non-deterministic methods. Metaheuristic algorithms fall in the non-deterministic solution methods. Prey-predator algorithm is one of the well-known metaheuristic algorithms developed for optimization problems. It has gained popularity within a short time and is used in different applications, and it is an easy algorithm to understand and also to implement. The grey systems theory was initialized as uncertain systems. Each grey system is described with grey numbers, grey equations, and grey matrices. A grey number has uncertain value, but there is an interval or a general set of numbers, within that the value lies is known. In this chapter, the author will review and show that grey system modeling is very useful to use with prey-predator algorithm. The benchmark functions, grey linear programming, and grey model GM (1,1) are used as examples of grey system.

INTRODUCTION

The grey systems theory is designed to study uncertain systems which focus on the incomplete information that is due to small samples and poor information (Julong, 1982, 1989; K. Li, Liu, Zhai, Khoshgoftaar, & Li, 2016; Liu & Forrest, 2010; Liu, Yang, & Forrest, 2017). Grey systems have incomplete parameters, structure, or boundary of systems (Liu & Forrest, 2010; Y. Yang, 2010). They have been

DOI: 10.4018/978-1-5225-5091-4.ch002

widely applied in areas like engineering, economics, and computer sciences (Liu & Forrest, 2010; Thissen, Pepers, Üstün, Melssen, & Buydens, 2004; Xie & Liu, 2009; Zavadskas, Kaklauskas, Turskis, & Tamošaitienė, 2009). There are many scientific applications of the grey systems for analysis, and modeling (Stanujkic, Magdalinovic, Jovanovic, & Stojanovic, 2012). For example Bing Liu developed the first grey systems modeling software for the Windows (Liu & Forrest, 2010);(Stanujkic et al., 2012) combine concept of interval grey numbers and MOORA method; (Kumar, 2016) developed the Grey Wolf Algorithm (GWA); (Razi & Shahabi, 2016) present an appropriate practical approach to select the optimal stock portfolio based on Grey Relational Analysis and C5 algorithm which is a model of decision tree; (K. Li et al., 2016) developed grey model based on particle swarm optimization algorithm; (Zhou, Ren, & Yao, 2017) integrated multi-objective optimization method with grey relational analysis, radial basis function neural network, and particle swarm optimization algorithm.

Optimization problems can be divided into two categories in terms of the level of available information, namely deterministic and non-deterministic (X.-S. Yang, 2010; Yang, 2011). Deterministic approaches include grid search, covering methods, and trajectory-based methods(Tilahun & Ong, 2014; X.-S. Yang, 2010). The deterministic techniques seek the minimum point based on the information given by the negative of the gradient (or sub-gradient) of the objective function. Naturally, the efficiency of these algorithms depends on several factors, such as the starting point, the accuracy of the descent direction evaluation and the method used to execute the line search as well as the stopping criteria. Non-deterministic methods include random search, clustering, and methods based on probabilistic models of the objective function(Yang, 2011). Metaheuristic algorithms are from the class of non-deterministic methods (W. A. Khan, Hamadneh, Tilahun, & Ngnotchouye, 2016; Tilahun & ONG, 2013; X.-S. Yang, 2010). Metaheuristic algorithms are formally defined to find the optimal solutions by systematically exploring and exploiting the search space (Tilahun, Ngnotchouye, & Hamadneh, 2017). It is efficient, not affected much by the behavior of the problem and an easy to use in different application (Durkota, 2011; Nawaf Hamadneh et al., 2013; Nawaf Hamadneh et al., 2012; W. S. Khan, Hamadneh, & Khan, 2017). Prey-predator algorithm uncomplicated metaheuristic algorithms with effectiveness in applying and use (Tilahun & ONG, 2013). The algorithm is designed for continuous optimization problems, and also to use for non-continuous problems (Nawaf Hamadneh, 2013; Nawaf Hamadneh, Tilahun, Sathasivam, & Choon, 2013; Tilahun & ONG, 2013). . In this chapter prey predator algorithm will be used to solve grey optimization problems

GREY SYSTEMS

Grey Numbers

A grey system is described with grey numbers, grey sequences, grey equations or matrices (Julong, 1989; K. Li et al., 2016; Liu et al., 2017; Stanujkic et al., 2012; Zhou et al., 2017). Grey numbers are the elementary parameters with unknown values, and indeterminate its possible value within a specific range (Kumar, 2016; Xie & Liu, 2009; Y. Yang, 2010). A grey number is generally represented using the symbol "$G^{\pm}$". There are several types of grey numbers:

- **Closed Interval Grey Numbers:** In the form of $G^{\pm} = [G^-, G^+]$
- **Clopen interval grey numbers:** With only a lower bound or only an upper bound, (in the form of $G^{\pm} = [G^-, \infty$ or $(-\infty^+])$
- **Continuous:** A grey number possibly taking any value between the upper and the lower bound
- **Discrete Grey Numbers:** Not continuous grey number (i.e. The grey numbers taking on a finite number of values or a countable number of values in a set);
- **Black White Grey Numbers:** White grey numbers have upper and lower limited values, while black grey numbers neither have upper limit nor lower limit values.
- **Essential and Non-Essential Grey Numbers:** An essential grey number is a grey number that is impossible or temporarily not possible to find a white number to represent (Liu & Forrest, 2010).

Closed Interval grey numbers are any interval in the form $[G^-, G^+]$, where G^- is defined as known lower bound of the grey number "G^*", and G^+ is defined as known upper bound on the grey number "G^*" or "$G^{\pm}$". The width of grey number is defined as the difference between G^- and G^+ (width of grey number $= G^+ - G^-$). Clopped interval grey numbers are the interval that has only a lower bound or only an upper bound in the forms $[G^-, \infty]$ and (∞, G^+) respectively. The black grey number is that number which neither has an upper nor has a lower bound; that is, $G^* \in (-\infty, \infty)$. In interval $G^* \in [G^-, G^+]$, if $G^- = G$, then G^* is called white grey number or deterministic number with a value lying between upper and lower limited values.

Grey number has been involved and studied in different scenarios including linear programming, grey model GM(1,1), and benchmark functions are some of the grey systems applications (G.-H. Huang & Loucks, 2000; G. Huang, Baetz, &

Patry, 1992; Ishibuchi & Tanaka, 1990; Mirjalili et al., 2014; Rosenberg, 2009). In linear programming, the grey numbers are incorporated into all decision variables in the logic programming. The grey model GM(1,1) is an important model used by Grey systems, requires a relatively small amount of data to establish a prediction model and employs a simple calculation process to achieve high accuracy(K. Li et al., 2016). The accuracy of the prediction of GM(1,1) can be improved by using the optimization algorithms(K. Li et al., 2016; Liu & Forrest, 2010).) Li et al. (2016) proposes an improved method for calculating the parameters of the grey model GM(1,1) by using particle swarm optimization (PSO) algorithm in order to reduce the error between the restored value and real value of the model. And optimize the initial value of the GM(1,1), and introduce sliding window to the model to improve both accuracy and adaptability.

Different methods have been proposed and used for these problems. Chapter 1 of this book gives a good review on grey optimization models and their corresponding solution methods. However, for the sake of completeness two methods will briefly discussed below.

Grey Linear Programming

The second application in this study is grey linear programming. There are many ways can be used to solve the logic programming such as decomposing it into two deterministic sub-models(Maqsood, Huang, & Zeng, 2004; Rosenberg, 2009). Then we call it grey logic programming which has the uncertain grey objective function f^* constraint matrix, and right-hand sides of constraints (Eq.1) (G. Huang et al., 1992; Rosenberg, 2009).

$$f^* = \sum_{i=1}^{n} c_i x_i^*, x_i^* = \in \left\{ x_i^+, x_i^- \right\} \tag{1a}$$

$$\sum_{i=1}^{n} a_{ij} x_j^* \leq b_j \tag{1b}$$

$$x_j^* \geq 0 \tag{1c}$$

where f^* is the uncertain grey objective function with lower- and upper bounds; similarly for the other decision variables and input coefficients.

We will propose PPA based solution methods, where PPA can generate solutions for grey variables $x_k^*, \forall k,$ and grey objective function f^*. The following is an example that can be solved using PPA(G. H. Huang, 1994).

$$\max f^* = [50, 60] x_1^* - [70, 90] x_2^* \tag{2a}$$

$$[4, 6] x_1^* + x_2^* \leq 150 \tag{2b}$$

$$6x_1^* + [5, 7] x_2^* \leq 280 \tag{2c}$$

$$x_1^* + [3, 4] x_2^* \leq 90 \tag{2d}$$

$$[1, 2] x_1^* - 10x_2^* \leq -1 \tag{2e}$$

Grey Model GM (1,1)

GM (1, 1) type of grey model is a kind of homogeneous exponential growth model based on the accumulation generation sequence and the least squares method(Julong, 1989; Wang, Wei, Sun, & Li, 2016). The Grey GM (1, 1) model has been widely applied in many fields, because of the model has the simple principle, easy calculation, and high forecasting accuracy (Kayacan, Ulutas, & Kaynak, 2010; M. Madhi & N. Mohamed, 2017; Wang et al., 2016). There are many ways can be used to estimate the accuracy of the GM (1, 1) model such as relative error size test, posterior deviation test, and correlation test (Wang et al., 2016). In addition, Many scholars proposed novel approaches for improving the accuracy of GM(1,1) (H.-w. Li, Liu, & Mao, 2010; M. H. Madhi & N. Mohamed, 2017). The grey model GM(1,1) is demonstrated as follows(K. Li et al., 2016; Liu et al., 2017)

1. A non-negative sequence of raw data be in the form

$$x^0 = \left\{ x^0 \left(k \right), k = 1, 2, ..., n, n \geq 4 \right\} \tag{3}$$

$$x^1 = \left\{ x^1 \left(k \right) = \sum_{i=1}^{k} x^0 \left(i \right), k = 1, 2, ..., n \right\} \tag{4}$$

2. The sequence of generated mean value of consecutive neighbors can be expressed as

$$z^1 = \left\{ z^1\left(k\right), = \eta x^1\left(k-1\right) + \left(1-\eta\right)x^1\left(k\right), \eta \int \left[0,1\right] \right\} \tag{5}$$

3. The whitened equation of GM(1,1) model can be expressed as

$$\frac{dx^1}{dt} + ax^1\left(t\right) = b \tag{6}$$

where x^1 has an approximately exponential variation. and Eq.6 is called as albinism differential equation of GM (1,1), and its solution is expressed as the following:

4.   Calculate the values of parameters a and b by using the least square estimation method
5.   5. Calculate the time response equation of GM(1,1) based on parameters a and b, then the solution of x^1 can be express as

$$\hat{x}^1\left(k\right) = \left(x^0\left(1\right) - \frac{b}{a}\right)e^{-a\left(k-1\right)} + \frac{b}{a} \tag{7}$$

6.   6. The restored values of raw data is given by equation:

$$\hat{x}^0\left(k+1\right) = \hat{x}^1\left(k+1\right) - \hat{x}^0\left(k\right) \tag{8}$$

PREY-PREDATOR ALGORITHM

Prey-predator algorithm (PPA) is a new metaheuristic algorithm developed for handling a complex optimization applications in different applications including engineering, transportation, management, economics, artificial intelligence, and decision science (Nawaf Hamadneh et al., 2013; W. S. Khan et al., 2017; Tilahun & ONG, 2013, 2014). The algorithm uses the concept of following and exploring by running away from the predator (Ong, Tilahun, Lee, & Ngnotchouye, 2017). It has better exploration properties compared to other algorithms, such as particle swarm optimization algorithm and genetic algorithm (Bean, 1994; Nawaf Hamadneh et al., 2013; Nawaf Hamadneh et al., 2012; K. Li et al., 2016). It is inspired by the interaction between a carnivorous predator and its prey. The algorithm mimics the ways in which a predator runs after and hunt its prey where each prey tries to stay within the pack, search for a hiding place, and also run away from the predator. The following is some of the advantages of PPA:

- It can quickly scan a wide range of solutions.
- The bad solution helps the algorithm to explore the solution speed by forcipes other solution to run away.
- It has better exploration properties compared to other algorithms which allow it not to be stuck in local optimum solutions.
- Do not require complex mathematics to execute.
- Get a good set of answers, as opposed to a single optimal answer.
- Deals with a large number of variables.

In the algorithm, a set of initial feasible solutions will be generated and for each solution, x_i, is assigned a numerical value to show its performance in the objective function called survival value ($SV(x_i)$). Better performance in the objective function implies higher survival value. This means for solutions x_i and x_j, if x_i performs better than x_j in the objective function, $SV(x_i) > SV(x_j)$. A solution with the smallest survival value will be assigned as a predator, $x_{predator}$, and the rest as prey. Among these prey, a prey, say x_b, where $SV(x_b) \geq SV(x_i)$, for all i, is called the best prey. This means the best prey is a prey with the highest survival value among the solutions. The pseudo-code of the algorithm is given in Figure 1.

Once the prey and the predator are assigned, each prey (except the best prey) needs to escape from the predator and try to follow other prey with better survival values or find a hiding place. While the predator hunts the weak prey and scares the others which contribute to the exploration of the solution space. Exploitation is carried out by the preys, especially the best prey, by using a local search. The best prey is considered as the one who has found a secure place and is safe from the predator. Thus it will only focus on conducting a local search to improve its survival value. However, the other prey will follow the prey population with better-surviving values and run away from the predator.

In the algorithm, the movement of an ordinary prey (not the best prey) depends on an algorithm parameter called the probability of follow-up (or follow-up probability). If the follow up probability is met, which is if a randomly generated number between zero and one from a uniform distribution is less than or equal to the probability of follow up, then the prey will follow other prey with better survival values and also does a local search; else it will randomly run away from the predator.

Figure 1. Pseudo-code of PPA for a minimization problem

Generate a random solution set $X = \{\overline{x_i} \mid i \in \{1, 2, \ldots, m\}\}$

Calculate survival value of each particle, $SV(x_i)$ depending on the objective function.

index=0

Do while (index ≤ MaxGen)

$\quad x_{predator} = \overline{x_j}$ such that $SV(\overline{x_j}) \geq SV(\overline{x_i}), \forall i$

$\quad x_{best} = \overline{x_j}$ such that $SV(\overline{x_j}) \leq SV(\overline{x_i}), \forall i$

$\quad$ Set of prey $= Sp = X \setminus \{x_{predator}, x_{best}\} = \{x_1, x_2, \ldots, x_{m-2}\}$

$\quad x_{predator} = x_{predator} + \lambda_{max} rand + \lambda_{min}(x' - x_{predator})$, for $SV(x') \geq SV(x_i), \forall i$

$\quad$ for i=1:m-2 (for all prey)

$\quad\quad$ if (rand ≤ p_f)

$\quad\quad\quad$ compute $y = \{x_j \mid SV(x_j) \leq SV(x_i)\}$

$\quad\quad\quad x_i = x_i + \sum_j \lambda_{max}(y_j - x_i) + \lambda_{min} rand$

$\quad\quad$ else

$\quad\quad\quad x_i = x_i + \lambda_{max} y_r$, where y_r is a random direction away from $x_{predator}$

$\quad\quad$ end

$\quad$ end

$\quad$ Generate $\{u_1, u_2, \ldots, u_t\}$ random unit directions

$\quad$ If ($SV(x_{best} + u_j rand) \leq SV(x_{best})$ for some j)

$\quad\quad x_{best} = x_{best} + u_j rand$

$\quad$ end

Update set X. index=index+1

PREY-PREDATOR ALGORITHM FOR GREY SYSTEMS

One of the main objectives of PPA is that the algorithm easily finds the best solutions, and can get local optima (Tilahun & ONG, 2013). In addition, PPA best solutions don't depend on the initial training values. In this section, we overviewed some of the grey systems application that can be optimized by PPA.

With the success of prey predator algorithm in different applications, it can be very useful in handling grey numbers as well. The main idea or modification used to make the problem suitable for prey predator algorithm is to consider the grey number as a stochastic number from a uniform distribution i.e. each number in the interval will have equal probability of occurrence. In each of the iterations of the algorithm a specific values for the grey number will be generated from these uniform distribution and the problem will be optimized. The maximum number of iteration will be used as a termination criterion.

SIMULATION RESULTS

Benchmark Functions

One of the grey numbers applications is the benchmarks numbers. The benchmark functions listed in Table 1 as examples of grey systems applications (Tilahun & Ong, 2014). The benchmark functions used are maximization functions. The functions that need to be maximized is called the objective functions, the variables, x, are called decision variables and the set of possible values for the decision variables is called feasible set. A solution for a maximization problem is a value from the feasible set which maximizes the objective function (Dorigo, Birattari, & Stutzle, 2006; Joshi, 2013; Tilahun, Kassa, & Ong, 2012). Note that, by multiplying the function by negative one, then the maximization problem switch to minimization problem, where a solution for a maximization problem is a value that maximizes the objective function. The benchmark problems are given in Table 1. The problems are taken from literature and some of the coefficients are made grey numbers.

Table 1. Benchmark test functions

Function	Range
$f_1 = [4,6] e^{(x_1-\pi)^2-(x_2-\pi)^2} + \sum\limits_{j=1}^{2}\sum\limits_{i=0}^{2}\xi_{ij} e^{(x_1-i)^2-(x_2-j)^2}$, where ξ_{ij} is a random number from a uniform distribution between 0 and 1	[0,10]
$f_2 = -\left[\sum\limits_{i=1}^{5}\left(i\cos\left(i+1\right)x_1 + i\right)\right]\left[\sum\limits_{i=1}^{5}\left(i\cos\left(i+1\right)x_2 + [0.5,1.5]\right)i\right]$	[-10,10]
$f_3 = \sum\limits_{i=1}^{m}\left[\sin x_i \sin\dfrac{[0.5,1.5]\,ix_i^2}{\pi}\right]^{20}$	[-5.12,5.12]
$f_4 = [0.5,1.5]\cos x_1 \cos x_1 e^{(x_1-\pi)^2-(x_2-\pi)^2}$	[-10,10]
$f_5 = \sum\limits_{i=1}^{2} int\left(x_i\right)$	[4.5,5.12]

Parameter Setting

In the simulation of using benchmark functions, each problem has the same 20 randomly generated feasible initial solutions. Follow-up probability; $\lambda_{max} = \lambda_{min}$ =0.5 with 100 number of local randomly search directions. The results are analysis with 100 trials each time. The parameters which the author used with benchmark problems is used also with the grey logic programming accept the follow-up probability ($\lambda_{max} = \lambda_{min}$ =0.9).

Results and Discussion

The After the 100 trials of running PPA, the average solution with a standard deviation and CPU time of running PPA of the functions are listed in Table 2.

From the results, PPA is efficient for solving the benchmarks test functions with smaller CPU time and also with good average functional values compared with the optimal solutions.

For solving linear programming by using PPA, the author has used successfully PPA to solve Eq.2.We found that the optimal solution of f^* is 2185.081 with $x_1 = 41.2, x_2 = 3$. And also, the readers can show the solutions for two trails; the first trial is shown in Figure 2 and the second in Figure 3.

PSO algorithm was employed successively to optimize the parameters of GM (1,1)(Bahrami, Hooshmand, & Parastegari, 2014; K. Li et al., 2016; Niu, Zhao, Zhang, & Wang, 2007). PSO has the same structure of exploration with a preference for PPA (Goel, Jain, & Srivastava, 2017; Nawaf Hamadneh et al., 2013; Kennedy

Table 2. Benchmark test functions solution by using Prey-Predator algorithm

Function	Average Solution With a Standard Deviation Using PPA	Optimal Solution	CPU Time
f_1	(5.0541, 0.0219)	[5, 5.0794]	0.2028
f_2	(186.5112, 185.1899)	186.73067	0.0995
f_3	(4.6954, 4.5984)	4.687	0.1185
f_4	(0.99996, 0.000283)	1	-
f_5	(10,0)	10	-

Figure 2. The first trail Solutions of Eq.2 by using PPA

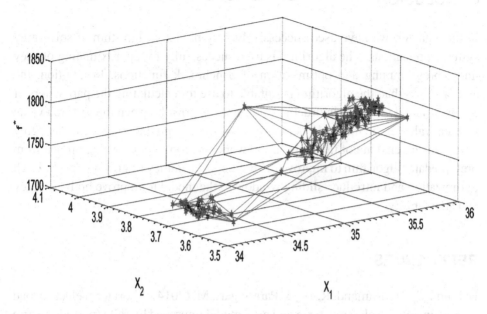

Figure 3. The second trail solutions of Eq.2 by using PPA

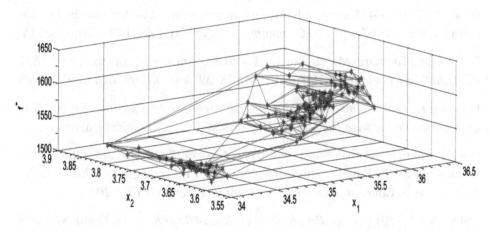

& Eberhart, 1995; K. Li et al., 2016; Tilahun & ONG, 2013). Therefore, PPA is suitable to use for calculating the parameters of the grey model GM(1,1) in order to minimize the error between the restored value and real value of the model.

The convergence property of the proposed algorithm needs further study and is one of the possible future works. Dealing with clopen or open problems, system forecast, grey clustering, systems design techniques are another which needs further study.

CONCLUSION

In this chapter, we have used successively prey predator algorithm to solve grey system applications. The algorithm is used successfully for approximating of grey linear programming and optimization of benchmark functions. In addition, the author shows that, the algorithm is suitable to use for calculating the parameters of the grey model GM(1,1) in order to minimize the error between the restored value and real value of the model. A detailed review of prey-predator algorithm and grey systems is given. One of the main future works is proposed a novel approach from prey-predator algorithm to improve the prediction accuracy of grey models through optimization and introduce sliding window to the model to improve both accuracy and adaptability.

REFERENCES

Bahrami, S., Hooshmand, R.-A., & Parastegari, M. (2014). Short term electric load forecasting by wavelet transform and grey model improved by PSO (particle swarm optimization) algorithm. *Energy*, *72*, 434–442. doi:10.1016/j.energy.2014.05.065

Bean, J. C. (1994). Genetic algorithms and random keys for sequencing and optimization. *ORSA Journal on Computing*, *6*(2), 154–160. doi:10.1287/ijoc.6.2.154

Dorigo, M., Birattari, M., & Stutzle, T. (2006). Ant colony optimization. *IEEE Computational Intelligence Magazine*, *1*(4), 28–39. doi:10.1109/MCI.2006.329691

Durkota, K. (2011). *Implementation of a discrete firefly algorithm for the QAP problem within the sage framework* (BSc thesis). Czech Technical University.

Goel, L., Jain, N., & Srivastava, S. (2017). A novel PSO based algorithm to find initial seeds for the k-means clustering algorithm. *Proceedings of the International Conference on Communication and Computing Systems (ICCCS 2016)*.

Hamadneh, N. (2013). *Logic Programming in Radial Basis Function Neural Networks*. Universiti Sains Malaysia.

Hamadneh, N., Khan, W. A., Sathasivam, S., & Ong, H. C. (2013). Design optimization of pin fin geometry using particle swarm optimization algorithm. *PLoS One*, *8*(5).

Hamadneh, N., Sathasivam, S., Tilahun, S. L., & Choon, O. H. (2012). Learning Logic Programming in Radial Basis Function Network via Genetic Algorithm. *Journal of Applied Sciences (Faisalabad)*, *12*(9), 840–847. doi:10.3923/jas.2012.840.847

Hamadneh, N., Tilahun, S. L., Sathasivam, S., & Choon, O. H. (2013). Prey-Predator Algorithm as a New Optimization Technique Using in Radial Basis Function Neural Networks. *Research Journal of Applied Sciences, 8*(7), 383–387.

Huang, G., Baetz, B. W., & Patry, G. G. (1992). A grey linear programming approach for municipal solid waste management planning under uncertainty. *Civil Engineering Systems, 9*(4), 319–335. doi:10.1080/02630259208970657

Huang, G. H. (1994). *Grey mathematical programming and its application to municipal solid waste management planning.* McMaster University.

Huang, G.-H., & Loucks, D. P. (2000). An inexact two-stage stochastic programming model for water resources management under uncertainty. *Civil Engineering Systems, 17*(2), 95–118. doi:10.1080/02630250008970277

Ishibuchi, H., & Tanaka, H. (1990). Multiobjective programming in optimization of the interval objective function. *European Journal of Operational Research, 48*(2), 219–225. doi:10.1016/0377-2217(90)90375-L

Joshi, R. (2013). Optimization Techniques for Transportation Problems of Three Variables. *IOSR Journal of Mathematics, 9*(1), 46–50. doi:10.9790/5728-0914650

Julong, D. (1982). Control problems of Grey Systems, systems and Control Letters, (1) 5, 288-94.

Julong, D. (1989). Introduction to grey system theory. *Journal of Grey System, 1*(1), 1–24.

Kayacan, E., Ulutas, B., & Kaynak, O. (2010). Grey system theory-based models in time series prediction. *Expert Systems with Applications, 37*(2), 1784–1789. doi:10.1016/j.eswa.2009.07.064

Kennedy, J., & Eberhart, R. (1995). *Particle swarm optimization.* Paper presented at the International Conference on Neural Networks IV, Perth, Australia. 10.1109/ICNN.1995.488968

Khan, W. A., Hamadneh, N. N., Tilahun, S. L., & Ngnotchouye, J. M. T. (2016). A Review and Comparative Study of Firefly Algorithm and its Modified Versions. In O. Baskan (Ed.), Optimization Algorithms- Methods and Applications. Rijeka: InTech. doi:10.5772/62472

Khan, W. S., Hamadneh, N. N., & Khan, W. A. (2017). Prediction of thermal conductivity of polyvinylpyrrolidone (PVP) electrospun nanocomposite fibers using artificial neural network and prey-predator algorithm. *PLoS One, 12*(9), e0183920. doi:10.1371/journal.pone.0183920 PMID:28934220

Kumar, V. (2016). *Modified Grey Wolf Algorithm for optimization problems.* Paper presented at the International Conference on Inventive Computation Technologies (ICICT), India.

Li, H.-w., Liu, Q.-y., & Mao, W.-j. (2010). *An Optimized GM(1,1) Model Based on the Modified Construction Method of Background Value.* Paper presented at the Computational and Information Sciences (ICCIS), Chengdu, China. 10.1109/ICCIS.2010.17

Li, K., Liu, L., Zhai, J., Khoshgoftaar, T. M., & Li, T. (2016). The improved grey model based on particle swarm optimization algorithm for time series prediction. *Engineering Applications of Artificial Intelligence, 55,* 285–291. doi:10.1016/j.engappai.2016.07.005

Liu, S., & Forrest, J. Y. L. (2010). *Grey systems: theory and applications.* Springer. doi:10.1007/978-3-642-13938-3

Liu, S., Yang, Y., & Forrest, J. (2017). *Grey Numbers and Their Operations. In Grey Data Analysis* (pp. 29–43). Springer. doi:10.1007/978-981-10-1841-1_3

Madhi, M., & Mohamed, N. (2017). An Initial Condition Optimization Approach for Improving the Prediction Precision of a GM (1, 1) Model. *Mathematical and Computational Applications, 22*(1), 21. doi:10.3390/mca22010021

Madhi, M. H., & Mohamed, N. (2017). A Modified Grey Model Gm (1, 1) Based on Reconstruction of Background Value. *Far East Journal of Mathematical Sciences, 101*(1), 189–199. doi:10.17654/MS101010189

Maqsood, I., Huang, G. H., & Zeng, G. (2004). An inexact two-stage mixed integer linear programming model for waste management under uncertainty. *Civil Engineering and Environmental Systems, 21*(3), 187–206. doi:10.1080/10286600410001730698

Mirjalili, S., Mirjalili, S. M., & Lewis, A. (2014). Grey wolf optimizer. *Advances in Engineering Software, 69,* 46–61. doi:10.1016/j.advengsoft.2013.12.007

Niu, D.-x., Zhao, L., Zhang, B., & Wang, H.-f. (2007). The application of particle swarm optimization based grey model to power load forecasting. *Chinese Journal of Management Science, 1,* 12.

Ong, H. C., Tilahun, S. L., Lee, W. S., & Ngnotchouye, J. M. T. (2017). Comparative Study of Prey-Predator Algorithm and Firefly Algorithm. *Intelligent Automation & Soft Computing,* 1-8.

Razi, F. F., & Shahabi, V. (2016). Forming the stock optimized portfolio using model Grey based on C5 and the Shuffled frog leap algorithm. *Journal of Statistics and Management Systems, 19*(3), 397–421. doi:10.1080/09720510.2015.1086165

Rosenberg, D. E. (2009). Shades of grey: A critical review of grey-number optimization. *Engineering Optimization, 41*(6), 573–592. doi:10.1080/03052150902718125

Stanujkic, D., Magdalinovic, N., Jovanovic, R., & Stojanovic, S. (2012). An objective multi-criteria approach to optimization using MOORA method and interval grey numbers. *Technological and Economic Development of Economy, 18*(2), 331–363. doi:10.3846/20294913.2012.676996

Thissen, U., Pepers, M., Üstün, B., Melssen, W., & Buydens, L. (2004). Comparing support vector machines to PLS for spectral regression applications. *Chemometrics and Intelligent Laboratory Systems, 73*(2), 169–179. doi:10.1016/j.chemolab.2004.01.002

Tilahun, S. L., & Ong, H. C. (2013). Prey-predator algorithm: A new metaheuristic algorithm for optimization problems. *International Journal of Information Technology & Decision Making*, 1–22.

Tilahun, S. L., Kassa, S. M., & Ong, H. C. (2012). *A new algorithm for multilevel optimization problems using evolutionary strategy, inspired by natural adaptation. In PRICAI 2012: Trends in Artificial Intelligence* (pp. 577–588). Springer.

Tilahun, S. L., Ngnotchouye, J. M. T., & Hamadneh, N. N. (2017). Continuous versions of firefly algorithm: A review. *Artificial Intelligence Review*, 1–48.

Tilahun, S. L., & Ong, H. C. (2014). Comparison between genetic algorithm and prey-predator algorithm. *Malaysian Journal of Fundamental and Applied Sciences, 9*(4). doi:10.11113/mjfas.v9n4.104

Wang, Y., Wei, F., Sun, C., & Li, Q. (2016). The Research of Improved Grey GM (1, 1) model to predict the postprandial glucose in Type 2 diabetes. *BioMed Research International*. PMID:27314034

Xie, N., & Liu, S. (2009). Discrete grey forecasting model and its optimization. *Applied Mathematical Modelling, 33*(2), 1173–1186. doi:10.1016/j.apm.2008.01.011

Yang, X.-S. (2010). *Nature-inspired metaheuristic algorithms*. Luniver press.

Yang, X.-S. (2011). Review of meta-heuristics and generalised evolutionary walk algorithm. *International Journal of Bio-inspired Computation, 3*(2), 77–84. doi:10.1504/IJBIC.2011.039907

Yang, X.-S. (2013). Multiobjective firefly algorithm for continuous optimization. *Engineering with Computers*, *29*(2), 175–184. doi:10.100700366-012-0254-1

Yang, Y. (2010). Extended Grey Numbers. *Advances in Grey Systems Research*, 73-85.

Zavadskas, E. K., Kaklauskas, A., Turskis, Z., & Tamošaitienė, J. (2009). Multi-attribute decision-making model by applying grey numbers. *Informatica*, *20*(2), 305–320.

Zhou, J., Ren, J., & Yao, C. (2017). Multi-objective optimization of multi-axis ball-end milling Inconel 718 via grey relational analysis coupled with RBF neural network and PSO algorithm. *Measurement*, *102*, 271–285. doi:10.1016/j.measurement.2017.01.057

Chapter 3
Optimality Principles for Fuzzy Dual Uncertain Systems

Félix Mora-Camino
Durban University of Technology, South Africa

Hakim Bouadi
Ecole Militaire Polytechnique, Algeria

Roger Marcelin Faye
Cheikh Anta Diop University, Senegal

Lunlong Zhong
Civil Aviation University of China, China

ABSTRACT

This chapter considers the extension of the calculus of variations to the optimization of a class of fuzzy systems where the uncertainty of variables and parameters is represented by symmetrical triangular membership functions. The concept of fuzzy dual numbers is introduced, and the consideration of the necessary differentiability conditions for functions of dual variables leads to the definition of fuzzy dual functions. It is shown that when this formalism is adopted to represent performance indexes for uncertain optimization problems, the calculus of variations can be used to establish necessary optimality conditions as an extension to this case of the Euler-Lagrange equation. Then the chapter discusses the propagation of uncertainty when the fuzzy dual formalism is adopted for the state representation of a time continuous system. This leads to the formulation of a fuzzy dual optimization problem for which necessary optimality conditions, corresponding to an extension of Pontryagine's optimality principle, are established.

DOI: 10.4018/978-1-5225-5091-4.ch003

INTRODUCTION

One major challenge when leading with optimization of uncertain systems has been to take profit of previous theoretical results obtained in deterministic frameworks, mainly when these results have an analytical form. In this direction, few effective studies have been performed until today while in this chapter an original approach is developed to extend the main results of continuous systems optimization theory to a class of uncertain systems. More specifically, in this chapter is considered the extension of the calculus of variations to the optimization of a class of fuzzy systems where the uncertainty of variables and parameters is represented by symmetrical triangular membership functions. In many situations, the basic uncertainty representation with respect to variables and parameters is given by real intervals with a central value which is naturally expected to be more representative. This can result either from the fact that possible intervals are effectively the only information about these variables and parameters or from the fact that diverse levels of uncertainty are attached to them and their symmetrical triangular approximation is a way to have a common representation of uncertainty. It is also important to note that for optimization purpose, different total orders can be defined for this class of fuzzy numbers allowing the definite comparison of different performance levels expressed in this formalism. In this chapter, first a connection is established between dual numbers (introduced originally for the design and analysis of kinematics for mechanical systems) and symmetrical triangular fuzzy numbers. This leads to the concept of *fuzzy dual numbers* to which the main dual calculus operations can be applied, easing the manipulation of this class of fuzzy numbers. Then, the consideration of the necessary differentiability conditions for functions of dual variables leads to the definition of *fuzzy dual functions*. The way in which uncertainty effects are produced as well as other mathematical properties of this type of functions are discussed. At this point it is shown that when this formalism is adopted to represent performance indexes for uncertain optimization problems, the calculus of variations can be used to establish of an extension of the Euler-Lagrange equation to this case. These necessary conditions for optimality can be easily completed in the same formalism with local second order optimal conditions. Then is discussed the propagation of uncertainty when the fuzzy dual formalism is adopted for the state representation of a time continuous system. Linear and nonlinear dynamics involving either initial variable uncertainty or parameter uncertainty, are considered. This leads to the formulation of a so called *fuzzy dual optimization problem* for which necessary optimality conditions, corresponding to an extension of Pontryagin's optimality principle, are established. The main concepts presented is this chapter will be illustrated through examples while the solution of different uncertain optimization problems will be discussed to display the effectiveness of the proposed approach.

The Hamilton-Jacobi-Bellman equation (HJB in abbreviation) (Pontryagin, 1986) results from the dynamic programming principle established by Richard Bellman (1954) in the fifties to solve sequential optimization problems. This equation which generalizes previous results in classical mechanics by William Hamilton and Carl Gustav Jacobi, is usually called Hamilton-Jacobi-Bellman equation in recognition of the complementary contributions of these three major scientists. The Hamilton-Jacobi-Bellman equation has played an important role in the understanding of the conditions for the optimal operation of dynamical systems. Historically applied first in engineering and then in other fields of applied mathematics, the Hamilton-Jacobi-Bellman equation has become an important tool to solve decision problems in economics and finance.

In many situations, real systems are submitted to perturbations which are not completely known, generating uncertainty in their future performance when solutions computed from nominal values are applied. Different approaches have been proposed in the literature to cope with this class of difficulty. A first approach has been to perform around the nominal optimal solution numerical post optimization sensibility analysis. When some probabilistic information is available, stochastic optimization techniques (Stengel, 1993) may provide the most expected optimal solution. In that case the stochastic version of the Bellman's principle resulting in the stochastic Hamilton-Jacobi-Bellman equation allows to choose the values of the decision variables so that the probabilistic mean value of a performance index is optimized (Peng, 1992). The fuzzy formalism has been also considered in this case as an intermediate approach to represent the parameter uncertainties and provide fuzzy solutions (Ying, 2000). These different approaches result in general in the adoption of unrealistic assumptions as well as in a very large amount of computation which turns them practically unfeasible. In (Cosenza and Mora-Camino, 2016) a new formalism based on fuzzy-dual numbers has been proposed to diminish the computational burden when dealing with uncertainty in mathematical programming problems. Then in this paper a similar approach is developed to cope with fuzzy optimization of continuous dynamical systems. First a connection is established between dual numbers encountered in the design and analysis of kinematics for mechanical systems (Fisher, 1999) and triangular fuzzy numbers, which result in real intervals for which total orders can be easily adopted. Then fuzzy-dual functions, fuzzy-dual functionals and fuzzy-dual differential equations are introduced. Then, following the variational calculus approach, necessary conditions for the extremum of fuzzy-dual differential functionals, the Euler's equations for fuzzy-dual optimization, are established. The next step then is to traduce the Bellman's principle of optimality into the fuzzy-dual framework and to develop the corresponding fuzzy-dual version of the Hamilton-Jacobi-Bellman equation. Finally, considering that this equation is, even in the classical case, rather difficult to be solved, a fuzzy dual optimal control problem is introduced leading to the application of Pontryagin's maximum principle to the three resulting classical optimal control problems.

FUZZY DUAL NUMBERS

Dual Numbers and Fuzzy-Dual Numbers

Definition 1: Dual numbers. The set of dual numbers Ω is the set of R^2 with specific addition (+) and multiplication (•) laws given by:

$$\forall (x_1, y_1), (x_2, y_2) \in \Omega : (x_1, y_1) + (x_2, y_2) = (x_1 + x_2, y_1 + y_2)$$
$$and \tag{1}$$
$$(x_1, y_1) \cdot (x_2, y_2) = (x_1 \cdot x_2, x_1 \cdot y_2 + x_2 \cdot y_1)$$

The set Ω has a structure of unity commutative ring with respect to these two laws. Its unitary element is (1,0). The dual number $\varepsilon = (0,1)$ is nilpotent of order two with respect to multiplication, then Ω has divisors of (0,0) and it is not an integral ring.

The subset of Ω, $\left\{ (x,0) \middle| x \in \mathbb{R} \right\}$, is a sub-ring of Ω and is isomorph to $\mathbb{R}$. The adopted notation for a dual number (x,y) of Ω is in this paper is $x + \varepsilon \cdot y$ where $x + \varepsilon \cdot y$ and the zero element (0,0) is written $\tilde{0}$.

To each dual number $a + \varepsilon \cdot b$, $b \neq 0$, can be associated a triangular fuzzy number whose membership function is given by:

$$\mu(u) = 0 \ if \ u \leq a - |b| \tag{2}$$

$$\mu(u) = \left(u - a + |b| \right) / |b| \ if \ a - |b| \leq u \leq a \tag{3}$$

$$\mu(u) = \left(a + |b| - u \right) / |b| \ if \ a \leq u \leq a + |b| \tag{4}$$

$$\mu(u) = 0 \ if \ u \geq a + |b| \tag{5}$$

Definition 2: Fuzzy dual numbers. The set of fuzzy-dual numbers can be seen as the set $\tilde{\Omega}$ of dual numbers of the form $a + \varepsilon \cdot b$ such as $a \in \mathbb{R}, b \in \mathbb{R}^+$ where a is the primal part and $|b|$ is the dual part of the fuzzy dual number. Here a is its mean value, the most probable of the fuzzy number according to its triangular membership function, while $2|b|$ is the size of its basis or uncertainty interval. A crisp fuzzy-dual number is such as b is equal to zero.

Orders for Fuzzy-Dual Numbers

When considering optimization problems we will be naturally led to compare numbers, here fuzzy-dual numbers, and the above definition provides different ways to compare them according to what is pursued through the optimization.

Definitions 3: Weak/strong orders for fuzzy dual numbers. Different weak total orders can be defined over $\tilde{\Omega}$, one is relative to the mean value of the fuzzy-dual number, the mean order is such as:

$$x_1 + \varepsilon \cdot y_1 \underset{mean}{\leq} x_2 + \varepsilon \cdot y_2 \Leftrightarrow x_1 \leq x_2 \tag{6}$$

others are relative to their extreme values. The minimal order is such as:

$$x_1 + \varepsilon \cdot y_1 \underset{min}{\leq} x_2 + \varepsilon \cdot y_2 \Leftrightarrow x_1 - |y_1| \leq x_2 - |y_2| \tag{7}$$

while the maximal order is such as:

$$x_1 + \varepsilon \cdot y_1 \underset{max}{\leq} x_2 + \varepsilon \cdot y_2 \Leftrightarrow x_1 + |y_1| \leq x_2 + |y_2| \tag{8}$$

These total orders are weak in the sense that they do not allow to compare completely two fuzzy-dual numbers and another total order may be added with respect to the degree of uncertainty:

$$x_1 + \varepsilon \cdot y_1 \overset{\smile}{\leq} x_2 + \varepsilon \cdot y_2 \Leftrightarrow |y_1| \leq |y_2| \tag{9}$$

A strong partial order can be defined over $\tilde{\Omega}$ for fuzzy-dual numbers:

$$x_1 + \varepsilon \cdot y_1 \underset{str}{\leq} x_2 + \varepsilon \cdot y_2 \Leftrightarrow x_1 + |y_1| \leq x_2 - |y_2| \tag{10}$$

In that case, these two numbers are non-overlapping, while in general comparing accurately close solutions will lead to overlapping fuzzy-dual numbers.

FUZZY-DUAL FUNCTIONS

Differentiability of a Dual Function

Definition 4: Dual function. A dual function f is here a function of a dual variable $x + \varepsilon \cdot y$ is such as:

$$f(x + \varepsilon \cdot y) = \phi(x, y) + \varepsilon \cdot \psi(x, y) \tag{11}$$

where ϕ and ψ are two functions of the real variables x and y supposed smooth with respect to x and y.

This function has a limit equal to $z_1 + \varepsilon \cdot z_2$ when $x + \varepsilon \cdot y$ goes to $x_1 + \varepsilon \cdot y_1$ if and only if:

$$\lim_{x \to x_1, y \to y_1} \phi(x, y) = z_1 \text{ and } \lim_{x \to x_1, y \to y_1} \psi(x, y) = z_2 \tag{12}$$

Properties of a dual function:

- **Continuity:** This function will be continuous at $x_1 + \varepsilon \cdot y_1$ if and only if:

$$\lim_{x \to x_1, y \to y_1} f(x + \varepsilon \cdot y) = f(x + \varepsilon \cdot y_1) \tag{13}$$

- **Differentiability:** Such a function will be differentiable at $x_1 + \varepsilon \cdot y_1$ if there exists a dual number $p + \varepsilon \cdot q$ and a function δ of a dual variable $h + \varepsilon \cdot l$ such as:

$$f(x_1 + h, y_1 + l) = f(x_1, y_1) + ((p + \varepsilon \cdot q) + \delta(h + \varepsilon \cdot l) \cdot (h + \varepsilon \cdot l) \quad \text{w i t h}$$
$$\lim_{h \to 0, l \to 0} \delta(h + \varepsilon \cdot l) = \tilde{0} \tag{14}$$

The function of the dual variable defined by $f' : \Omega \to p + \varepsilon \cdot q$ is then the derivative function of f over Ω.

- **Theorem:** The dual function $f(x + \varepsilon \cdot y) = \phi(x,y) + \varepsilon \cdot \psi(x,y)$ is differentiable if and only if it can be written under the form (Zadeh, 1965).

$$f(x + \varepsilon \cdot y) = \phi(x) + \varepsilon \cdot (\phi_x(x) \cdot y + \theta(x)) \tag{15}$$

where $\theta(x)$ is a real valued smooth function.

- **Proof:** Let $p + \varepsilon \cdot q$ be the value of the derivative of f at $x_1 + \varepsilon \cdot y_1$, then from (11) we can write also:

$$\begin{aligned} f(x_1 + h, y_1 + l) = \\ f(x_1, y_1) + (\phi_x \cdot h + \phi_y \cdot l) + \varepsilon \cdot (\psi_x \cdot h + \psi_y \cdot l) + O^2(h + \varepsilon \cdot l) \end{aligned} \tag{16}$$

and comparing with (14), it appears that:

$$p = \phi_x = \psi_y, q = \psi_x \text{ and } \phi_y = 0 \tag{17}$$

and f will be differentiable over a subset of Ω if at any of its points $\phi_x = \psi_y$ and $\phi_y = 0$. Then $f(x + \varepsilon \cdot y)$ can be written under the form (15). Reciprocally, a dual function such as (15) admits the derivative function given by $p = \phi_x$ and $q = \phi_{xx} \cdot y + \theta_x$.

Fuzzy-Dual Functions

Definition 5: Fuzzy dual function.

When function $\theta(x)$ is zero, we will say that f is a *fuzzy-dual function* and we will write:

$$\tilde{f}(x + \varepsilon \cdot y) = f(x) + \varepsilon \cdot y \cdot f_x(x) \text{ for } x \in O \subset \mathbb{R}, y \in \mathbb{R} \tag{18}$$

Observe that this expression recalls a first order approximation of $f(x)$. In fact, (18) represent any first order approximation of $f(x + \delta x)$ around x for $|\delta x| \leq |y|$ as well as a local linearized view of the Extension Principle of Zadeh (1965).

Figure 1 proposes a view of a fuzzy-dual function where the fuzzy-dual input is related with the fuzzy-dual output of the considered function.

Observe that the partial derivative of a fuzzy-dual function is a fuzzy dual function:

$$f_x(x + \varepsilon \cdot y) = f_x(x) + \varepsilon \cdot y \cdot f_{xx}(x) \tag{19}$$

Relation (18) can be generalized to a fuzzy-dual function f of n dual variables $x_i + \varepsilon \cdot y_i, i = 1, \cdots, n$:

$$f(x_1 + \varepsilon \cdot y_1, \cdots, x_n + \varepsilon \cdot y_n) = f(x_1, \cdots, x_n)$$
$$+ \varepsilon \cdot \sum_{i=1}^{n} y_i \cdot f_{x_i}(x_1, \cdots, x_n) \; for \; x_i \in O \subset \mathbb{R}, y_i \in \mathbb{R}, i = 1, \cdots, n \tag{20}$$

Figure 1. A fuzzy-dual function with the associated memberships

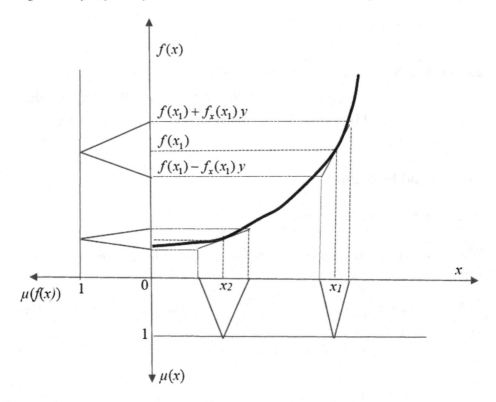

FUZZY DUAL MINIMUM OF A FUNCTIONAL

Minimum of a Fuzzy Dual Functional

Consider now a fuzzy-dual functional given by:

$$J(x,y) = \int_{t_0}^{t_f} f(x(t) + \varepsilon \cdot y(t)) \cdot dt \tag{21}$$

where f is a fuzzy-dual function of $x(t)$ and $y(t)$ while x and y are real valued functions of time, both at least of class C^2. Since the values of the considered fuzzy-dual functions f can be parametrized over [0, 1] by the left and right functions of its α-sets which are continuous, integrability of fuzzy-dual function $\tilde{f}$ is guaranteed (Messelmi, 2013). For given functions x and y, from (16) we write J as a fuzzy dual number:

$$J(x,y) = \int_{t_0}^{t_f} f(x) + \varepsilon \cdot y' \cdot f_x(x)) \cdot dt = \int_{t_0}^{t_f} f(x) \cdot dt + \varepsilon \cdot \int_{t_0}^{t_f} y' \cdot f_x(x) \cdot dt \tag{22}$$

which is a fuzzy-dual number.

Definition 6: Fuzzy dual minimum of a functional.

The fuzzy dual minimum of $J(x,y)$ over $X \times Y$ where X and Y are bounded subsets of $\mathbb{R}^n$ is written as:

$$J^* = \widetilde{\min_{x \in X, y \in Y}} \int_{t_0}^{t_f} f(x) + \varepsilon \cdot y' \cdot f_x(x)) \cdot dt \tag{23}$$

and is defined by:

$$J^* = \frac{1}{2}\left(J^*_+ + J^*_-\right) + \frac{\varepsilon}{2} \cdot \left|J^*_+ - J^*_-\right| \tag{24}$$

where

$$J_+^* = \min_{x \in X, y \in Y} \int_{t_0}^{t_f} f(x) + y' \cdot f_x(x)) \cdot dt \tag{25}$$

and

$$J_-^* = \min_{x \in X, y \in Y} \int_{t_0}^{t_f} f(x) - y' \cdot f_x(x)) \cdot dt \tag{26}$$

with obviously

$$\frac{1}{2}(J_+^* + J_-^*) = \min_{x \in X} \int_{t_0}^{t_f} f(x) \cdot dt \tag{27}$$

Fuzzy-Dual Variation of a Functional and Fuzzy-Dual Euler Equation

The increment of J defined in (21) and resulting from deviations Δx and Δy is such a s:

$$\Delta J = \int_{t_0}^{t_f} f(x + \Delta x + \varepsilon \cdot (y + \Delta y) \cdot dt - \int_{t_0}^{t_f} f(x + \varepsilon \cdot y) \cdot dt \tag{28}$$

or

$$\Delta J = \int_{t_0}^{t_f} (f(x + \Delta x) - f(x)) \cdot dt + \varepsilon \cdot \int_{t_0}^{t_f} ((y + \Delta y)' \cdot f_{x + \Delta x} - y' \cdot f_x) \cdot dt \tag{29}$$

and

$$\Delta J = \int_{t_0}^{t_f} (f_x' \cdot \Delta x + O^2(\Delta x)) \cdot dt + \varepsilon \cdot \int_{t_0}^{t_f} (y' \cdot f_{xx} \cdot \Delta x + \Delta y' \cdot f_x) \cdot dt \tag{30}$$

The fuzzy-dual variation δJ is finally given by the first order terms of ΔJ (Farhadinia, 2014)

$$\delta J = \int_{t_0}^{t_f} f_x{}' \cdot \Delta x \cdot dt + \varepsilon \cdot \int_{t_0}^{t_f} (y' \cdot f_{xx} \cdot \Delta x + \Delta y' \cdot f_x) \cdot dt \tag{31}$$

and

$$J(x + \Delta x, y + \Delta y) = J(x, y) + \delta J(x, \Delta x, y, \Delta y) + O^2(\Delta x, \Delta y) \tag{32}$$

Consider now a fuzzy-dual functional given by:

$$J(x, y) = \int_{t_0}^{t_f} f(x + \varepsilon \cdot y(t), \dot{x}(t) + \varepsilon \cdot \dot{y}(t)) \cdot dt \tag{33}$$

Here we suppose that like it happens very frequently with physical systems, the level of uncertainty evolves from an initial level according to time and to the value of $x(t)$, so that we have:

$$y(t) = g(x(t), t) \tag{34}$$

where g is supposed to be at least of class C^2 with respect to x and t.

The fuzzy-dual variation of J is now given by:

$$\delta J =$$

$$\int_{t_0}^{t_f} (f_x{}' \cdot \Delta x + f_{\dot{x}}{}' \cdot \Delta \dot{x}) \cdot dt + \tag{35}$$

$$\varepsilon \cdot \int_{t_0}^{t_f} (y' \cdot f_{xx} \cdot \Delta x + \dot{y}' \cdot f_{\dot{x}\dot{x}} \cdot \Delta \dot{x} + f_x{}' \cdot \Delta y + f_{\dot{x}}{}' \cdot \Delta \dot{y}) \cdot dt$$

with

$$\Delta y = g_x \cdot \Delta x \text{ and } \Delta \dot{y} = \dot{g}_x \cdot \Delta x + g_x{}' \cdot \Delta \dot{x} \tag{36}$$

Then it is possible to write:

$$\delta J = \left[f_x \,{}'\cdot \Delta x(t) \right]_{t_0}^{t_f} + \int\limits_{t_0}^{t_f} \left(f_x - \frac{d}{dt} f_{\dot{x}} \right) \cdot \Delta x(t) \cdot dt +$$

$$\varepsilon \cdot \Big(\left[(\dot{y}\,{}'\cdot f_{\dot{x}\dot{x}} + f_{\dot{x}}\,{}'\cdot g_x) \cdot \Delta x(t) \right]_{t_0}^{t_f} \tag{37}$$

$$+\varepsilon \cdot \left[\int\limits_{t_0}^{t_f} (y\,{}'\cdot f_{xx} + f_x\,{}'\cdot g_x + f_{\dot{x}}\,{}'\cdot \dot{g}_x - \frac{d}{dt}(\dot{y}\,{}'\cdot f_{\dot{x}\dot{x}} + f_{\dot{x}}\,{}'\cdot g_x)) \cdot \Delta x(t) \cdot dt \right]$$

Then adopting the assumptions that deviations at times t_0 and t_f are zero, we get:

$$\delta J =$$

$$\int\limits_{t_0}^{t_f} \left(f_x - \frac{d}{dt} f_{\dot{x}} \right) \cdot \Delta x(t) \cdot dt + \tag{38}$$

$$\varepsilon \cdot \left[\int\limits_{t_0}^{t_f} (y\,{}'\cdot f_{xx} + f_x\,{}'\cdot g_x + f_{\dot{x}}\,{}'\cdot \dot{g}_x - \frac{d}{dt}(\dot{y}\,{}'\cdot f_{\dot{x}\dot{x}} + f_{\dot{x}}\,{}'\cdot g_x)) \cdot \Delta x(t) \cdot dt \right]$$

In that case, equations (35) and (36) are replaced by the two fuzzy dual extensions of the Euler equation:

$$f_x + (y\,{}'\cdot f_{xx} + f_x\,{}'\cdot g_x + f_{\dot{x}}\,{}'\cdot \dot{g}_x) - \frac{d}{dt}(f_{\dot{x}} + y\,{}'\cdot f_{\dot{x}\dot{x}} + f_{\dot{x}}\,{}'\cdot g_x) = 0 \tag{39}$$

$$f_x - (y\,{}'\cdot f_{xx} + f_x\,{}'\cdot g_x + f_{\dot{x}}\,{}'\cdot \dot{g}_x) + \frac{d}{dt}(-f_{\dot{x}} + y\,{}'\cdot f_{\dot{x}\dot{x}} + f_{\dot{x}}\,{}'\cdot g_x) = 0 \tag{40}$$

Let $x_+^*(t)$ and $x_-^*(t)$, $t \in [t_0, t_f]$ be the respective solutions of these equations which corresponds to extensions of the Euler's necessary conditions of optimality $f_x - \frac{d}{dt} f_{\dot{x}} = 0$ and let $x^*(t)$ be the solution of the nominal problem:

$$\min_x \int\limits_{t_0}^{t_f} f(x(t), \dot{x}(t), t) \cdot dt \tag{41}$$

In the case in which f and g are linear, $x_+^*(t)$ and $x_-^*(t)$, $t \in \left[t_0, t_f\right]$ will constitute the extreme values of a fuzzy dual trajectory of center $x^*(t)$.

When f or g are nonlinear, this will no more be the case and an index can be computed as:

$$I(t) = 2 \cdot \left\| x^*(t) - (x_+^*(t) + x_-^*(t)) / 2 \right\| / \left\| x_+^*(t) - x_-^*(t) \right\| \tag{42}$$

while a global index will be given by:

$$I = \frac{\displaystyle\int_{t_0}^{t_f} \left\| \ddot{x}^*(t) - (x_+^*(t) + x_-^*(t)) / 2 \right\| \cdot dt}{(1/2) \cdot \displaystyle\int_{t_0}^{t_f} \left\| x_+^*(t) - x_-^*(t) \right\| \cdot dt} \tag{43}$$

DYNAMICS OF FUZZY DUAL SYSTEMS

Definition 7: Fuzzy dual dynamics. Here it is considered that the state dynamics of an uncertain process are given by:

$$\dot{z} = a(z, u, t) \tag{44}$$

where a represents a fuzzy-dual function which is at least of class C^2 with respect to z and u where z is a fuzzy-dual variable. They are such as:

$$z = x + \varepsilon \cdot y \in \Delta^n, u \in \mathbb{R}^m \tag{45}$$

where x represents the nominal value of the system state while y represents, through a fuzzy-dual vector, the half span of the uncertainty on the state, u is the control vector which is supposed to be known when applied to the process. Introducing the Jacobian matrix:

$$a_x = \left[(\partial a_i / \partial z_j)_{x,u} \right] \tag{46}$$

the state equation can be rewritten in R^{2n} as:

$$\dot{x} = a(x, u, t) \qquad (47)$$

and

$$\dot{y} = a_x(x, u, t) \cdot y \qquad (48)$$

while the initial conditions are given by x_0 and y_0.

It is considered here that the uncertainty about the future value of x originates in its initial value and the dynamics of the process. Then it is assumed a low level of knowledge with respect to the uncertainty relative to the initial state value by adopting fuzzy-dual numbers associated to real intervals. In the case in which the systems dynamics are linear and given by:

$$\dot{z} = A(t) \cdot z + B(t) \cdot u \qquad (49)$$

The dynamics of the uncertainty over the state will be independent of the state and the input:

$$\dot{y} = A \cdot y \qquad (50)$$

In the nonlinear case, the uncertainty will be a function of the state. For example, consider:

$$a(x, u, t) = \alpha \cdot x^2 + u \; with \; \alpha \neq 0 \qquad (51)$$

then:

$$\dot{y} = 2 \cdot \alpha \cdot x \cdot y \; and \; y(t) = y_0 \cdot e^{\left(\alpha \cdot (x(t)^2 - x(t_0)^2)\right)} \qquad (52)$$

FUZZY DUAL HAMILTON-JACOBI-BELLMAN EQUATION

Fuzzy Dual Bellman's Principle

It is supposed here that times t_0 and t_f are given and the initial and final conditions are such as:

$$x(t_0) = x_0, \quad x(t_f) = x_f, \quad y(t_0) = y_0, \quad y(t_f) \tag{53}$$

is free. It is supposed that $\underline{v}$ is given over the interval $[t_0, t_f]$, while the optimization criterion is such as:

$$\varphi(x(t_f), y(t_f), t_f) + \int_{t_0}^{t_f} f(x(t) + \varepsilon \cdot y(t), u(t), t) \cdot dt \tag{54}$$

with (44), (45) and (46).

Consider the functional J defined over $[t, t_1] \subset [t_0, t_1]$ by:

$$J\left(x(\omega), y(\omega), \omega \in [t, t_f]\right) + \int_{t}^{t_f} f(x(\omega) + \varepsilon \cdot y(\omega), u(\omega), \omega) \cdot d\omega \tag{55}$$

Its fuzzy-dual optimal value for $t \leq t_f$ is such as:

$$J^*(x(t), y(t), t) = \widetilde{\min_{u(\omega), t \leq \omega \leq t_f}} \left(\int_{t}^{t_f} f(x(\omega) + \varepsilon \cdot y(\omega), u(\omega), \omega) \cdot d\omega \right) \tag{56}$$

The Bellman's optimality principle can be written in this framework as:

$$J^*(x(t), y(t), t) =$$
$$\widetilde{\min_{u(\omega), t \leq \omega \leq t_f}} \tag{57}$$
$$\left(\int_{t}^{t+\Delta t} f(x(\omega) + \varepsilon \cdot y(\omega), u(\omega), \omega) \cdot d\omega + J^*(x(t+\Delta t), y(t+\Delta t), t + \Delta t) \right)$$

since this principle can be applied separately to the problems:

$$\min_{u(\omega), t \leq \omega \leq t_f} \int_t^{t_f} \Big(f(x(\omega), u(\omega), \omega) - f_x(x(\omega), u(\omega), \omega) \cdot y(\omega) \Big) \cdot d\omega \tag{58}$$

and to

$$\min_{u(\omega), t \leq \omega \leq t_f} \int_t^{t_f} \Big(f(x(\omega), u(\omega), \omega) + f_x(x(\omega), u(\omega), \omega) \cdot y(\omega) \Big) \cdot d\omega \tag{59}$$

Fuzzy Dual HJB Equation

A first order development of the term:

$$J^*(x(t + \Delta t), y(t + \Delta t), t + \Delta t) \tag{60}$$

gives:

$$J^*(x(t + \Delta t), y(t + \Delta t), t + \Delta t) =$$

$$\widetilde{\min_{u(\omega), \leq \omega \leq t + \Delta t}} \begin{pmatrix} \int_t^{t+\Delta t} f(x(\omega) + \varepsilon \cdot y(\omega), u(\omega), \omega) \cdot d\omega \\ + J^*(x(t)), y(t), t) + \dfrac{\partial}{\partial t}\Big(J^*(x, y, t)\Big) \cdot \Delta t \\ + \dfrac{\partial}{\partial x}\Big(J^*(x, y, t)\Big) \cdot \Big(x(t + \Delta t) - x(t)\Big) \\ + \dfrac{\partial}{\partial y}\Big(J^*(x, y, t)\Big) \cdot \Big(y(t + \Delta t) - y(t)\Big) + O^2(\Delta t) \end{pmatrix} \tag{61}$$

and for a small Δt:

$$J^*(x(t + \Delta t), y(t + \Delta t), t + \Delta t) =$$

$$\widetilde{\min_{u(t)}} \begin{pmatrix} f(x(t) + \varepsilon \cdot y(t), u(t), t) \cdot \Delta t \\ +J^*(x(t)), y(t), t) + \frac{\partial}{\partial t}\Big(J^*(x, y, t)\Big) \cdot \Delta t \\ +\frac{\partial}{\partial x}\Big(J^*(x, y, t)\Big)' \cdot a(x(t), u(t), t) \cdot \Delta t \\ +\frac{\partial}{\partial y}\Big(J^*(x, y, t)\Big)' \cdot a_x(x(t), u(t), t) \cdot \Delta t \\ +O^2(\Delta t) \end{pmatrix} \tag{62}$$

Then:

$$\frac{\partial}{\partial t}J^*(x, y, t) + \widetilde{\min_{u(t)}} \begin{pmatrix} f(x(t) + \varepsilon \cdot y(t), u(t), t) \\ +\frac{\partial}{\partial x}\Big(J^*(x, y, t)\Big)' \cdot a(x(t), u(t), t) \\ +\frac{\partial}{\partial y}\Big(J^*(x, y, t)\Big)' \cdot a_x(x(t), u(t), t) \end{pmatrix} = 0 \tag{63}$$

with

$$J^*(x(t_f), y(t_f), t_f) = \varphi(x(t_f), y(t_f), t_f) \tag{64}$$

Then introducing the auxiliary function Z given by:

$$Z(x(t), y(t), u(t), \frac{\partial}{\partial x}J^*(x, y, t), \frac{\partial}{\partial x}J^*(x, y, t)) =$$

$$\begin{bmatrix} \ddot{}f(x(t) + \varepsilon \cdot y(t), u(t), t) \\ +\frac{\partial}{\partial x}J^*(x, y, t) \cdot a(x(t), u(t), t) \\ +\frac{\partial}{\partial y}J^*(x, y, t) \cdot a_x(x(t), u(t), t) \end{bmatrix} \tag{65}$$

and defining respectively the optimal solutions of:

$$J_+^*(x,y,t) = \min_{u(\omega),t\leq\omega\leq t_f} \int_t^{t_f} \Big(f(x,u,\omega) + f_x(x,u,\omega)\cdot y(\omega)\Big)\cdot d\omega \tag{66}$$

and

$$J_-^*(x,y,t) = \min_{u(\omega),t\leq\omega\leq t_f} \int_t^{t_f} \Big(f(x,u,\omega) - f_x(x,u,\omega)\cdot y(\omega)\Big)\cdot d\omega \tag{67}$$

as

$$u_+^*(\omega), u_-^*(\omega)\omega \in \Big[t,t_f\Big] \tag{68}$$

Now defining J* as in (61), we write:

$$Z(x(t),y(t),u^*(t),\frac{\partial}{\partial x}J^*(x,y,t),\frac{\partial}{\partial y}J^*(x,y,t),t)$$
$$= \widetilde{\min_{u(t)}} Z(x(t),y(t),u(t),\frac{\partial}{\partial x}J^*(x,y,t),\frac{\partial}{\partial y}J^*(x,y,t),t) \tag{69}$$

Then relation (63) is rewritten as the fuzzy-dual Hamilton-Jacobi-Bellman (FD-HJB) equation:

$$\frac{\partial}{\partial t}J^*(x,y,t) + Z(x(t),y(t),u^*(t),\frac{\partial}{\partial x}J^*(x,y,t),\frac{\partial}{\partial y}J^*(x,y,t)) = 0 \tag{70}$$

CONSTRAINED OPTIMIZATION PROBLEMS

Going a step further, we consider the case in which the previous optimization problem is subject to m constraints according to the fuzzy dual expression:

$$g(x(t) + \varepsilon y(t),t) = o(t) + \varepsilon z(t) \tag{71}$$

where $o(t)$, $t \in [t_0, t_f]$ is the zero real vector function of R^m and $z(t)$, $t \in [t_0,t_f]$, is a bounded real function of R^m, eventually the zero real function. Expression (29) can be rewritten as:

$$g(x(t),t) = 0 \text{ and } G_x(t)y(t) = z(t) \ \forall t \in [t_0, t_f]$$ (72)

where G_x is the Jacobian of g. Here we introduce a fuzzy dual Lagrange multiplier $\lambda + \varepsilon\,\mu$ where $\lambda \in R^m, \mu \in R^m$, to build the augmented fuzzy dual functional:

$$J(x,y,\lambda,\mu) = \int_{t_0}^{t_f} (f(x + \varepsilon\,y, \dot{x} + \varepsilon\,\dot{y}, t) + (\lambda + \varepsilon\,\mu)'\, g(x + \varepsilon\,y, t))dt$$ (73)

or

$$J(x,y,\lambda,\mu) = \int_{t_0}^{t_f} r(x,\dot{x},\lambda,t)\,dt + \varepsilon \int_{t_0}^{t_f} d(x,\dot{x},y,\dot{y},\lambda,\mu)\,dt$$ (74)

with:

$$r(x,\dot{x},\lambda,t) = f(x,\dot{x},t) + \lambda'\, g(x,t)$$ (75)

and

$$d(x,\dot{x},y,\dot{y},\lambda,\mu,t) = (f_x' + \lambda'\, G_x)y + f_{\dot{x}}'\,\dot{y} + \mu'\, g(x,t)$$ (76)

The fuzzy dual variation of the augmented functional which is associated to deviations $\Delta x, \Delta\dot{x}, \Delta y, \Delta\dot{y}, \Delta\lambda$ and $\Delta\mu$ is now given by:

$$\delta J =$$

$$\int_{t_0}^{t_f} \left(r_x'\,\Delta x + r_{\dot{x}}'\,\Delta\dot{x} + g'\,\Delta\lambda \right)dt +$$ (77)

$$\varepsilon \int_{t_0}^{t_f} \left(d_x'\,\Delta x + d_{\dot{x}}'\,\Delta\dot{x} + y'\,G_x'\,\Delta\lambda + g'\,\Delta\mu \right)dt$$

or

$$\delta J =$$

$$+ \int\limits_{t_0}^{t_f} \left(r_x - \frac{d}{dt}(r_{\dot{x}}) \right)' \Delta x + g' \Delta \lambda \right) dt +$$

$$\varepsilon \int\limits_{t_0}^{t_f} \left[(d_x - \frac{d}{dt}(d_{\dot{x}}))' \Delta x + y' G_x ' \Delta \lambda + g' \Delta \mu \right] dt \qquad (78)$$

$$+ \left[r_{\dot{x}} ' \Delta x(t) \right]_{t_0}^{t_f} + \varepsilon \left[d_{\dot{x}} ' \Delta x(t) \right]_{t_0}^{t_f}$$

Considering again that the deviations at times t_0 and t_f are taken equal to zero and that the considered solutions are feasible, the variation of the augmented functional can be written:

$$\delta J = \int\limits_{t_0}^{t_f} \left[r_x - \frac{d}{dt}(r_{\dot{x}}) \right]' \Delta x(t) dt + \varepsilon \int\limits_{t_0}^{t_f} \left[\left(d_x - \frac{d}{dt}(d_{\dot{x}}) \right)' \Delta x(t) \right] dt \qquad (79)$$

The necessary condition to have a mean extremum for *J* is given by the classical Euler equation applied to function *r*:

$$r_x - \frac{d}{dt}(r_{\dot{x}}) = 0 \qquad (80)$$

The necessary conditions to have a minimal extremum for *J* are given by the augmented Euler equations:

$$(r_x - d_x) - \frac{d}{dt}(r_{\dot{x}} - d_{\dot{x}}) = 0 \qquad (81)$$

The necessary conditions to have a maximal extremum for *J* are given by the augmented Euler equations:

$$(r_x + d_x) - \frac{d}{dt}(r_{\dot{x}} + d_{\dot{x}}) = 0 \qquad (82)$$

while conditions (26) must be satisfied.

FUZZY DUAL OPTIMAL CONTROL PROBLEM

Problem Formulation

In this section we consider a class of optimal control problems where the system to be controlled is subject to perturbations whose uncertainty is imbedded in a fuzzy dual function representing the dynamics of the considered process to be controlled. Let the formulation be given by:

$$\min_{u \in R^m} J(u) \text{ with } J(u) = \int_{t_0}^{t_f} f(z, u, t) dt \text{ with } f \in C^2 \tag{83}$$

where the fuzzy dual state dynamics of the process are such as:

$$\dot{z} = a(z, u, v + \varepsilon w, t) \tag{84}$$

where $a \in C^2$ with

$$z = x + \varepsilon y \in \Delta^n, u \in R^m, v \in R^p$$

and $w \in R^p$ is a fuzzy dual function.

It is supposed here that instant t_0 and t_f are given and the initial and final conditions are such as: $x(t_0) = x_0$, $x(t_f) = x_f$, $y(t_0) = y_0$ with $y(t_f)$ free. It is supposed that $\underline{v}$ and $\underline{w}$ are given over the interval $[t_0, t_f]$. Introducing the Jacobians $A_x = [\alpha_{ij}] = [a_{ix_j}]$ and $A_v = [\beta_{ik}] = [a_{iv_k}]$, the state equation can be rewritten as:

$$\dot{x} = a(x, u, v, t) \text{ and } \dot{y} = A_x(x, u, v, t) y + A_v(x, u, v, t) w \tag{85}$$

while the optimization criterion is such as:

$$J(u) = \int_{t_0}^{t_f} f(x, u, t) \, dt + \varepsilon \int_{t_0}^{t_f} f_x ' \underline{y} y dt \tag{86}$$

Mean Optimal Control Problem

In that case, the optimal control problem reduces to a classical optimization problem:

$$\min_{u} \int_{t_0}^{t_f} f(x, u, t)\, dt \text{ with } \dot{x} = a(x, u, v),\ x(t_0) = x_0 \text{ and } x(t_f) = x_f \tag{87}$$

Then introducing the classical Hamiltonian function (Farhadinia, 2014).

Here for sake of brevity we treat simultaneously the minimal and maximal extremum problems by introducing the $\pm$ symbol. In these cases, the optimal control problem can be written as:

$$\min_{\underline{u}} \int_{t_0}^{t_f} \left(f(x, u, t) \pm f_x{}' y \right) dt \tag{90}$$

with $\dot{x} = a(x, u, v)$ and $\dot{y} = A_x y + A_v w$ (91)

$$x(t_0) = x_0,\ x(t_f) = x_f,\ y(t_0) = y_0 \tag{92}$$

Then introducing the two different Hamiltonian functions given by:

$$H = f(x, u, t) \pm f_x{}' y + \lambda' a(x, u, v, t) + \mu' \left(A_x y + A_v w \right) \tag{93}$$

where λ and μ are classical dual variables with values in R^n, we get the necessary conditions for an extremal optimal control solution:

$$\dot{x} = H_\lambda(x, u, \lambda, \mu, t)\ ,\qquad \dot{y} = H_\mu(x, u, \lambda, \mu, t)\ ,\qquad \dot{\lambda} = -H_x(x, u, \lambda, \mu, t)\ ,$$
$$\dot{\mu} = -H_y(x, u, \lambda, \mu, t) \tag{94}$$

with the transversality condition $\mu(t_f) = \underline{0}$.

Let $\left(x^{\min}, u^{\min} \right)$ and $\left(x^{\max}, u^{\max} \right)$ be the solutions of the above optimal control problems to which are attached performance levels written $J^{\min}$ and $J^{\max}$, a fuzzy dual solution of the optimal control problem will be given by:

$$\tilde{u}(t) = (u^{\min}(t) + u^{\max}(t) / 2) + \varepsilon \left| u^{\max}(t) - u^{\min}(t) \right| / 2t \in [t_0, t_f] \tag{95}$$

with an expected fuzzy dual performance given by:

$$\tilde{J} = (J^{\min} + J^{\max} / 2) + \varepsilon \left| J^{\max} - J^{\min} \right| / 2 \tag{96}$$

Finally, J^{min}, J^{max} and $\tilde{J}$ can be compared with J^{mean} to assess the influence of uncertainty in the expected performance.

EXAMPLE OF APPLICATION: INITIAL STATE UNCERTAINTY

Consider the following optimal control problem:

$$\min \frac{1}{2} \int_0^{+\infty} e^{-\delta t} (x^2 + u^2) \cdot dt \text{ with } \delta > 0, \; \dot{x} = u \text{ and } x(0) = x_0 \tag{97}$$

The Hamilton-Jacobi-Bellman equations is here:

$$\frac{\partial}{\partial t} J^* + \min_{u(t)} \left\{ \frac{1}{2} (x^2 + u^2) e^{-\delta t} + \left(\frac{\partial}{\partial x} J^*(x,t) \right) \cdot u \right\} = 0 \tag{98}$$

It is easy to show (Farhadinia, 2014) that its solution is such as:

$$u^*(t) = \frac{1}{2} (\delta - \sqrt{\delta^2 + 4}) \cdot x(t) \tag{99}$$

So that the optimal behavior of the system is given by:

$$x^*(t) = e^{\frac{1}{2} \left(\delta - \sqrt{\delta^2 + 4} \right) \cdot t} \cdot x_0 \tag{100}$$

In the case in which there is an uncertainty on the initial value of the state x, such as $y(0) = \lambda \cdot x_0$, the dynamics of the fuzzy dual term will be such as:

$$\dot{y} = \frac{1}{2}\left(\delta - \sqrt{\delta^2 + 4}\right) \cdot y \text{ with } y(0) = \lambda \cdot x_0 \tag{101}$$

and the uncertainty at time t will be:

$$y(t) = \lambda \cdot e^{\frac{1}{2}\left(\delta - \sqrt{\delta^2 + 4}\right) \cdot t} \cdot x_0 \tag{102}$$

Following the proposed approach, the Hamilton-Jacobi-Bellman equation becomes:

$$\frac{\partial}{\partial t} J^* + \min_{u(t)} \left[\frac{1}{2}(x^2 + u^2)e^{-\delta t} + \varepsilon \cdot xy + \left(\frac{\partial}{\partial x} J^*(x,t) \right) \cdot u \right] = 0 \tag{103}$$

The solutions of (66) and (67) can be summarized here by:

$$u^*(t) = \frac{1}{2}\left(\delta - \sqrt{\delta^2 + 4 \mp \lambda}\right) \cdot x(t) \tag{104}$$

with a resulting evolution for the state summarized by:

$$x^*(t) = e^{\frac{1}{2}\left(\delta - \sqrt{\delta^2 + 4 \pm \lambda}\right) \cdot t} \cdot x_0 \tag{105}$$

and a state uncertainty at time *t* given by:

$$\frac{1}{2}\left[(1+\lambda) \cdot e^{\frac{1}{2}\left(\delta - \sqrt{\delta^2 + 4 - \lambda}\right) \cdot t} - (1-\lambda) \cdot e^{\frac{1}{2}\left(\delta - \sqrt{\delta^2 + 4 + \lambda}\right) \cdot t} \right] \cdot x_0 \tag{106}$$

which is always less than the value given by (100) for $t > 0$.

CONCLUSION

In this chapter a new approach has been developed to cope with uncertain optimal control problems. First a connection has been established between dual numbers encountered in the design and analysis of kinematics for mechanical systems and triangular fuzzy numbers for which different total orders have been considered. Fuzzy-dual functions, fuzzy-dual functionals and fuzzy-dual differential equations have been introduced, leading to the formulation of fuzzy-dual optimal control problems where the criteria of optimization is a fuzzy dual functional and the state representation function is a fuzzy dual function.

Adopting first a variational calculus approach, the fuzzy dual extension of the Euler's necessary conditions has been established, then the introduction of the fuzzy-dual Bellman's optimality principle has led to the formulation of a fuzzy-dual Hamilton-Jacobi-Bellman equation characterizing fuzzy-dual optimal solutions. Finally, a fuzzy dual version of the Pontryagin's optimality principle has been established.

The developed approach, by handling fuzzy-dual numbers where uncertainty represented by a single parameter limits the computational burden associated with fuzzy optimal control problems and should allow to treat large uncertain optimal control problems by developing an integrated sensitivity analysis of the proposed solution to the optimal control problem formulated as a fuzzy dual optimal control problem.

The authors acknowledge Tianjin Research Program of Application Foundation and Advanced Technology for Youths (Grant No. 15JCQNJC04400), Fundamental Research Funds for the Central Universities (Grant No. 3122015C004).

REFERENCES

Bellman, R. E. (1954). Dynamic Programming and a new formalism in the calculus of variations. *Proceedings of the National Academy of Sciences of the United States of America*, *40*(4), 231–235. doi:10.1073/pnas.40.4.231 PMID:16589462

Cosenza, C. A. N., & Mora-Camino, F. (2016). *Fuzzy Dual Numbers: Theory and Applications*. COPPE/UFRJ.

Farhadinia, B. (2014). Pontryagin's Minimum Principle for Fuzzy Optimal Control Problems. *Iranian Journal of Fuzzy Sets*, *11*(2), 27–43.

Fisher, I. S. (1999). *Dual-Number Methods in Kinematics, Statics and Dynamics*. CRC Press.

Messelmi, F. (2013). *Analysis of Dual Functions*, Annual Review of Chaos Theory. *Bifurcations and Dynamical Systems*, *4*, 37–54.

Mora-Camino, F., & Faye, R. M. (2017). Commande optimale: Approche Variationnelle. Harmattan.

Peng. (1992). Stochastic Hamilton-Jacobi-Bellman Equation. *SIAM J. Control Optim.*, *30*(2), 284–304.

Pontryagin, L. S. (1986). *The Mathematical Theory of Optimal Processes*. Gordon and Breach Science Publishers.

Stengel, R. (1993). *Optimal Control and Estimation*. New York: Dover publications.

Ying, H. (2000). *Fuzzy Control and Modelling: Analytical Foundations and Applications*. Wiley-IEEE Press. doi:10.1109/9780470544730

Zadeh, L. A. (1965). Fuzzy sets. *Information and Control*, *8*(3), 338–353. doi:10.1016/S0019-9958(65)90241-X

Chapter 4

A Study of Fully Fuzzy Linear Fractional Programming Problems by Signed Distance Ranking Technique

Moumita Deb
Karimganj Polytechnic, India

ABSTRACT

The aim of this chapter is to study fully fuzzy linear fractional programming (FFLFP) problems where all coefficients of the decision variables and parameters are characterized by triangular fuzzy numbers. To deal with this, the authors have first to transform FFLFP problems to fuzzy linear programming (FLP) problems by using Charnes and Cooper method and then use signed distance ranking to convert fuzzy linear programming (FLP) problems to crisp linear programming (LP) problems. The proposed method is solved by using the simplex method to find the optimal solution of the problem. The authors have studied sensitivity analysis to determine changes in the optimal solution of the fully fuzzy linear fractional programming (FFLFP) problems resulting from changes in the parameters. To demonstrate the proposed method, one numerical example is solved.

INTRODUCTION

Mathematical optimization is the process of -finding the conditions that give the maximum or the minimum value of a function. A number of methods have been developed for solving different types of optimization problems (Astolfi, 2006).

DOI: 10.4018/978-1-5225-5091-4.ch004

The technique of Linear programming (LP) may be used for solving broad range of problems arising in business, government, industry, hospitals, libraries, etc. As a decision making(DM) tool, it has demonstrated its value in various fields such as production, finance, marketing, research and development and personnel management. The goal of LP is to determine the values of decision variables that maximize or minimize a linear objective function, where decision variables are subject to linear constraints. The Hungarian mathematician Bela Martos (1960, 1961) has first formulated a linear fractional programming (LFP) problem. In mathematical optimization, LFP is a generalization of LP. Whereas the objective function in a linear programming problem is a linear function, the objective function in a linear-fractional programming problem is a ratio of two linear functions. A linear programming problem can be regarded as a special case of a linear-fractional programming problem in which the denominator is a constant. The mathematical form of linear fractional programming problem is stated by Charnes and Cooper (1962) is given below:

$$\text{Max or Min } Z(x) = \frac{cx + \alpha}{dx + \beta} = \frac{N^r}{D^r}$$

subject to the constraints:

$$Ax \begin{pmatrix} \leq \\ = \\ \geq \end{pmatrix} b, x \geq 0$$

where $x \in R^n$ represents the vector of variables to be determined, $c, d \in R^n$ and $b \in R^m$ are vectors of (known) coefficients, $A \in R^{m \times n}$ is a (known) matrix of coefficients and $\alpha, \beta \in R$ are constants. The constraints have to restrict the feasible region to $dx + \beta > 0$, i.e., the region on which the D^r is positive.

Zadeh (1965) introduced the notion of fuzzy sets to describe vagueness mathematically in its very abstractness and tried to solve such problems by giving a certain grade of membership to each member of a given set. Zadeh (1965) has defined a fuzzy set as a generalization of the characteristic function of a subset. A fuzzy set can be defined mathematically by assigning to each possible individual in the universe of discourse, a value representing its grade of membership in the fuzzy set. The membership grades are very often represented by real numbers in the closed interval between 0 and 1. The nearer the value of an element to unity, the higher the grade of its membership.

Characteristic function of a set A is denoted by χ_A (x) and is defined as follows (Ross, 2005):

$$\chi_A(x) = \begin{cases} 1 \ if \ x \in X \\ 0 \ if \ x \notin X \end{cases}$$

i.e., the characteristic function maps elements of X to elements of the set {0, 1} which is expressed as-

$$\mu_A(x) : X \to \{0,1\}.$$

For each $x \in X$, when $\chi_A(x) = 1$, x is said to be a member of A; when $\chi_A(x) = 0$, x is as a non-member of A.

Zadeh extended the notion of binary membership to accommodate various "degrees of membership" on the real continuous interval [0, 1], where the endpoints 0 and 1 corresponds no membership and full membership, respectively. The sets on the universe X that can accommodate ''degrees of membership'' were termed by Zadeh as Fuzzy Sets. The membership function is denoted by $\mu_A(x)$. The properties of this membership functions are (Ross, 2005):

1. Normal, i.e., $\mu_A(x) = 1$,
2. Monotonic and
3. Symmetric.

Fuzzy sets are always functions, which map a universe of objects, say X, onto the unit interval [0, 1]. Hence, every function that maps X onto [0, 1] is a fuzzy set, i.e.,

$$\mu_{\tilde{A}}(x) : X \to \left[0,1\right].$$

The symbol $\mu_{\tilde{A}}(x)$ is the degree of membership function of element x in the fuzzy set $\tilde{A}$. Thus $\mu_{\tilde{A}}(x)$ is a value on the unit interval that measures the degree to which element x belongs to fuzzy set $\tilde{A}$; equivalently $\mu_{\tilde{A}}(x)$ = degree to which $x \in \tilde{A}$. A fuzzy number is a quantity whose value is imprecise, rather than exact as is the case with ordinary or single valued numbers. Any fuzzy number can be thought of as a function whose domain is a specified set (usually the set of real numbers), and whose range is the span of non-negative real numbers between real numbers between,- a lower and an upper bound, for example [0,1000]. Each numerical value in the domain is assigned a specific grade or degree of membership function where 0 represents the smallest possible grade, and 1000 is the largest possible grade.

Many real-world problems require handling and evaluation of fuzzy data for making decisions. To evaluate and compare different alternatives, it is necessary to rank fuzzy numbers. Ranking of fuzzy numbers is an important tool in decision making. Fuzzy numbers are partially ordered and cannot be compared like real numbers which can be linearly ordered. In order to rank fuzzy quantities, each fuzzy quantity is converted into a real number and compared by defining a ranking function from the set of fuzzy numbers to a set of real numbers which assign a real number to each fuzzy number where a natural order exists. Ranking fuzzy numbers were first proposed by Jain (1976) for decision making in fuzzy situations by representing the ill-defined quantity as a fuzzy set. The formulation of fuzzy linear programming (FLP) problem was introduced by Zimmermann (1978). After that, many researchers have studied the FLP problem and proposed several approaches for solving FLP problems.

Sensitivity analysis in FLP problems with crisp parameters and soft constraints was first considered by Hamacher et al. (1978). Tanaka et al. (1986) have formulated a fuzzy linear programming problem with fuzzy coefficients and the value of information was discussed via sensitivity analysis. Sakawa and Yano (1988) presented fuzzy approach for solving multi-objective linear fractional programming (MOLFP) problem. Dutta et al. (1992) have studied sensitivity analysis for FLFP problems. Gupta and Bhatia (2001) studied the measurement of sensitivity for changes of violations in the aspiration level for FMOLFP problem. Lotfi et al . (2010) developed sensitivity analysis approach for the additive model in a fuzzy environment. Kheirfam and Hasani (2010) studied the basis invariance sensitivity analysis for FLP problems. Kumar et al. (2011) discussed some important cases of sensitivity analysis which includes deletion of a fuzzy variable and deletion of a fuzzy constraint. Ebrahimnejad (2011) has generalized the concept of sensitivity analysis in fuzzy number linear programming (FNLP) problems by applying primal simplex algorithm and the fuzzy dual simplex algorithm and showed the post- optimality analysis on LP problems with fuzzy numbers. Bhatia et al. (2012) have studied sensitivity analysis of fuzzy LP problems in which all the parameters are represented by LR-flat fuzzy numbers. Farhadinia (2014) proposed a method for solving the interval-valued trapezoidal fuzzy number LP problem based on the comparison of the interval-valued trapezoidal fuzzy numbers by the help of signed distance ranking and hence studied sensitivity analysis for the level interval-valued trapezoidal fuzzy number LP problems.

The objective of this paper is to study the FFLFP problems where parameters and variables are characterized by triangular fuzzy number (TFN). By suitable transformation, the FFLFP problem reduces to FFLP problem and the transformed FFLP problem is again reduces to its crisp LP problem by using signed distance ranking. The problem is then solved by the simplex method to find the optimal solution and hence we have studied sensitivity analysis for the linear fractional programming problem.

DEFINITIONS AND PRELIMINARIES

The following few definitions are related to the present methodology used in this article which are taken from Zimmermann (2001) and Lee (2005).

Definition 2.1: (Zimmermann, 2001) If X is a collection of objects denoted generally by x, then a fuzzy set $\tilde{A}$ in X is defined as a set of ordered pairs:

$$\tilde{A} = \left\{ (x, \mu_{\tilde{A}}(x)) : x \in X \right\}$$

$\mu_A(x)$ is called the membership function or grade of membership of x in $\tilde{A}$ that maps X to the membership space.

Definition 2.2: (Zimmermann, 2001) The support of a fuzzy set $\tilde{A}$ is the crisp set of all points x in X such that $\mu_{\tilde{A}}(x) > 0$ and is denoted by Supp($\tilde{A}$).

i.e., $Supp(\tilde{A}) = \left\{ x \mid \mu_{\tilde{A}}(x) > 0 \right\}$.

Definition 2.3: (Zimmermann, 2001) The (crisp) set of elements that belong to the fuzzy set $\tilde{A}$ at least to the degree α is called the α-cut (α-level) set and is denoted by

$$A_\alpha = \left\{ x \in X \mid \mu_{\tilde{A}}(x) \geq \alpha \right\}.$$

Fuzzy Numbers

The notion of fuzzy numbers was introduced by Dubois and Prade (1979).

Definition 2.4: (Dubois and Prade, 1979) A fuzzy subset $\tilde{A}$ of the real line R with membership function $\mu_{\tilde{A}}(x) : X \to [0,1]$ is called a fuzzy number if

1. $\tilde{A}$ is normal, i.e., there exists an element x_0 such that $\mu_{\tilde{A}}(x_0) = 1$,
2. $\tilde{A}$ is convex, i.e.,
3. $\mu_{\tilde{A}}[\lambda x + (1-\lambda)y] \geq \mu_{\tilde{A}}(x) \cap \mu_{\tilde{A}}(y)$, $x, y \in R, \forall \lambda \in [0,1]$,
4. $\mu_{\tilde{A}}(x)$ is upper continuous, and
5. $Supp(\tilde{A})$ is bounded, where $Supp(\tilde{A}) = \{x \in R \mid \mu_{\tilde{A}}(x) > 0\}$.

Definition 2.5: (Lee, 2005) A fuzzy number $\tilde{A}$ is a convex normalized fuzzy set on the real line R such that

1.   It exists at-least one $x_0 \in R$ with $\mu_{\tilde{A}}(x_0) = 1$.
2. $\mu_{\tilde{A}}(x)$ is piecewise continuous.

Triangular Fuzzy Number

Triangular fuzzy numbers (TFNs) are introduced by Dubois and Prade (1980).

The following few definitions are stated by Chiang et al. (2005), Lee (2005) and Nagoor Gani et al. (2012).

Definition 2.6: (Chiang et al., 2005) Let $\tilde{A} = (a_1, a_2, a_3), a_1 < a_2 < a_3$ be a fuzzy set on $R = (-\infty, \infty)$. It is called a triangular fuzzy number, if its membership function is given by:

$$\mu_{\tilde{A}}(x) = \begin{cases} \dfrac{x - a_1}{a_2 - a_1}, & if \, a_1 \leq x \leq a_2 \\ \dfrac{a_3 - x}{a_3 - a_2}, & if \, a_2 \leq x \leq a_3 \\ 0, & otherwise \end{cases}$$

If $a_1 = a_2 = a_3$ then $\tilde{A} = (a_1, a_1, a_1)$.

Figure 1. Triangular fuzzy number a= a1, a2, a3

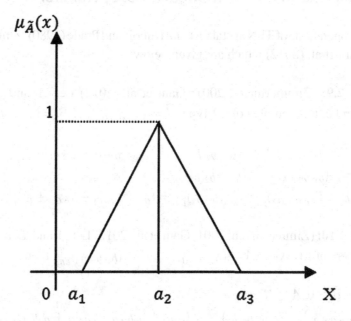

Definition 2.7: (Lee, 2005) From Definition of triangular fuzzy number, the α- cut operation of interval A_α is obtained as follows $\forall \alpha \in [0,1]$.

$$A_\alpha = [a_1^\alpha, a_3^\alpha] = [(a_2 - a_1)\alpha + a_1, -(a_3 - a_2)\alpha + a_3].$$

Definition 2.8: (Gani et al., 2012) A fuzzy number $\tilde{A}$ is said to be a LR- type fuzzy number iff,

$$\mu_{\tilde{A}}(x) = \begin{cases} L\left(\dfrac{a_2 - x}{a_1}\right), & if\, a_2 - a_1 \leq x \leq a_2 \\ R(\dfrac{x - a_2}{a_3}), & if\, a_2 \leq x \leq a_2 + a_3 \\ 0, otherwise \end{cases}$$

L is for left and R for right reference.

Arithmetic Operations of Triangular Fuzzy Number

Arithmetic operations of TFN are taken from Dubois and Prade (1980), Zimmermann (2001), Gani et al. (2012) which are given below:

Definition 2.9: (Zimmermann, 2001; Gani et al., 2012) Let $\tilde{A}$ and $\tilde{B}$ are two triangular fuzzy number of LR-type: $\tilde{A} = (a_1, a_2, a_3)_{LR}$, $\tilde{B} = (b_1, b_2, b_3)_{LR}$, then

1. $\tilde{A} \oplus \tilde{B} = (a_1, a_2, a_3)_{LR} \oplus (b_1, b_2, b_3)_{LR} = (a_1 + b_1, a_2 + b_2, a_3 + b_3)_{LR}$,
2. $-\tilde{B} = -(b_1, b_2, b_3)_{LR} = (b_3, -b_2, b_3)_{LR}$,
3. $\tilde{A} - \tilde{B} = (a_1, a_2, a_3)_{LR} - (b_1, b_2, b_3)_{LR} = (a_1 + b_3, a_2 - b_2, a_3 + b_1)_{LR}$.

Definition 2.10: (Zimmermann, 2001; Gani et al., 2012) Let $\tilde{A}$ and $\tilde{B}$ are be fuzzy numbers of LR-type: $\tilde{A} = (a_1, a_2, a_3)_{LR}$, $\tilde{B} = (b_1, b_2, b_3)_{LR}$, then

1. for $\tilde{A}, \tilde{B} > 0, \tilde{A} \otimes \tilde{B} =$
   $(a_1, a_2, a_3)_{LR} \otimes (b_1, b_2, b_3)_{LR} \approx (a_1 b_2 + a_2 b_1, a_2 b_2, a_2 b_3 + a_3 b_2)_{LR}$
2. for $\tilde{A} < 0, \tilde{B} > 0, \tilde{A} \otimes \tilde{B} =$
   $(a_3, -a_2, a_1)_{LR} \otimes (b_1, b_2, b_3)_{LR} \approx (a_3 b_2 - a_2 b_1, -a_2 b_2, a_1 b_2 - a_2 b_3)_{LR}$
3. for $\tilde{A}, \tilde{B} < 0, \tilde{A} \otimes \tilde{B} =$
   $(a_3, -a_2, a_1)_{LR} \otimes (b_3, -b_2, b_1)_{LR} \approx (-a_2 b_3 - a_3 b_2, a_2 b_2, -a_2 b_1 - a_1 b_2)_{LR}$

Figure 2. LR representation of fuzzy number

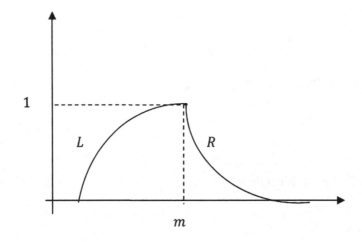

The following operations are given by Gani et al. (2005).

Definition 2.11: (Gani et al., 2005) Let $\tilde{A}$ be a triangular fuzzy number of LR-type:

$$\tilde{A} = (a_1, a_2, a_3)_{LR}, \text{ then } \tilde{A}^{-1} = \frac{1}{\tilde{A}} = \left(\frac{1}{a_1}, \frac{1}{a_2}, \frac{1}{a_3}\right)_{LR}.$$

Definition 2.12: (Gani et al., 2005) Let $\tilde{A}$ and $\tilde{B}$ are fuzzy numbers of LR-type:

$$\tilde{A} = (a_1, a_2, a_3)_{LR}, \tilde{B} = (b_1, b_2, b_3)_{LR}, \text{ then}$$

1. For $\tilde{A}, \tilde{B} > 0, \tilde{A} \div \tilde{B} = (a_1, a_2, a_3)_{LR} \div (b_1, b_2, b_3)_{LR}$
$\approx (a_1 / b_2 + a_2 / b_1, a_2 / b_2, a_2 / b_3 + a_3 / b_2)_{LR}$

2. For $\tilde{A} < 0, \tilde{B} > 0, \tilde{A} \div \tilde{B} = (a_3, -a_2, a_1)_{LR} \div (b_1, b_2, b_3)_{LR}$
$\approx (a_3/b_2 - a_2 / b_1, -a_2 / b_2, a_1 / b_2 - a_2 / b_3)_{LR}$

3. For $\tilde{A}, \tilde{B} < 0, \tilde{A} \div \tilde{B} = (a_3, -a_2, a_1)_{LR} \div (b_3, -b_2, b_1)_{LR}$
$\approx (-a_2/b_3 - a_3/b_2, a_2/b_2, -a_2/b_1 - a_1 / b_2)_{LR}$

Definition 2.13: (Gani et al., 2005) Let $\tilde{A}$ be a triangular fuzzy number of LR-type:

$$\tilde{A} = (a_1, a_2, a_3)_{LR} \text{ and } \lambda \text{ be any scalar then } \lambda\tilde{A} = \begin{cases} (\lambda a_1, \lambda a_2, \lambda a_3), if \lambda > 0 \\ (\lambda a_3, -\lambda a_2, \lambda a_1), if \lambda < 0 \end{cases}.$$

METHODOLOGY

Defuzzification

Defuzzification is the process of producing a quantifiable result in crisp logic, given fuzzy sets and corresponding membership degrees. It is the process that maps a fuzzy set to a crisp set. It is typically needed in fuzzy control systems. These will have a number of rules that transform a number of variables into a fuzzy result, i.e., the result is described in terms of membership in fuzzy sets. For example, rules designed to decide how much pressure to apply might result in "Decrease Pressure, Maintain Pressure, Increase Pressure, etc." Thus, the defuzzification method provides a correspondence from the set of all fuzzy sets into the set of all real numbers.

Signed Distance Ranking

Yao and Wu (2000) used signed distance to define ordering. This signed distance has some similar properties to the properties induced by the signed distance in real numbers. Also they define "signed distance" as both positive and negative values to define ordering.

The Ranking System of Fuzzy Numbers on R

We give some preliminary definitions and results on signed distance which can be found in Yao and Wu (2000), Pu and Liu (1980) and Kauffman and Gupta (1991) are listed below.

Definition 3.1: (Kauffman and Gupta, 1991) For each $p, q \in R = (-\infty, \infty)$, define the signed distance of d_0 of p, q by $d_0(p, q) = p - q$.

Since

$$d_0(p, 0) = p, d_0(p, q) = p - q = d_0(p, 0) - d_0(q, 0)$$

i.e. $d_0(p, 0)$ denotes the signed distance of p from 0.

If $p > 0, d_0(p, 0) = p$ implies that p is on the right-hand side of 0 with distance p.

If $p < 0, d_0(p, 0) = -p$ implies that p is on the left-hand side of 0 with distance -p.

Therefore, we call $d_0(p, 0) = p$ is the signed distance of 'p' measured from 0. Thus, we have the following way to define the rank of any two numbers on R. For each $p, q \in R$,

$d_0(p, q) > 0 \; iff d_0(q, 0) < d_0(p, 0) \; iff \; q < p,$
$d_0(p, q) < 0 \; iff d_0(p, 0) < d_0(q, 0) \; iff \; p < q,$
$d_0(p, q) = 0 \; iff d_0(p, 0) = d_0(q, 0) \; iff \; p = q$

We convert this crisp ranking system into ranking of fuzzy numbers on R.

Definition 3.2: (Pu and Liu, 1980) Fuzzy Point: Let $\tilde{p}$ be a fuzzy point on $R = (-\infty, \infty)$ .It is called a fuzzy point if its membership function is

$$\mu_{\tilde{p}}(x) = \begin{cases} 1 & if \ x = p \\ 0 & if \ x \neq p \end{cases}$$

Let $F_p(\alpha)$ be the family of all level α fuzzy points.

Definition 3.3: (Kauffman and Gupta, 1991) The fuzzy set $\tilde{p}_\alpha$ of $R, 0 \leq \alpha \leq 1$ is called a level α fuzzy point if

$$\mu_{\tilde{p}_\alpha}(x) = \begin{cases} \alpha & if \ x = p \\ 0 & if \ x \neq p \end{cases}.$$

Definition 3.4: (Kauffman and Gupta, 1991) The fuzzy set $[p_\alpha, q_\alpha]$ of R, $0 \leq \alpha \leq 1$ is called a level α fuzzy interval if- $\mu_{[p_\alpha, q_\alpha]}(x) = \begin{cases} \alpha & if \ x = p \\ 0 & if \ x \neq p \end{cases}$

For each $\alpha \in [0,1] \in [0,1]$, let $F_I(\alpha) = \left\{ [p_\alpha, q_\alpha] \ \forall p < q, p, q \in R \right\}$

Definition 3.5: (Yao and Wu, 2000) (i) A fuzzy subset $\tilde{A}$ of R is convex iff every ordinary subset $A(\alpha) = \{ x \mid \mu_{\tilde{A}}(x) \geq \alpha \}, \forall \alpha \in [0,1]$ is convex, that is, it is a closed interval of R.

A fuzzy subset $\tilde{A}$ of R is normal $\vee_{x \in R} \mu_{\tilde{A}}(x) = 1$.

A fuzzy number in R is a fuzzy subset of R which is convex and normal.

Definition 3.6: (Yao and Wu, 2000) Let F_N be the family of fuzzy numbers of R satisfying Definition 3.5 and $F_p(1)$ be the family of all level 1 fuzzy point.

$$\begin{bmatrix} (0.5, 1, 1.5) \\ (2, 3, 4) \end{bmatrix}$$
$$\begin{bmatrix} (1.5, 2, 2.5) \\ (1, 2, 3) \end{bmatrix}$$
$$\begin{bmatrix} (0.2, 1, 1.2) \\ (1, 3, 5) \end{bmatrix} \begin{bmatrix} (1.3, 2, 2.5) \\ (0.5, 2, 4.5) \end{bmatrix}$$

Let $F = F_N \cup F_p(1)$, and the left end point of the α-cut of $\tilde{S}_R(\alpha)$.

By Definition 3.5 (i), this α-cut $S(\alpha) = [S_L(\alpha), S_R(\alpha)]$ is a closed interval, where $(0 \leq \alpha \leq 1)$. If $\tilde{S} = p_1 \in F_p(1)$, then both the left and right end points of its α-cut are the same point p, i.e. $S(\alpha) = [p, p] = p, \forall \alpha \in [0,1]$. Here the level 1 fuzzy point q_1 may be regarded as the degenerated case of the triangular fuzzy number (p, q, r) in which $p = q = r$ so that $F_p(1) \subset F_N$.

Property 3.7: (Yao and Wu, 2000) For $\tilde{S}, \tilde{T} \in F$ and if $\tilde{S}, \tilde{T} \in F_N$ then the α-cut of

$$\tilde{S}(+)\tilde{T} = [S_L(\alpha)(+)T_L(\alpha), S_R(\alpha)(+)T_R(\alpha)], (0 \leq \alpha \leq 1).$$

Property 3.8: (Yao and Wu, 2000) For $\tilde{S}, \tilde{T} \in F$ and if $\tilde{S}, \tilde{T} \in F_N$ then the α-cut of

$$\tilde{S}(-)\tilde{T} = [S_L(\alpha)(-)T_L(\alpha), S_R(\alpha)(-)T_R(\alpha)], (0 \leq \alpha \leq 1).$$

Property 3.9: (Yao and Wu, 2000) If $p_1, q_1 \in F_p(1)$ and $\tilde{P} \in F_N$ then

1.   If $p > 0$, then the α-cut of $p_1(.)\tilde{S} = [pS_L(\alpha), pS_R(\alpha)]$,
2.   2. If $p < 0$, then the α-cut of $p_1(.)\tilde{S} = [pS_R(\alpha), pS_L(\alpha)]$,

where $0 \leq \alpha \leq 1$.

The following Decomposition Principle is stated by Yao and Wu (2000).

Theorem: Decomposition Principle

For $\tilde{P} \in F_N, \mu_{\tilde{P}}(z) = \vee_{\alpha \in [0,1]}(\alpha \wedge C_{P_\alpha}(z)) = \vee_{\alpha \in [0,1]} \mu_{[P_L(\alpha)_\alpha, P_R(\alpha)_\alpha]}(z)$

$= \mu_{\cup_{\alpha \in [0,1]}[P_L(\alpha)_\alpha, P_R(\alpha)_\alpha]}(z)$

or,

$$\tilde{P} = \bigcup_{\alpha \in [0,1]}[P_L(\alpha)_\alpha, P_R(\alpha)_\alpha]$$

where $C_{P_\alpha} = 1$ *if* $z \in P_\alpha$ and $C_{P_\alpha} = 0$ *if* $z \neq P_\alpha$.

Remark 3.11: (Yao and Wu, 2000)

1. For $p_1 \in F_p(1)$, the above theorem becomes $p_1 = \vee_{\alpha \in [0,1]}[p_\alpha, p_\alpha]$.
2. For each $\alpha \in [0,1]$, there is one-one mapping between the level α fuzzy interval $[p_\alpha, p_\alpha]$ and real interval $[p, q], p < q$.

For $\tilde{S}, \tilde{T} \in F$, by Decomposition Principle (Yao and Wu 2000), we can write $\tilde{S}, \tilde{T}$ as

$$\tilde{S} = \bigcup_{\alpha \in [0,1]}[S_L(\alpha)_\alpha, S_R(\alpha)_\alpha], \ \tilde{T} = \bigcup_{\alpha \in [0,1]}[T_L(\alpha)_\alpha, T_R(\alpha)_\alpha].$$

The level α fuzzy intervals $[S_L(\alpha)_\alpha, S_R(\alpha)_\alpha]$ and $[T_L(\alpha)_\alpha, T_R(\alpha)_\alpha]$ correspond to real intervals $[S_L(\alpha), S_R(\alpha)]$ and $[T_L(\alpha), T_R(\alpha)]$ respectively.

The mid-points are-

$$M(S(\alpha)) = \frac{1}{2}[S_L(\alpha) + S_R(\alpha)], \ M(T(\alpha)) = \frac{1}{2}[T_L(\alpha) + T_R(\alpha)].$$

By Definition of signed distance, the crisp signed distance between $M(S(\alpha))$ and $M(T(\alpha))$ is

$$d_0(M(S(\alpha)), M(T(\alpha))) = M(S(\alpha)) - M(T(\alpha)), \forall \alpha \in [0,1].$$

Hence, by using $\tilde{P} = \bigcup_{\alpha \in [0,1]}[P_L(\alpha)_\alpha, P_R(\alpha)_\alpha]$, in Decomposition Principle, we may assign the signed distance of any two fuzzy sets $\tilde{S}, \tilde{T} \in F$ by considering the mean of the distance of these two mid-points $M(S(\alpha)), M(T(\alpha))$ over $\alpha \ in \ [0,1]$

Definition 3.11: (Yao and Wu, 2000) For $\tilde{S}, \tilde{T} \in F$, the signed distance of $\tilde{S}, \tilde{T}$ is defined as follows:

$$d(\tilde{S}, \tilde{T}) =$$

$$\frac{1}{1-0} \int_0^1 [M(S(\alpha)) - M(T(\alpha))] d\alpha = \qquad .$$

$$\frac{1}{2} \int_0^1 [S_L(\alpha) + S_R(\alpha) - T_L(\alpha) - T_R(\alpha)] d\alpha$$

Property 3.12: (Yao and Wu, 2000) For $\tilde{S}, \tilde{T} \in F$, $d(\tilde{S}, \tilde{T}) = d(\tilde{S}, 0_1) - d(\tilde{T}, 0_1)$.

Remark 3.13: (Yao and Wu, 2000) For $\tilde{S} \in F$, from Definition, we have that the signed distance of $S_L(\alpha)$ *and* $S_R(\alpha)$ measured from 0 is

$$d_0(S_L(\alpha), 0) = S_L(\alpha) \text{ and } d_0(S_R(\alpha), 0) = S_R(\alpha) \text{ respectively.}$$

Therefore, we may define the signed distance of the interval $[S_L(\alpha), S_R(\alpha)]$ which is measured from the origin 0, by

$$d_0[[S_L(\alpha), S_R(\alpha)], 0) = \frac{1}{2}[d_0(S_L(\alpha), 0) + d_0(S_R(\alpha), 0)] = \frac{1}{2}[S_L(\alpha) + S_R(\alpha)].$$

Its average over $\alpha \in [0, 1]$ is $d(\tilde{S}, 0_1) = \frac{1}{2} \int_0^1 [S_L(\alpha) + S_R(\alpha)] d\alpha$.

It means that the signed distance of fuzzy set $\tilde{S}$ from 0_1 (y-axis).

By Property 3.12, we have $d(\tilde{S}, \tilde{T}) = d(\tilde{S}, 0_1) - d(\tilde{T}, 0_1)$ is the difference of signed distance $d(\tilde{S}, 0_1)$ of $\tilde{S}$ from 0_1 and signed distance $d(\tilde{T}, 0_1)$ of $\tilde{T}$ from 0_1, i.e., the difference of the signed distances of two fuzzy sets $\tilde{S}, \tilde{T}$ fro m0_1 (y-axis). For each $\alpha \in [0, 1]$, the crisp interval $[S_L(\alpha), S_R(\alpha)]$ and the level α fuzzy interval $[[S_L(\alpha), S_R(\alpha)]; \alpha]$ are in one to one correspondence. Therefore, the signed distance from $[[S_L(\alpha), S_R(\alpha)]; \alpha]$ to $\tilde{0}$ may be defined as follows-

$$d_0([[S_L(\alpha), S_R(\alpha)]; \alpha], \tilde{0}) = d_0([S_L(\alpha), S_R(\alpha)], 0) = \frac{1}{2}[S_L(\alpha) + S_R(\alpha)].$$

Since $\tilde{S} \in F$, $S_L(\alpha)$ *and* $S_R(\alpha)$ exist and are integrable for $\alpha \in [0, 1]$, we have the following definition

Definition 3.14: (Yao and Wu, 2000) Let $\tilde{S} \in F$, the signed distance of $\tilde{S}$ measured from $\tilde{0}$ is defined as $d(\tilde{S}, 0) = \dfrac{1}{2} \displaystyle\int_0^1 [S_L(\alpha) + S_R(\alpha)] d\alpha$.

Remark 3.15: Let $\tilde{C} = (c_1, c_2, c_3)$ be a triangular fuzzy number, then the left and the right α -cut of $\tilde{C}$ are given by

$$C_L(\alpha) = [(c_2 - c_1)\alpha + c_1], C_R(\alpha) = [-(c_3 - c_2)\alpha + c_3]$$

respectively.

By Definition 3.14, the signed distance of $\tilde{C}$ is

$$d(\tilde{C}, 0) = \frac{1}{2} \int_0^1 [(c_2 - c_1)\alpha + c_1, -(c_3 - c_2)\alpha + c_3] d\alpha = \frac{1}{4}[c_1 + 2c_2 + c_3].$$

The Fuzzy Linear Fractional Programming Problem

Phase-I

The fuzzy linear fractional programming is defined as below:

$$\text{Max } \tilde{Z}(x) = \frac{\tilde{c}x + \tilde{\alpha}}{\tilde{d}x + \tilde{\beta}} = \frac{(c_1, c_2, c_3)x + (\alpha_1, \alpha_2, \alpha_3)}{(d_1, d_2, d_3)x + (\beta_1, \beta_2, \beta_3)} \qquad (1.1)$$

subject to the constraints:

$$x \in S = \{x \mid \tilde{A}x \le \tilde{b}, x \ge 0\} = \{x \mid (a_1, a_2, a_3)x \le (b_1, b_2, b_3)\} \qquad (1.2)$$

$$x \ge 0 \qquad (1.3)$$

where

$$x \in R^n, \tilde{c}, \tilde{d} \in R^n \text{ and } \tilde{b} \in R^m, \tilde{A} \in R^{m \times n}, \alpha, \beta \in R$$

By using Charnes and Cooper method (1962), the fuzzy linear fractional programming (FLFP) problem (1.1)-(1.3) is reduced to a fuzzy linear programming (FLP) problem is as follows:

$$\text{Max } \tilde{z} = \tilde{c}y + \tilde{\alpha}t = (c_1, c_2, c_3)y + (\alpha_1, \alpha_2, \alpha_3)t \tag{1.4}$$

subject to the constraints:

$$(a_1, a_2, a_3)y - (b_1, b_2, b_3)t \leq 0, \tag{1.5}$$

$$(d_1, d_2, d_3)y + (\beta_1, \beta_2, \beta_3)t = 1, \tag{1.6}$$

$$y, t \geq 0 \tag{1.7}$$

where

$$t = \frac{1}{(d_1, d_2, d_3)x + (\beta_1, \beta_2, \beta_3)}, y = tx$$

By using signed distance ranking of triangular fuzzy number, the problem (1.4)-(1.7) reduces to a crisp linear programming (LP) problem as follows:

$$\text{Max } z = \frac{1}{4}\left[c_1 + 2c_2 + c_3\right]y + \frac{1}{4}\left[\alpha_1 + 2\alpha_2 + \alpha_3\right]t \tag{1.8}$$

subject to the constraint:

$$\frac{1}{4}[a_1 + 2a_2 + a_3]y - \frac{1}{4}[b_1 + 2b_2 + b_3]t \leq 0, \tag{1.9}$$

$$\frac{1}{4}[d_1 + 2d_2 + d_3]y + \frac{1}{4}[\beta_1 + 2\beta_2 + \beta_3]t = 1 \tag{1.10}$$

$$\text{Max } z = C'y + \alpha't \tag{1.11}$$

subject to the constraints:

$$A'y - B't \leq 0, \tag{1.12}$$

$$D'y + \beta't = 1 \tag{1.13}$$

where $y, t \geq 0$

$$A' = \frac{1}{4}[a_1 + 2a_2 + a_3], B' = \frac{1}{4}[b_1 + 2b_2 + b_3], C' = \frac{1}{4}[c_1 + 2c_2 + c_3],$$

$$D' = \frac{1}{4}[d_1 + 2d_2 + d_3], \alpha' = \frac{1}{4}[\alpha_1 + 2\alpha_2 + \alpha_3], \beta' = \frac{1}{4}[\beta_1 + 2\beta_2 + \beta_3].$$

By using LP package, the optimal solution is obtained.

The following few definitions are related to the present article which are as follows:

Definition 3.15: (Bajalinov, 2001) If a given vector $x = (x_1, x_2, \ldots, x_n)$ satisfies constraints (1.2) and (1.3), we will say that the vector x is a feasible solution of LFP problem (1.1)-(1.3).

Definition 3.16: (Bajalinov, 2001) If a given vector $x = (x_1, x_2, \ldots, x_n)$ is a feasible solution of maximization LFP problem (1.1)-(1.3), and provides maximal value for objective function $Z(x)$ over the feasible set S, we say that the vector x is an optimal solution of maximization LFP problem (1.1)-(1.3).

Definition 3.17: (Bajalinov, 2001) If the feasible set S is empty, i.e., $S = \varphi$, we say that the LFP problem is infeasible.

Definition 3.18: (Bajalinov, 2001) If objective function $Z(x)$ of a maximization (minimization) LFP problem has no upper finite (lower) bound, we say that the problem is unbounded.

Definition 3.19: (Bajalinov, 2001) The given vector $x = (x_1, x_2, \ldots, x_n)^T$ is a basic solution (or a basic vector) to system $Ax \leq b$, if vector x satisfies system –

$$\sum_{j \in J_B} A_j x_j = b$$

and

$$x_j = 0, \forall j \in J_N.$$

Those variables x_j whose indices are in the set J_B are said to be basic variables. If variable x_j is such that $j \in J_N$, then this variable is a non-basic variable.

Definition 3.20: (Bajalinov, 2001) The basic solution x is degenerate, if at least one of its basic variables is equal to zero, i.e., $\exists j \mid j \in J_B$, such that $x_j = 0$. In that case if $x_j \neq 0, \forall j \in J_B$, basic solution x is said to be non-degenerate .

Definition 3.21: (Bajalinov, 2001) Basic solution $x = (x_1, x_2, \dots\dots, x_n)^T$ of system $Ax \leq b$ is said to be a basic feasible solution (BFS) of problem (1.1)-(1.3) if all elements x_j, j=1,2,....,n, of vector x satisfy non-negativity constraints (1.3).

Theorem: (Ebrahimnejad, 2011) Let a linear programming (LP) problem have a basic feasible solution with fuzzy objective value $\tilde{Z}$ such that $\tilde{Z}_j - \tilde{C}_j > 0$ for some non-basic variable x_j, and if $y_j \leq 0$, then it is possible to obtain a new basic feasible solution with new fuzzy objective value $\tilde{Z}' \leq \tilde{Z}$.

Theorem: (Ebrahimnejad, 2011) Let there exists a basic feasible solution to a given LP problem with $\tilde{Z}_j - \tilde{C}_j > 0$ for some non-basic variable x_j and if $y_j \leq 0$, then the problem (1.4)-(1.6) has an unbounded optimal solution.

Theorem: Criteria of Optimality (Gupta et al., 1997; Bajalinov, 2001) Let a LP problem have a basic feasible solution to be an optimum is that $\tilde{Z}_j - \tilde{C}_j > 0$ for all j for which the column vector a_j not in the basis B.

The Fuzzy Simplex Algorithm

The steps for the computation of a fuzzy optimal solution are as follows:

Step 1: Convert the FFLFP problem into an FFLP problem by using $\tilde{y} = \tilde{t}\tilde{x}$.

Step 2: Convert the FFLP problem into a crisp LP problem by using signed distance ranking where both objective function and constraints are characterised by TFN.

Step 3: Check whether the objective function of the given LP problem is to be maximized or minimized. If it minimized then we convert it into a problem of maximizing it by using the result, Min $\tilde{z} = -$Max $(-\tilde{z})$.

Step 4: Check whether all $\tilde{b}_i$ (i=1, 2,...., m) are non-negative. If any one of $\tilde{b}_i$ is negative then multiply the corresponding in-equation of the constraints by -1, so as to get all $\tilde{b}_i$ (i=1, 2,.....,m) non-negative.

Step 5: Convert all the in-equations of the constraints into equations by introducing slack and/or surplus variables in the constraints. The costs of these variables equal to zero.

Step 6: Obtain an initial basic feasible solution to the given problem in the form $x_B = B^{-1}b$ and put it in the first column of the simplex table.

Step 7: Compute the net evaluation Δ_j, (j=1, 2,...., n) where $\Delta_j = z_j - c_j$.

Step 8: Examine the sign $\Delta_j = z_j - c_j$

If all $z_j - c_j \geq 0$ then the initial basic feasible solution x_B is an optimum basic feasible solution.

If at-least one $z_j - c_j < 0$, proceed to the next step.

Step 9: If there are more than one negative Δ_j then choose the most negative of them.it be Δ_r for some j= r.

If all $y_{ir} \leq 0$, (i=1, 2,...., m) then there is an unbounded solution to the given problem.

If at least one $y_{ir} > 0$, (i=1, 2,...., m) then the corresponding vector y_r enters the basis y_B.

Step 10: Compute the ratios $\left\{ \dfrac{x_{Bi}}{y_{ir}}, y_{ir} > 0, i = 1, 2, ..., m \right\}$ and choose the minimum

of them. Let the minimum of these ratios be $\dfrac{x_{Bk}}{y_{kr}}$. Then the vector y_k will

leave the basis y_B. The common element y_{kr} and this must be k^{th} and r^{th} column is known as leading or (pivotal) element of the table.

Step 11: Convert the leading element to unity by dividing its row by the leading element itself and all other elements in its column to zeroes by making the use of the relations-

$$\tilde{y}_{ij} = y_{ij} - \frac{y_{kj}}{y_{kr}} y_{ir}, i = 1, 2, ..., m + 1; i \neq k \text{ and } \hat{y}_{kj} = \frac{y_{kj}}{y_{kr}}, j = 0, 1, 2, ..., n.$$

Step 12: Go to Step 7 and repeat the computational procedure until either an optimum solution is obtained or the solution is unbounded.

Step 13: Compute the values of $x_1, x_2, ..., x_m$ by substituting the values of $y_1, y_2, ..., y_n$ and hence find the values of $\tilde{Z}_1, \tilde{Z}_2, ..., \tilde{Z}_m$.

NUMERICAL EXAMPLE

Consider the following fully fuzzy linear fractional programming problem as follows:

$$\text{Max } \tilde{Z}(x) = \frac{(5,6,7)\tilde{x}_1 + (3,5,6)\tilde{x}_2}{(1,2,3)\tilde{x}_1 + (5.5,7,8.5)}$$

subject to the constraints:

$$(0.5,1,1.5)\tilde{x}_1 + \left(1.5,2,2.5\right)\tilde{x}_2 \leq (2,3,5),$$

$$(2,3,4)\tilde{x}_1 + (1,2,3)\tilde{x}_2 \leq (5,6,7),$$

$$\tilde{x}_1, \tilde{x}_2 \geq 0.$$

Solution: By using Charnes and Cooper method (1962), the FLFP problem reduced to a FLP problem as follows:

$$\text{Max } \tilde{z} = (5,6,7)\tilde{y}_1 + (3,5,6)\tilde{y}_2$$

subject to the constraints:

$$(0.5,1,1.5)\tilde{y}_1 + \left(1.5,2,2.5\right)\tilde{y}_2 - (2,3,5)t \leq 0,$$

$$(2,3,4)\tilde{y}_1 + (1,2,3)\tilde{y}_2 - (5,6,7)t \leq 0,$$

$$(1,2,3)\tilde{y}_1 + (5.5,7,8.5)t = 1,$$

$$\tilde{y}_1, \tilde{y}_2, t \geq 0$$

where

$$t = \frac{1}{(1,2,3)\tilde{x}_1 + (5.5,7,8.5)}, \tilde{y}_1 = t\tilde{x}_1, \tilde{y}_2 = t\tilde{x}_2$$

Using signed distance ranking, the FLP problem is reduced to an LP problem as follows-

$$\text{Max } Z = 6y_1 + 4.75y_2$$

subject to the constraints:

$$y_1 + 2y_2 - 3.25t \le 0,$$

$$3y_1 + 2y_2 - 6t \le 0,$$

$$2y_1 + 7t = 1,$$

$$y_1, y_2, t \ge 0.$$

Solving the above problem by LP package, we get,

$$y_1 = 0.14, y_2 = 0.10, t = 0.10$$

Therefore the optimal solution is

$\tilde{x}_1 = 1.4, \tilde{x}_2 = 1$ and hence Max $\tilde{Z}(x) = (2.96, 1.37, 2.67)$.

SENSITIVITY ANALYSIS

Sensitivity analysis is to determine changes in the optimal solution of the fully fuzzy linear fractional programming (FFLFP) problem resulting from changes in the parameters. In particular, following variations in the FFLFP problem will be considered:

1. Change in the right hand side of the constraints ($\tilde{b}$),
2. Change in the fuzzy constraints matrix ($\tilde{A}$),
3. Addition of a new fuzzy constraints,
4. Change in fuzzy cost co-efficient ($\tilde{c}$),
5. Addition of a new fuzzy variable.

Generally, these parameter changes result in one of the following three cases-

1. The fuzzy optimal solution remains unchanged, i.e., the basic variables and their values remain unchanged.
2. The basic variables remain unchanged but their values are changed.
3. The basic variables as well as their values are changed.

While dealing with these changes, one important objective is to find the maximum extent to which a parameter or a set of parameters can be changed so that the current optimal solution remains optimal. In other words, the objective is to determine how sensitive is the optimal solution to the changes in those parameters.

Phase-II

Change in the Right-Hand Side of the Constraints ($\tilde{b}$)

Suppose that a fuzzy optimal solution to a FLP problem has already been found and it is desired to find the effect of increasing or decreasing some resource. Clearly, this will affect not only the objective function but also the solution. Large changes in the limiting resource may even change the solution variables. Let RHS vector $\tilde{b}$ in Equation (2) is replaced by (b'_1, b'_2, b'_3) and $\tilde{b}_i \in F(R)$.

By using Charnes and Cooper (1962) method, the fully fuzzy linear fractional programming (FFLFP) problem is reduced to a fuzzy linear programming (FLP) problem as follows:

Max $\tilde{z} = \tilde{c}y + \tilde{\alpha}t = (c_1, c_2, c_3)y + (\alpha_1, \alpha_2, \alpha_3)t$

subject to the constraints:

$(a_1, a_2, a_3)y - (b'_1, b'_2, b'_3)t \leq 0,$

$(d_1, d_2, d_3)y + (\beta_1, \beta_2, \beta_3)t = 1,$

$y, t \geq 0$

where

$$t = \frac{1}{(d_1, d_2, d_3)x + (\beta_1, \beta_2, \beta_3)}, y = tx$$

By using signed distance ranking, the FLP problem is reduced to a crisp LP problem as follows:

$$\text{Max } z = C'y + \alpha't$$

subject to the constraints:

$$A'y - B''t \leq 0,$$

$$D'y + \beta't = 1$$

where

$$y, t \geq 0$$

$$A' = \frac{1}{4}[a_1 + 2a_2 + a_3], B'' = \frac{1}{4}[b'_1 + 2b'_2 + b'_3], C' = \frac{1}{4}[c_1 + 2c_2 + c_3],$$

$$D' = \frac{1}{4}[d_1 + 2d_2 + d_3], \alpha' = \frac{1}{4}[\alpha_1 + 2\alpha_2 + \alpha_3], \beta' = \frac{1}{4}[\beta_1 + 2\beta_2 + \beta_3].$$

By using simplex method we can find the fuzzy optimal solution of FLFP problem.

Change in the Fuzzy Constraints Matrix ($\tilde{A}$)

When change takes place in the constraints of a non-basic variable in the current optimal solution, feasibility of the solution is not affected. The effect, if any, may be on the optimality of the solution.

Let (a_1, a_2, a_3) is replaced by (a'_1, a'_2, a'_3) in Equation (1.2) and $\tilde{A} \in R^{m \times n}$.

By using Charnes and Cooper (1962) method in Equation (1.2), the fuzzy linear fractional programming (FLFP) problem is reduced to a fuzzy linear programming (FLP) problem as follows:

Max $\tilde{z} = \tilde{c}y + \tilde{\alpha}t = (c_1, c_2, c_3)y + (\alpha_1, \alpha_2, \alpha_3)t$

subject to the constraints:

$(a'_1, a'_2, a'_3)y - (b_1, b_2, b_3)t \leq 0,$

$(d_1, d_2, d_3)y + (\beta_1, \beta_2, \beta_3)t = 1,$

$y, t \geq 0$

where

$$t = \frac{1}{(d_1, d_2, d_3)x + (\beta_1, \beta_2, \beta_3)}, y = tx$$

By using signed distance ranking, the FLP problem is reduced to a crisp LP problem as follows:

Max $z = C'y + \alpha't$

subject to the constraints:

$A''y - B't \leq 0,$

$D'y + \beta't = 1$

where

$y, t \geq 0$

$$A'' = \frac{1}{4}[a'_1 + 2a'_2 + a'_3], B' = \frac{1}{4}[b_1 + 2b_2 + b_3], C' = \frac{1}{4}[c_1 + 2c_2 + c_3],$$

$$D' = \frac{1}{4}[d_1 + 2d_2 + d_3], \alpha' = \frac{1}{4}[\alpha_1 + 2\alpha_2 + \alpha_3], \beta' = \frac{1}{4}[\beta_1 + 2\beta_2 + \beta_3].$$

By using simplex method we can find the fuzzy optimal solution of FLFP problem.

Addition of a New Fuzzy Constraint

Suppose that a new fuzzy constraint is added to the FFLFP problem whose optimal solution has been obtained. Addition of this new constraint may or may not affect the feasibility of the current fuzzy optimal solution. For this, it is sufficient to check whether the new constraint is satisfied by the current optimal solution or not. If it is satisfied, the current optimal solution is also an optimal solution to the new FFLFP problem, the additional constraint being a redundant constraint. If however the constraint is not satisfied, the optimal solution is infeasible.

Let,

$$\text{Max } \tilde{Z}(x) = \frac{\tilde{c}x_i + \tilde{\alpha}}{\tilde{d}x_i + \tilde{\beta}} = \frac{(c_1, c_2, c_3)x_i + (\alpha_1, \alpha_2, \alpha_3)}{(d_1, d_2, d_3)x_i + (\beta_1, \beta_2, \beta_3)}$$

subject to the constraints:

$$x \in S = \{x \mid \tilde{A}x \leq \tilde{b}, x \geq 0\} = \{x \mid (a_1, a_2, a_3)x_i \leq (b_1, b_2, b_3),$$

$$(a_1, a_2, a_3)x \leq (b_1, b_2, b_3)$$
$$x_i \geq 0, i = 1, 2, \ldots, n$$

where

$$x \in R^n, \tilde{c}, \tilde{d} \in R^n \text{ and } \tilde{b} \in R^m, \tilde{A} \in R^{m \times n}, \alpha, \beta \in R$$

By using Charnes and Cooper method (1962), the fuzzy linear fractional programming (FLFP) problem is reduced to a fuzzy linear programming (FLP) problem is as follows:

$$\text{Max } \tilde{z} = \tilde{c}y_i + \tilde{\alpha}t = (c_1, c_2, c_3)y_i + (\alpha_1, \alpha_2, \alpha_3)t$$

subject to the constraints:

$$(a_1, a_2, a_3)y_i - (b_1, b_2, b_3)t \leq 0,$$

$$(a_1, a_2, a_3)y - (b_1, b_2, b_3)t \leq 0,$$

$$(d_1, d_2, d_3)y_i + (\beta_1, \beta_2, \beta_3)t = 1,$$

$$y, t \geq 0$$

where

$$t = \frac{1}{(d_1, d_2, d_3)x_i + (\beta_1, \beta_2, \beta_3)}, y_i = tx_i$$

By using signed distance ranking of triangular fuzzy number, the problem reduced to a crisp linear programming (LP) problem as follows:

Max $z = C'y_i + \alpha't$

subject to the constraints:

$$A'y_i - B't \leq 0,$$

$$A'y - B't \leq 0,$$

$$D'y_i + \beta't = 1$$

where

$$y_i, y, t \geq 0, i = 1, 2, \ldots, m$$

$$A' = \frac{1}{4}[a_1 + 2a_2 + a_3], B' = \frac{1}{4}[b_1 + 2b_2 + b_3], C' = \frac{1}{4}[c_1 + 2c_2 + c_3]$$
$$D' = \frac{1}{4}[d_1 + 2d_2 + d_3], \alpha' = \frac{1}{4}[\alpha_1 + 2\alpha_2 + \alpha_3], \beta' = \frac{1}{4}[\beta_1 + 2\beta_2 + \beta_3]$$

By using simplex method we can find the fuzzy optimal solution of FLFP problem.

Change in the Fuzzy Cost Co-Efficient ($\tilde{c}$)

Changes in the co-efficient of the objective function may take place due to a change in cost of either basic variables or non- basic variables.

Case I: Changes in the fuzzy cost co-efficient of a non-basic variable:

In this case, change in the fuzzy cost of x_i, (i=1,2,.....,m) doesn't change the c_B and d_B and thus $\tilde{z}_j$ doesn't change for any j. If the new fuzzy optimal solution is negative then the old solution is still optimal with respect to the new problem.

Case II: Changes in the fuzzy cost co-efficient of a basic variable:

Change in the fuzzy cost of x_i, (i=1,2,.....,m) changes the $\tilde{c}_B$ to $\tilde{c}'_B$ and d_B to $\tilde{d}'_B$ and thus $\tilde{z}_j$ changes to $\tilde{z}'_j$ for any j. Thus the new fuzzy optimal solution is the corresponding solution to the non-basic variable x_i. If these values satisfy the optimal conditions then the old solution is still optimal with respect to the new problem.
Let,

$$\text{Max } \tilde{Z}(x) = \frac{\tilde{c}x + \tilde{\alpha}}{\tilde{d}x + \tilde{\beta}} = \frac{(c'_1, c'_2, c'_3)x + (\alpha_1, \alpha_2, \alpha_3)}{(d'_1, d'_2, d'_3)x + (\beta_1, \beta_2, \beta_3)}$$

subject to the constraints:

$$x \in S = \{x \mid \tilde{A}x \leq \tilde{b}, x \geq 0\} = \{x \mid (a_1, a_2, a_3)x \leq (b_1, b_2, b_3)\}$$

$$x \geq 0,$$

where

$$x \in R^n, \tilde{c}, \tilde{d} \in R^n \text{ and } \tilde{b} \in R^m, \tilde{A} \in R^{m \times n}, \alpha, \beta \in R$$

By using Charnes and Cooper method (1962), the fuzzy linear fractional programming (FLFP) problem is reduced to a fuzzy linear programming (FLP) problem as follows:

$$\text{Max } \tilde{z} = \tilde{c}y + \tilde{\alpha}t = (c'_1, c'_2, c'_3)y + (\alpha_1, \alpha_2, \alpha_3)t$$

subject to the constraints:

$$(a_1, a_2, a_3)y - (b_1, b_2, b_3)t \leq 0,$$

$$(d'_1, d'_2, d'_3)y + (\beta_1, \beta_2, \beta_3)t = 1,$$

$$y, t \geq 0$$

where

$$t = \frac{1}{(d'_1, d'_2, d'_3)x + (\beta_1, \beta_2, \beta_3)}, y = tx$$

By using signed distance ranking of triangular fuzzy number, the problem reduced to a crisp linear programming (LP) problem as follows:

$$\text{Max } z = C''y + \alpha't$$

subject to the constraints:

$$A'y - B't \leq 0,$$

$$D''y + \beta't = 1$$

where

$$y, t \geq 0$$

$$A' = \frac{1}{4}[a_1 + 2a_2 + a_3], B' = \frac{1}{4}[b_1 + 2b_2 + b_3], C'' = \frac{1}{4}[c'_1 + 2c'_2 + c'_3]$$

$$D'' = \frac{1}{4}[d'_1 + 2d'_2 + d'_3], \alpha' = \frac{1}{4}[\alpha_1 + 2\alpha_2 + \alpha_3], \beta' = \frac{1}{4}[\beta_1 + 2\beta_2 + \beta_3]$$

By using simplex method we can find the fuzzy optimal solution of FLFP problem.

Addition of a New Fuzzy Variable

Suppose that a new variable is added to FFLFP problem, after an optimal feasible solution has been obtained then the solution remains feasible but may no longer be optimal. This new variable will enter the solution if it improves the value of the objective function. If it doesn't, it remains at zero value and is just like a non-basic variable.

Suppose that a non-negative fuzzy variable x_{i+1} is added in Equation (1.1) and let the corresponding cost is (c'_1, c'_2, c'_3) and $\tilde{A}_{i+1}$ is the column associated with x_{i+1} then the FFLFP problem as follows:

Let,

$$\text{Max } \tilde{Z}(x) = \frac{(c_1, c_2, c_3)x_i + (c'_1, c'_2, c'_3)x_{i+1} + (\alpha_1, \alpha_2, \alpha_3)}{(d_1, d_2, d_3)x_i + (\beta_1, \beta_2, \beta_3)}$$

subject to the constraints:

$$x \in S = \{x \mid \tilde{A}x \leq \tilde{b}, x \geq 0\} = \{x \mid (a_1, a_2, a_3)x_i \leq (b_1, b_2, b_3)\}$$

$$(a_1, a_2, a_3)x_{i+1} \leq (b_1, b_2, b_3),$$

$$x_i, x_{i+1} \geq 0, i = 1, 2, ..., m$$

where

$$x \in R^n, \tilde{c}, \tilde{d} \in R^n \ and \ \tilde{b} \in R^m, \tilde{A} \in R^{m \times n}, \alpha, \beta \in R$$

By using Charnes and Cooper method (1962), the fuzzy linear fractional programming (FLFP) problem is reduced to a fuzzy linear programming (FLP) problem as follows:

Max $\tilde{z} = (c_1, c_2, c_3)y_i + (c'_1, c'_2, c'_3)y_{i+1} + (\alpha_1, \alpha_2, \alpha_3)t$

subject to the constraints:

$$(a_1, a_2, a_3)y_i - (b_1, b_2, b_3)t \leq 0,$$
$$(a_1, a_2, a_3)y_{i+1} - (b_1, b_2, b_3)t \leq 0,$$
$$(d_1, d_2, d_3)y_i + (\beta_1, \beta_2, \beta_3)t = 1,$$

where

By using signed distance ranking of triangular fuzzy number, the problem reduced to a crisp linear programming (LP) problem as follows:

Max $z = C'y_i + C''y_{i+1} + \alpha't$

subject to the constraints:

$$A'y_i - B't \leq 0,$$
$$A'y_{i+1} - B't \leq 0,$$
$$D'y_i + \beta't = 1$$

where

$$y_i, y_{i+1}, t \geq 0, \ i = 1, 2, ..., m$$

$$A' = \frac{1}{4}[a_1 + 2a_2 + a_3],$$

$$B' = \frac{1}{4}[b_1 + 2b_2 + b_3],$$

$$C' = \frac{1}{4}[c_1 + 2c_2 + c_3],$$

$$C'' = \frac{1}{4}[c'_1 + 2c'_2 + c'_3]$$

$$D' = \frac{1}{4}[d_1 + 2d_2 + d_3],$$

$$\alpha' = \frac{1}{4}[\alpha_1 + 2\alpha_2 + \alpha_3],$$

$$\beta' = \frac{1}{4}[\beta_1 + 2\beta_2 + \beta_3]$$

By using simplex method we can find the fuzzy optimal solution of FLFP problem.

Remark: The other cases of variations in the FLFP problem are: (1) deletion of a fuzzy variable, (2) deletion of a fuzzy constraint, (3) simultaneous change in coefficients of the fuzzy decision variables in the objective function and requirement vectors etc. can also be solved by the above method.

NUMERICAL EXAMPLE

Same example is solved by our approach which is as follows:

Consider the following fully fuzzy linear fractional programming problem as follows:

$$\text{Max } \tilde{Z}(x) = \frac{(5,6,7)\tilde{x}_1 + (3,5,6)\tilde{x}_2}{(1,2,3)\tilde{x}_1 + (5.5,7,8.5)}$$

subject to the constraints:

$$(0.5, 1, 1.5)\tilde{x}_1 + \left(1.5, 2, 2.5\right)\tilde{x}_2 \le (2, 3, 5),$$

$$(2, 3, 4)\tilde{x}_1 + (1, 2, 3)\tilde{x}_2 \le (5, 6, 7),$$

$\tilde{x}_1, \tilde{x}_2 \geq 0$.

1. Discuss the effect of changing the requirement vector ( ) from (2,3,5) and (5,6,7) to (1,4,6) and (4,6,8) on the fuzzy optimal solution and fuzzy optimal value of resulting FFLFP problem.

2. Discuss the effect of changing co-efficient of decision variables $\tilde{x}_1$ and $\tilde{x}_2$ from $\begin{bmatrix} (0.5,1,1.5) \\ (2,3,4) \end{bmatrix}$ and $\begin{bmatrix} (1.5,2,2.5) \\ (1,2,3) \end{bmatrix}$ to $\begin{bmatrix} (0.2,1,1.2) \\ (1,3,5) \end{bmatrix}$ and $\begin{bmatrix} (1.3,2,2.5) \\ (0.5,2,4.5) \end{bmatrix}$ on the fuzzy optimal solution and fuzzy optimal value of resulting FFLFP problem.

3. Find the effect of addition of a new fuzzy constraint $(4,7,9) + (2,3,5.5) \leq (7,8,9)$ on the fuzzy optimal solution and fuzzy optimal value of resulting FFLFP problem.

4. Discuss the effect of changing the cost co-efficient (5,6,7),(3,5,6) and (1,2,3) to (5,7,9), (9,12,15) and (2,4,6) of the fuzzy decision variables $\tilde{x}_1$, $\tilde{x}_2$ for numerator, $\tilde{x}_1$ for denominator respectively on the fuzzy optimal solution and fuzzy optimal value of resulting FFLFP problem.

5. Find the effect of addition of a new fuzzy variable $\tilde{x}_3$ with cost (7, 8, 9) and column vectors [(3.5,4,4.5), (4,5,7)]on the fuzzy optimal solution and fuzzy optimal value of resulting FFLFP problem.

Solution: The solution of the fully fuzzy linear fractional programming problem is solved by the proposed method is as follows:

Changes in the Requirement Vector ($\tilde{b}$)

Since the requirement vector ($\tilde{b}$) is changes from (2,3,5) to (1,4,6) and (5,6,7) to (4,6,8) in the FFLFP problem then by Step 1, the problem reduces to the FLP problem as follows:

Max $\tilde{z} = (5,6,7)\tilde{y}_1 + (3,5,6)\tilde{y}_2$

subject to the constraints:

$(0.5,1,1.5)\tilde{y}_1 + (1.5,2,2.5)\tilde{y}_2 - (1,4,6)t \leq 0,$
$(2,3,4)\tilde{y}_1 + (1,2,3)\tilde{y}_2 - (4,6,8)t \leq 0,$
$(1,2,3)\tilde{y}_1 + (5.5,7,8.5)t = 1$

$\tilde{y}_1, \tilde{y}_2, t \geq 0,$

where

$$t = \frac{1}{(1,2,3)_{\tilde{x}_1} + (5.5,7,8.5)}, \tilde{y}_1 = t_{x_1}, \tilde{y}_2 = t_{x_2}.$$

Using signed distance ranking in the FLP problem, we get

Max $z = 6y_1 + 4.75y_2$

subject to the constraints:

$y_1 + 2y_2 - 3.75t \leq 0,$
$3y_1 + 2y_2 - 6t \leq 0,$
$2y_1 + 7t = 1,$
$y_1, y_2, t \geq 0$

Solving the above problem by an LP package, we get,

$y_1 = 0.12, y_2 = 0.14, t = 0.11$

$\tilde{x}_1 = 1.09, \tilde{x}_2 = 1.27$

and

Max $\tilde{Z}(x) = (2.97, 1.40, 2.75).$

Change in the Fuzzy Constraint Matrix ($\tilde{A}$)

Replacing $\begin{bmatrix} (0.5,1,1.5) \\ (2,3,4) \end{bmatrix}$ and $\begin{bmatrix} (1.5,2,2.5) \\ (1,2,3) \end{bmatrix}$ to $\begin{bmatrix} (0.2,1,1.2) \\ (1,3,5) \end{bmatrix}$ and $\begin{bmatrix} (1.3,2,2.5) \\ (0.5,2,4.5) \end{bmatrix}$ in the

FFLFP problem then by Step 1, the problem reduces to the FLP problem as follows:

Max $\tilde{z} = (5,6,7)\tilde{y}_1 + (3,5,6)\tilde{y}_2$

subject to the constraints:

$$(0.2, 1, 1.2)\tilde{y}_1 + (1.3, 2, 2.5)\tilde{y}_2 - (2, 3, 5)t \leq 0,$$
$$(1, 3, 5)\tilde{y}_1 + (0.5, 2, 4.5)\tilde{y}_2 - (5, 6, 7)t \leq 0,$$
$$(1, 2, 3)\tilde{y}_1 + (5.5, 7, 8.5)t = 1$$

$$\tilde{y}_1, \tilde{y}_2, t \geq 0,$$

where

$$t = \frac{1}{(1, 2, 3)\tilde{x}_1 + (5.5, 7, 8.5)}, \tilde{y}_1 = t\tilde{x}_1, \tilde{y}_2 = t\tilde{x}_2$$

Using signed distance ranking in the FLP problem, we get

Max $z = 6y_1 + 4.75y_2$

subject to the constraints:

$$0.85y_1 + 1.95y_2 - 3.25t \leq 0,$$
$$3y_1 + 2.25y_2 - 6t \leq 0,$$
$$2y_1 + 7t = 1,$$
$$y_1, y_2, t \geq 0$$

Solving the above problem by an LP package, we get,

$$y_1 = 0.12, y_2 = 0.13, t = 0.11$$

$$\tilde{x}_1 = 1.09, \tilde{x}_2 = 1.18$$

and

Max $\tilde{Z}(x) = (2.87, 1.36, 2.66)$.

Addition of a New Fuzzy Constraint

Suppose that a new constraint $(4,7,9)+(2,3,5.5) \leq (7,8,9)$ added in the FFLFP problem, then by Step 1, the problem reduces to the FLP problem as follows:

Max $\tilde{z} = (5,6,7)\tilde{y}_1 + (3,5,6)\tilde{y}_2$

subject to the constraints:

$$(0.5,1,1.5)\tilde{y}_1 + (1.5,2,2.5)\tilde{y}_2 - (2,3,5)t \leq 0,$$
$$(2,3,4)\tilde{y}_1 + (1,2,3)\tilde{y}_2 - (5,6,7)t \leq 0,$$
$$(1,2,3)\tilde{y}_1 + (5.5,7,8.5)t = 1,$$
$$\left(4,7,9\right)\tilde{y}_1 + \left(2,3,5.5\right)\tilde{y}_2 \leq \left(7,8,9\right),$$

$$\tilde{y}_1, \tilde{y}_2, t \geq 0$$

where

$$t = \frac{1}{(1,2,3)\tilde{x}_1 + (5.5,7,8.5)}, \tilde{y}_1 = t\tilde{x}_1, \tilde{y}_2 = t\tilde{x}_2$$

Using signed distance ranking in the FLP problem, we get

Max $z = 6y_1 + 4.75y_2$

subject to the constraints:

$$y_1 + 2y_2 - 3.75t \leq 0,$$
$$3y_1 + 2y_2 - 6t \leq 0,$$
$$2y_1 + 7t = 1,$$
$$6.75y_1 + 3.375y_2 - 8t \leq 0,$$

$$y_1, y_2, t \geq 0$$

Solving the above problem by an LP package, we get,

$$y_1 = 0.04, y_2 = 0.22, t = 0.13$$

$$\tilde{x}_1 = 0.31, \tilde{x}_2 = 1.69$$

and

$$\text{Max } \tilde{Z}(x) = (2.64, 1.35, 2.78).$$

Change in the Fuzzy Cost Co-Efficient ($\tilde{c}$)

Replacing the cost co efficient (5,6,7),(3,5,6) and (1,2,3) to (5,7,9),(9,12,15) and (2,4,6) of the decision variables of numerator and denominator in the FFLFP problem then by Step 1, the problem reduces to the FLP problem as follows:

$$\text{Max } \tilde{z} = (5,7,9)\tilde{y}_1 + (9,12,15)\tilde{y}_2$$

subject to the constraints:

$$(0.5,1,1.5)\tilde{y}_1 + (1.5,2,2.5)\tilde{y}_2 - (2,3,5)t \leq 0,$$
$$(2,3,4)\tilde{y}_1 + (1,2,3)\tilde{y}_2 - (5,6,7)t \leq 0,$$
$$(2,4,6)\tilde{y}_1 + (5.5,7,8.5)t = 1,$$

$$\tilde{y}_1, \tilde{y}_2, t \geq 0$$

where

$$t = \frac{1}{(1,2,3)\tilde{x}_1 + (5.5,7,8.5)}, \tilde{y}_1 = t\tilde{x}_1, \tilde{y}_2 = t\tilde{x}_2$$

Using signed distance ranking in the FLP problem, we get

$$\text{Max } z = 7y_1 + 12y_2$$

subject to the constraints:

$$y_1 + 2y_2 - 3.25t \leq 0,$$
$$3y_1 + 2y_2 - 6t \leq 0,$$
$$4y_1 + 7t = 1,$$

$$y_1, y_2, t \geq 0$$

Solving the above problem by an LP package, we get,

$$y_1 = 0, y_2 = 0.23, t = 0.14$$

$$\tilde{x}_1 = 0, \tilde{x}_2 = 1.64$$

and

$$\text{Max } \tilde{Z}(x) = (2.19, 1.17, 2.36).$$

Addition of a New Fuzzy Variable

Let $\tilde{x}_3$ be introduced in the numerator of objective function and also in both the constraints of FFLFP problem then by Step 1, the problem reduces to the FLP problem as follows:

$$\text{Max } \tilde{z} = (5, 6, 7)\tilde{y}_1 + (3, 5, 6)\tilde{y}_2 + (7, 8, 9)\tilde{y}_3$$

subject to the constraints:

$$(0.5, 1, 1.5)\tilde{y}_1 + (1.5, 2, 2.5)\tilde{y}_2 + (3.5, 4, 4.5)\tilde{y}_3 - (2, 3, 5)t \leq 0,$$
$$(2, 3, 4)\tilde{y}_1 + (1, 2, 3)\tilde{y}_2 + (4, 5, 7)\tilde{y}_3 - (5, 6, 7)t \leq 0,$$
$$(1, 2, 3)\tilde{y}_1 + (5.5, 7, 8.5)t = 1,$$

$$\tilde{y}_1, \tilde{y}_2, \tilde{y}_3, t \geq 0$$

where

$$t = \frac{1}{(1,2,3)\tilde{x}_1 + (5.5,7,8.5)}, \tilde{y}_1 = t\tilde{x}_1, \tilde{y}_2 = t\tilde{x}_2, \tilde{y}_3 = t\tilde{x}_3$$

Using signed distance ranking in the above problem, we get

$$\text{Max } z = 6\,y_1 + 4.75\,y_2 + 8\,y_3$$

subject to the constraints:

$$y_1 + 2y_2 + 4y_3 - 3.25t \leq 0,$$
$$3y_1 + 2y_2 + 5.25y_3 - 6t \leq 0,$$
$$2y_1 + 7t = 1,$$

$$y_1, y_2, y_3, t \geq 0.$$

Solving the above problem by an LP package, we get,

$$y_1 = 0.14, y_2 = 0.10, y_3 = 0, t = 0.10$$

$$\tilde{x}_1 = 1.4, \tilde{x}_2 = 1$$

and

$$\text{Max } \tilde{Z}(x) = (2.96, 1.37, 2.67).$$

From Table 1, we see that the optimal values of Phase I are the same as those of Phase II: Addition of a new fuzzy variable in FFLFP problem.

Table 1. Optimal solution

Observation		Different Variations	Values of y_1, y_2, t	Optimal Values	
Phase I	1	FFLFP	$y_1 = 0.14, y_2 = 0.10, t = 0.10$	$\tilde{x}_1 = 1.4, \tilde{x}_2 = 1$	Max $\tilde{Z}(x) = (2.96, 1.37, 2.67)$ =2.09
Phase II	1	Changes in the requirement vector ($\tilde{b}$)	$y_1 = 0.12, y_2 = 0.14, t = 0.11$	$\tilde{x}_1 = 1.09, \tilde{x}_2 = 1.27$	Max $\tilde{Z}(x) = (2.97, 1.40, 2.75)$ =2.13
	2	Change in the fuzzy constraint matrix ($\tilde{A}$)	$y_1 = 0.12, y_2 = 0.13, t = 0.11$	$\tilde{x}_1 = 1.09, \tilde{x}_2 = 1.18$	Max $\tilde{Z}(x) = (2.87, 1.36, 2.66)$ 2.06
	3	Addition of a new fuzzy constraint	$y_1 = 0.04, y_2 = 0.22, t = 0.13$	$\tilde{x}_1 = 0.31, \tilde{x}_2 = 1.69$	Max $\tilde{Z}(x) = (2.64, 1.35, 2.78)$ =2.03
	4	Change in fuzzy the cost co-efficient ($\tilde{c}$)	$y_1 = 0, y_2 = 0.23, t = 0.14$	$\tilde{x}_1 = 0, \tilde{x}_2 = 1.64$	Max $\tilde{Z}(x) = (2.19, 1.17, 2.36)$ =1.72
	5	Addition of a new fuzzy variable	$y_1 = 0.14, y_2 = 0.10, y_3 = 0, t = 0.10$	$\tilde{x}_1 = 1.4, \tilde{x}_2 = 1$	Max $\tilde{Z}(x) = (2.96, 1.37, 2.67)$ =2.09

CONCLUSION

In this paper, we introduced a theory of fully fuzzy linear fractional programming (FFLFP) problem where coefficients and parameters are triangular fuzzy number (TFN). Such type of FFLFP problem is the general form of a triangular fuzzy number linear fractional programming (TFNLFP) problem. In Phase-I, TFNLFP problem is solved by the proposed method. We have studied the measurement of sensitivity analysis of Phase-II and investigate that the results obtained in Phase-II and Phase-I. In this study, the maximum value is 2.13 and the minimum value is 1.72. But the numerical is a Maximization problem. So the optimal value is 2.13 which we have obtained in changes in the requirement vector ().

We want to find the feasible region in our present case and so this is our future research work.

REFERENCES

Astolfi, A. (2006). *Optimization- An Introduction*. Retrieved from www3.imperial. ac.uk/pls/portallive/docs/1/7288263.pdf

Bellman, R. E., & Zadeh, L. A. (1970). Decision making in fuzzy environment. *Management Science*, *17*(4), 141–146. doi:10.1287/mnsc.17.4.B141

Bajalinov, E. B. (2001). *Linear-Fractional Programming: Theory, Methods, Applications and Software*. Kluwer Academic Publishers.

Bhatia, N., & Kumar, A. (2012). Mehar's method for solving fuzzy sensitivity analysis with LR flat fuzzy numbers. *Applied Mathematical Modelling*, *36*(9), 4087–4095. doi:10.1016/j.apm.2011.11.038

Charnes, A., & Cooper, W. W. (1962). Programming with linear fractional functions. *Naval Research Logistics Quarterly*, *9*(3-4), 181–186. doi:10.1002/nav.3800090303

Chiang, J., Yao, J.-S., & Lee, H.-M. (2005). Fuzzy inventory with backorder defuzzification by signed distance method. *Journal of Information Science and Engineering*, *21*, 673–694.

Craven, B. D., & Mond, B. (1975). On fractional programming and equivalence. *Naval Research Logistics Quarterly*, *2*(2), 405–410. doi:10.1002/nav.3800220216

Craven, B. D. (1988). Fractional Programming. *Sigma Series in Applied Mathematics*, *4*, 145.

Dantzig, G. B. (1947). Maximization of a linear function of variables subject to linear equalities. In Activity analysis of production and allocation. New York: Wiley.

De, P. K., & Deb, M. (2013). Solving fuzzy linear fractional programming problem using signed distance ranking. *3rd IEEE International Advance Computing Conference*, 806-812. 10.1109/IAdCC.2013.6514330

Deb, M., & De, P. K. (2015). Optimal solution of a fully fuzzy linear fractional programming problem by using graded mean integration representation method. *Applications and Applied Mathematics*, *10*(1), 571–587.

Deb, M., & De, P.K. (2014). Study of possibility programming in stochastic fuzzy multi-objective linear fractional programming problems by possibility programming. *8th IEEE Intelligent Systems and Control (ISCO)*, 331-337.

De, P. K., & Deb, M. (2015). Solution of fuzzy multi-objective linear fractional programming problems by Taylor series approach. *International Conference on Man and Machine Interfacing, IEEE- MAMI*, 1-5.

Deb, M., Das, D., & De, P. K. (2017). An approach to study the optimal solution of linear fractional programming problems under Intutionistic fuzzy setting. *Far East Journal of Mathematical Sciences, 101*(11), 24212443.

Dubois, D., & Prade, H. (1979). Fuzzy real algebra: Some results. *Fuzzy Sets and Systems, 2*(4), 327–348. doi:10.1016/0165-0114(79)90005-8

Dubois, D., & Prade, H. (1980). *Fuzzy Sets and Systems: Theory and Applications.* London: Academic Press.

Dutta, D., Rao, J. R., & Tiwari, R. N. (1992). Sensitivity analysis in fuzzy linear fractional programming problem. *Fuzzy Sets and Systems, 48*(2), 211–216. doi:10.1016/0165-0114(92)90335-2

Ebrahimnejad, A. (2011). Sensitivity analysis in fuzzy number linear programming problems. *Mathematical and Computer Modelling, 53*(9-10), 1878–1888. doi:10.1016/j.mcm.2011.01.013

Farhadinia, B. (2014). Sensitivity analysis in interval-valued trapezoidal fuzzy number linear programming problems. *Applied Mathematical Modelling, 38*(1), 50–62. doi:10.1016/j.apm.2013.05.033

Gupta, P. K. (1987). *Linear Programming and Theory of Games* (1st ed.). Khanna Publishers.

Gupta, P., & Bhatia, D. (2001). Sensitivity analysis in fuzzy multi-objective linear fractional programming problem. *Fuzzy Sets and Systems, 122*(2), 229–236. doi:10.1016/S0165-0114(99)00164-5

Gani, A. N., Duraisamy, C., & Veeramani, C. (2009). A note on fuzzy linear programming problem using LR-fuzzy number. *International Journal of Algorithms, Computing and Mathematics, 2*(3), 93–106.

Gani, A. N., & Assarudeen, S. N. M. (2012). A new operation on triangular fuzzy number for solving fuzzy linear programming problem. *Applied Mathematical Sciences, 6*(11), 525–532.

Hamacher, H., Leberling, H., & Zimmermann, H.-J. (1978). Sensitivity analysis in fuzzy linear programming problem. *Fuzzy Sets and Systems, 1*(4), 269–281. doi:10.1016/0165-0114(78)90018-0

Jain, R. (1976). Decision making in the presence of fuzzy variable. *IEEE Transactions on Systems, Man, and Cybernetics, 6*, 698–703.

Jershan, C., Yao, J.-S., & Lee, H.-M. (2005). Fuzzy inventory with backorder. *Journal of Information Science and Engineering, 21,* 673–694.

Kantorrovich, L. V. (1940). A new method of solving some classes of extremal problems. *Doklady Akad Science, 28,* 211–214.

Kaufmann, A., & Gupta, M. M. (1991). *Introduction to Fuzzy Arithmetic, Theory and Applications.* New York: Van Nostrand Reinhold.

Kheirfam, B. (2010). Multi-parametric sensitivity analysis of the constraint matrix in piecewise linear fractional programming problem. *Journal of Industrial and Management Optimization, 6*(2), 347–361. doi:10.3934/jimo.2010.6.347

Kheirfam, B., & Hasani, F. (2010). Sensitivity analysis for fuzzy linear programming problems with fuzzy variables. *Advanced Modelling and Optimization, 12,* 257–272.

Kumar, A., & Bhatia, N. (2011). A new method for solving sensitivity analysis for fuzzy linear programming problems. *International Journal of Applied Science and Engineering, 9*(3), 169–176.

Lotfi, F. H., Jondabeh, M. A., & Faizrahnemoon, M. (2010). Sensitivity analysis in fuzzy environment. *Applied Mathematical Sciences, 4,* 1635–1646.

Lee, K. H. (2005). First Course on Fuzzy Set Theory and Applications. Springer.

Martos, B. (1960). Hyperbolic programming. *Publications of the Research Institute for Mathematical Sciences, 5*(B), 386-40.

Martos, B. (1960). Hyperbolic programming by simplex method. Deuxieme Congress Mathematique Hongrois, 2, 44-48.

Maleki, H. R., Tata, M., & Mashinchi, M. (2000). Linear programming with fuzzy variables. *Fuzzy Sets and Systems, 109*(1), 21–33. doi:10.1016/S0165-0114(98)00066-9

Nasseri, S. H., Ardil, E., Yazdani, A., & Zaefarian, R. (2005). Simplex method for solving fuzzy variable linear programming problems. *World Academy of Science, Engineering and Technology, 10,* 284–288.

Pu, P. M., & Liu, Y. M. (1980). Fuzzy topology 1, neighbourhood structure of a fuzzy point and moore-smith convergence. *Journal of Mathematical Analysis and Applications, 76*(2), 571–599. doi:10.1016/0022-247X(80)90048-7

Pattnaik, M. (2013). Fuzzy multi-objective linear programming problems: Sensitivity analysis. *Journal of Mathematics and Computer Science, 7,* 131–137.

Ross, T. J. (2005). *Fuzzy Logic with Engineering Applications* (2nd ed.). Singapore: John Wiley and Sons Private Limited.

Swarup, K., Gupta, P. K., & Mohan, M. (1997). *Operations Research* (8th ed.). S.Chand and Publishers.

Sakawa, M., & Yano, H. (1988). An interactive fuzzy satisficing method for multi-objective linear fractional programming problems. *Fuzzy Sets and Systems*, *28*(2), 129–144. doi:10.1016/0165-0114(88)90195-9

Tanaka, H., Ichihashi, H., & Asai, K. (1986). A value of information in FLP problems via sensitivity analysis. *Fuzzy Sets and Systems*, *18*(2), 119–129. doi:10.1016/0165-0114(86)90015-1

Taha, H. M. (n.d.). *Operations Research- An Introduction with AMPL, Solver, Excel and Tora Implementations* (8th ed.). Prentice Hall.

What is Fuzzy Number? (n.d.). Retrieved from http://whatis.techtarget.com/definition/fuzzy-number

Yao, J.-S., & Wu, K. (2000). Ranking fuzzy numbers based on decomposition principle and signed distance. *Fuzzy Sets and Systems*, *116*(2), 275–288. doi:10.1016/S0165-0114(98)00122-5

Zadeh, L. A. (1965). Fuzzy Sets. *Information and Control*, *8*(3), 338–353. doi:10.1016/S0019-9958(65)90241-X

Zimmermann, H.-J. (1978). Fuzzy programming and linear programming with several objective functions. *Fuzzy Sets and Systems*, *1*(1), 45–55. doi:10.1016/0165-0114(78)90031-3

Zimmermann, H.-J. (1983). Fuzzy mathematical programming. *Computers & Operations Research*, *10*(4), 291–298. doi:10.1016/0305-0548(83)90004-7

Zimmermann, H.-J. (2001). *Fuzzy Set Theory and Its Applications*. Boston: Kluwer Academic Publishers. doi:10.1007/978-94-010-0646-0

Chapter 5
Advances in Fuzzy Dynamic Programming

Felix Mora-Camino
Durban University of Technology, South Africa

Elena Capitanul Conea
ENAC, France

Fabio Krykhtine
COPPE UFRJ, Brazil

Walid Moudani
Lebanese University, Lebanon

Carlos Alberto Nunes Cosenza
COPPE UFRJ, Brazil

ABSTRACT

This chapter considers the use of fuzzy dual numbers to model and solve through dynamic programming process mathematical programming problems where uncertainty is present in the parameters of the objective function or of the associated constraints. It is only supposed that the values of the uncertain parameters remain in known real intervals and can be modelled with fuzzy dual numbers. The interest of adopting the fuzzy dual formalism to implement the sequential decision-making process of dynamic programming is discussed and compared with early fuzzy dynamic programming. Here, the comparison between two alternatives is made considering not only the cumulative performance but also the cumulative risk associated with previous steps in the dynamic process, displaying the traceability of the solution under construction as it is effectively the case with the classical deterministic dynamic programming process. The proposed approach is illustrated in the case of a long-term airport investment planning problem.

DOI: 10.4018/978-1-5225-5091-4.ch005

INTRODUCTION

While deterministic optimization problems are formulated with known parameters, very often real-world problems include unknown parameters (Delgado et al., 1987). When the parameters are only known to remain within given bounds, one way to tackle such problems is through robust optimization (Ben-Tal et al., 2009). When probability distributions are available for their values, stochastic optimization techniques (Ruszczynski et al., 2003) may be used to provide the most expected feasible solution. An intermediate approach adopting the fuzzy formalism to represent the parameter uncertainties has been also developed (Zimmermann, 1986). These three approaches lead in general to cumbersome computations. Also, in many situations the optimal solution cannot be applied exactly according to implementation constraints which have not been considered explicitly in the formulation of the problem. In that case post optimization sensibility analysis (Gal et al., 1997) resulting often in an important computational effort must be performed.

In this chapter, the fuzzy dual formalism is proposed to treat parameter uncertainty and solution diversion in mathematical optimization problems. This formalism adopting a simplified version of fuzzy numbers provides feasible solution approaches with respect to the resulting computational needs. The case of dynamic programming is more particularly considered in this chapter. Since its development in the mid-fifties by Richard Bellman, Dynamic Programming has become one of the main tool to cope with the optimization of dynamical systems and sequential decision problems, either in the control field or in the Operations Research field. Fuzzy Set Theory has been developed by Zadeh in the early sixties and has established itself as an important mathematical tool to address uncertainties and imprecision in treating real world problems. So, as soon as 1970, Bellman and Zadeh put together these concepts to propose a sequential decision tool under uncertainty leading to what has been called *fuzzy dynamic programming*. Although many decision problems are both sequential and uncertain, it has to be recognized that this promising technique has not encountered the expected popularity. So in this chapter, fuzzy dynamic programming with fuzzy dual numbers, i.e. Fuzzy Dual Programming is introduced and a case study is produced. At first, the general approach proposed by Bellman and Zadeh, leading to the fuzzy optimality principle, will be stated. Then different settings of fuzzy dynamic programming problems in conjunction with the corresponding solution approaches have been introduced, while more recent contributions in that field (in general Kacprzyk and Esogbue) will be discussed. Then the main limitations and difficulties common to these approaches will be outlined and analyzed. Beyond the computational burden generated by these approaches, the traceability of the proposed results is extremely poor. These have been the main negative factors for the adoption of Fuzzy Dynamic Programming techniques. Here, to improve both aspects, conceptual questions regarding first the equal logical treatment applied to constraints and performance indexes, and then regarding the fuzzy comparison process of different partial performance indexes, will be analyzed and directions for improvement will be proposed. With respect to the first point, either or not the optimization problem has a fuzzy character, only feasible solutions are of interest for the decision maker, so a first step before comparing the performances of solutions is to assess in a clear and independent way their feasibility, even when it is assessed in fuzzy terms. Then the current approach where performance levels and feasibility are merely merged using a logical *and* is considered questionable, so a new logical operator will be discussed. The second point is central in the dynamic programming process since it allows not only to progress towards the whole solution but also to weed out partial non optimal solutions and lessen the remaining computational burden. So to make effective the fuzzy dynamical programming process, the use of a class of fuzzy numbers easily comparable appears of utmost interest. The comparison of overlapping fuzzy numbers incurs the evaluation of the risk of wrong selection and its computation should be also performed as simply as possible. So for given stage and state, the comparison between two alternatives can be made considering not only the cumulative performance but also the cumulative risk associated with previous steps in the dynamic process. The final part of the proposed chapter will consider the implementation of the above proposals in the case of fuzzy dynamic programming using fuzzy dual numbers, displaying the traceability of the proposed solution as it is effectively the case with the classical dynamic programming process. This will be illustrated in the case of a long term investment planning problem.

FUZZY DUAL NUMBERS

Definition 1: Fuzzy dual numbers.

A set of fuzzy dual numbers is defined as the set $\widetilde{\Delta}$ of numbers of the form $a+\varepsilon.b$, where a is the primal part and b is the dual part of the fuzzy dual number, $\forall\ a \in \mathbb{R}$, $\forall\ b \in \mathbb{R}^+$. Here ε represents the unity pure dual number. A fuzzy dual number loses both its dual and fuzzy attributes if b equals zero. The lower and upper bounds of $a+\varepsilon b$ are given respectively by $B^{low}(a+\varepsilon.b) = a\text{-}b$ and $B^{high}(a+\varepsilon.b) = a+b$ while the pseudo norm of a fuzzy dual number is given by:

$$\|a + \varepsilon b\| = |a| + \rho b \in \mathbb{R}^+ \tag{1}$$

Here ρ is a real positively valued shape parameter given by:

$$\rho = (1/b) \int_{a-b}^{a+b} \mu(u) \cdot du \tag{2}$$

where μ is the membership function in the sense of Zadeh (1965). The following properties of the pseudo norm are met no matter the values the shape parameters take:

$$\forall a + \varepsilon \cdot b \in \widetilde{\Delta} : \|a + \varepsilon \cdot b\| \geq 0 \tag{3}$$

$$\forall a \in \mathbb{R}, \forall b \in \mathbb{R}^+, \|a + \varepsilon \cdot b\| = 0 \Rightarrow a = b = 0 \tag{4}$$

$$\|(a + \varepsilon \cdot b) + (\alpha + \varepsilon \cdot \beta)\| \leq \|a + \varepsilon \cdot b\| + \\ \|\alpha + \varepsilon \cdot \beta\| \; \forall a, \alpha \in \mathbb{R}, \forall b, \beta \in \mathbb{R}^+ \tag{5}$$

$$\|\lambda \cdot (a + \varepsilon \cdot b)\| = \lambda \cdot \|a + \varepsilon \cdot b\| \; \forall a \in \mathbb{R}, \forall b \in \mathbb{R}^+ \tag{6}$$

Definitions 2: Orders between fuzzy dual numbers.

Total orders between fuzzy dual numbers can be introduced using the above pseudo norm. The strong partial written $\overset{\sim}{\geq}$ can be defined over $\widetilde{\Delta}$ by:

$$\forall a_1 + \varepsilon \cdot b_1, a_2 + \varepsilon \cdot b_2 \in \widetilde{\Delta} : a_1 + \\ \varepsilon \cdot b_1 \overset{\sim}{\geq} a_2 + \varepsilon \cdot b_2 \Leftrightarrow a_1 - \rho \cdot b_1 > a_2 + \rho \cdot b_2 \tag{7}$$

The *mean* partial order of *case b*, written $\overset{\frown}{\geq}$, is defined over $\widetilde{\Delta}$ by:

$$\forall a_1 + \varepsilon \cdot b_1, a_2 + \varepsilon \cdot b_2 \in \widetilde{\Delta} : a_1 + \\ \varepsilon \cdot b_1 \overset{\frown}{\geq} a_2 + \varepsilon \cdot b_2 \Leftrightarrow a_1 + \rho \cdot b_1 > a_2 + \rho \cdot b_2 > a_1 - \rho \cdot b_1 \tag{8}$$

The *weak* partial order of *case c*, written $\overset{\smile}{>}$, is such as:

$$a_1 > a_2, a_1 - \rho \cdot b_1 > a_2 - \rho \cdot b_2, a_1 + \rho \cdot b_1 < a_2 + \rho \cdot b_2 \tag{9}$$

The *fuzzy equality* between two fuzzy dual numbers, corresponding to case *d*, is symbolized by $\cong$ and is characterized by:

$$a_1 = a_2 \tag{10}$$

Then, it appears that it is *always possible* to rank with a minimum of computational effort two fuzzy dual numbers and to assign a qualitative evaluation to this comparison (strong, mean or weak). When either (7), (8) or (9) is satisfied, it will be said that *fuzzy dual number* $a_1 + \varepsilon \cdot b_1$ *is greater than fuzzy dual number* $a_2 + \varepsilon \cdot b_2$ and we will write:

$$a_1 + \varepsilon \cdot b_1 > a_2 + \varepsilon \cdot b_2 \tag{11}$$

A degree of certainty *c* can be attached to assertion (11). A candidate expression for this degree of certainty is given by:

$$c = 1 - \frac{1}{2} \min \left\{ \frac{\alpha}{b_1}, \frac{\alpha}{b_2} \right\} \ if \ a_1 \geq a_2 \ and \ c = \frac{1}{2} \min \left\{ \frac{\alpha}{b_1}, \frac{\alpha}{b_2} \right\} \ if \ a_1 < a_2 \tag{12}$$

where α is the area of the intersection between fuzzy dual numbers $a_1 + \varepsilon \cdot b_1$ and $a_2 + \varepsilon \cdot b_2$.

Since two fuzzy dual numbers can be easily compared, even introducing a degree of certainty, this allows the consideration of mathematical programming problems with parameter and variable uncertainties represented by fuzzy dual numbers and open the way to the application of the dynamic programming paradigm to sequential decision problems where performance is assessed using fuzzy dual numbers leading to the concept of fuzzy dual dynamic programming.

PROGRAMMING WITH FUZZY DUAL PARAMETERS

It is now possible to introduce fuzzy dual formulations of uncertain mathematical programming problems. Here we will consider only the case of linear programming, but the formalism can be applied to other classes of objective functions and restrictions. Let then consider problem D_0 which is a fuzzy dual linear programming problem with fuzzy dual constraints and real decision variables:

$$\min_{x \in \mathbb{R}^{+n}} \left\| \sum_{i=1}^{n} (c_i + \varepsilon \cdot d_i) \cdot x_i \right\| \qquad (13)$$

under strong constraints:

$$\sum_{i=1}^{n} \left(a_{ki} + \varepsilon \cdot \alpha_{ik} \right) \cdot x_i \gtrsim b_k + \varepsilon \cdot \beta_k, k \in \{1, \cdots, m\} \qquad (14)$$

and

$$x_i \in \mathbb{R}^+, i \in \{1, \cdots, n\} \qquad (15)$$

In this case uncertainty is attached to cost coefficients c_i, to technical parameters a_{ki} and to constraint levels b_k.

The above problem corresponds to the minimization of the worst estimate of total cost with satisfaction of strong level constraints. Here variables x_i are supposed to be real positive but they could be either fully real or integer. In the case in which the d_i are zero, the fuzziness is restricted to the feasible set.

Problem D_0 is equivalent to the following problem in $\mathbb{R}^{+n}$:

$$\min_{x \in \mathbb{R}^{+n}} \left| \sum_{i=1}^{n} c_i \cdot x_i \right| + \rho \cdot \sum_{i=1}^{n} d_i \cdot x_i \qquad (16)$$

under the constraints:

$$\sum_{i=1}^{n} (a_{ki} - \rho \cdot \alpha_{ki}) \cdot x_i \geq b_k + \rho \cdot \beta_k, k \in \{1, \cdots, m\} \qquad (17)$$

and

$$x_i \geq 0, i \in \{1, \cdots, n\} \qquad (18)$$

Then it can be seen that the proposed formulation leads to minimize a combination of the values of the nominal criterion and of its degree of uncertainty. In the case in which the cost coefficients are positive this problem reduces to a classical linear programming problem over $\mathbb{R}^{+n}$. In the general case, since the quantity $\sum_{i=1}^{n} c_i \cdot x_i$ will have at solution a particular sign, the solution x^* of problem D_0 will be such as:

$$\arg \min \left\{ \overset{..}{\min_{\overleftarrow{x} \in \mathbb{R}^{+n}}} \left(\sum_{i=1}^{n} c_i \overleftarrow{x}_i + \rho \sum_{i=1}^{n} d_i \overleftarrow{x}_i \right), \min_{\overrightarrow{x} \in \mathbb{R}^{+n}} \left(\rho \sum_{i=1}^{n} d_i \overrightarrow{x}_i - \sum_{i=1}^{n} c_i \overrightarrow{x}_i \right) \right\} \qquad (19)$$

where $\overleftarrow{x}$ is solution of problem:

$$\min_{x \in R^{+n}} \left(\sum_{i=1}^{n} c_i x_i + \rho \sum_{i=1}^{n} d_i x_i \right) \qquad (20)$$

under the constraints:

$$\sum_{i=1}^{n} (a_{ki} - \rho \alpha_{ki}) x_i \geq b_k + \rho \beta_k, k \in \left\{ 1, \cdots, m \right\} \qquad (21)$$

$$\sum_{i=1}^{n} c_i x_i \geq 0 \text{ and } x_i \geq 0, i \in \left\{ 1, \cdots, n \right\} \qquad (22)$$

and where $\overrightarrow{x}$ is solution of problem:

$$\min_{x \in R^{n+}} \left(\rho \sum_{i=1}^{n} d_i x_i - \sum_{i=1}^{n} c_i x_i \right) \qquad (23)$$

under the constraints:

$$\sum_{i=1}^{n} (a_{ki} - \rho \alpha_{ki}) x_i \geq b_k + \rho \beta_k, k \in \left\{ 1, \cdots, m \right\} \qquad (24)$$

$$\sum_{i=1}^{n} c_i x_i \leq 0 \text{ and } x_i \geq 0, i \in \left\{ 1, \cdots, n \right\} \qquad (25)$$

The fuzzy dual optimal performance of this program will be given by:

$$\sum_{i=1}^{n}(c_i + \varepsilon \cdot d_i) \cdot x_i^* = \sum_{i=1}^{n}c_i x_i^* + \varepsilon \cdot \sum_{i=1}^{n}d_i x_i^* \qquad (26)$$

Problems (20) and (23) are here again classical linear programming problems. Considering other linear constraints involving the other partial order relations over $\tilde{\Delta}$ (weak inequality and fuzzy equality) the solution of the fuzzy dual programming problem will lead to the consideration of at most two classical linear programming problems. The integer version of problem D_0 will lead also to classical integer linear programming problems.

PROGRAMMING WITH FUZZY DUAL VARIABLES

Now we consider fuzzy dual programming problems with fuzzy dual variables. In that case we formulate problem D_1:

$$\min_{x \in R^n, y \in R^{+n}} \left\| \sum_{i=1}^{n}(c_i + \varepsilon d_i)(x_i + \varepsilon y_i) \right\| \qquad (27)$$

under the strong constraints:

$$\sum_{i=1}^{n}(a_{ki} + \varepsilon \cdot \alpha_{ki})(x_i + \varepsilon \cdot y_i) \gtrsim b_k + \varepsilon \cdot \beta_k, k \in \left\{ 1, \cdots, m \right\} \qquad (28)$$

and

$$x_i \in \mathbb{R}, y_i \in \mathbb{R}^+, i \in \left\{ 1, \cdots, n \right\} \qquad (29)$$

The above problem corresponds to the minimization of the worst estimate of total cost with satisfaction of strong level constraints when there is some uncertainty not only on the values of the parameters but also on the capability to implement exactly the best solution.

Problem D_1 can be rewritten as:

$$\min_{x \in R^n, y \in R^{+n}} \left\| \sum_{i=1}^{n} \left(c_i x_i + \varepsilon \left(|x_i| d_i + |c_i| y_i \right) \right) \right\| \qquad (30)$$

under constraints (29) and:

$$\sum_{i=1}^{n}\left(a_{ki}x_i + \varepsilon \cdot \left(\alpha_{ki}\left|x_i\right| + \left|a_{ki}\right|y_i\right)\right) \gtrsim b_k + \varepsilon \cdot \beta_k, k \in \left\{\ddot{}1,\cdots,m\right\} \tag{31}$$

which is equivalent in $\mathbb{R}^n \times \mathbb{R}^{+n}$ to the following mathematical programming problem:

$$\min_{\underline{x}\in\mathbb{R}^n, \underline{y}\in\mathbb{R}^{+n}} C\left(\underline{x},\underline{y}\right) = \left|\sum_{i=1}^{n}c_ix_i\right| + \rho\sum_{i=1}^{n}\left(d_i\left|x_i\right| + \left|c_i\right|y_i\right) \tag{32}$$

under constraints (29) and:

$$\sum_{i=1}^{n}\left(a_{ki}x_i - \rho\left(\alpha_{ki}\left|x_i\right| + \left|a_{ki}\right|y_i\right)\right) \geq b_k + \rho\beta_k, k \in \left\{\ddot{}1,\cdots,m\right\} \tag{33}$$

Let

$$A\left(\underline{x},\underline{y}\right) = \left[\begin{array}{l}\underline{x}\in\mathbb{R}^n, \underline{y}\in\mathbb{R}^{+n} : \\ \sum_{i=1}^{n}\left(a_{ki}x_i - \rho\left(\alpha_{ki}\left|x_i\right| + \left|a_{ki}\right|y_i\right)\right) \geq b_k + \rho\beta_k, k \in \left\{1,\cdots,m\right\}\end{array}\right] \tag{34}$$

since

$$\forall x \in \mathbb{R}^n, \forall y \in \mathbb{R}^{+n}, A(\underline{x},\underline{y}) \subset A(\underline{x},\underline{0}) \text{ and } C(\underline{x},\underline{y}) \geq C(\underline{x},\underline{0}) \tag{35}$$

it appears, as expected, that the case of no diversion of the nominal solution is always preferable. In the case in which the diversion from the nominal solution is fixed to $\overline{y}_i, i \in \left\{1,\cdots,n\right\}$, problem D_1 has the same solution than problem $D_1{}'$:

$$\min_{\underline{x}\in\mathbb{R}^n} \left|\sum_{i=1}^{n}c_ix_i\right| + \rho\sum_{i=1}^{n}d_i\left|x_i\right| \tag{36}$$

under constraints (29) and:

$$\sum_{i=1}^{n}\left(a_{ki}x_i - \rho\alpha_{ki}\left|x_i\right|\right) \geq b_k + \rho\left(\beta_k + \sum_{i=1}^{n}\left|a_{ki}\right|\bar{y}_i\right), k \in \left\{1,\cdots,m\right\} \tag{37}$$

The fuzzy dual optimal performance of problem (30) will be given by:

$$\sum_{i=1}^{n} c_i x_i^* + \varepsilon\sum_{i=1}^{n}\left(\left|x_i^*\right|d_i + \left|c_i\right|y_i\right) \tag{38}$$

where $\underline{x}^*$ of problem $D_0^{'}$.

In the case in which p of the n decision variables are of undetermined sign, the solution of this problem can be obtained by solving 2^{p+1} classical linear programming problems. Here also other linear constraints involving the other partial order relations over $\tilde{\Delta}$ (weak inequality and fuzzy equality) could be introduced in the formulation of problem D_I while the consideration of he integer version of problem D_I will lead also to solve families of classical integer linear programming problems. The performance of the solution of problem D_I will be potentially diminished by the reduction of the feasible set defined by (29) and (37).

FUZZY DUAL DYNAMIC PROGRAMMING

In this case, we consider the following fuzzy dual formulation of an N steps optimization problem:

$$\max \sum_{n=1}^{N-1}\left(c_n(s_n,x_n) + \varepsilon \cdot d_n(s_n,x_n)\right) \tag{39}$$

with $s_{n+1} = \Gamma(s_n,x_n) \in S$ and $x_n \in X_{s_n}$, s_1 being given. (40)

Here:

- Γ represents the transition of the process from state s_n when decision x_n is taken to the resulting state s_{n+1}.
- X_{s_n} is the set of feasible decisions according to current state s_n of the process.

A key issue for developing dynamic programming in the context of fuzzy dual numbers is to be able to rank always and easily two fuzzy numbers. Here it is considered that only four different situations, represented in Figure 1, can appear.

Figure 1. Relative situations of two fuzzy dual numbers

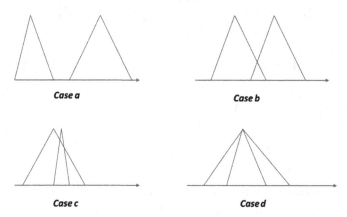

Here, case a, corresponds to a strong partial order, written $\breve{>}$, which is be defined over $\tilde{\Delta}$ by:

$$\forall a_1 + \varepsilon\, b_1, a_2 + \varepsilon\, b_2 \in \tilde{\Delta} : a_1 + \varepsilon\, b_1 \breve{>} a_2 + \varepsilon\, b_2 \Leftrightarrow a_1 - \rho\, b_1 > a_2 + \rho\, b_2 \qquad (41)$$

Case b corresponds to a mean partial order, it is written $\hat{\geq}$, and is defined over $\tilde{\Delta}$ by:

$$\forall a_1 + \varepsilon\, b_1, a_2 + \varepsilon\, b_2 \in \tilde{\Delta} : a_1 + \varepsilon\, b_1 \hat{>} a_1 + \\ \varepsilon\, b_2 \Leftrightarrow a_1 + \rho\, b_1 > a_2 + \rho\, b_2 > a_1 - \rho\, b_1 \qquad (42)$$

Case c corresponds to a *weak* partial order of *case c*, it is written $\breve{>}$, and is such as:

$$a_1 > a_2, \;\; a_1 - \rho\, b_1 > a_2 - \rho\, b_2, \;\; a_1 + \rho\, b_1 < a_2 - \rho\, b_2 \qquad (43)$$

Case d corresponds to the *fuzzy equality* between two fuzzy dual numbers, it is symbolized by $\cong$ and is characterized by:

$$a_1 = a_2 \text{ and } b_1 = b_2 \qquad (44)$$

Then, it appears that it is always possible to rank two fuzzy dual numbers and to assign a qualitative evaluation to this comparison (strong, mean or weak). When either (7.29), (7.30) or (7.31) is satisfied, it can be said that the fuzzy dual number $a_1 + \varepsilon \cdot b_1$ is greater than the fuzzy dual number $a_2 + \varepsilon b_2$ and we will write:

$$a_1 + \varepsilon \cdot b_1 > a_2 + \varepsilon \cdot b_2 \tag{45}$$

- **Degree of Certainty:** Since there are different degrees of comparison, a degree of certainty c can be attached to this assertion. A candidate expression for this degree is given by:

$$c = 1 - \frac{1}{2} \min \left\{ \frac{\alpha}{b_1}, \frac{\alpha}{b_2} \right\} \text{ if } a_1 \geq a_2 \text{ and } c = \frac{1}{2} \min \left\{ \frac{\alpha}{b_1}, \frac{\alpha}{b_2} \right\} \text{ if } a_1 < a_2 \tag{46}$$

where α is the area of the intersection between fuzzy dual numbers $a_1 + \varepsilon \cdot b_1$ and $a_2 + \varepsilon \cdot b_2$.

In Figure 1, in case a: $c = 1$, in case b: $c = 0.9$, in case c: $c = 0.7$ and in case d: $c = 0.5$.

Then a transition graph $G = [S, X]$ can be built from the initial state s_1 by considering all feasible decisions from each state of each stage to the states of the next stage:

$$S = \bigcup_{n=0}^{N-1} \Gamma^n(s_1) \text{ and } X = \bigcup_{n=0}^{N-1} \left(\Gamma^n(s_1), X_{S_n} \right) \tag{47}$$

The optimality principle of dynamic programming can be put into action here to generate from stage to stage an optimal solution tree since fuzzy dual performances can always be compared according to (41) to (44).

In that graph, in fact a tree, when the performance of a path to a state is considered superior to any other path to this state with a degree of certainty c higher than a threshold value (let say for instance 0.6), this path with the corresponding decision to reach it from the previous stage is retained. When comparing two fuzzy dual performances with a degree of certainty near 0.5, any of them can be chosen as pivot to build further branches searching for the optimal solution.

Then, supposing that Γ_{nj} is the set of states of stage n-1 from which it is possible to reach state j of stage n, the retained decision from stage n-1 to state j of stage n will be associated to a state of stage n-1 such as:

$$k_n^* = \underset{k \in \Gamma_{n-1j}}{\arg \max} \left\{ G_{n-1}^k + g_n(k,(k,j)) \right\} \tag{48}$$

where

$$G_{n-1}^k = \sum_{m=1}^{n-1} g_m(k_{m-1}^*,(k_{m-1}^*,k_m^*)) \tag{49}$$

and where a resulting degree of certainty is given by:

$$c_n^j = \underset{k \in \Gamma_{n-1,j}, k \neq k_n^*}{\min} c_{n,k,j} \tag{50}$$

Here $c_{n,k,j}$ is attached to the degree of certainty of the fuzzy dual comparison of $G_{n-1}^k + g_n(k,(k,j))$ with $G_{n-1}^{k_n^*} + g_n(k_n^*,(k_n^*,j))$. Then to each state j of each stage n is attached:

- a fuzzy dual performance given by $G_{n-1}^{k_n^*} + g_n(k_n^*,(k_n^*,j))$, representing the deterministic aspects (the real part of the performance index) as well as the degree of uncertainty (the dual part of the performance index),
- a degree of certainty c_n^j of having chosen the best solution to reach state j at stage n.

The optimal sequence of decisions will follow from one stage to the next, a path composed of decisions corresponding locally to the highest degree of certainty. The analysis of the developed tree with the degree of certainty values associated to its nodes will provide useful information for generating alternate decision scenarios.

CASE STUDY

In this section, the overall assumptions allowing to characterize the airport planning case study are established.

The Considered Background

For the numerical illustration the case of a national airport expected to gain an international position has been considered. The airport is expected to be managed under a BOT agreement (Build – Operate – Transfer) over a period of thirty years. In this situation, the BOT project financing involves a private entity which has received a concession from the public sector to finance, design, construct, and operate the complex of airport infrastructure facilities, according to the concession contract. The financial risk of the concessionaire is to be unable to recover its investment, operating and maintenance expenses in the project. In this type of situation, the project proponent is facing a significant amount of risk that needs to be assessed and mitigated.

The considered case consists in constructing a Master Plan which must incorporate the main elements encountered in airport projects, focusing on infrastructure needs. It sets the problem of the timing of the construction of facilities in order to meet future traffic demand, covering a 25 years time span. The Master Plan is built on a flexible framework by no committing in advance to any particular project, but following a comprehensive decision-making process that will avoid situations in which short-term initiatives could preclude long-term opportunities.

The major constraint the airport development project is facing is the fact that the airport operational area is restricted by the land the airport owns. For the initial stages of the development project additional land has already been acquired to facilitate infrastructure expansion. Further land will be acquired to allow or safeguard the potential airport expansion as long as it remains a commercially viable option. A factor to be noted is the location of the airport in an urban area, which imposes aerodrome and navigational constraints beyond the boundary of the airport operational area. Also, the operational area is currently constrained by the adjoined land use, including rail network and highway. Completing the 25-year Master Plan based on the potential traffic will definitely require acquisition of land to the south and safeguarding also land to the east as a way of not risking future airport and airport-related development projects.

As seen, the traffic mix is generating specific costs and revenues, with primary focus on passengers and freight flows as well as aircraft traffic that is related with the level of these flows.

The Airport Planning Scenario

The region the airport is serving is expected to become increasingly important at regional and national level with a catchment area of 8 million people living within one-hour travel time of the airport, and 40 million living within two-hours travel time. Currently, less than 40% of the region's demand for air travel is served by the local airport. A significant air travel demand is therefore underserved in the region, contributing to an overgrowing number of unnecessary surface trips and congestion. An overall unsustainable situation is expected within a decade. In this context, guaranteed access to markets are more and more relevant for economic development both from a business and commercial perspective but also for boosting tourism and creating a more efficient transportation system.

The airport is strategically located, which generates the potential of becoming the principal international gateway for the region it is serving. The need for access to sustainable air travel is expected to continue its positive trend, the airport becoming a basic driver for economic growth in the region. The airport is already providing access to air travel in an integrated way, acting as a regional transport hub with interchange facilities across all modes. The airport has a mixed ownership with the majority share belonging to private investors. A Master Plan covering a 25 years time-span details future airside and landside infrastructure requirements and flexible and sustainable expansion strategies necessary to implement in order to accommodate the forecasted traffic growth while mitigating potential risks that may jeopardize irreversibly the chances of success of the entire development project. The main objective of the airport is to claw back traffic, which currently travels to other regions for access to air travel with the benefit of decongesting the over capacitated airports and creating the premises for a sustainable regional economic development and increased environment awareness and mitigation. Current passenger throughput is 9 million, expected to reach the 35 million passengers level in 25 years. This will suggest the addition of a new runway and the possibility of adding a new terminal building to the current airport configuration. The airport has experienced strong growth of passenger traffic, over the last two decades averaging at 8% per year, with the national market share increasing from 3% to 4%. Currently, the air traffic breakdown by market sector at this airport is: low cost: 45%, short haul: 35%, long haul:10% and charter: 10%. Long-haul is expected to be the most potent sector of growth. This sector is currently limited by the lack of proper airside infrastructure – the existing length of the runway is precluding operation of commercial flights both east and west and severely limits access to emerging markets. Short haul traffic historically has been the fastest growing market sector for the airport and going forward the assumption that the sector will continue its steady growth will stand. A similar trend can be identified for the low cost sector who is looking to further expand its network. The only sector who is predicted to contract will be the charter flights due to continuous consolidation and expansion of low-cost carriers. Overall, the focus and opportunities for growth are identified solely in the international sector, while domestic traffic is forecasted to have the slowest growth, reaching complete maturity.

The forecasted growth of long-haul flights will also trigger an increase of future freight activity. This is also supported by the progressive addition of new routes, giving the airport access to new markets and positioning it as a regional cargo hub.

Traffic Forecast

The traffic forecast provides estimates every five years. This forecast is one of the key indicators that will deem which phase of the master plan is the best trade-off between commercial viability and associated risks.

Fuzzy dual demand levels will be directly associated with these uncertainty levels. For instance in the case of passenger demand we have:

$$\overline{D_k}^{Pax} = D_k^{Pax} + \varepsilon \cdot (\delta Pax / Pax) \cdot D_k^{Pax} \tag{51}$$

Table 1. Forecast of nominal passenger, ATM and freight activity levels

Current	9 million	100,000	15,000 t
5 year mark	12 million	130,000	30,000 t
10 year mark	15 million	160,000	55,000 t
15 year mark	20 million	180,000	80,000 t
20 year mark	25 million	200,000	100,000 t
25 year mark	35 million	220,000	125,000 t

Table 2. Uncertainty for passenger, ATM and freight activity levels

	$\delta Pax/Pax$	$\delta ATM/ATM$	$\delta Freight/Freight$
Current	0%	0%	0%
5 year mark	10%	9%	6%
10 year mark	15%	12%	10%
15 year mark	20%	18%	15%
20 year mark	25%	20%	16%
25 year mark	30%	28%	20%

SOLUTION PROCESS AND NUMERICAL APPLICATION

Fuzzy dual dynamic programming has been used to solve the proposed airport planning problem.

The Sequential Decision Problem

Figure 2 displays the dynamic programming decision graph associated to the airport plan development including two new runways, two terminal buildings (one passengers, one cargo) control buildings, fire and rescue facilities, multi-store car parks, taxiways, hangars, rail access over a period of 25 years divided in five stages of five years duration and corresponding to five different operational configurations for the airport. Here 31 different paths lead to the states of the final stage while 20 different states at equal or different stages must be evaluated following relations (48), (49) and (50). To each state is associated the corresponding passengers and cargo capacity.

Figure 2. Dynamic programming decision graph

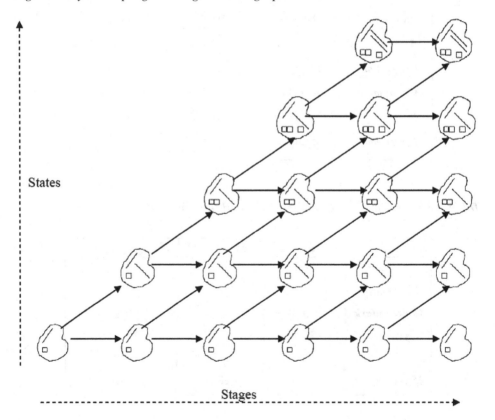

The expected passengers and cargo capacities associated to each of these states are the following:

states (i, 1): Passenger capacity = 10 million, Cargo capacity = 30, 000 t.

states (i+1, 2): Passenger capacity = 15 million, Cargo capacity = 45, 000 t.

states (i+2, 3): Passenger capacity = 25 million, Cargo capacity = 65, 000 t.

states (i+3, 4): Passenger capacity = 25 million, Cargo capacity = 125, 000 t.

states (i+4, 5): Passenger capacity = 35 million, Cargo capacity =135, 000 t.

The Solution Through Fuzzy Dual Dynamic Programming

The application of the proposed fuzzy dual dynamic programming approach leads to the optimal decision tree represented in Figure 4 where each potential state corresponding to every stage has associated a fuzzy dual performance, a degree of certainty and a fuzzy dual net present value.

Figure 3. Identification of potential options

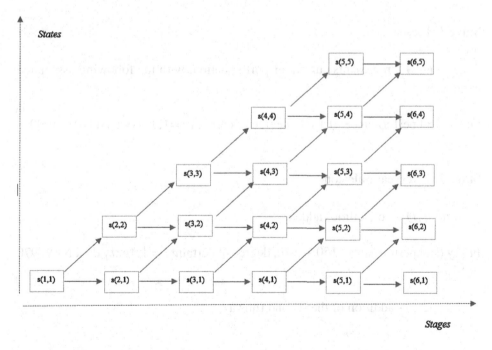

Figure 4. Fuzzy dual dynamic programming solutions tree

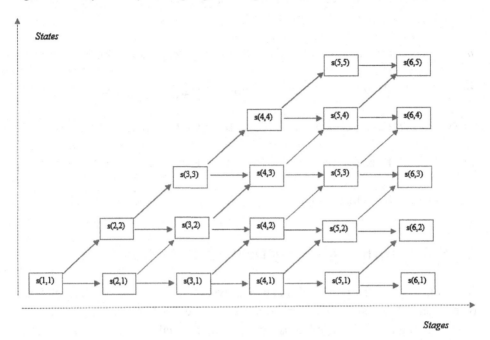

The breakdown for every stage and states in the optimal decision tree is detailed bellow:

Stage 1: Present state

state (1,1) – represents current airport situation, with the following associated parameters:

Fuzzy dual performance: $0 + \varepsilon\, 0$, degree of certainty $=1$, fuzzy dual NPV: $1000 + 0\,\varepsilon$.

Stage 2: Five-year milestone

state (2,1) – no facilities added

Fuzzy dual performance: $150 + \varepsilon\, 20$, degree of certainty $= 1$, fuzzy dual NPV: $970 + \varepsilon\, 150$.

state (2,2) - addition of the second runway

Fuzzy dual performance: -250 + ε 30, degree of certainty =1, fuzzy dual NPV: 1280 + ε 140.

Stage 3: Ten-year milestone

    state (3,1) – no facilities added

Fuzzy dual performance: 135 + ε 32, degree of certainty =1, fuzzy dual NPV: 950 + ε 310.

    state (3,2) – addition of the second runway

Fuzzy dual performance: 125 + ε 34, degree of certainty = 0.90, fuzzy dual NPV: 1210 + ε 275.

    state (3,3) – addition of the second passenger terminal

Fuzzy dual performance: -230 + ε 35, degree of certainty = 1, fuzzy dual NPV: 1450 + ε 190.

Stage 4: Fifteen-year milestone

    state (4,1) – no facilities added

Fuzzy dual performance: 128 + ε 56, degree of certainty =1, fuzzy dual NPV: 925 + ε 525.

    state (4,2) – addition of the second runway

Fuzzy dual performance: -235 + ε 48, degree of certainty =0.84, fuzzy dual NPV: 1210 + ε 490.

    state (4,3) – addition of the second passenger terminal

Fuzzy dual performance: -25 +ε 41, degree of certainty = 0.83, fuzzy dual NPV:1400 + ε 320.

    state (4,4) - addition of the cargo terminal

Fuzzy dual performance: -220 + ε 35, degree of certainty = 1, fuzzy dual NPV: 1750 + ε 260.

Stage 5: Twenty-year milestone

state (5,1) – no facilities added

Fuzzy dual performance: 123 + ε 97, degree of certainty =1, fuzzy dual NPV: 905 + ε 840.

state *(5,2)* – addition of the second runway

Fuzzy dual performance: -227+ ε 84, degree of certainty = 0.75, fuzzy dual NPV: 1195 + ε 766.

state (5,3) – addition of the second passenger terminal

Fuzzy dual performance: 115 + ε 73, degree of certainty = 0.75, fuzzy dual NPV: 1380 + ε 470.

state (5,4) - addition of the cargo terminal

Fuzzy dual performance: 110 + ε 42, degree of certainty = 0.77, fuzzy dual NPV: 1675 + ε 365.

state (5,5) – addition of the third runway

Fuzzy dual performance: -210 + ε 55, degree of certainty = 1, fuzzy dual NPV: 1800 + ε 466.

Stage 6: Twenty-five-year milestone

state (6,1) – no facilities added

Fuzzy dual performance: 120 + ε 129, degree of certainty between =1, fuzzy dual NPV: 894+ ε 962.

state (6,2) – addition of the second runway

Fuzzy dual performance: 115 + ε 105degree of certainty = 0.66, fuzzy dual NPV: 1185 + ε 971.

state (6,3) – addition of the second passenger terminal

Fuzzy dual performance: $110 + \varepsilon\ 92$, degree of certainty $= 0.59$, fuzzy dual NPV: $1370 + \varepsilon\ 750$.

state (6,4) - addition of the cargo terminal

Fuzzy dual performance: $108 + \varepsilon\ 65$, degree of certainty $= 0.68$, fuzzy dual NPV: $1650 + \varepsilon\ 582$.

state (6,5) – addition of the third runway

Fuzzy dual performance: $-200 + \varepsilon\ 75$, degree of certainty $= 0.67$, fuzzy dual NPV: $1810 + \varepsilon\ 684$.

Then it appears that (degree of certainty 0.67) to get at the horizon of 25 years with the project entirely complete (i.e. airport with three runways, two passenger terminals and a cargo terminal) the best solution is to start immediately the construction process by adding each five years a new element (second runway, second passenger terminal, cargo terminal in this particular order), then wait for five years before constructing the third runway. There is no financial risk in this case. In the case in which it is considered that the third runway will not be taken into consideration (traffic deficit, environmental considerations, lack of quantifiable economic benefits, difficulties in funding, etc.), then the best solution appears to be (degree of certainty 0.59) starting as soon as possible the second runway (+5), the second passenger terminal (+10) and the cargo terminal (+15). Here also, there is no financial risk attached. However, the do nothing solution (state (6,1)) has a financial risk attached. In this particular case, airport congestion will generate increasing operating costs.

CONCLUSION

In this chapter, the fuzzy dual formalism has been considered to treat parameter uncertainty and solution diversion in mathematical programming optimization problems. This formalism adopting a simplified version of fuzzy numbers appears to provide computational feasible solution approaches to deal with uncertainty. The case of dynamic programming has more particularly been considered in this chapter and an application to the long term airport planning problem has been displayed and analyzed. It appears that this approach allows to take explicitly into account the degree of uncertainty in the prediction of activity levels while proposing milestones for the different stages of the airport project in view of maximizing profit over the planning horizon while assessing the resulting financial risk. Here uncertainty is represented through fuzzy dual numbers which limits the problem complexity and the computational burden to get a solution. The sequential decision process is performed using what can be considered as a fuzzy dual extension of dynamic programming. Following the proposed approach to tackle uncertainty, future works should consider fuzzy dual LMI domains to represent uncertain constraints and fuzzy dual probabilities to compare possible outcomes and associated performances (Mora-Camino et al., 2017).

REFERENCES

Bellman, R. (2010). Dynamic Programming. In First Princeton Landmarks in Mathematics. Princeton University Press.

Bellman, R., & Zadeh, L. A. (1970). Decision-Making in a Fuzzy Environment. *Management Science*, *17B*(4), 141–164. doi:10.1287/mnsc.17.4.B141

Ben-Tal, A., El Ghaoui, L., & Nemirovski, A. (2009). *Robust Optimization*. Princeton University Press.

Bilegan, I., Faye, R. M., Cosenza, A. C. N., & Mora-Camino, F. (2003). A Dynamic Booking Model Revenue for Airline Management. *Journal of Decision Systems*, *12*(3-4), 417–428. doi:10.3166/jds.12.417-428

Capitanul, E. M. (2016). *Airport Strategic Planning under Uncertainty: Fuzzy dual dynamic programming approach* (PhD Thesis). Toulouse University-ENAC.

Capitanul, E. M., Cosenza, C. A. N., El Moudani, W., & Mora-Camino, F. (2014). Airport Investment Risk Assessment under Uncertainty. *International Journal of Mathematical, Computational, Physical, Electrical and Computer Engineering*, *8*(9), 1202–1206.

Capitanul-Conea, E., Krykhtine, F., Alfazari, H., Cosenza, C. A. N., & Mora-Camino, F. (2016). *Airport Planning using Fuzzy Dual Dynamic Programming*. Brazil: XV SITRAER, São Luis do Maranhão.

Cosenza, K., El Moudani, & Mora-Camino. (2016). Introduction to Fuzzy Dual Mathematical Programming. In *Fuzzy Systems and Data Mining, Proceedings of FSDM 2016*. IOS Press.

Delgado, M., Verdegay, J. L., & Vila, M. A. (1987). Imprecise Costs in Mathematical Programming Problems. *Control and Cybernetics*, *16*, 114–121.

El Moudani, W., & Mora-Camino, F. (2000). A dynamic approach for aircraft assignment and maintenance scheduling by airlines. *Journal of Air Transport Management*, *6*(4), 233–237. doi:10.1016/S0969-6997(00)00011-9

Esogbue & Bellman. (n.d.). Fuzzy Dynamic Programming and its Extensions. *TIMS/ Studies in the Management Sciences*, 20, 147-167.

Faye, R. M., Sawadogo, S., Lishou, C., & Mora-Camino, F. (2003). Long-term Fuzzy Management of Water Resource Systems. *J. of Applied Mathematics and Computation*, 137(2-3), 459–475. doi:10.1016/S0096-3003(02)00151-0

Faye, R. M., Sawadogo, S., & Mora-Camino, F. (2002). Logique floue Appliquée à la Gestion à Long-terme des Resources en Eau. *Revue des Sciences de l'Eau*, 15(3), 579–596. doi:10.7202/705470ar

Gal, T., & Greenbers, H. J. (Eds.). (1997). *Advances in Sensitivity Analysis and Parametric Programming*. Kluwer Academic Publishers. doi:10.1007/978-1-4615-6103-3

Hagelauer, P., & Mora-Camino, F. (1998). A Soft Dynamic Programming Approach for On-line Aircraft 4D-trajectory Optimization. *European Journal of Operational Research*, 107(1), 87–95. doi:10.1016/S0377-2217(97)00221-X

Kacprzyk, J. (1983). *Multistage Decision Making under Fuzziness. Verlag TÜV*.

Kacprzyk, J., & Esogbue, A. O. (1996). Fuzzy Dynamic Programming: Main Developments and Applications. *Fuzzy Sets and Systems*, 81(1), 31–45. doi:10.1016/0165-0114(95)00239-1

Kosinsky, W. (2006). On Fuzzy Number Calculus. *International Journal of Applied Mathematics and Computer Science*, 16(1), 51–57.

Mora-Camino, F., & Nunes Cosenza, C. A. (2017). Fuzzy Dual Numbers, Theory and Applications. In Studies in Fuzziness and Soft Computing. Springer.

Nasseri, H. (2006), Fuzzy Numbers: Positive and Nonnegative. *International Mathematical Forum*, 3, 1777-1780.

Parida. (2013). Fuzzy Dynamic System Approach to Multistage Decision Making Problems. *Ultra Scientist,* 25(2), 350-360.

Ruszczynski, A., & Shapiro, A. (2003). Stochastic Programming. *Handbooks in Operations Research and Management Science, 10*.

Tanaka, H., Ichihashi, H., & Asai, K. (1974). On Fuzzy Mathematical Programming. *Journal of Cybernetics*, 3(4), 37–46. doi:10.1080/01969727308545912

Zimmermann, H. J. (1986). Fuzzy Sets Theory and Mathematical Programming. In A. Jones & ... (Eds.), *Fuzzy Sets Theory and Applications* (pp. 99–114). D.Reidel Publishing Company. doi:10.1007/978-94-009-4682-8_7

Chapter 6
Selected Topics in Robust Optimization

Ihsan Yanikoglu
Ozyegin University, Turkey

ABSTRACT

In this chapter, the authors give a brief introduction to important concepts of RO paradigm. The remainder of the chapter is organized as follows: Section 2 gives an introduction on optimization under uncertainty, and presents brief comparisons among the well-known sub-fields of optimization under uncertainty such as RO, stochastic programming (SP), and fuzzy optimization (FO). Section 3 presents important methodologies of RO paradigm. Section 4 gives insights about alternative ways of choosing the uncertainty set. Section 5 shows alternative methods of assessing the quality of a robust solution and presents miscellaneous topics. Finally, Section 6 summarizes conclusions and gives future research directions.

INTRODUCTION

Robust optimization (RO) is an active research field that has been mainly developed in the course of last twenty years. The goal of robust optimization is to find solutions that are 'immune' to uncertainty of parameters in a given mathematical optimization problem. RO is well-known because it yields computationally tractable solution methods for uncertain optimization problems. RO does not suffer from the curse of dimensionality, and its methods are very useful for real-life applications and tailored to the information at hand. There have been many publications that show the value of RO in many fields of application including finance (Lobo 2000),

DOI: 10.4018/978-1-5225-5091-4.ch006

energy (Bertsimas et al. 2013, Babonneau et al. 2010), supply chain (Ben-Tal et al. 2005, Lim 2013), inventory management (Bertsimas and Thiele 2006) healthcare (Fredriksson et al. 2011), engineering (Ben-Tal and Nemirovski 2002a), scheduling (Yan and Tang 2009), marketing (Wang and Curry 2012), etc. For a quick overview of the associated literature on RO, we refer to the survey papers by Ben-Tal and Nemirovski (2002b), Bertsimas et al. (2011), Beyer and Sendhoff (2007), Gabrel et al. (2014), and Gorissen et al. (2015).

OPTIMIZATION UNDER UNCERTAINTY

Mathematical optimization problems often have uncertainty in problem parameters because of measurement/rounding, estimation/forecasting, or implementation errors. *Measurement/rounding errors* are often caused when an actual measurement is rounded to a nearest value according to a rule, e.g., the nearest tenth or hundredth, or when the actual value of the parameter cannot be measured with a high precision as it appears in reality. For example, if the reported parameter value is 1.5 according to the nearest tenth, then the actual value can be anywhere between 1.45 and 1.55, i.e., it is uncertain. *Estimation/forecasting errors* come from the lack of true knowledge about the problem parameter or the impossibility to estimate the true characteristics of the actual data. For example, demand and cost parameters are often subject to such estimation/forecasting errors. *Implementation errors* are often caused by "ugly" reals that can be hardly implemented with the same precision in reality. For example, suppose the optimal voltage in a circuit, that is calculated by an optimization tool, is 3.81231541. The decimal part of this optimal solution can be hardly implemented in practice, since you cannot provide the same precision. Aside from the above listed errors, a parameter can also be *inherently stochastic or random*. For example, the hourly number of customers arriving at a bank may follow a Poisson distribution.

Optimization based on nominal values often lead to "severe" infeasibilities. Notice that a small uncertainty in the problem data can make the nominal solution completely useless. A case study in Ben-Tal and Nemirovski (2000) shows that perturbations as low as 0.01% in problem coefficients result constraint violations more than 50% in 13 out of 90 *NETLIB* Linear Programming problems considered in the study. In 6 of these 13 problems violations were over 100%, where 210,000% being the highest (i.e., seven scale higher than the tested uncertainty). Therefore, a practical optimization methodology that proposes immunity against uncertainty is needed when the uncertainty heavily affects the quality of the nominal solution.

Flaw of Using Nominal Values

Consider an uncertain linear optimization problem with a single constraint:

$$a^T x \leq b \tag{1}$$

where $a = \bar{a} + \rho\zeta$ is the vector of uncertain coefficients and $\bar{a}$ being the nominal vector, $\zeta \in \mathbb{R}^2$ is the uncertain parameter that is uniformly distributed in a unit box $\left\| \zeta_\infty \right\|_2 \leq 1$, and ρ is a scalar shifting parameter. Now (say) we ignore the uncertainty in the constraint coefficients and solve the associated problem according to the nominal data, i.e. $a = \bar{a}$, and assume that the constraint is binding for the associated nominal optimal solution $\bar{x}$, i.e. $\bar{a}^T \bar{x} = b$. Figure 1 shows the original constraint $\left[a^T x \leq b \right]$ in the uncertainty space when x is fixed to the nominal optimal solution $\bar{x}$.

The solid line in Figure 1 represents ζ values where the uncertain constraint is binding when x is fixed to the nominal solution $\bar{x}$, and the dashed lines represent the feasible uncertainty region for the same constraint. Therefore, the area that is

Figure 1. Feasible region of the uncertain constraint $\left(\bar{a} + \rho\zeta \right)^T \bar{x} \leq b$ in the uncertainty space $[-1,1]^2$

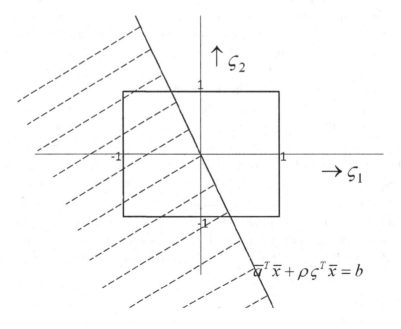

determined by the intersection of the unit box with the dashed region gives the subset for which the nominal $\bar{x}$ is robust. From the figure we can conclude that the probability of violating this constraint can be as high as 50%, since ζ follows a uniform distribution. This shows that uncertainty may severely affect the quality of the nominal solution, and there exists a crucial need for an optimization methodology that yields solutions that are immunized against the uncertainty.

Now let us consider the following figure that presents another illustrative example.

In Figure 2, there are three constraints and their binding values are represented by the solid lines. The constraint on the right-hand side is uncertain, and the other two are certain. For the uncertain constraint, the solid line represents the binding value of the constraint for the nominal data and the dashed line represents the same for a different realization of the uncertain data. Notice that, different than in Figure 1, in Figure 2 we are in the space of the decision variable x. We assume that the problem at hand is an uncertain linear problem, therefore, the optimal solutions are obtained at the extreme points of the feasible region where the constraints are binding. Suppose x^1 denotes the unique nominal optimal solution of the problem. It is easy to see that x^1 may be highly infeasible when the associated constraint is uncertain. The new (robust) optimal solution may become x^3. Now consider the case where x^1 and x^2 are both optimal for the nominal data, i.e., the optimal facet is the line segment that connects x^1 and x^2. In this case, the decision maker would always prefer x^2 over x^1, since its feasibility performance is less affected by the uncertainty. This shows that staying away from "risky" solutions that have uncertain binding constraints may be beneficial.

There are three complementary approaches in optimization that deals with data uncertainty, namely, *robust optimization* (RO), *stochastic programming* (SP), and *fuzzy optimization* (FO). Each method has its own assumptions, and the way uncertainty

Figure 2. Effects of uncertainty on feasibility and optimality performance of solutions (this figure is represented in the decision variable space)

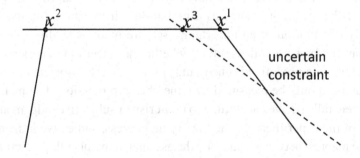

is modelled in FO is substantially different than the other two approaches, which shall be explained later in this section.

To begin with, as it is pointed out by Ben-Tal et al. (2009, p. xiii), basic SP has the following assumptions: 1) The underlying probability distribution or a family of distributions of the uncertain parameter must be known. 2) The associated distribution or a family of distributions should not change over the time horizon that the decisions are made. 3) The decision maker should be ready to accept probabilistic guarantees as the performance measure against the uncertainty. If these conditions are met and the deterministic counterpart of the stochastic problem is tractable, then SP is the right optimization methodology to solve the problem at hand. For additional details on SP we refer to Prékopa (1995), Birge and Louveaux (2011), Shapiro and Ruszczyński (2003), and Charnes and Cooper (1959).

On the other hand, the 'orthodox' RO approach has the following three implicit assumptions (Ben-Tal et al. 2009, p. xii):

A.1: All decision variables represent "here and now" decisions: they should get specific numerical values as a result of solving the problem before the actual data "reveals itself".

A.2: The decision maker is fully responsible for consequences of the decisions to be made when, and only when, the actual data is within the prespecified uncertainty set.

A.3: The constraints of the uncertain problem in question are "hard" – the decision maker cannot tolerate violations of constraints when the data is in the prespecified uncertainty set.

It is important to point out that assumption [A.1] can be extended by *adjustable robust optimization* (ARO); a brief introduction on ARO will be given in Section 3.2. In addition, assumption [A.3] can be relaxed by *globalized robust optimization* (Ben-Tal et al. 2009, Ch. 3 & 11), as well as by using safe approximations of chance constraints that shall be briefly explained in Section 4.

FO is used when data is vague or ambiguous, i.e., unlike RO and SP, the structural properties of the uncertainty such as a probability distribution, the moments of a probability distribution or an uncertainty set, are unknown. More precisely, in FO, one may not be sure with certainty whether an uncertain parameter does or does not belong to a predefined (uncertainty) set since the associated information is 'fuzzy' and can only be measured by a membership function. The membership function is generally derived according to non-crisp or subjective judgements of the 'members' of the experiment. In the fuzzifying process, subjective judgements of the users are mapped between 0 and 1 by the associated membership function which is often modelled as triangular or trapezoid shaped curves. In fuzzy optimization, the membership functions of fuzzy objective and/or constraints are derived in the fuzzifying step, and then the associated fuzzy mathematical optimization problem is optimized to derive crisp 'defuzzified' outputs from the initial non-crisp information at hand. Notice that fuzzifying and defuzzifying steps are conceptually similar to deriving the deterministic counterpart in SP and RO, which shall be explained in Section 3.1 for RO. Nevertheless, instead of using duality and complex mathematical optimization techniques, FO uses simple operators and 'basic' OR techniques to optimize membership functions. For further details on FO, we refer reader to the other chapters of this book on FO.

In the remainder of this section, we compare the three main approaches that are mentioned above:

Optimization Under Uncertainty vs. Sensitivity Analysis

While the objective of RO, SP, and FO is to find the optimal solution that is immunized against the uncertainty of problem data. Sensitivity analysis checks feasibility of the nominal optimal solution for changing values of the nominal data. Therefore, it is misleading to compare sensitivity analysis with optimization under uncertainty approaches since these methods are aimed at completely different questions than sensitivity analysis.

Robust Optimization vs. Stochastic Programming

If we compare the basic versions of RO and SP, the latter seems to be less conservative than the former since it is not worst-case oriented. However, it is important to point out that the SP approach is valid only when the probability distribution is known. Notice that RO does not have such a restriction since it works with uncertainty sets that can be derived by expert opinion or using historical data. Moreover, the RO paradigm is computationally more tractable than the SP approach; for details on such examples we refer to Ben-Tal et al. (2009, pp. xiii - xv), and Chen et al. (2006). On the other hand, the two approaches may also complement each other under mild assumptions on the uncertainty; see Yanıkoğlu and Kuhn (2017), and the list of references can be easily extended.

Robust Optimization and Stochastic Programming vs. Fuzzy Optimization

RO, SP and FO distinguish from each other by the way they model ambiguity in the uncertainty. We explain similarities and differences among these approaches in threefold: 1) To begin with, SP uses ambiguous chance constraints to model ambiguity in probability distributions; see Section 4. More precisely, different than the classic chance constraint approach, the ambiguity set define a family of probability distributions instead of a unique "known" distribution. Even though an ambiguity set allows the uncertainty to be unknown to some extent, certain probabilistic assumptions are still required for tractability. Nevertheless, ambiguous chance constraints are generally intractable for general classes of probability distributions that are different than Gaussian; for a quick overview, see Nemirovski (2012). Therefore, the SP approach to model ambiguity is impractical when available information at hand is limited and does not follow a specific family of distributions. 2) To model ambiguous uncertain parameters, RO uses the so-called *distributionally robust optimization* (DRO) framework. Similar to FO, the associated RO methods can be also used when available data is limited. In addition, the associated methods are generally tractable under mild conditions. To model ambiguity sets, DRO uses certain distance measures such as phi-divergence, Wasserstein metric and etc. to quantify the distance between the nominal data and other realizations defined in the (bounded) ambiguity set; see, Esfahani and Kuhn (2015) and Yanıkoğlu and den Hertog (2013) for applications, and Delage and Ye (2010), Goh and Sim (2010), Wiesemann et al. (2014) for the general theory. 3) Different than RO and SP, FO uses membership functions to model ambiguity in uncertainty. In addition, unlike RO and SP, the way ambiguity is modelled in FO is also subject to vagueness in itself because it is based on vague inputs that do not exhibit any structural properties. On the contrary, SP and RO allow ambiguity to be modelled using certain measures, and the structural properties of the uncertain parameter and the mathematical optimization problem. This is why, the similarities and differences that we have mentioned in this subsection are based on conceptual comparisons.

ROBUST OPTIMIZATION PARADIGM

In this section, we first give a brief introduction to RO by presenting the three core steps of deriving the robust counterpart, i.e., the deterministic equivalent of the uncertain optimization problem at hand, which lie at the heart of RO paradigm. Then we present the adjustable robust optimization methodology that enables formulating the wait-and-see decisions, and finalize the section with a procedure for applying RO in practice.

For the sake of exposition, we use an uncertain linear optimization problem, but we point out that our discussions in the sequel can be generalized to uncertain nonlinear optimization problems. The "general" formulation of the uncertain linear optimization problem is

$$\min_{x} \left\{ c^T x : Ax \leq b \right\} (c, A, b) \in \mathcal{U}, \tag{2}$$

where $c \in \mathbb{R}^n$ is a vector of uncertain objective coefficients, $A \in \mathbb{R}^{m \times n}$ is a matrix of constraint coefficients, and $b \in \mathbb{R}^m$ denotes an uncertain RHS vector, and $\mathcal{U}$ denotes the user specified uncertainty set. As it is explained earlier in Section 2, the RO paradigm is based on the three basic assumptions [A.1], [A.2] and [A.3], namely, $x \in \mathbb{R}^n$ is a "here and now" decision, true data is assumed to be within the specified uncertainty set $\mathcal{U}$, and constraints are 'hard', i.e., constraints violations are not allowed when the data is in $\mathcal{U}$; respectively. In addition to the main "basic" assumptions, we may assume without loss of generality (w.l.o.g.) that: 1) the objective and the right-hand side of the constraint are certain; 2) $\mathcal{U}$ is a compact and convex set; and 3) the uncertainty is constraint-wise. Now, we explain why these three assumptions are w.l.o.g.

E.1: Suppose the objective coefficients c and the right-hand side vector b are uncertain and (say) they reside in the uncertainty sets C and B; respectively, i.e., the robust reformulation of the uncertain optimization problem is

$$\min_{x} \max_{c \in C} \left\{ c^T x : Ax \leq b \forall A \in \mathcal{U}, \forall b \in B \right\}$$

Without loss of generality we may assume that the uncertain optimization problem can be equivalently reformulated with a certain objective function and right-hand side:

$$\min_{x,t} \left\{ t : c^T x - t \leq 0 \forall c \in C, Ax + bx_{n+1} \leq 0 \forall (A, b) \in \mathcal{U} \times B \right\}$$

using an epigraphic reformulation and extra variables $t \in \mathbb{R}$ and $x_{n+1} = -1$.

E.2: The uncertainty set can be replaced by the smallest convex set $conv(\mathcal{U})$, i.e., the convex hull, that includes $\mathcal{U}$ because the RC with respect to $\mathcal{U}$ is equivalent to taking the supremum of the left-hand side of a constraint over $\mathcal{U}$, which is also equivalent to maximizing the left-hand side over $conv(\mathcal{U})$. For the formal proof, see (Ben-Tal et al. 2009, pp. 12–13).

E.3: Robust counterparts of different constraints with respect to the uncertainty set can always be formulated constraint-wise. E.g., consider a problem with two constraints and with uncertain parameters b_1 and b_2: $x_1 + b_1 \leq 0, x_2 + b_2 \leq 0$, and let

$$\mathcal{U} = \left\{ b \in \mathbb{R}^2 : b_1 \geq 0, b_2 \geq 0, b_1 + b_2 \leq 1 \right\}$$

be the uncertainty set. It is easy to see that robustness of the ith $(i = 1, 2)$ constraint with respect to $\mathcal{U}$ is equivalent to robustness with respect to the projection of $\mathcal{U}$ on b_i, i.e., it can be modelled *constraint-wise*. For the general proof, see (Ben-Tal et al. 2009, pp. 11–12).

Notice that the above assumptions are also w.l.o.g. for nonlinear uncertain optimization problems, except the second assumption [E.2].

Deriving Robust Counterpart

The robust reformulation of (2) that is generally referred to as the *robust counterpart* (RC) problem is given as follows:

$$\min_{x} \left\{ c^T x : A(\zeta) x \leq b \forall \zeta \in Z \right\} \tag{3}$$

where $\zeta \in \mathbb{R}^L$ is the 'primitive' uncertain parameter, $Z \subset \mathbb{R}^{m \times n}$ denotes the user specified uncertainty set, and $A(\zeta) \in \mathbb{R}^{m \times n}$ is the uncertain coefficient matrix and for the sake of simplicity (say) $A(\zeta)$ is affine in ζ. A solution $x \in \mathbb{R}^n$ is called *robust feasible* if it satisfies the uncertain constraints $\left[A(\zeta) x \leq b \right]$ for all realizations of $\zeta \in Z$.

As it is mentioned above, we may focus on a single constraint because RO can be applied constraint-wise. To this end, a single constraint extracted from (3) can be modeled as follows:

$$\left(a + P\zeta \right)^T x \leq b \forall \zeta \in Z. \tag{4}$$

We use a factor model to formulate a single constraint as an affine function $a + P\zeta$ of the *primitive* uncertain parameter $\zeta \in Z$, where $a \in \mathbb{R}^n$, $b \in \mathbb{R}$ and $P \in \mathbb{R}^{n \times L}$; for a real-life application of factor models, see Fama and French (1993). Notice that the dimension of the general uncertain parameter $P\zeta$ is often much higher than that of the primitive uncertain parameter ζ, i.e., $n \gg L$. Notice that (4) contains infinitely many constraints due to the *for all* ($\forall$) quantifier, i.e., it is a semi-infinite optimization problem that seems intractable in its current form. There are two ways to tackle with such semi-infinite constraints. The first way is to apply robust reformulation techniques to remove the for all quantifier, and the second way is to apply the *adversarial approach*. In this section, we describe the details of these two approaches.

The first approach consists of three steps and the final result will be a computationally tractable RC of (4) that contains a finite number of tractable constraints. Note that this reformulation technique constitutes the core of RO paradigm. We illustrate the three steps of deriving the RC via a polyhedral uncertainty set:

$$Z = \left\{ \zeta : D\zeta + q \geq 0 \right\},$$

where $D \in \mathbb{R}^{m \times n}, \zeta \in \mathbb{R}^{L}$ and $q \in \mathbb{R}^{m}$.

Step 1: (Worst-Case Reformulation). Notice that (4) is equivalent to the following worst-case reformulation:

$$a^T x + \max_{\zeta : D\zeta + q \geq 0} \left(P^T x \right)^T \zeta \leq b. \tag{5}$$

Step 2: (Duality). We take the dual of the inner maximization problem in (5). The inner maximization problem and its dual yield the same optimal objective value by strong duality. Therefore, (5) is equivalent to

$$a^T x + \min_{w} \left\{ q^T w : D^T w = -P^T x, w \geq 0 \right\} \leq b. \tag{6}$$

Step 3: (Robust Counterpart). It is important to point out that we can omit the minimization term in (6), since it is sufficient that the constraint holds for at least one w. Hence, the final formulation of the RC becomes

$$\exists w : a^T x + q^T w \leq b, D^T w = -P^T x, w \geq 0. \tag{7}$$

Note that the constraints in (7) are linear in $x \in R^n$ and $w \in R^m$.

Table 1 presents the tractable robust counterparts of an uncertain linear optimization problem for box and ellipsoidal uncertainty sets. These robust counterparts are derived using the three steps that are described above. However, we need conic duality instead of LP duality in Step 2 to derive the tractable robust counterparts for the ellipsoidal uncertainty set; see the second row of Table 1. Notice that both formulations in Table 1 are tractable mathematical optimization problems that can

Table 1. Tractable reformulations for the uncertain constraint $\left[\left(a + P\zeta\right)^T x \leq b \forall \zeta \in \mathcal{Z}\right]$

Uncertainty	$\mathcal{Z}$	Robust Counterpart	Tractability
Box	$\left\|\zeta\right\|_\infty \leq 1$	$a^T x + \left\|P^T x_1\right\|_1 \leq b$	LP
Ellipsoidal	$\left\|\zeta\right\|_2 \leq 1$	$a^T x + \left\|P^T x_2\right\|_2 \leq b$	CQP

easily solved by commercial solvers for medium to large sized instances. To derive the RC for different classes of uncertainty sets and problem types, one may apply the three steps that are mentioned above by adjusting the second step ('duality') of the procedure in order to meet the problem requirements.

If the robust counterpart cannot be written as or approximated by a tractable reformulation, we advocate to perform the so-called *adversarial approach*. The adversarial approach starts with a finite set of scenarios $S_i \subset Z_i$ for the uncertain parameter in constraint i. For example, at the start, S_i only contains the nominal scenario. Then, the robust optimization problem, which has a finite number of constraints since Z_i has been replaced by S_i, is solved. If the resulting solution is robust feasible, we have found the robust optimal solution. If that is not the case, we can find a scenario for the uncertain parameter that makes the last found solution infeasible, e.g., we can search for the scenario that maximizes the infeasibility. We add this scenario to S_i, and solve the resulting robust optimization problem, and so on. For a more detailed description, we refer to Bienstock and Ozbay (2008). It appeared that this simple approach often converges to¨ optimality in a few number of iterations. The advantage of this approach is that solving the robust optimization problem with S_i instead of Z_i in each iteration, preserves the structure of the original optimization problem. Only constraints of the same type are added, since constraint i should hold for all scenarios in S_i. This approach could be faster than reformulating, even for polyhedral uncertainty sets. See Bertsimas et al. (2016) for a comparison. Alternatively, if the probability distribution of the uncertain parameter is known, one may also use the *randomized sampling* of the uncertainty set proposed by Calafiore and Campi (2005). The randomized approach substitutes the infinitely many robust constraints with a finite set of constraints that are randomly sampled. It is shown that such a randomized approach is an accurate approximation of the original uncertain problem provided that a sufficient number of samples is drawn; see Campi and Garatti (2008, Theorem 1).

Adjustable Robust Optimization

The first assumption [A.1] of the RO paradigm, i.e., the decisions are *here-and-now*, can be relaxed by *adjustable robust optimization*. Namely, in multistage decision-making problems, some (or all) decision variables can be modelled as *wait-and-see*, i.e., one may decide on the value of a wait-and-see decision variable after uncertain data reveals itself. For example, the amount of product a factory will manufacture next month may not be a here-and-now decision, but a wait-and-see decision that shall be taken based on the demand of the current month. Therefore, some (or all) decision variables can be adjusted in the time horizon according to a decision rule, which is a function of (some or all part of) the uncertain data. The semi-infinite representation of the *adjustable robust counterpart* (ARC) is given as follows:

$$\min_{x,y(\cdot)} \left\{ c^T x : A(\zeta)x + By(\zeta) \leq b \forall \zeta \in Z \right\} \tag{8}$$

where $x \in \mathbb{R}^n$ is the here-and-now decision that is made before $\zeta \in R^L$ is realized, $y(\cdot) \in \mathbb{R}^k$ denotes the wait-and-see decision that can be taken when the actual data reveals itself, and $B \in \mathbb{R}^{m \times k}$ denotes a certain coefficient matrix, i.e., fixed recourse. Nevertheless, the ARC formulation (8) is a complex mathematical optimization problem unless we restrict the function $y(\zeta)$ to specific classes such as affine (or linear) decision rules. More precisely, $y(\zeta)$ is often approximated by

$$y(\zeta) := y0 + Q\zeta \tag{9}$$

where $y^0 \in \mathbb{R}^k$ and $Q \in \mathbb{R}^{k \times L}$ are the coefficients in the affine decision rule that are optimized. *Affinely adjustable* RC (AARC) is famous because it yields tractable reformulations and has many applications in real-life; for more details, see Ben-Tal et al. (2009, Ch. 14) and references therein. Eventually, the tractable reformulation of the constraints in (8):

$$\min_{x,y^0,Q} \left\{ c^T x : A(\zeta)x + By^0 + BQ\zeta \leq d \forall \zeta \in Z \right\}$$

can be derived by the three step procedure that is described in Section 3.1, since the problem is linear in the uncertain parameter ζ, and the decision variables x, y^0 and Q. AARC is equivalent to RC when $Q = 0$ in (9) and this is why AARC is less conservative than the 'classic' RC approach and yields more flexible decisions that can be adjusted according to the realized portion of data at a given stage. Moreover, AARC is a tractable and it does not affect the mathematical optimization complexity of the problem compared with that of the RC, even though, it introduces additional variables. Notice that affine decision rules may also be optimal in some applications areas such as inventory management (Bertsimas et al. 2010)

Last but not least, ARO has many applications in real-life, e.g., supply chain management (Ben-Tal et al. 2005), project management (Ben-Tal et al. 2009, Ex. 14.2.1), and engineering (Ben-Tal and Nemirovski 2002a). For a comprehensive survey on ARO, we refer reader to Yanıkoğlu et al. (2017).

Remark 1: Tractable ARC reformulations for nonlinear decision rules also exist for specific classes; see Ben-Tal et al. (2009, Ch. 14.3) and Georghiou et al. (2015) for details.

Remark 2: A parametric decision rule like (9) cannot be used for integer 'adjustable' variables, since we have then to enforce that the decision rule to be integer for all $\zeta \in Z$. For alternative methods on modelling adjustable integer variables, we refer to Bertsimas and Caramanis (2007), Vayanos et al. (2011), Bertsimas and Georghiou (2014), Gorissen et al. (2015).

Illustrative Example

As it is pointed out above, ARO formulation of an uncertain optimization problem yields an optimal objective function value that is at least as good as that of a classic RO formulation. The following example taken from Ben-Tal et al. (2009) illustrates how far the difference between the two objective function values can get according to the given problem data.

$$\min_{x \geq 0, y \geq 0} x : y \geq \frac{1}{2}\zeta x + 1, x \geq \left(2 - \zeta\right)y \forall \zeta : 0 \leq \zeta \leq \rho \tag{10}$$

We have a simple example with two decision variables, two constraints, and an interval uncertainty set. Instead of deriving the explicit RC and ARC using the three step procedure presented in Section 3.1 (i.e., the standard procedure), here we present discussions over specific realizations of ζ and numeric values of the decision variables.

Let's begin with the orthodox RO formulation where both variables x and y are here-and-now, i.e., they are decided before uncertain data $\zeta \in \left[0, \rho\right]$ reveals itself. Now, suppose that $\zeta = \rho$ for the first constraint and $\zeta = 0$ for the second constraint; notice that a robust solution must satisfy the constraints for all realizations of the uncertainty set $\zeta \in [0, \rho]$ and this is why it must also be feasible for the given realizations. Consequently, when the data is implemented, the two constraints in (10) are as follows:

$$y \geq 0.5\rho x + 1, x \geq 2y, \tag{11}$$

and it is easy to see that

$$x \geq 2/1 - \rho \tag{12}$$

when both sides of the first constraint in (11) are multiplied by 2 (i.e., $x \geq 2y \geq \rho x + 2$) and the terms with x are collected at one side of the inequality. Therefore, the objective function value of the RC is at least $\dfrac{2}{1-\rho}$ because we minimize x and use specific realization of ζ. Therefore, Obj(RC) goes to ∞ as ρ goes to 1; see, Obj(RC) $\geq 2(1-\rho)^{-1}$ from (12).

Now let's focus on an ARO reformulation of the same problem. Suppose x is here-and-now, i.e., decided before the uncertain data reveals itself; y is a wait-and-see decision that is adjustable, i.e., decided after the uncertain data ζ reveals itself; and also suppose that y is linearly adjustable in ζ that can be modelled as $y = y_0 + y_1\zeta$ where y_0 and y_1 are coefficient variables (i.e., ARC is equivalent to RC when $y_1 = 0$). Suppose the linear decision rule (LDR) is given by $y = 1 + \dfrac{1}{2}\zeta x$ (i.e., $y_0 = 1$ and $y_1 = \dfrac{1}{2}x$) that is one possible option among infinitely many LDRs. Notice that such a decision rule satisfies the first constraint in (10) as binding for all realizations of the uncertainty, and for the second constraint we have the following when the given LDR for y is implemented in:

$$x \geq (2 - \zeta)(1 + 0.5\zeta x) \forall \zeta : 1 \leq \zeta \leq \rho.$$

It is easy to see that $x = 4$ is feasible for (13) when $\rho = 1$:

$$4 \geq (2 - \zeta)(2\zeta + 1) \forall \zeta : 1 \leq \zeta \leq \rho = 1.$$

Therefore, one may conclude that $\text{Obj(ARC)} \leq 4$. Consequently, the difference between the two objective function values can get as high as infinity according to the given values of the parameters, e.g., when $\rho = 1 \xrightarrow{\text{yields}} \text{Obj(RC)} = \infty$ while $\text{Obj(ARC)} \leq 4$.

CHOOSING UNCERTAINTY SET

In this section, we describe possible uncertainty sets and their advantages and disadvantages.

There is a trade-off between the size (and properties) of the uncertainty set and the optimality performance of the robust optimal solution with respect to this uncertainty set. For example, the *box uncertainty set* contains the full range of realizations for each individual component of the uncertain parameter. It is the most robust choice because it allows each uncertain component to take its worst-case realization independent from the other components. The box uncertainty set yields tractable RCs with LP complexity for uncertain linear optimization problems, nevertheless, the associated RCs may result in over-conservative objective function values because they yield optimal solutions which are robust against 'full' uncertainties where all parameters can take their worst-case realizations at the same time. To overcome the associated over-conservatism, one may use smaller uncertainty sets such as the *ellipsoid* and the *co-axial box*, i.e., the intersection of an ellipsoid with a box. Both ellipsoid and co-axial box uncertainty sets introduce some sort of dependence among different components of the uncertainty parameter so that all components cannot take their worst-case realizations at the same time because the total dispersion is bounded by the radius of the ellipsoid. The ellipsoid and co-axial box uncertainty sets are often preferred in practice because they are less conservative than the box and yield tractable RCs that fall in the realm of *second-order cone programming* (SOCP) given that the original uncertain problem is linear both in terms of the decision variables and the parameters.

The practical and theoretical implications behind using the ellipsoid and the co-axial box uncertainty sets are inspired by the chance constraint which is first introduced by Charnes and Cooper (1959). A chance constraint can be represented as:

$$\Pr_{\zeta \sim \mathbb{P}} \left\{ \zeta : a\left(\zeta\right)^{T} x \leq b \right\} \geq \varepsilon, \tag{14}$$

where $\zeta \in \mathbb{R}^{L}$ is the 'primitive' uncertain parameter, $a \in \mathbb{R}^{n}$ denotes a vector of uncertain coefficients, $x \in \mathbb{R}^{n}$ is a vector of decision variables, is the prescribed probability bound, and $\mathbb{P}$ is a 'known' probability distribution. Different than the classical approach, in the ambiguous chance constraint:

$$\Pr_{\zeta \sim \mathbb{P}} \left\{ \zeta : a(\zeta)^T x \leq b \right\} \geq \varepsilon, \forall \mathbb{P} \in P. \tag{15}$$

$\mathbb{P}$ belongs to a family of distributions P. It is important to stress that the ambiguous approach is computationally more challenging than the classical approach because it generalizes one probability distribution to a family of distributions, and is only tractable when the associated family is Gaussian. (Ambiguous) chance constraints are generally intractable because the feasible set is nonconvex, or it is computationally expensive to check the feasibility of constraint, e.g., (14) is bilinear in x and ζ, and ζ follows a uniform distribution. In addition, underlying probability distribution of an uncertain parameter is often unknown or non-existent due to limited data availability or structural properties of the uncertain parameter.

To overcome the associated limitations, one way is to use RO to find tractable and (distributionally) safe approximations of the chance constraint. More precisely, we aim to find the uncertainty set $\mathcal{U}_\varepsilon$ such that if x satisfies

$$a(\zeta)^T x \leq b \forall \zeta \in \mathcal{U}_\varepsilon, \tag{16}$$

then x also satisfies (14). Ben-Tal et al. (2009, Chapter 2) show that when U_ε is equivalent to the *co-axial box uncertainty set*:

$$\mathcal{U}_\varepsilon^{coax} := \left\{ \zeta \in \mathbb{R}^L : \|\zeta\|_2 \leq \Omega_\varepsilon, \|\zeta\|_\infty \leq 1 \right\} \tag{17}$$

a feasible solution for the RC of (16):

$$\sum_{j=1}^{\ell} |z_j| + \Omega_f = \sqrt{\sum_{j=1}^{\ell} w_j^2} \leq b - [a^0] x, \tag{18}$$

tisfies the chance constraint with at least probability ε, where (z, w). are the additional dual variables, $a(\zeta) = a^0 + \sum_{j=1}^{\ell} \zeta_j a^j$ is affine in the uncertain parameter

155

$\zeta, \Omega_\varepsilon$ is the radius of the ellipsoid that is equivalent to $\exp\left(-\Omega^2 / 2\right)$ (i.e., $\Omega_\varepsilon = \sqrt{-2\ln\varepsilon}$), and the uncertain parameter satisfies

$E\left[\zeta i\right] = 0$, $\left|\zeta i\right| \leq 1$ and ζ_i's are independent $\forall i \in \left\{1, ..., L\right\}$.

Another way is to use a polyhedral set (Ben-Tal et al. 2009, Proposition 2.3.4), called budgeted uncertainty set or the *Bertsimas and Sim* uncertainty set (Bertsimas and Sim 2004):

$$Z_\varepsilon = \left\{\zeta : \left\|\zeta\right\|_1 \leq \Gamma, \left\|\zeta\right\|_\infty \leq 1\right\}, \tag{19}$$

where $\varepsilon = \exp\left(-\Gamma^2 / 2L\right)$. The probability guarantee of the Bertismas and Sim uncertainty set is only valid when the uncertain parameters are independent and symmetrically distributed. The advantage of the co-axial box is that it is less conservative than the Bertsimas and Sim uncertainty for a fixed ε. Nevertheless, the RC with respect to Bertsimas and Sim uncertainty set is computationally less challenging than the SOCP in (18) because it yields an LP.

Bandi and Bertsimas (2012) propose uncertainty sets based on the *central limit theorem*. When the components of ζ are independent and identically distributed with mean μ and variance σ^2, the uncertainty set is given by:

$$Z\epsilon = \left\{\zeta : \left|\sum_{i=1}^{L}\zeta_i - L\mu\right| \leq \rho\sqrt{n}\sigma\right\}, \tag{20}$$

where ρ controls the probability of constraint violation $1 - \varepsilon$. Bandi and Bertsimas also show variations on (20) that incorporate correlations, heavy tails, or other distributional information. The advantage of this uncertainty set is its tractability, since the robust counterpart of an LP with this uncertainty set is also LP. A disadvantage of this uncertainty set is that it is unbounded for $L > 1$.

Ben-Tal et al. (2013) propose phi-divergence *uncertainty sets*. The phi-divergence between the vectors p and q is:

$$I_\phi\left(p, q\right) = \sum_{i=1}^{m}q_i\phi\left(\frac{p_i}{q_i}\right) \tag{21}$$

where ϕ in (21) is the (convex) phi-divergence function; for details on phi-divergence, we refer to Pardo (2005). Let p denote a probability vector and let q be the vector with observed frequencies when N items are sampled according to p. Under certain regularity conditions,

$$\frac{2N}{\phi''(1)} I_\phi(p,q) \xrightarrow{d} \chi^2_{m-1} \; as \; N \to \infty$$

This motivates the use of the following uncertainty set:

$$Z_\epsilon = \left\{ p : p \geq 0,^T p = 1, \frac{2N}{\phi''(1)} I_\phi(p,\hat{p}) \leq \chi^2_{m-1;1-\epsilon} \right\}, \tag{22}$$

where $\hat{p}$ in (22) is an estimate of p based on N observations, and $\chi^2_{m-1;1-\epsilon}$ is the $1-\epsilon$ percentile of the χ^2 distribution with $m-1$ degrees of freedom. The uncertainty set contains the true p with (approximate) probability $1-\epsilon$. Ben-Tal et al. (2013) give many examples of phi-divergence functions that lead to tractable robust counterparts. This approach is later extended to general uncertainties in Yanıkoğlu and den Hertog (2013) to safely approximate ambiguous chances constraints by using historical data. An alternative to phi-divergence is using the *Anderson-Darling test* to construct the uncertainty set; see, (Ben-Tal et al. 2015, Ex. 15).

$$z_j + w_j = -\left[a^j\right]^T x, \forall j \in \{1,\ldots,\ell\}$$

MISCELLANEOUS TOPICS

How to Compare Robust and Nominal Solutions

A common mistake that is often made in practice is to compare the optimal objective function value of a nominal problem with that of its robust reformulation. Notice that a direct comparison is misleading because it is known that both models favors their own objective and it is also known that the robust objective is essentially more conservative than the nominal one. Moreover, we compare objective function values of two different solutions with respect two different data which are likely to be realized with 0 probability.

To fairly compare nominal and robust optimization problems, the best way is to use a Monte Carlo simulation that compares the 'average' performance of two mathematical optimization models with respect to a given criterion by sampling uncertain data from a given distribution. The performance criteria can be the average objective function value if the uncertainty is in the objective. If the uncertainty is in the constraints, then the performance criteria can be the average number of constraint violations or the average size of the constraint violations.

The simulation outcomes can also be analyzed using statistical tests. Gorissen et al. (2015) provide corresponding statistical tests to verify whether one solution is better than the other solution. Suppose the data for a statistics test is available as n pairs $(R_i, N_i)(i = 1, 2, \ldots, n)$, where R_i and N_i are the performance characteristics in the ith simulation for the robust and the nominal solutions; respectively. Even though it is not necessary for the statistical test that R_i and N_i are based on the same simulated uncertainty vector ζ, it increases the power of the test because R_i and N_i will be positively correlated. It reduces the variance of the difference, i.e.,

$$Var\left(R_i - N_i\right) = Var\left(R_i\right) + Var\left(N_i\right) - 2Cov\left(R_i, N_i\right),$$

which is used in the following statistical tests:

- The sign test for the median validates $H_0 : m_R = m_N$ against $H_1 : m_R < m_N$ with confidence level α, where m_R and m_N are the medians of the distributions of R_i and N_i, respectively. This tests the conjecture that the probability that solution X outperforms solution Y is larger than 0.5. Let $n_=$ be the number of observations for which $R_i = N_i$ and let Z be the number of negative signs of $R_i - N_i$. Under the null hypothesis, Z follows a binomial distribution with parameters $n - n_=$ and 0.5. That means that the null hypothesis gets rejected if Z is larger than the $(1 - \alpha)$ percentile of the binomial distribution.

- The t-test for the mean validates $H_0 : \mu_R = \mu_N$ against $H_1 : \mu_R < \mu_N$ with confidence level α, where μ_x and μ_y are the means of the distributions of R_i and N_i, respectively. This tests the conjecture that solution R outperforms solution N in long run average behavior. This test assumes that   follows a normal distribution. Let

$$Z_i = R_i - N_i, \bar{Z} = \left(\sum_{i=1}^{n} Z_i / n \right)$$

and

$$s^2 = \sum_{i=1}^{n} \left(Z_i - \bar{Z} \right)^2 / \left(n - 1 \right),$$

then

$$T = \sqrt{n} \sum_{i=1}^{n} \left(Z_i - \bar{Z} \right) / s$$

follows a t-distribution with $n - 1$ degrees of freedom under the null hypothesis. This means that H_0 gets rejected if T is smaller than the α percentile of the t-distribution with $n-1$ degrees of freedom.

Robust Counterparts of Equivalent Deterministic Problems Are Not Necessarily Equivalent

In this section, we show that deterministically equivalent reformulations of a given problem are not necessarily equivalent when we take their robust counterparts. Following examples, taken form Gorissen et al. (2015), provide nice illustrative examples on the associated issue.

The first one is similar to the example in Ben-Tal et al. (2009, p. 13). Consider the following constraint:

$$\left(2 + \zeta \right) x_1 \leq 1,$$

where ζ is an (uncertain) parameter. This constraint is equivalent to:

$$\left(2 + \zeta \right) x_1 + s = 1, \, s \geq 0$$

However, the robust counterparts of these two constraint formulations, i.e.

$$\left(2+\varsigma\right)x_1 + s = 1 \forall \varsigma : |\varsigma| \le 1 \tag{23}$$

and:

$$\left(2+\varsigma\right)x_1 + s = 1, s \ge 0 \forall \varsigma : |\varsigma| \le 1 \tag{24}$$

in which the uncertainty set for ς is the set $\left\{\varsigma : |\varsigma| \le 1\right\}$, are not equivalent. It can easily be verified that the feasible set for robust constraint (23) is: $x_1 \le 1/3$, while for the robust constraint (20) this is $x_1 = 0$. The reason why (23) and (24) are not equivalent is that by adding the slack variable, the inequality becomes an equality that has to be satisfied for all values of the uncertain parameter, which is very restrictive. The general message is therefore: *do not introduce slack variables in uncertain constraints, unless they are adjustable like in Kuhn et al. (2011), and avoid uncertain equalities.*

Another example is the following constraint:

$$|x_1 - \varsigma| + |x_2 - \varsigma| \le 2,$$

which is equivalent to:

$$y_1 + y_2 \le 2$$

$$y_1 \ge x_1 - \varsigma$$

$$y_1 \ge \varsigma - x_1$$

$$y_2 \ge x_2 - \varsigma$$

$$y_2 \ge \varsigma - x_2.$$

However, the robust versions of these two formulations, namely:

$$|x_1 - \varsigma| + |x_2 - \varsigma| \le 2 \forall \varsigma : |\varsigma| \le 1, . \tag{25}$$

and:

$$y_1 + y_2 \leq 2.$$

$$y_1 \geq x_1 - \zeta \forall \zeta : |\zeta| \leq 1$$

$$y_1 \geq \zeta - x_1 \forall \zeta : |\zeta| \leq 1 \tag{26}$$

$$y_2 \geq x_2 - \zeta \forall \zeta : |\zeta| \leq 1$$

$$y_2 \geq \zeta - x_2 \forall \zeta : |\zeta| \leq 1$$

are not equivalent. Indeed, it can easily be checked that the set of feasible solutions for (25) is $(\theta, -\theta), -1 \leq \theta \leq 1$, but the only feasible solution for (26) is $x = (0,0)$. The reason for this is that in (26) the uncertainty is split over several constraints, and since the concept of RO is constraint-wise, this leads to different problems, and thus different solutions. The following linear optimization reformulation, however, is equivalent to (25):

$$x_1 - \zeta + x_2 - \zeta \leq 2 \forall \zeta : |\zeta| \leq 1$$

$$x_1 - \zeta + \zeta - x_2 \leq 2 \forall \zeta : |\zeta| \leq 1 \tag{27}$$

$$\zeta + x_2 - x_1 - \zeta \leq 2 \forall \zeta : |\zeta| \leq 1$$

$$\zeta - x_1 + \zeta - x_2 \leq 2 \forall \zeta : |\zeta| \leq 1$$

For more details on such reformulation issues in different optimization settings, we refer to Gorissen et al. (2015, §6).

Pareto Efficiency

Iancu and Trichakis (2013) discovered that "the inherent focus of RO on optimizing performance only under worst-case outcomes might leave decisions unoptimized in case a non-worst-case scenario materialized". Therefore, the "classical" RO framework might lead to a Pareto inefficient solution; i.e., an alternative robust optimal solution may guarantee an improvement in the objective or slack size for (at least) one scenario without deteriorating it in other scenarios. Given a robust optimal solution, Iancu and Trichakis propose optimizing a new problem to find a solution that is Pareto efficient. In this new problem, the objective is optimized for a scenario in the interior of the uncertainty set, e.g., for the nominal scenario, while the worst-case objective is constrained to be not worse than the robust optimal objective value. For more details on Pareto efficiency in robust linear optimization we refer to Iancu and Trichakis (2013).

CONCLUSION

In this chapter, we have presented the core methodologies to successfully apply RO paradigm. In addition, we have also presented advantages and disadvantages of the associated methods as well as limitations and common wrong doings while applying the RO procedure. Presented topics are based on current advances of RO and for new comers they are good outlet for applying RO in practice. Future research directions on RO could be on ARO, as it is explained before, more research is needed on adjustable integer variables and applications of ARO for MIP problems. To point out, efficient local search algorithms to solve MIP formulations are generally not viable in RO because at each stage the worst-case realization has to be found and this may be costly. This is why efficient solution methodologies tailored for RO to solve challenging uncertain MIP formulations are also required. Last but not least, applications or RO (and specifically ARO) are still lagging behind, especially research on semi-conductor manufacturing, engineering design optimization, and humanitarian logistics are scarce, and more research on these topics is needed. Other research directions would be on applying modern distributionally robust optimization methodologies to real life problems from energy, healthcare, and supply chain fields, as well as, reformulating ambiguous chance constraints with DRO perspective and their applications.

ACKNOWLEDGMENT

This work is supported by Scientific and Technological Research Council of Turkey (TUBITAK) through BIDEB 2232 Research Grant (115C100) of the author. Some sections are taken from (or related to) Gorissen et al. (2015), the author acknowledges Omega Journal for their permission. The author thanks to the editors and two anonymous referees for their valuable comments and suggestions in the realization of this chapter. Finally, the author thanks to his Master student Botan Çıtıl for proof-reading and editing the document to the publisher's file format.

REFERENCES

Babonneau, F., Vial, J.-P., & Apparigliato, R. (2010). Robust optimization for environmental and energy planning. In *Uncertainty and Environmental Decision Making* (pp. 79–126). Springer.

Bandi, C., & Bertsimas, D. (2012). Tractable stochastic analysis in high dimensions via robust optimization. *Mathematical Programming, 134*(1), 23–70. doi:10.100710107-012-0567-2

Ben-Tal, A., den Hertog, D., De Waegenaere, A. M. B., Melenberg, B., & Rennen, G. R. (2013). Robust solutions of optimization problems affected by uncertain probabilities. *Management Science, 59*(2), 341–357. doi:10.1287/mnsc.1120.1641

Ben-Tal, A., den Hertog, D., & Vial, J.-P. (2015). Deriving robust counterparts of nonlinear uncertain inequalities. *Mathematical Programming, 149*(1-2), 265–299. doi:10.100710107-014-0750-8

Ben-Tal, A., El Ghaoui, L., & Nemirovski, A. (2009). *Robust Optimization. Princeton Series in Applied Mathematics*. Princeton University Press.

Ben-Tal, A., Golany, B., Nemirovski, A., & Vial, J.-P. (2005). Retailer-supplier flexible commitments contracts: A robust optimization approach. *Manufacturing & Service Operations Management: M & SOM, 7*(3), 248–271. doi:10.1287/msom.1050.0081

Ben-Tal, A., & Nemirovski, A. (2000). Robust solutions of linear programming problems contaminated with uncertain data. *Mathematical Programming, 88*(3), 411–424. doi:10.1007/PL00011380

Ben-Tal, A., & Nemirovski, A. (2002a). Robust optimization–methodology and applications. *Mathematical Programming, 92*(3), 453–480. doi:10.1007101070100286

Ben-Tal, A., & Nemirovski, A. (2002b). Robust optimization – methodology and applications. *Mathematical Programming, 92*(3), 453–480. doi:10.1007101070100286

Bertsimas, D., Brown, D., & Caramanis, C. (2011). Theory and applications of robust optimization. *SIAM Review, 53*(3), 464–501. doi:10.1137/080734510

Bertsimas, D., & Caramanis, C. (2007). Adaptability via sampling. *46th IEEE Conference on Decision and Control*, 4717–4722.

Bertsimas, D., Dunning, I., & Lubin, M. (2016). Reformulations versus cutting planes for robust optimization: A computational and machine learning perspective. *Computational Management Science, 13*(2), 195–217. doi:10.100710287-015-0236-z

Bertsimas, D., & Georghiou, A. (2014). Binary decision rules for multistage adaptive mixed-integer optimization. *Mathematical Programming*, 1–39.

Bertsimas, D., Iancu, D. A., & Parrilo, P. A. (2010). Optimality of affine policies in multistage robust optimization. *Mathematics of Operations Research, 35*(2), 363–394. doi:10.1287/moor.1100.0444

Bertsimas, D., Litvinov, E., Sun, X. A., Zhao, J., & Zheng, T. (2013). Adaptive robust optimization for the security constrained unit commitment problem. *IEEE Transactions on Power Systems, 28*(1), 52–63. doi:10.1109/TPWRS.2012.2205021

Bertsimas, D., & Sim, M. (2004). The price of robustness. *Operations Research, 52*(1), 35–53. doi:10.1287/opre.1030.0065

Bertsimas, D., & Thiele, A. (2006). A robust optimization approach to inventory theory. *Operations Research, 54*(1), 150–168. doi:10.1287/opre.1050.0238

Beyer, H.-G., & Sendhoff, B. (2007). Robust optimization – a comprehensive survey. *Computer Methods in Applied Mechanics and Engineering, 196*(33–34), 3190–3218. doi:10.1016/j.cma.2007.03.003

Bienstock, D., & Ozbay, N. (2008). Computing robust basestock levels. *Discrete Optimization, 5*(2), 389–414. doi:10.1016/j.disopt.2006.12.002

Birge, J. R., & Louveaux, F. V. (2011). *Introduction to Stochastic Programming*. Springer. doi:10.1007/978-1-4614-0237-4

Calafiore, G., & Campi, M. C. (2005). Uncertain convex programs: Randomized solutions and confidence levels. *Mathematical Programming, 102*(1), 25–46. doi:10.100710107-003-0499-y

Campi, M. C., & Garatti, S. (2008). The exact feasibility of randomized solutions of uncertain convex programs. *SIAM Journal on Optimization, 19*(3), 1211–1230. doi:10.1137/07069821X

Charnes, A., & Cooper, W. W. (1959). Chance-constrained programming. *Management Science, 6*(1), 73–79. doi:10.1287/mnsc.6.1.73

Chen, X., Sim, M., Sun, P., & Zhang, J. (2006). A tractable approximation of stochastic programming via robust optimization. *Operations Research.*

Delage, E., & Ye, Y. (2010). Distributionally robust optimization under moment uncertainty with application to data-driven problems. *Operations Research, 58*(3), 595–612. doi:10.1287/opre.1090.0741

Esfahani, P. M., & Kuhn, D. (2015). *Data-driven distributionally robust optimization using the Wasserstein metric: Performance guarantees and tractable reformulations.* arXiv preprint arXiv:1505.05116

Fama, E. F., & French, K. R. (1993). Common risk factors in the returns on stocks and bonds. *Journal of Financial Economics, 33*(1), 3–56. doi:10.1016/0304-405X(93)90023-5

Fredriksson, A., Forsgren, A., & H˚ardemark, B. (2011). Minimax optimization for handling range and setup uncertainties in proton therapy. *Medical Physics, 38*(3), 1672–1684. doi:10.1118/1.3556559 PMID:21520880

Gabrel, V., Murat, C., & Thiele, A. (2014). Recent advances in robust optimization: An overview. *European Journal of Operational Research, 235*(3), 471–483. doi:10.1016/j.ejor.2013.09.036

Georghiou, A., Wiesemann, W., & Kuhn, D. (2015). Generalized decision rule approximations for stochastic programming via liftings. *Mathematical Programming, 152*(1-2), 301–338. doi:10.100710107-014-0789-6

Goh & Sim. (2010). Distributionally robust optimization and its tractable approximations. *Operations Research, 58*(4-part-1), 902–917.

Gorissen, B. L., Yanıkoğlu, İ., & den Hertog, D. (2015). A practical guide to robust optimization. *Omega, 53*, 124–137. doi:10.1016/j.omega.2014.12.006

Iancu, D., & Trichakis, N. (2013). Pareto efficiency in robust optimization. *Management Science, 60*(1), 130–147. doi:10.1287/mnsc.2013.1753

Kuhn, D., Wiesemann, W., & Georghiou, A. (2011). Primal and dual linear decision rules in stochastic and robust optimization. *Mathematical Programming, 130*(1), 177–209. doi:10.100710107-009-0331-4

Lim, S. (2013). A joint optimal pricing and order quantity model under parameter uncertainty and its practical implementation. *Omega, 41*(6), 998–1007. doi:10.1016/j.omega.2012.12.003

Lobo, M. S. (2000). *Robust and convex optimization with applications in finance* (PhD thesis). Stanford University. Retrieved from http://sousalobo.com/thesis/thesis.pdf

Nemirovski, A. (2012). On safe tractable approximations of chance constraints. *European Journal of Operational Research, 219*(3), 707–718. doi:10.1016/j.ejor.2011.11.006

Pardo, L. (2005). *Statistical inference based on divergence measures*. CRC Press. doi:10.1201/9781420034813

Prékopa, A. (1995). *Stochastic Programming*. Kluwer Academic Publishers. doi:10.1007/978-94-017-3087-7

Shapiro, A., & Ruszczynśki, A. P. (2003). *Stochastic Programming*. Elsevier.

Vayanos, P., Kuhn, D., & Rustem, B. Decision rules for information discovery in multi-stage stochastic programming. In *Decision and Control and European Control Conference (CDC-ECC), 2011 50th IEEE Conference on* (pp. 7368–7373). IEEE. 10.1109/CDC.2011.6161382

Wang, X., & Curry, D. J. (2012). A robust approach to the share-of-choice product design problem. *Omega, 40*(6), 818–826. doi:10.1016/j.omega.2012.01.004

Wiesemann, W., Kuhn, D., & Sim, M. (2014). Distributionally robust convex optimization. *Operations Research, 62*(6), 1358–1376. doi:10.1287/opre.2014.1314

Yan, S., & Tang, C.-H. (2009). Inter-city bus scheduling under variable market share and uncertain market demands. *Omega, 37*(1), 178–192. doi:10.1016/j.omega.2006.11.008

Yanıkoğlu, Gorissen, & den Hertog. (2017). *Adjustable Robust Optimization – A Survey and Tutorial*. Available online at ResearchGate.

Yanıkoğlu, İ., & den Hertog, D. (2013). Safe approximations of ambiguous chance constraints using historical data. *INFORMS Journal on Computing, 25*(4), 666–681. doi:10.1287/ijoc.1120.0529

Yanıkoğlu, İ., & Kuhn, D. (2017). Decision rule bounds for two-stage stochastic bilevel programs. *SIAM Journal on Optimization*. (in press)

Chapter 7
A Fuzzy Measure of Vulnerability for the Optimization of Vehicle Routing Problems With Time Windows

Kris Braekers
Hasselt University, Belgium

Gerrit K. Janssens
Hasselt University, Belgium

ABSTRACT

In a vehicle routing problem (VRP) with time windows, the start of service needs to take place within the customer time window. Due to uncertainty on travel times, vehicles might arrive late at a customer's site. A VRP is mostly solved to minimize a total cost criterion (travel time, travel distance, fixed and variable vehicle costs). But the dispatcher might also take into consideration the risk of non-conformance with the service agreement to start service within the time window. Therefore, a measure of risk, called "vulnerability of a solution," is developed to serve as a second criterion. This chapter develops such a measure based on a distance metric and investigates its strengths and weaknesses.

DOI: 10.4018/978-1-5225-5091-4.ch007

INTRODUCTION

While the Vehicle Routing Problem (VRP) has been under study for several decades, its solution methods in recent times have been able to deal with real-time complexities (e.g. Hartl et al. (2006), Drexl (2012)). The problems have become richer by including time windows, time-dependent travel times, multiple vehicle types, vehicle loading constraints, etc. The scientific literature publishes from time to time reviews on the evolution of either solution methods for the variants of the VRP or on a classification of various types of VRPs. The most recent review can be found in Braekers et al. (2016), in which the interested reader can find references to most of the earlier reviews and classifications.

Like many combinatorial problems, also the vehicle routing problem can be formulated as a mixed-integer linear program including a huge amount of binary variables which make that a fast solution of the problem is hardly possible. Therefore, in recent times, VRPs are solved by advanced (meta)heuristic methods. Moreover, the optimal solution depends on input data which are assumed to be deterministic but mostly are only an approximation of the reality. A small perturbation on the input could result in impractical or suboptimal solutions. To cope with uncertainty in the input data of a VRP, one wants to find solutions which are robust to perturbations caused by the uncertainty. In robust optimisation, there is a trade-off between robustness and quality of the solution. Therefore, the stochastic VRP has been defined and solution methods have been proposed. Stochastic Vehicle Routing Problems include different models: VRP with Stochastic Demands, VRP with Stochastic Customers and VRP with Stochastic Travel Times.

Demand uncertainty is a serious problem in the VRP as it may lead to unmet demands. Due to the limited vehicle capacity, the main issue is that a vehicle might have to pay an extra visit to the depot for restocking, which requires algorithms for re-optimisation (Haughton, 1998). Exact solutions for the VRP with stochastic demand and customers have been proposed by Gendreau et al. (1995) and Sungur et al. (2008). Metaheuristics like tabu search have been proposed by Gendreau et al. (1996) and particle swarm optimization by Moghaddam et al. (2012).

Stochastic travel times have been studied in Laporte and Louveaux (1992). Van Woensel et al. (2008) studied the VRP with travel times resulting from a stochastic process due to traffic congestion. Also, combinations of various sources of uncertainty have been studied, for example in Erera (2010) and in Sörensen and Sevaux (2009).

Any VRP problem becomes more complex in case it involves time windows. The constraints of the problem are to service all customers within the earliest and latest (start of service) time of the customer without exceeding the route time of the vehicle. The route time of the vehicle is defined as the sum of the waiting times, the service times and the travel times. A vehicle that reaches a customer before the earliest time, after the latest time and after the route time incurs waiting time, tardiness time and overtime, respectively. In this chapter the VRP with stochastic travel times is considered in combination with time windows (VRPTW).

Ando and Taniguchi (2006) consider the VRPTW with uncertain travel times. The objective is to minimize the total cost which includes penalty costs due to the early and late arrivals, operational costs and the fixed cost of vehicles used. A genetic algorithm has been proposed to solve the described problem. Russell and Urban (2008) studied the VRPTW with random travel times with a known probability distribution. The number of vehicles used and the total distance travelled are minimized along with penalties due to arrivals outside the time windows. The authors developed a tabu search method. The VRPTW with stochastic travel and service times is studied by Li et al. (2010). Two formulations based on stochastic programming have been proposed. A heuristic algorithm based on tabu search has been developed to obtain the results effectively. Manisri et al. (2011) propose an approach to the robust VRPTW problem with uncertain travel times. The main objective is to find a robust solution for the min-max optimisation problem under robustness criteria by using a two-phase algorithm, including an insertion heuristic, local descent improvement method and a tabu search heuristic.

BACKGROUND

In this chapter a Vehicle Routing Problem (VRP) is considered as one of finding a set of routes for a fleet of m vehicles (identical or non-identical) which have to service a set of customers $V = \{ v_1, .., v_n \}$ from a central depot v_0. The number of vehicles is limited or unlimited. The vehicles depart and arrive at a single depot. A non-negative demand quantity $q_i (i=1..n, q_0=0)$ at each stop is known in advance and is deterministic. No single demand quantity exceeds the vehicle capacity. The type of VRP considered in this paper makes use of customer time windows and a depot window. A time window then represents the time interval in which the service at a customer must start. It has a lower bound and an upper bound. The depot window indicates the time period in which vehicles leave from and return to the depot. The time windows are of the hard type.

An approach is proposed to evaluate a vehicle routing solution in terms of a concept called 'vulnerability'. The concept of 'vulnerability' relates to the possibility of not being able to fulfil all service requests in all routes within the predetermined time windows, due to uncertainty in travel times. The VRP solution is generated by a (heuristic) algorithm. Evaluation in terms of feasibility of the solution and of the objective function value is straightforward in the deterministic case, but is less obvious in the case uncertainties are included. A vulnerability measure for a VRP solution is presented so that a set of solutions can be ranked in terms of vulnerability.

The process of evaluation works as follows. In the next section, a graphical representation of a VRP solution is introduced. It is explained how, making use of this graphical network representation, a solution is evaluated in the case of deterministic travel times. Afterwards, uncertainty in the travel times is introduced by representing the travel times as interval numbers on a finite support.

GRAPHICAL REPRESENTATION AND EVALUATION: DETERMINISTIC CASE

A VRP solution may be graphically represented as a graph $G=(A, V)$. Let V be the set of nodes of the graph: they represent customers and the depot. Let A be the set of edges which represent the connections between two different nodes. With every arc between two nodes is associated a non-negative travel time. The travel time may be deterministic or may contain some uncertainty. The VRP consists of designing a set of vehicle routes in such a way that: every route starts and ends at the depot; every customer is visited exactly once by exactly one vehicle, within the time window set by the customer, and satisfying the constraint that the total demand of any vehicle route cannot exceed the vehicle capacity.

The explanation how to construct the graphical representation is based on a single route of a VRP solution. The route contains three customers. In this route a vehicle leaves the depot towards customer K1, then continues its journey to customers K2 and K3 before returning to the depot. The deterministic travel times are indicated on the edges of the graph in Figure 1. The lower and upper bounds of the time-window

Figure 1. A route with three customers

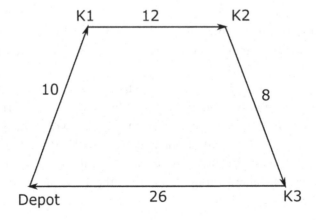

intervals of the customers K1, K2 and K3, as well as the time window of the depot, are shown in Table 1 (ETA stands for Earliest Time of Arrival; LTA stands for Latest Time of Arrival).

For easy reference, the result of the graphical representation is shown in Figure 2 before the step-by-step explanation.

A single route is represented by a directed, connected, acyclic graph $G(A,V)$. In this graph V is a set of nodes and $A \subset V x V$ is a set of arcs. Two special nodes are identified in the graph G: a start node and a finish node. Let the set of nodes $V = \{v_1, v_2, ..., v_k\}$ represent the service activity at a customer's site (of zero duration). Two special nodes are defined in V: v_1 is a source node denoting start of the travel activity from the depot, and v_k is a sink node denoting start of the activity at the depot (which in fact means the end of the travel activity towards the depot). In Figure 2 the source node is indicated by D_1 and the sink node by D_2.

The set of arcs A consists of several subsets related to various concepts of the route and its customers. A partition $A = (A^a, A^d, A^{ce}, A^{cl})$ is defined where:

A^a: The set of arcs related to travel activities, with $A^a \subset V \times V$

Table 1. Data for the illustrative example

Location	ETA	LTA
K1	0	40
K2	10	55
K3	20	90
Depot	0	100

Figure 2. Graphical representation of a route with time windows

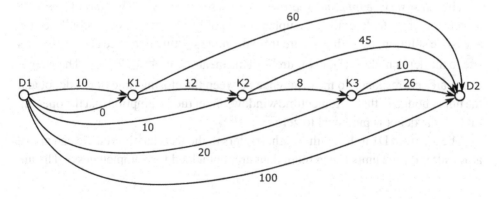

A^d: A single arc representing the time period that the depot is open (depot time window),

A^{ce}: The set of arcs related to the earliest arrival times of the customers (lower bound of the customer time window),

A^{cl}: The set of arcs related to the latest arrival times of the customers (upper bound of the customer time window).

The procedure to construct the network consists of the following steps:

1. Construct the backbone of the network (A^a)
2. Add the depot time window to the network (A^d)
3. Add the earliest customer arrival times to the network (A^{ce})
4. Add the latest customer arrival times to the network (A^{cl}).

The *backbone* of the network is made up of arcs belonging to A^a. The backbone consists of alternating travel and service activities. The service activities are omitted here as they are assumed to have zero durations. The weights of the arcs correspond to travel times. In Figure 2 the backbone consists of the sequence of arcs (D_1, K_1), (K_1, K_2), (K_2, K_3) and (K_3, D_2).

The *depot time window* is represented by a single arc $A^d_{=(v_1, v_k)}$. The weight of the arc is equal to the time period that the depot is open. The depot opens at time 0. In Figure 2 the depot window is represented by the arc (D_1, D_2).

The *earliest service times* are represented by a set of arcs A^{ce}. The start of a service at a customer's site, earlier than the lower bound of its time window, is prohibited (in a feasible solution) by adding an arc from the depot node v_1 (D_1 in Figure 2) to the node starting service at a customer's site. This means that A^{ce} ⊂ $v_1 \times V$. The weight of the arcs corresponds to the lower bound of the customer time window, under the assumption that the opening time of the depot is put equal to zero.

The *latest service times* are represented by a set of arcs A^{cl}. The start of a service at a customer's site, later than the upper bound of its time window, is prohibited (in a feasible solution) by adding an arc from the node starting a service at a customer's site to the depot node v_k (D_2 in Figure 2). This means that $A^{cl} \subset V \times v_k$. The weight of the arcs corresponds to the difference between the closing time of the depot and the upper bound of the customer time window, under the assumption that the opening time of the depot is put equal to zero.

The arc from D1 to K1 with weight 0 refers to the fact that the vehicle can arrive at K1 after 0 time units (i.e. a redundant arc, but added for completeness). The arc from K1 to D2 with weight 60 tells that K1 should be left at least 60 time units before the closing of the depot (100) or, in others words, not leave after 40.

The arc from D1 to K2 with weight 10 refers to the fact that the vehicle can arrive at K2 after 10 time units. The arc from K2 to D2 with weight 45 tells that K2 should be left at least 45 time units before the closing of the depot (100) or, in others words, not leave after 55.

The arc from D1 to K3 with weight 20 refers to the fact that the vehicle can arrive at K3 after 20 time units. The arc from K3 to D2 with weight 10 tells that K3 should be left at least 10 time units before the closing of the depot (100) or, in others words, not leave after 90.

A *path* in G is defined as a path from source node to sink node. Let us denote by $P(n)$ the set of all paths in G from source node to sink node. A deterministic duration time t_{ij} is associated with each arc $(i,j) \in A$. The length of a path is defined as the sum of the duration times of the arcs on the path. Investigation is required whether a path $p \in P(n)$, different from the arc representing the depot time window, can be the longest path in the graph G. If no such path exists the route (part of the VRP solution) is a feasible route satisfying all time window constraints.

For the route in Figure 2 to be feasible, the arc at the bottom (weight $= 100$) should be the longest path from node D1 to node D2. In Figure 2 it can be noticed that multiple arcs exist between pairs of nodes (between D_1 and K_1, and between K_3 and D_2). The node sequences from source node to sink node are enumerated in Table 2.

Due to multiple arcs in total 13 paths (next to the path D_1-D_2) can be identified. No path length is larger than 100, so the route is a feasible route. This fact can be verified in Table 3. Table 3 shows all paths, their length and their sequence of type of arcs (either a travel arc (TR) or a time window arc (TW)).

Table 2. Paths in the network as developed in Figure 2

Sequence ID	Node	Node	Node	Node	Node	Type
S1	D1	K1	D2			Multiple
S2	D1	K1	K2	D2		Multiple
S3	D1	K1	K2	K3	D2	Multiple
S4	D1	K2	D2			Single
S5	D1	K2	K3	D2		Multiple
S6	D1	K3	D2			Multiple
S7	D1	D2				Single

Table 3. Enumeration of the paths in the graph

Path	Length	Type of Arc Sequence
D1K1D2	70	TR-TW
D1K1D2	60	TW-TW
D1K1K2D2	67	TR-TR-TW
D1K1K2D2	57	TW-TR-TW
D1K1K2K3D2	40	TR-TR-TR-TW
D1K1K2K3D2	56	TR-TR-TR-TR
D1K1K2K3D2	30	TW-TR-TR-TW
D1K1K2K3D2	46	TW-TR-TR-TR
D1K2D2	55	TW-TW
D1K2K3D2	28	TW-TR-TW
D1K2K3D2	44	TW-TR-TR
D1K3D2	30	TW-TW
D1K3D2	46	TW-TR

EVALUATION IN THE CASE OF UNCERTAINTY ON TRAVEL TIMES

The uncertainty in travel time causes a problem when it comes to deciding whether the weight on the depot time window arc is the longest path. In case probability distributions were available, the evaluation of the probability, with which a specific path is the longest path, becomes very complicated from a computational point of view, even if the functional form of all probability distributions of the travel times is known. The simplest way of representing uncertainty with respect to a travel time is by means of an interval.

Let the route again be represented as a graph $G(A, V)$. A travel activity is denoted by (i,j) where $(i,j) \in A$. But, in this case, travel times are given by means of interval numbers. The interval $I_{ij} = [a_{ij}, b_{ij}]$ contains possible duration times of (i,j) associated with a travel activity.

Let us use the notion of interval-criticality, as introduced by Chanas and Zielinski (2002). A path p is *interval-critical* if there exists a set of times t_{ij} with $t_{ij} \in [a_{ij}, b_{ij}]$, $(i,j) \in A$, such that p is critical (read 'is longest path' in our case) after replacing the interval times I_{ij} with the deterministic values t_{ij} by means of:

$$t_{ij} = b_{ij} \text{ if } (i,j) \in p$$

a_{ij} if $(i,j) \notin p$

The evaluation on interval-criticality needs to be performed over all paths from source node to sink node, which contain at least one arc with an uncertain weight. The node sequences S_1 until S_6 (see Table 2) contain at least one arc with an uncertain weight.

Let uncertainty be introduced on the travel times as follows. The lower bounds of the intervals correspond to the values as shown in Figure 1. The upper bounds are determined by adding, to the lower bound, a value of 25 time units for the trips from D_1 to K_1 and from K_1 to K_2, and a value of 30 time units for the trips from K_2 to K_3 and from K_3 to D_2. This leads to the following updated path lengths, as shown in Table 4.

Under these uncertainty assumptions, five paths have the possibility to lead to a non-feasible solution (i.e. they have a length > 100).

TOWARDS A MEASURE OF VULNERABILITY

Time windows make part of the service from a supplier to a customer. It specifies a lower and an upper bound on the time of start of delivery of goods at a customer's site. Sometimes these time windows are specified by regulations. For example, in

Table 4. Enumeration of the paths in the graph with updated path lengths

Path	Length	Type of Arc Sequence
D1K1D2	95	TR-TW
D1K1D2	60	TW-TW
D1K1K2D2	117	TR-TR-TW
D1K1K2D2	82	TW-TR-TW
D1K1K2K3D2	120	TR-TR-TR-TW
D1K1K2K3D2	166	TR-TR-TR-TR
D1K1K2K3D2	85	TW-TR-TR-TW
D1K1K2K3D2	131	TW-TR-TR-TR
D1K2D2	55	TW-TW
D1K2K3D2	58	TW-TR-TW
D1K2K3D2	104	TW-TR-TR
D1K3D2	30	TW-TW
D1K3D2	76	TW-TR

a shopping walking street goods should be delivered to the shops, either before 9 a.m. of after 7 p.m. In other cases, it relates to the working hours of the warehouse labor at the customer's location. Sometimes it makes part of the contract between supplier and customer for the customer convenience. A planning, made up by the distributor, might be disturbed by longer than expected travel times, for example due to an incident on the road or due to bad weather conditions. In that way the truck or van might not be able to meet the agreed time windows. In the example of the walking street, the distributor might not be allowed anymore into the street by closed barriers or the driver can get a fine from the local authorities when neglecting the time window. In the example of the warehouse, the driver might arrive at a closed warehouse requiring a second visit the next day. In the example of the contract, a penalty might be included per time unit late. In all three cases, the uncertainty in travel times means a risk to the distributor. Mostly a distributor makes up a delivery plan deciding which trucks have to visit which customers and in which sequence. In case the plan makes part of an optimization problem, then this decision is called a solution to the vehicle routing problem (VRP). Mostly the objective to be optimized is a cost function expressed in term of total distance travelled or total time travelled. In case of uncertainty the distributor also might take the risk of not meeting the windows into consideration. In that case there is a need for a numerical expression of this risk. To say that a route is more risky than another in not meeting the time windows, it is called here that one route is more vulnerable than the other.

Vulnerability refers to risk: the risk of not meeting the time windows. In the graphical representation, some paths are more vulnerable than others. A need emerges to define a measure to identify how vulnerable a path is. This measure allows for a ranking of paths, of routes and of VRP solutions. One might state, for example, that a VRP solution S_A is more vulnerable than a VRP solution S_B if the most vulnerable path in S_A is 'more vulnerable' than the most vulnerable path in S_B. But more complex ways of comparison and ranking are possible. The graphical representation in Figure 2 contains a number of paths from node D_1 to node D_2. Each path consists of arcs which represent either time windows or travel times. As the travel times are uncertain and expressed as a time interval, also the length of all paths can be represented as time intervals. The depot time window in the example equals 100. So, if a time interval of a path length has its lower and upper bound both less than 100, this path is considered safe. Even in the worst conditions the time windows are respected. If however the upper bound of the path length is greater than 100, there is a risk that the time windows cannot be respected. It is said that this path contains a risk and it is called 'vulnerable'. The risk can be small or can be big: that is why a measure of vulnerability is needed.

The measure of vulnerability might be defined in terms of a distance measure. More specifically, a distance measure needs to be defined between an interval (the interval between the lower and upper bounds of the length of a path) and a fixed value (the length of the depot time window). In the following paragraphs a distance measure from literature is introduced and explained how it can be used or cannot be used. The distance measure originates from a comparison of interval numbers. It will be defined first. Then it will be polished to our specific situation and applied. Finally some conclusions are drawn why this measure is useful or not. The measure has been introduced in Tran and Duckstein (2002).

Let an interval number be denoted as <name>(<lowerbound>,<upperbound>) which means that it can take any real value between the <lowerbound> and the <upperbound>. Assume two interval numbers $A(a_1, a_2)$ and $B(b_1, b_2)$ and the distance between both defined as:

$$D^2(A,B) = \int_{-1/2}^{1/2} \int_{-1/2}^{1/2} \left\{ \left[\left(\frac{a_1 + a_2}{2} \right) + x(a_2 - a_1) \right] - \left[\left(\frac{b_1 + b_2}{2} \right) + y(b_2 - b_1) \right] \right\}^2 dx\, dy$$

$$= \left[\left(\frac{a_1 + a_2}{2} \right) - \left(\frac{b_1 + b_2}{2} \right) \right]^2 + \frac{1}{3} \left[\left(\frac{a_2 - a_1}{2} \right)^2 + \left(\frac{b_2 - b_1}{2} \right)^2 \right]$$

In the case under study the interval number A is a constant, which means $a_1 = a_2$. This number A corresponds to the length of the depot path (in our case = 100). The distance measure 'as such' is worthless related to the concept of 'vulnerability', due to its symmetric character. It may be illustrated by the following example. Take the path D1K1K2D2 as an example. Its length falls in the interval [67,117]. Assume the value of A is varied between 57 and 127. Then the distance measure in function of A is shown in Figure 3.

Figure 3. Example of the distance measure (y-axis) on a specific path in function of a threshold value A (x-axis)

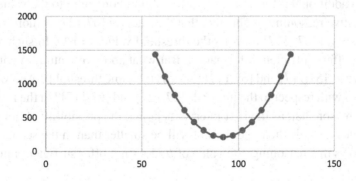

For example, the distances between the interval and $A=62$ and $A=122$ have both value 1108.33. In terms of vulnerability the reality is completely different. If $A=122$, the worst case of the path length (which is 117) is still feasible, while if $A=62$, even the best case (which is 67) of the path length is not feasible. In fact the danger appears only at path lengths greater than 100. This means that the number A needs to be compared in distance with an interval $(A,<upperbound>)$ in case $<upperbound>$ is greater than A (otherwise the distance is zero). This means that, in the above notation, also $b_1 = A$.

More specifically, this means that

$$\frac{a_1 + a_2}{2} = A$$

$$\frac{b_1 + b_2}{2} = \frac{A + b_2}{2}$$

$$\frac{a_2 - a_1}{2} = 0$$

$$\frac{b_2 - b_1}{2} = \frac{b_2 - A}{2}$$

The distance measure takes the form:

$$D^2\left(A, B\right) = \frac{4}{3}\left(\frac{b_2 - A}{2}\right)^2$$

The value of the measure is increasing in b_2 (which is the only parameter), so it offers no additional information on vulnerability compared to the value of b_2.

An intuitive reasoning might state that the interval [67,127] is more vulnerable than the interval [67, 117] towards the threshold value $A=100$. In such a case the value of b_2 offers sufficient information. But what about the intuition with respect to the intervals [57,117] and [67,117] towards the same threshold ? And what about the intuition with respect to the intervals [57,127] and [67,117]? In the former case, one might reason that, as the first interval is larger, the possibility of obtaining the higher values towards the upper bound will be smaller than in the second interval. If one follows this reasoning, the value of b_2 does not offer sufficient information.

In the latter case, most probably no intuition is available to come with an answer which interval is the most vulnerable.

When considering both the lower and the upper bound of the path length, it may be useful to express the uncertainty as a fuzzy number. When the lower bound changes, but the upper bound is kept constant, the membership function value of the values towards the upper bound also changes. The inclusion of membership function values into the distance measure might lead to an acceptable 'measure of vulnerability'.

A MEASURE OF VULNERABILITY BASED ON A DISTANCE BETWEEN FUZZY NUMBERS

Sometimes it is required to construct a distance between two vaguely described objects. In the world of fuzzy sets, various types of fuzzy distances have been defined. They can be divided in three distinct groups: (1) generalization of a classic distance between subsets of a metric space (e.g. Gerla and Volpe, 1984); (2) distance between membership functions of fuzzy sets (e.g. Szmidt and Kacprzyk, 2000); and (3) fuzzy metrics introduced by generalizing a metric space to a fuzzy-metric one (Kaleva and Seikkala, 1984). This section makes use of fuzzy numbers. Distances between fuzzy numbers are, for example, used in ranking fuzzy numbers. Various types of distances have been defined, for example in Heilpern (1997), Yao and Wu (2000), and de Campos and Gonzalez Munoz (1998). Next to ranking purposes, other ways of calculating a distances between two fuzzy numbers have been defined, for example in Chakraborty and Chakraborty (2006), Cheng (1998), Tran and Duckstein (2002) and Voxman (1998).

Basic Definitions

First a few definitions are mentioned, which are required in the construction of the measure.

Definition: Let X be a universal set. Then the fuzzy subset A of X is defined by its membership function:

$$\mu_A : X \to [0,1]$$

which assigns a real number $\mu_A(x)$ in the interval [0,1], to each element $x \in X$, where the value of $\mu_A(x)$ at x shows the grade of membership of x in A.

Definition: Given a fuzzy set A in X and any real number $\alpha \in [0,1]$, then the α-level, denoted by $^{\alpha}A$ is the crisp set

$$^{\alpha}A = \left\{ x \in X : \mu_A(x) \geq \alpha \right\}$$

The concept of the *α-level* is illustrated in Figure 4. The membership μ_z is shown on the vertical axis. The variable under consideration z is defined on an interval $[z^-, z^+]$ on the horizontal axis. The interval $[z^-_\alpha, z^+_\alpha]$ represent the set of values of z which have a membership of at least α.

Definition: A fuzzy number F possesses the following three properties:

1. *F* must be a normal fuzzy set, (normal = there is an x for which $\mu_F(x) = 1$)
2. The alpha levels *F(α)* must be closed for every $\alpha \in (0,1]$
3. The support of *F*, *F(0+)*, must be bounded.

Definition: A generalized left right fuzzy numbers (GLRFN), defined as A(a$_1$, a$_2$, a$_3$, a$_4$), has a membership function specified as follows:

$$\mu(x) = \begin{cases} L\left(\dfrac{a_2 - x}{a_2 - a_1}\right) & for\ a_1 \leq x \leq a_2 \\ 1 & for\ a_2 \leq x \leq a_3 \\ R\left(\dfrac{x - a_3}{a_4 - a_3}\right) & for\ a_3 \leq x \leq a_4 \\ 0 & else \end{cases}$$

Figure 4. Illustration of the concept of the α-level

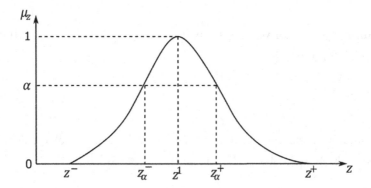

where L ad R are strictly decreasing functions on $[0,1]$.

The measure, developed in this chapter, makes use of Triangular Fuzzy Numbers (TFN), which is a special case of the GLRFN. The choice for TFN is not made on logical reasoning but because of the ease of calculation. The conditions for a GLRFN to be a TFN are:

$$L\left(x\right) = R\left(x\right) = 1 - x$$

and

$$a_2 = a_3$$

The conditions lead to:

$$L\left(\frac{a_2 - x}{a_2 - a_1}\right) = \frac{x - a_1}{a_2 - a_1}$$

and

$$R\left(\frac{x - a_2}{a_4 - a_2}\right) = \frac{a_4 - x}{a_4 - a_2}$$

Definition: The sum of two TFNs is a TFN. Its values are developed below.

Let $X = [a,b,c]$ and $Y = [p,q,r]$ be two TFNs with membership functions:

$$\mu_X\left(x\right) = \frac{x - a}{b - a} \; if \; a \leq x \leq b$$
$$= \frac{c - x}{c - b} \; if \; b \leq x \leq c$$

$$\mu_Y\left(x\right) = \frac{x - p}{q - p} \; if \; p \leq x \leq q$$
$$= \frac{r - x}{r - q} \; if \; q \leq x \leq r$$

Then the sum is a TFN with membership function:

$$\mu_{X+Y}\left(x\right) = \frac{x - \left(a + p\right)}{\left(b + q\right) - \left(a + p\right)} \; if \left(a + p\right) \le x \le \left(b + q\right)$$

$$= \frac{\left(c + r\right) - x}{\left(c + r\right) - \left(b + q\right)} \; if \left(b + q\right) \le x \le \left(c + r\right)$$

Let A be the crisp threshold value. The α-level interval of TFN B is denoted as (following Tran & Duckstein, 2002, p. 333):

$$B\left(\alpha\right) = \left(B_L\left(\alpha\right), B_U\left(\alpha\right)\right) = \left(b_2 - \left(b_2 - b_1\right)L_B^{-1}\left(\alpha\right), b_3 + \left(b_4 - b_3\right)R_B^{-1}\left(\alpha\right)\right)$$

which, because of the assumption of symmetry, with

$$b_2 = b_3$$

reduces to

$$B\left(\alpha\right) = \left(b_2 - \left(b_2 - b_1\right)\left(1 - \alpha\right), b_2 + \left(b_4 - b_2\right)\left(1 - \alpha\right)\right) = \left(b_1 + \left(b_2 - b_1\right)\alpha, b_4 - \left(b_4 - b_2\right)\alpha\right)$$

Development of the Measure for General Weighted A-Levels

For each relevant value of α, the distance is measured following our revised version of equation (2) in Tran and Duckstein (2002). The relevance of an α-value is determined as follows:

- If $A \le b_2$ then all α-values ($0 \le \alpha \le 1$) are relevant *(the former case)*
- If $A > b_2$ only the α-values ($0 \le \alpha \le R_B(A)$) are relevant *(the latter case)*.

The distance needs to be calculated between A and an interval. In the *former case*, the interval is defined as:

- If $L_B^{-1}\left(\alpha\right) \le A$, the interval is $\left(A, R_B^{-1}\left(\alpha\right)\right)$
- If $L_B^{-1}\left(\alpha\right) > A$, the interval is $\left(L_B^{-1}\left(\alpha\right), R_B^{-1}\left(\alpha\right)\right)$.

In the *latter case*, the interval is defined as $\left(A, R_B^{-1}(\alpha) \right)$.

In relation to formula (6) of Tran and Duckstein (2002), in both the *former case* and the *latter case*:

$$A_L(\alpha) = A_U(\alpha) = A$$

In the *former case*, the integral exists of two sub-integrals covering the interval for α to be [0,1], while for the *latter case* only a single interval is required covering the interval for α to be [0,α'], where α' is the solution of $R^{-1}(\alpha') = A$. For ease of understanding the former case is illustrated in Figure 5, the latter case in Figure 6.

Different choices can be made for the weighting function f in order to weigh the distances according to the level α. Two simple functional forms for f are: a constant i.e. $f(\alpha) = 1$, and a linearly increasing function i.e. $f(\alpha) = \alpha$.

In the *former case*, the first sub-integral needs the following values:

$$B_L(\alpha) = A \ and \ B_U(\alpha) = b_4 - \left(b_4 - b_2 \right)\alpha .$$

Figure 5. Illustration of the former case (A < b₂)

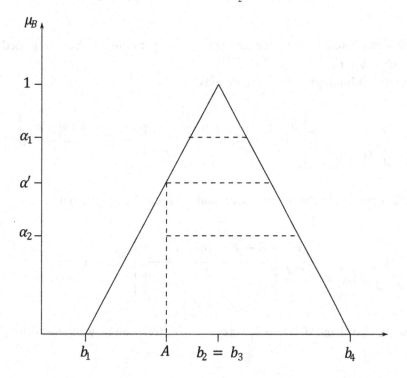

Figure 6. Illustration of the former case (A > b_2)

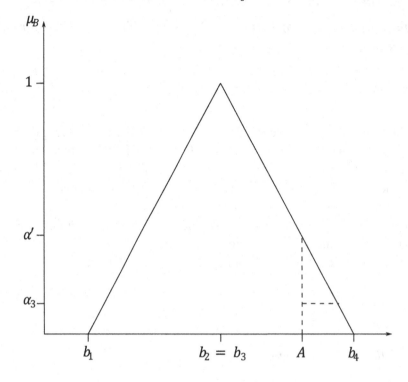

The lower bound of the integral is 0 and its upper bound is α', determined by $A = b_1 + (b_2 - b_1) \alpha'$.

The first sub-integral can be written as:

$$I_1 = \frac{1}{\int_0^1 f(\alpha) d\alpha} \times \int_0^{\alpha'} \left\{ \left[\frac{A - \left[b_4 - \left(b_4 - b_2 \right) \alpha \right]}{2} \right]^2 + \frac{1}{3} \left[\frac{\left[b_4 - \left(b_4 - b_2 \right) \alpha \right] - A}{2} \right]^2 \right\} f(\alpha) d\alpha$$

Both terms under the integral are equal, so I_1 can be rewritten as:

$$I_1 = \frac{1}{\int_0^1 f(\alpha) d\alpha} \times \frac{4}{3} \int_0^{\alpha'} \left\{ \left[\frac{A - \left[b_4 - \left(b_4 - b_2 \right) \alpha \right]}{2} \right]^2 \right\} f(\alpha) d\alpha$$

Use the shorthand $B(\alpha) = b_4 - \left(b_4 - b_2 \right) \alpha$, so I_1 can be written shorter as:

$$I_1 = \Bigg/ \!\!\int_0^1 f(\alpha)\, d\alpha \times \frac{4}{3}\int_0^{\alpha'} \left\{ \frac{A^2}{4} - \frac{A.B(\alpha)}{2} + \frac{B^2(\alpha)}{4} \right\} f(\alpha)\, d\alpha$$

Note that

$$B^2(\alpha) = b_4^2 - 2b_4\left(b_4 - b_2\right)\alpha + \left(b_4 - b_2\right)^2 \alpha^2$$

Making use of sub-sub-integrals, I_1 may be written as:

$$I_1 = \Bigg/ \!\!\int_0^1 f(\alpha)\, d\alpha \times \left\{ I_{11} + I_{12} + I_{13} \right\}$$

where

$$I_{11} = \frac{A^2}{3}\int_0^{\alpha'} f(\alpha)\, d\alpha$$

$$I_{12} = -\frac{2A}{3}\int_0^{\alpha'} \left[b_4 - \left(b_4 - b_2\right)\alpha \right] f(\alpha)\, d\alpha$$

$$I_{13} = \frac{1}{3}\int_0^{\alpha'} \left[b_4^2 - 2b_4\left(b_4 - b_2\right)\alpha + \left(b_4 - b_2\right)^2 \alpha^2 \right] f(\alpha)\, d\alpha$$

The second sub-integral needs the following values:

$$B_L(\alpha) = b_1 + \left(b_2 - b_1\right)\alpha \ \text{ and } \ B_U(\alpha) = b_4 - \left(b_4 - b_2\right)\alpha$$

The second sub-integral can be written as:

$$I_2 = \Big/ {\int_0^1 f(\alpha)d\alpha} \times \int_{\alpha'}^1 \left\{ \left[A - \frac{\big[b_1 + (b_2 - b_1)\alpha\big] + \big[\overline{b_4} - (b_4 - b_2)\alpha\big]}{2} \right]^2 + \tfrac{1}{3} \left[\frac{\big[b_4 - (b_4 - b_2)\alpha\big] - \big[b_1 + (b_2 - b_1)\alpha\big]}{2} \right]^2 \right\} f(\alpha)d\alpha$$

Use the shorthand $B(\alpha) = (b_1 + b_4) + (2b_2 - b_4 - b_1)\alpha$ (the latter term vanishes in case of symmetrical TFN), I_2 can be written shorter as:

$$I_2 = \Big/ {\int_0^1 f(\alpha)d\alpha} \times \int_{\alpha'}^1 \left\{ \left[A - \frac{B(\alpha)}{2} \right]^2 + \tfrac{1}{3}\left[-\frac{B(\alpha)}{2} \right]^2 \right\} f(\alpha)d\alpha$$

or

$$I_2 = \Big/ {\int_0^1 f(\alpha)d\alpha} \times \int_{\alpha'}^1 \left\{ A^2 - A.B(\alpha) + \frac{B^2(\alpha)}{3} \right\} f(\alpha)d\alpha$$

Note that

$$B^2(\alpha) = (b_1 + b_4)^2 + 2(b_1 + b_4)(2b_2 - b_4 - b_1)\alpha + (2b_2 - b_4 - b_1)^2 \alpha^2$$

Making use of sub-sub-integrals, I_2 may be written as:

$$I_2 = \Big/ {\int_0^1 f(\alpha)d\alpha} \times \{I_{21} + I_{22} + I_{23}\}$$

where

$$I_{21} = A^2 \int_{\alpha'}^1 f(\alpha)d\alpha$$

$$I_{22} = -A \int_{a'}^{1} \left[(b_1 + b_4) + (2b_2 - b_4 - b_1) \alpha \right] f(\alpha) \, d\alpha$$

$$I_{23} = \frac{1}{3} \int_{a'}^{1} \left[(b_1 + b_4)^2 + 2(b_1 + b_4)(2b_2 - b_4 - b_1) \alpha + (2b_2 - b_4 - b_1)^2 \alpha^2 \right] f(\alpha) \, d\alpha$$

In the *latter case*, the integral needs the following values:

$$B_L(\alpha) = A \text{ and } B_U(\alpha) = b_4 - (b_4 - b_2) \alpha.$$

The lower bound of the integral is 0 and its upper bound is α', determined by $A = b_4 + (b_4 - b_2) \, α'$.
The integral can be written as:

$$I = \frac{1}{\int_0^1 f(\alpha) \, d\alpha} \times \int_0^{\alpha'} \left\{ \left[\frac{A - [b_4 - (b_4 - b_2) \alpha]}{2} \right]^2 + \frac{1}{3} \left[\frac{[b_4 - (b_4 - b_2) \alpha] - A}{2} \right]^2 \right\} f(\alpha) \, d\alpha$$

Use the shorthand $B(\alpha) = b_4 - (b_4 - b_2) \alpha$, so *I* can be written shorter as:

$$I = \frac{1}{\int_0^1 f(\alpha) \, d\alpha} \times \frac{4}{3} \int_0^{\alpha'} \left[\frac{A^2}{4} - \frac{A.B(\alpha)}{2} + \frac{B^2(\alpha)}{4} \right] f(\alpha) \, d\alpha$$

Note that

$$B^2(\alpha) = b_4^2 - 2b_4(b_4 - b_2) \alpha + (b_4 - b_2)^2 \alpha^2$$

Making use of sub-integrals, *I* may be written as:

$$I = \frac{1}{\int_0^1 f(\alpha) \, d\alpha} \times \left\{ I_{01} + I_{02} + I_{03} \right\}$$

where

$$I_{01} = \frac{A^2}{3} \int_0^{\alpha'} f(\alpha) \, d\alpha$$

$$I_{02} = -\frac{2A}{3} \int_0^{\alpha'} \left[b_4 - (b_4 - b_2) \alpha \right] f(\alpha) \, d\alpha$$

$$I_{03} = \frac{1}{3} \int_0^{\alpha'} \left[b_4^2 - 2b_4 (b_4 - b_2) \alpha + (b_4 - b_2)^2 \alpha^2 \right] f(\alpha) \, d\alpha$$

Calculation of a Specific Case for the A-Level Weight

Assume a choice is made for $f(\alpha) = \alpha$.

In the *former case*

$$I = 2 \times \left\{ I_{11} + I_{12} + I_{13} + I_{21} + I_{22} + I_{23} \right\}$$

and in the *latter case*

$$I = 2 * \left\{ I_{01} + I_{02} + I_{03} \right\}$$

In the *former case* the sub-sub-integrals take the following values, with $\alpha' = \dfrac{A - b_1}{b_2 - b_1}$,

$$I_{11} = \frac{A^2}{6} \left[\frac{A - b_1}{b_2 - b_1} \right]^2$$

$$I_{12} = \frac{-2A}{3} \left\{ \frac{b_4}{2} \left[\frac{A - b_1}{b_2 - b_1} \right]^2 - \frac{b_4 - b_2}{3} \left[\frac{A - b_1}{b_2 - b_1} \right]^3 \right\}$$

$$I_{13} = \frac{b_4^2}{6} \left[\frac{A - b_1}{b_2 - b_1} \right]^2 - \frac{2b_4 \left(b_4 - b_2\right)}{9} \left[\frac{A - b_1}{b_2 - b_1} \right]^3 + \frac{\left(b_4 - b_2\right)^2}{12} \left[\frac{A - b_1}{b_2 - b_1} \right]^4$$

$$I_{21} = \frac{A^2}{2} \left\{ 1 - \left[\frac{A - b_1}{b_2 - b_1} \right]^2 \right\}$$

$$I_{22} = -A \left\{ \frac{b_1 + b_4}{2} \left\{ 1 - \left[\frac{A - b_1}{b_2 - b_1} \right]^2 \right\} + \frac{2b_2 - b_4 - b_1}{3} \left\{ 1 - \left[\frac{A - b_1}{b_2 - b_1} \right]^3 \right\} \right\}$$

$$I_{23} = \frac{\left(b_1 + b_4\right)^2}{6} \left\{ 1 - \left[\frac{A - b_1}{b_2 - b_1} \right]^2 \right\} + \frac{2b_4 \left(b_1 + b_4\right)\left(2b_2 - b_4 - b_1\right)}{9} \left\{ 1 - \left[\frac{A - b_1}{b_2 - b_1} \right]^3 \right\}$$
$$+ \frac{\left(2b_2 - b_4 - b_1\right)^2}{12} \left\{ 1 - \left[\frac{A - b_1}{b_2 - b_1} \right]^4 \right\}$$

In the *latter case* the sub-sub-integrals take the following values, with $\alpha' = \dfrac{b_4 - A}{b_4 - b_2}$,

$$I_{01} = \frac{A^2}{6} \left[\frac{b_4 - A}{b_4 - b_2} \right]^2$$

$$I_{02} = \frac{-2A}{3} \left\{ \frac{b_4}{2} \left[\frac{b_4 - A}{b_4 - b_2} \right]^2 - \frac{b_4 - b_2}{3} \left[\frac{b_4 - A}{b_4 - b_2} \right]^3 \right\}$$

$$I_{03} = \frac{b_4^2}{6} \left[\frac{b_4 - A}{b_4 - b_2} \right]^2 - \frac{2b_4 \left(b_4 - b_2\right)}{9} \left[\frac{b_4 - A}{b_4 - b_2} \right]^3 + \frac{\left(b_4 - b_2\right)^2}{12} \left[\frac{b_4 - A}{b_4 - b_2} \right]^4$$

Solution for the Illustrative Example

Based on the data of the illustrative example the triangular fuzzy numbers representing the lengths of the individual paths are obtained in Table 5.

The length of the paths form the input to calculate the vulnerability measure as developed in the previous section. Table 6 shows, per path, the three values (b_1, b_2, and b_4) that define the triangular fuzzy number (TFN) for the length of the particular path. It further indicates whether the path length is of the fuzzy or of the crisp type and whether, according to our classification, it belongs to the former or the latter case. If the upper bound of the TFN is lower than 100, the path is in no danger so it is labelled 'safe', while the other ones are labeled 'risk'. Only for those labeled as 'risk', the distance is calculated. The rightmost column mentions 'NR' in case the distance is not relevant.

Table 6 shows the values of the vulnerability measure in the column 'Distance'. But the next question is how the vulnerability of this route can be evaluated. In some way the various measures, which are relevant (five in the illustrative example), should be combined to obtain a vulnerability measure for the route. Application of the 'sum' or 'average' operator, however, is most probably biased as many paths share the same links so the individual vulnerability measures are correlated. From a practical viewpoint, the only aggregation measure, which avoids this dependence, is the 'max' operator. In the illustrative example this means that we should evaluate the vulnerability of the route as 1831.34, which corresponds to the value belonging to path D1K1K2K3D2.

Table 5. Fuzzy path lengths for the illustrative example

Path	Length Components	Length
D1K1D2	[10,22.5,35]+60	[70,82.5,95]
D1K1D2	0+60	60
D1K1K2D2	[10,22.5,35]+[12,24.5,37]+45	[67,92,117]
D1K1K2D2	0+[12,24.5,37]+45	[57,69.5,82]
D1K1K2K3D2	[10,22.5,35]+[12,24.5,37]+[8,23,38]+10	[40,80,120]
D1K1K2K3D2	[10,22.5,35]+[12,24.5,37]+[8,23,38]+[26,41,56]	[56,111,166]
D1K1K2K3D2	0+[12,24.5,37]+[8,23,38]+10	[30,57.5,85]
D1K1K2K3D2	0+[12,24.5,37]+[8,23,38]+[26,41,56]	[46,88.5,131]
D1K2D2	10+45	55
D1K2K3D2	10+[8,23,38]+10	[28,43,58]
D1K2K3D2	10+[8,23,38]+[26,41,56]	[44,74,104]
D1K3D2	20+10	30
D1K3D2	20+[26,41,56]	[46,61,76]

Table 6. Vulnerability measure for the paths in the illustrative example

Path	b_1	b_2	b_4	Type	Case	Safe ?	Distance
D1K1D2	70	82.5	95	*fuzzy*	*latter*	*safe*	NR
D1K1D2	60	60	60	*crisp*	*latter*	*safe*	NR
D1K1K2D2	67	92	117	*fuzzy*	*latter*	*risk*	3.71
D1K1K2D2	57	69.5	82	*fuzzy*	*latter*	*safe*	NR
D1K1K2K3D2	40	80	120	*fuzzy*	*latter*	*risk*	2.78
D1K1K2K3D2	56	111	166	*fuzzy*	*former*	*risk*	1831.84
D1K1K2K3D2	30	57.5	85	*fuzzy*	*latter*	*safe*	NR
D1K1K2K3D2	46	88.5	131	*fuzzy*	*latter*	*risk*	14.21
D1K2D2	55	55	55	*crisp*	*latter*	*safe*	NR
D1K2K3D2	28	43	58	*fuzzy*	*latter*	*safe*	NR
D1K2K3D2	44	74	104	*fuzzy*	*latter*	*risk*	0.01
D1K3D2	30	30	30	*crisp*	*latter*	*safe*	NR
D1K3D2	46	61	76	*fuzzy*	*latter*	*safe*	NR

However the ultimate goal of the development is to obtain a vulnerability measure not only for a route but for a vehicle routing solution, i.e. for a set of routes. As the paths of the various routes do not contain any shared links, the problem of dependence does not appear, so any type of aggregation might be proposed. So if, for example, the vehicle routing solution consists of two routes. The second route is serving customers K4, K5, K6 and K7 and is evaluated to have a vulnerability of 1200. Any mathematical aggregation, be it the average operator, the max-operator or any other operator might be proposed.

Complexity of the Algorithm

Figure 2 serves as a basis for generating all paths in the graph. The graph is a 2-terminal series-parallel graph. Both a source and a sink are provided as terminal nodes. They both represent the depot in our case. If the route contains N customers, the number of nodes in the graph equals $N+2$. The number of arcs in the graph equals maximum $3N+2$. They include the depot time window arc, $N+1$ arcs which make up the backbone and $2N$ earliest and latest arrival arcs. With respect to the number of paths to be generated, the illustrative example is used. Let $P(Nx)$ denote the number of paths ending at node Nx. The number of arcs ending in node D_2 equals, $P(D_2) = 1 + 2 P(K_3) + P(K_2) + P(K_1)$. They include the depot time arc, the number of arcs to K_3 connected with D_2 by either the backbone arc or the latest arrival arc, and the number of arcs to K_2 and K_1, connected with D_2 by the latest arrival arc.

The number of arcs ending in node K_3 equals, $P(K_3) = P(K_2) + 1$. They include the number of arcs to K_2 and the earliest arrival arc for customer K_3. The number of arcs ending in K_2 equals $P(K_2) = P(K_1) + 1$. They include the number of arcs to K_1 and the earliest arrival arc to customer K_2. The number of arcs ending in K_1 equals 2, including the backbone arc and the earliest arrival arc to customer K_1. This leads, in our example, to 14 paths. In general, in case N customers belong to the route, the number of paths equals $(N+1)N/2 + 2(N+1)$. This means that the generation of the paths is of quadratic complexity.

FUTURE RESEARCH DIRECTIONS

The measure of vulnerability, as developed, in this chapter may appear in different versions. For example, the choice for symmetric triangular fuzzy numbers for travel times is based on simplicity. The measure can be extended towards asymmetric or non-triangular fuzzy numbers. For the weighting function of the α-levels functions, more complex than the linear one, are valid choices. However, one should be convinced that more complex versions bring an additional value. Like in probabilistic models probability distributions need to be chosen, most researchers make a choice related to tractability of obtaining meaningful results. In this application, this reasoning is also the case.

Future research mainly lies in how to combine the 'concept of vulnerability' with the usual cost-related objective function and how to integrate both in an optimization algorithm. A solution algorithm could generate a number of solutions in order to produce a Pareto front of non-inferior solutions. Then, the 'best' solution according to the responsible manager could be chosen by various multi-objective methods. Another approach is to integrate both objectives in a single algorithm. For example, the population of a generation in a genetic algorithm might be evaluated both in terms of cost and in terms of vulnerability. This bi-objective genetic algorithm produces finally a population of individual solutions which show low cost and low vulnerability. In meta-heuristic algorithms, which move from solution to solution, like tabu search or deterministic/simulated annealing, it is a challenge how to include the measure of vulnerability to guide the neighborhood search. For example, in Braekers et al. (2011) a two-phase solution algorithm using deterministic annealing is presented to solve a bi-objective problem, minimizing the number of vehicles used and minimizing total distance travelled. Results on random problem instances show that the algorithm is able to find sets of non-dominated solutions of good quality in a small amount of computation time. Similar approaches might be implemented in this case.

CONCLUSION

Most solution methods for the vehicle routing problem make use of deterministic travel times. In many parts of the world, and mostly in cities, the assumption of deterministic travel times is not a realistic assumption. Due to traffic congestion, uncertainty on travel time is present in most situations.

Practitioners as well as academics are aware of this situation but have no direct and not too complex solution to implement. The use of probability distributions in stochastic programming is a rigorous approach. For practical purposes, this approach has two disadvantages: (1) which probability distributions are to be used and how can their parameters be estimated, and (2) the optimization procedure is hard in computational terms, while in practice the dispatching of goods is under time pressure. Another option to include uncertainty in decision-making, is to go for a fuzzy approach. Fuzzy optimization to vehicle routing problems however also suffers from computational complexity. Therefore this chapter looks for an approach to include risk as a secondary criterion, out of the optimization algorithm but as part of the evaluation of a solution.

In order to quantify the risk of not being able to meet the customer time windows this chapter proposes a measure, which is called a measure of vulnerability. The chapter shows why the formulation of the uncertainty in terms of travel times expressed as a fuzzy number is a valid approach. A distance measure has been proposed to evaluate the vulnerability based on α-levels of fuzzy numbers, in this case representing the travel times.

The chapter develops the formulas for calculating this distance measure including a weighting of the α-levels, when wished by the decision-maker. For a specific case, the ready-to-use formulas have been developed. Most important is to realise that those formulas are of analytical nature. By this, they are easy to implement in a spreadsheet or in a computer program.

As a conclusion, it can be stated that the calculation of the measure of vulnerability is a rather easy task in case the weighting function $f(\alpha)$ takes a simple form like a constant or a linear increasing function or even any polynomial function in α (belonging to the set of functions increasing in α, for logical reasons). In this way, a measure of vulnerability can be calculated for each path in a route suggested by an algorithm, which forms a basis for evaluating a solution of a VRPTW on the risk of not satisfying the required time window constraints.

ACKNOWLEDGMENT

This work is supported by the Interuniversity Attraction Poles Programme initiated by the Belgian Science Policy Office (research project COMEX, Combinatorial Optimization: Metaheuristics & Exact Methods).

REFERENCES

Ando, N., & Taniguchi, E. (2006). Travel time reliability in vehicle routing and scheduling with time windows. *Networks and Spatial Economics*, *6*(3-4), 293–311. doi:10.100711067-006-9285-8

Braekers, K., Caris, A., & Janssens, G. K. (2011). A deterministic annealing algorithm for a bi-objective full-truckload vehicle routing problem in drayage operations. *Procedia: Social and Behavioral Sciences*, *20*, 344–353. doi:10.1016/j.sbspro.2011.08.040

Braekers, K., Ramaekers, K., & Van Nieuwenhuyse, I. (2016). The vehicle routing problem: State of the art classification and review. *Computers & Industrial Engineering*, *99*, 300–313. doi:10.1016/j.cie.2015.12.007

Chakraborty, C., & Chakraborty, D. (2006). A theoretical development on a fuzzy distance measure for fuzzy numbers. *Mathematical and Computer Modelling*, *43*(3-4), 254–261. doi:10.1016/j.mcm.2005.09.025

Chanas, S., & Zielinski, P. (2002). The computational complexity of the criticality problems in a network with interval activity times. *European Journal of Operational Research*, *136*(3), 541–550. doi:10.1016/S0377-2217(01)00048-0

Cheng, C. H. (1998). A new approach for ranking fuzzy numbers by distance method. *Fuzzy Sets and Systems*, *95*(3), 307–317. doi:10.1016/S0165-0114(96)00272-2

De Campos Ibanez, L. M., & Gonzalez Munoz, A. (1989). A subjective approach for ranking fuzzy numbers. *Fuzzy Sets and Systems*, *29*(2), 145–153. doi:10.1016/0165-0114(89)90188-7

Drexl, M. (2012). Rich vehicle routing in theory and practice. *Logistics Research*, *5*(1-2), 47–63. doi:10.100712159-012-0080-2

Erera, A. L., Morales, J. C., & Savelsbergh, M. (2010). The vehicle routing problem with stochastic demand and duration constraints. *Transportation Science*, *44*(4), 474–492. doi:10.1287/trsc.1100.0324

Gendreau, M., Laporte, G., & Séguin, R. (1995). An exact algorithm for the vehicle routing problem with stochastic demands and customers. *Transportation Science*, *29*(2), 143–155. doi:10.1287/trsc.29.2.143

Gendreau, M., Laporte, G., & Séguin, R. (1996). A tabu search heuristic for the vehicle routing problem with stochastic demands and customers. *Operations Research*, *44*(3), 469–477. doi:10.1287/opre.44.3.469

Gerla, G., & Volpe, R. (1986). The definition of distance and diameter in fuzzy set theory, *Studia Univ. Babes-Bolyai Ser. Math.*, *31*, 21–26.

Hartl, R. F., Hasle, G., & Janssens, G. K. (2006). Editorial to the Special Issue on Rich Vehicle Routing Problems. *Central European Journal of Operations Research*, *14*(2), 103–104. doi:10.100710100-006-0162-9

Haughton, M. A. (1998). The performance of route modification and demand stabilization strategies in stochastic vehicle routing. *Transportation Research Part B: Methodological*, *32*(8), 551–566. doi:10.1016/S0191-2615(98)00017-4

Heilpern, S. (1997). Representation and application of fuzzy numbers. *Fuzzy Sets and Systems*, *91*(2), 259–268. doi:10.1016/S0165-0114(97)00146-2

Kaleva, O., & Seikkala, S. (1984). On fuzzy metric spaces. *Fuzzy Sets and Systems*, *12*(3), 215–229. doi:10.1016/0165-0114(84)90069-1

Laporte, G., Louveaux, F., & Mercure, H. (1992). The vehicle routing problem with stochastic travel times. *Transportation Science*, *26*(3), 161–170. doi:10.1287/trsc.26.3.161

Li, X., Tian, P., & Leung, S. (2010). Vehicle routing problems with time windows and stochastic travel and service times: Models and algorithms. *International Journal of Production Economics*, *125*(1), 137–145. doi:10.1016/j.ijpe.2010.01.013

Manisri, T., Mungwattana, A., & Janssens, G. K. (2011). Minimax optimization approach for the robust vehicle routing problem with time windows and uncertain travel times. *International Journal of Logistics Systems and Management*, *10*(4), 461–477. doi:10.1504/IJLSM.2011.043105

Moghaddam, B. F., Ruiz, R., & Sadjadi, S. J. (2012). Vehicle routing with uncertain demands: An advanced particle swarm algorithm. *Computers & Industrial Engineering*, *62*(1), 306–317. doi:10.1016/j.cie.2011.10.001

Russell, R. A., & Urban, T. L. (2008). Vehicle routing with soft time windows and Erlang travel times. *The Journal of the Operational Research Society*, *59*(9), 1220–1228. doi:10.1057/palgrave.jors.2602465

Sörensen, K., & Sevaux, M. (2009). A practical approach for robust and flexible vehicle routing using metaheuristics and Monte Carlo sampling. *Journal of Mathematical Modelling and Algorithms*, *8*(4), 387–407. doi:10.100710852-009-9113-5

Sungur, F., Ordonez, F., & Dessouky, M. M. (2008). A robust optimization approach for the capacitated vehicle routing problem with demand uncertainty. *IIE Transactions*, *40*(5), 509–523. doi:10.1080/07408170701745378

Szmidt, E., & Kacprzyk, S. (2000). Distances between intuitionistic fuzzy sets. *Fuzzy Sets and Systems*, *114*(3), 505–518. doi:10.1016/S0165-0114(98)00244-9

Tran, L., & Duckstein, L. (2002). Comparison of fuzzy numbers using a fuzzy distance measure. *Fuzzy Sets and Systems*, *130*(3), 331–341. doi:10.1016/S0165-0114(01)00195-6

Van Woensel, T., Kerbache, L., Peremans, H., & Vandaele, N. (2008). Vehicle routing with dynamic travel times: A queueing approach. *European Journal of Operational Research*, *186*(3), 990–1007. doi:10.1016/j.ejor.2007.03.012

Voxman, W. (1998). Some remarks on distances between fuzzy numbers. *Fuzzy Sets and Systems*, *100*(1-3), 353–365. doi:10.1016/S0165-0114(97)00090-0

Yao, J., & Wu, K. (2000). Ranking fuzzy numbers based on decomposition principle and signed distance. *Fuzzy Sets and Systems*, *116*(2), 275–288. doi:10.1016/S0165-0114(98)00122-5

KEY TERMS AND DEFINITIONS

Fuzzy Number: Is a special case of a convex, normalized fuzzy set on the real line. A fuzzy number is a generalization of a real number in such a way that it can take several values in a connected set of possible values, each with their own weight defined by a membership function.

Time Window: Is an interval in time during which an activity can or must take place. In the case of routing problems with delivery of goods mostly it relates to the event of start of delivery. In some cases, however, the end of the activity also needs to fall within the interval.

Travel Time Uncertainty: Relates mostly to the mechanism through which causes the travel time not to be a deterministic value (for example, congestion or road disruption). For goods transport, the uncertainty is like a constraint for dispatchers, which in passenger traffic it relates to choices of routes or of modes of transport.

Vehicle Routing Problem: Is a combinatorial optimization and integer programming problem looking to service (pick-up or delivery of goods) a number of customers with a predetermined fleet of vehicles.

Vulnerability: Is mostly used related to physical damage. It means that the subject is capable or susceptible to being wounded or hurt (as by a weapon). Here, the term is used as not being able to meet the time constraints of a customer. It means that the customer is unsatisfied by the service and therefore mentally hurt.

Chapter 8
Experimental Investigation for Performance Optimization of Biodiesel–Fueled Diesel Engine Using Taguchi–Gray Relational Analysis

Rajesh Kumar
Indian Institute of Technology Roorkee, India

R. P. Gakkhar
Indian Institute of Technology Roorkee, India

ABSTRACT

The objective of this analysis is to determine optimum parameters for maximum performance and minimum emission for biodiesel-fueled diesel engine. The experiments were designed using Taguchi L25 orthogonal array. Five parameters— fuel blend, load, speed, injection timing, and injection pressure—each with five levels were selected. Cylinder pressure, exhaust temperature, brake thermal efficiency, brake specific fuel consumption, carbon monoxide, unburned hydrocarbons, nitric oxide, and smoke were response parameters. Optimum combination of parameters was determined by grey relational analysis. The confirmatory test was performed at optimum combination. The grey relational grade and signal-to-noise ratio was determined. The contribution of individual parameter was determined by ANOVA analysis. Optimum performance was obtained at 80% load and 1900 rpm speed with B50 fuel at injection timing of 15.5^0 BTDC with 225 bar injection pressure. Finally, grey relational grade was improved by 3.7%.

DOI: 10.4018/978-1-5225-5091-4.ch008

INTRODUCTION

Optimization of the operating parameters is necessary to find the optimum solution from the raw data. The conventional energy sources are depleting day by day. Therefore the optimization of energy sources is the demand in the current perspective. The problems having incomplete information are considered as black, while the problems having complete information are considered as white. But neither of these ideal situations really exists. The problem having incomplete information lies between these two situations. Since there is always an uncertainty which means problem is always in middle between black and white. This is the reason that the problem is termed as grey and the analysis is called Grey Relational Analysis. The operation mechanism, behavior document and structure message such as the human body, agriculture, economy can be Grey Systems. Here grey means incomplete, uncertain and poor (Julong, 1989). The Grey-taguchi method can be useful for optimization of multi response problems. Diesel engines are prominently used for power generation in industrial, agricultural and transportation sector because of their higher efficiency. However, diesel engines also produce more particulate matter, unburned hydrocarbons and oxides of nitrogen emissions than petrol engines. With increasing concerns about fast depleting natural reserves of crude oil and global climate change as a result of large amount of greenhouse gas emission, the efforts of researchers have been directed towards the use of eco-friendly alternative fuels from renewable sources. With these prime concerns environment friendly renewable sources of energy are being tried as an alternative to mineral diesel. Biodiesel has been recognized to be as one of such alternative.

Biodiesel is "mono alkyl ester of long chain fatty acids produced from renewable lipid feed stocks, such as vegetable oils and animal fats"(ASTM Standards, 2016). The viscosity of neat vegetable oil is very high and causes many problems in fuel flow and there is also the possibility of injector choking, gum formation and lubrication oil dilution. Hence transesterification can be done to reduce its viscosity. Biodiesel is renewable and biodegradable. It contains no sulphur, no aromatics and also having a higher content of oxygen. Raw stocks used for biodiesel production in India are non-edible vegetable oils and animal fats. Jatropha, Karanja, Mahua, Neem etc. are main sources of non-edible vegetable oils for biodiesel production. The kinematic viscosity, density and heating value are the main properties of biodiesel that affect engine performance and emission characteristics (Barnwal & Sharma, 2005; Tesfa, Mishra, Gu, & Powles, 2010). The higher viscosity of biodiesel affects injection characteristics which results in poor atomization and mixing of fuel and air. Hence biodiesel has poor combustion characteristics which further affect performance and exhaust emissions from diesel engines (An et al., 2013; Gumus, 2010; Lapuerta, Armas, & Rodríguez-Fernández, 2008; Sahoo & Das, 2009b). The biodiesel and its blends results in reduction of unburnt hydrocarbons (HC), carbon monoxide (CO) and particulate matters. However, there is a slight increase in oxides of nitrogen (NO_x) (N. Kumar, Varun, & Chauhan, 2013; Rajasekar, Murugesan, Subramanian, & Nedunchezhian, 2010). Graboski and McCormick (Graboski & McCormick, 1998) reviewed the combustion of fuel derived from fats and vegetable oils in diesel engines. The parameters mainly affecting the combustion of biofuels are fuel properties, flow properties, storage and stability. Biodiesel leads to increase in NO_x and lower the PM and soot formation which is mainly due to higher oxygen content.

Previous Work Done

The following work has been done previously on biodiesel fueled diesel engines:

Sun et al. (Sun, Caton, & Jacobs, 2010) studied the effects of injection timing, injection pressure, spray and fuel mixing, and ignition delay for biodiesel fuel. They found that the formation of NO_x is mainly due to atmospheric Nitrogen. The higher combustion efficiency and higher combustion temperature is the main cause of higher NO_x formation. Biodiesel produces lesser soot than that for diesel due to high oxygen content. That may reduce radiative heat transfer leading to increased flame temperature resulting in higher NO_x formation. Pali et.al (Pali, Kumar, & Alhassan, 2015) found improved brake thermal efficiency (BTE), brake specific fuel consumption (BSFC) but CO, HC emissions were lower at high loads. However increase in NOx emission was recorded in case of sal seed oil biodiesel and its blends. Dhar and Agarwal (Dhar & Agarwal, 2014) used karanja oil methyl ester and its blends to compare the combustion and performance characteristics with diesel in diesel engine. Engine cylinder pressure was lower at higher blend ratios and lower speeds. Fuel line pressure was higher than diesel due to higher bulk modulus of biodiesel fuel. In case of lower percentage blends start of combustion was earlier and it was slightly delayed for higher percentage blends. Combustion duration was shorter than diesel. B20 biodiesel blend was found to be optimum blend when it was used without any engine modification (Rakopoulos, Antonopoulos, & Rakopoulos, 2007; Sahoo & Das, 2009a). The above study explains the behaviour of biodiesel and its blends in diesel engine without any modifications. The following work has also been done on biodiesel fuelled diesel engine with modified engine parameters. Ganapathy et al. (Ganapathy, Gakkhar, & Murugesan, 2011) studied the effects of injection timing on combustion, performance and emission analysis with Jatropha biodiesel. They concluded that for 5^0 advance injection, there is a reduction in brake specific fuel consumption, HC, CO and smoke intensity while there is an increase in brake thermal efficiency, peak cylinder pressure, heat release rate and NOx emission. However the retarded injection timing results in an increase in brake specific fuel consumption, CO, HC and smoke. Further it can also reduce the brake thermal efficiency, P_{max}, HRR_{max} and NO_x emission. Raheman et.al (Raheman & Ghadge, 2008) experimentally investigated the performance of a diesel engine fuelled with mahua biodiesel and its blends at varying compression ratios and injection timing. brake specific fuel consumption decreased with decrease in compression ratio and injection timing. brake thermal efficiency increases as injection timing and compression ratio increases. Exhaust gas temperature decreases with increasing compression ratio and advanced injection timing. Sayin and Gumus (Sayin & Gumus, 2011) investigated the effects of compression ratio, injection timing and injection pressure with biodiesel and its blends. They concluded, that on increasing compression ratio in brake specific fuel consumption increases and was maximum for B100. For advanced, injection timing percentage change in brake specific fuel consumption was maximum for B100 and it was highest for B100 at 15^0 btdc. Percentage change in CO, HC, smoke and NOx emissions were maximum for B100 at 19:1 compression ratio, 25^0 CA btdc and 22MPa injection pressure. Qi et al. (Qi, Leick, Liu, & Lee, 2011) investigated the effect of exhaust gas temperature, injection timing and injection pressure on combustion and emission characteristics of biodiesel fuelled diesel engine. They concluded that as the rate of exhaust gas recirculation increases, there is an increment in brake specific fuel consumption and soot emission. A decrease in NOx emission was also observed. Peak cylinder pressure was higher at higher engine loads and increased EGR rates. For the retarded injection timing, brake specific fuel consumption and NOx increases. Finally it was found that higher rate of EGR and retardation in static injection timing are the effective methods for decreasing NOx emission for split injection strategy. Some other researchers (Agarwal, Dhar, Srivastava, Maurya, & Singh, 2013; Amarnath & Prabhakaran, 2012; N. Kumar & Chauhan, 2014; Saravanan, Nagarajan, Lakshmi Narayana Rao, & Sampath, 2014; Ye & Boehman, 2012) also worked on different engine parameters and find similar results in their study. Ozsezen et al. (Ozsezen, Canakci, Turkcan, & Sayin, 2009) revealed, for the same volume more biodiesel was injected into combustion chamber due to higher density. Hence higher viscosity and density influence the atomization rate which leads to slow mixing of fuel and air. Biodiesel leads higher brake specific fuel consumption due to lower heating value of waste cooking oil. Peak cylinder pressure was lower for biodiesel than diesel. Combustion starts earlier due to shorter ignition delay and early start of injection. CO, HC and smoke are reduced and NO and CO_2 increase for biodiesel. (An, Yang, Chou, & Chua, 2012; Can, 2014; Muralidharan, Vasudevan, & Sheeba, 2011) also found similar results for combustion of biodiesel in diesel engine. The major hurdle in commercialization of biodiesel is high cost of raw oils due to limited availability. Therefore the use the waste fried oils as raw oil for the production of biodiesel can reduce the cost of production. Hwang et al. (Hwang, Jung, & Bae, 2015) compared the spray and combustion characteristics of waste cooking oil biodiesel. The composition of biodiesel was found as 35% mono saturated, 44% poly saturated and 17% saturated fatty acids in which oleic and linoleic were major fatty acids. Spray behavior reveals that biodiesel has longer ignition delay, longer penetration length and narrow spray angle. This is the main reason for poor atomization and vaporization of biodiesel. It also has retarded combustion phase, lower cylinder peak pressure and heat release rate was lower than diesel. CO, HC and PM emissions were reduced but increase in NO_x was observed. Soot particles were reduced and visible flame duration was observed which shows that the generation of soot particles was suppressed and oxidation of PM was accelerated in case of waste cooking oil biodiesel. Hence the NO_x increased due to reduction in soot radiation heat transfer. It is clear from the above discussion that modifications in injection parameters can be helpful to enhance the performance and to reduce the emission. Therefore, to select the optimum injection system parameters various optimization methods such as Taguchi S-N ratio optimization (Ganapathy, Murugesan, & Gakkhar, 2009; Sathish Kumar, Sureshkumar, & Velraj, 2015; Win, Gakkhar, Jain, & Bhattacharya, 2005), Response surface methodology (Atmanli, Yüksel, Ileri, & Deniz Karaoglan, 2015; Hirkude & Padalkar, 2014; Karuppasamy & Basha, 2012), Artificial Neural Network (Ghobadian, Rahimi, Nikbakht, Najafi, & Yusaf, 2009; S. Kumar, P, & R, 2013; Mohamed Ismail, Ng, Queck, & Gan, 2012; Pachbhai, Deshmukh, & Dhanfule, 2014; Shivakumar, Srinivasa Pai, & Shrinivasa Rao, 2011), Genetic Algorithm (Betiku, Okunsolawo, Ajala, & Odedele, 2015) or the combination of these methods can be used. Most of the methods are mainly used for optimization of individual parameter. To optimize all the parameters together a multi-objective optimization is required. Taguchi method with Gray Relational Analysis for multi objective optimization can be used.

Taguchi Method

Dr. G. Taguchi was the inventor of this approach which is used to determine the effect of parameters of a process on performance characteristic that determines the effectiveness of the process. This method for design of experiments uses orthogonal arrays for the optimization of different parameters influencing the process and their variation. In this method, there is no need to investigate all the parameters combinations but only few pairs of combinations. This method paves way for collation of data for the determination of factors which most influence the quality of product with minimal number of experiments so as to reduce precious time and resources. This method is very effective with nominal number of parameters (3–50), few interactions between them and a very few contributing significantly. From the Orthogonal Arrays (OA), the required number of experiments and their layout is decided. The number of parameters and their variation is decided by orthogonal array. The minimum number of experiments N is decided by using the number of levels L and number of parameters P with the help of the relation:

N = (L-1) P +1.

This helps in optimizing the experimental problem through the determination of optimum parameters influencing the final output with the minimum number of experiments (Ross P.J., 1988). By minimizing the number of experiments, the efficiency of working system can be increased. The main aim is to reduce time and cost involved in performing the experiments. Taguchi method utilizes some standard tables called orthogonal array (Chamoli, Yu, & Kumar, 2016; Sivasakthivel, Murugesan, & Thomas, 2014; Verma & Murugesan, 2014).

Grey Relational Analysis

The Grey relational analysis explains the degree of approximation with the help of Grey relational grade. Grey relational analysis is a method for quantitatively describing and comparing to the development tendency of a system. The core idea is to compare the geometrical similarity between reference data sequence and several comparative data sequences. The higher the grey correlation, the closer these sequences about their development direction and rate, and their relationship will be closer to each other.

Deng Julong developed and proposed the concept of Grey relational analysis in 1982(Ju-long, 1982)-(Huang et al., 2004). Main advantage of using taguchi-GRA together is, a number of parameters can be optimized as a single parameter (A., N., & M.M., 2011; Masood et al., 2016; Patle, Sharma, Ahmad, & Rangaiah, 2014; Pohit & Misra, 2013). Yuvarajan et al. (Yuvarajan, Ravikumar, & Babu, 2016) also applied the Gray Relational Analysis with Taguchi to find optimum oxygenated fuel such as dimethyl ether (DME), diethyl ether (DEE) and diglyme (DGM), fuel percentage and injection timing. L9 orthogonal array was used and found 36% DGM with 10% fuel blend at -21^0 injection timing was the optimum engine operating conditions. It was observed from the above literature that a limited amount of work has been carried out on WCO biodiesel fueled diesel engine with increased injection pressure. Jadhav and Tandale (Jadhav & Tandale, 2016) applied taguchi GRA for L25 to optimize six engine parameters. In this analysis the experiments were designed using taguchi technique by selecting L_{25} orthogonal array. Five parameters namely biodiesel-diesel blend, load, speed, injection timing and injection pressure each with five levels were taken. Eight response parameters cylinder gas pressure, exhaust temperature, brake specific fuel consumption, brake thermal efficiency, carbon monoxide, unburned hydrocarbons, Nitric oxide and smoke were selected.

Optimum combination of parameters was determined by Grey Relational Analysis. The confirmatory test was performed at optimum combination. The Grey Relational Grade and Signal to noise ratio was determined. ANOVA analysis was also done to know the contribution of each parameter in the analysis.

METHODOLOGY

The waste cooking oil was collected from various restaurants. The oil was filtered to separate the impurities. Biodiesel was produced by transesterification using mechanical stirring method. The composition i.e. 6:1 molar ratio of methanol to oil (by Vol.) was selected (Phan & Phan, 2008).

Potassium hydroxide (KOH) 1% (by weight) was taken as a catalyst and the reaction temperature was kept 60-70°C for 2 hours. After the reaction glycerol present in oil was separated. The biodiesel was washed with water to remove alcohol present in biodiesel. The conversion efficiency (Yielding) was 89%. The properties of biodiesel were measured as per the provisions of ASTM standard number D6751 and shown in Table 1.

Test Engine Setup

The experiments were conducted on a single cylinder, variable speed, water cooled, small DI, 4-stroke diesel engine.

The variation of pressure inside the combustion chamber is most suitable parameter to analyse the combustion process (Heywood, 1988). The cylinder pressure was measured using AVL GM12D piezoelectric transducer. The pressure sensor was mounted flush with inside surface of the combustion chamber. Two pulse pick up sensors were used for signals of crank angle and TDC. All the signals were supplied

Table 1. Fuel specifications

Property	Testing Procedures	Diesel	B25	B50	B75	WCO Biodiesel	WCO
Kinematic viscosity at 40°C (mm²/s)	ASTM D445	2.4	3.39	4.52	5.12	6.58	39.7
Density at 15°C (kg/m³)	ASTM D1298	841	854	865	876	886	916
Calorific value (MJ/kg)	ASTM D240	42.3	40.7	38.1	37.4	36.62	36.10
Flash point (°C)	ASTM D93	76	102	125	168	180	277
Cloud point (°C)	ASTM D2500	-6	-5	-1	1	2	0
Pour point (°C)	ASTM D97	-21	-18	-14	-10	-8	-41

Table 2. Test engine specifications

Parameters	Specifications
Engine type	4-stroke, water cooled, DI- small, diesel engine
Number of cylinders	1
Bore (mm)	92
Stroke (mm)	92
Displacement (cc)	611
Compression ratio	18:1
Dynamometer type	Eddy current type
Maximum power (kW) at rated rpm	11
Fuel injection timing (degree BTDC)	13.5^0
Rated nozzle injection pressure (bar)	225

to AVL INDIMICRO for acquiring data from the sensors. Exhaust gases were measured using AVL DiTEST MDS GAS 1000. Smoke opacity was measured by AVL DiSmoke 480. The schematic diagram of engine test rig is shown in Figure 1.

The maximum possible error for the parameters was calculated by the procedure given by (Moffat, 1988). The maximum possible error was calculated for BSFC was around 0.35%. Further, the errors related to peak cylinder pressure and crank angle measurement was found to be 1.48% and 2% respectively. The range, accuracy with percentage in uncertainty of measuring instruments is shown in Table 3.

Figure 1. Schematic diagram of experimental engine setup

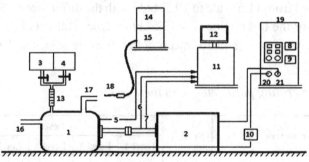

1. Diesel engine	9. Speed indicator	17. Engine exhaust
2. Eddy current dynamometer	10. Throttle actuator	18. Emission sampling probe
3. Diesel tank	11. Data acquisition system	19. Control panel
4. Biodiesel tank	12. Personal computer	20. Load controller
5. Pressure sensor	13. Burette	21. Speed controller
6. TDC sensor	14. Gas analyser	
7. Crank angle sensor	15. Smoke meter	
8. Load indicator	16. Engine Air inlet	

Table 3. List of range, accuracy, and percentage uncertainties of measuring instruments

Instruments	Measured Quantity	Range	Accuracy	Uncertainty (%)
Pressure sensor	Cylinder pressure	0-200 bar	±0.1 bar	±0.05
Crank angle encoder	Crank angle	0-360°	±0.2°	±0.05
K-type thermocouple	Exhaust gas temperature	0-1000°C	±1°C	±0.2
Burette	Fuel flow measurement	0-1000 cc	±0.1 cc	±1
Stop watch	Time	-	±0.1 sec	±0.2
Gas analyser	CO	0-15% vol.	±0.06%	±0.2
	HC	0-30,000 ppm	±12 ppm	±0.2
	NO	0-5000 ppm	±12 ppm	±0.2
Smoke meter	Smoke opacity	0-100%	±1%	±0.1

Procedure

Mainly five input variables namely fuel blend ratio, load, speed, static injection timing, injection pressure were selected with five levels of each variable as shown in Table 4.

The experimental layout was selected according to Taguchi L_{25} Orthogonal Array. All the experiments were performed according to the selected layout. The measurements were taken when the engine attained the steady state. Five fuel blends B0 (Diesel), B25, B50, B75, and B100 were used. Load was varied from 0 to 100% by taking the variation of 20% in each step. Variation in speed was from 1300 to 2100 revolutions/minute at the difference of 200 rev./min. Injection timing levels were selected from 11.5° btdc to 19.5° btdc with the difference of 2°. Standard injection timing for the test engine was 13.5° btdc. One retarded (11.5° btdc) and three advanced levels from standard injection timing were selected. The standard

Table 4. Engine operating parameters and their levels

Engine Parameters	Symbol	Levels				
		Level 1	Level 2	Level 3	Level 4	Level 5
Blend	A	B0	B25	B50	B75	B100
Load (%)	B	20	40	60	80	100
Speed (rpm)	C	1300	1500	1700	1900	2100
Static Injection timing (degree btdc)	D	11.5	13.5	15.5	17.5	19.5
Nozzle opening pressure (bar)	E	225	235	245	255	265

injection pressure for the test engine was 225 bar which was increased from 225 to 265 bar with an increase of 10 bar in each level. The static fuel injection timing was measured by spill out method. The static injection timing was changed by altering number of shims in fuel injection pump. An extra shim of thickness 0.25 mm was added to retard the injection timing by 2^0. Similarly to advance the injection timing by 2^0, a shim of thickness 0.25 mm was removed. The rated fuel injection pressure was 225 bar. The injection pressure was increased by increasing the spring tension inside the fuel injector. To increase the spring tension a washer was added to the spring. The injection pressure was increased by 10 bar by adding 1 washer. The nozzle opening pressure was increased from 225 bar to 265 bar at the difference of 10 bar.

EXPERIMENTAL DESIGN AND OPTIMIZATION

Taguchi approach is a suitable technique for experimental design to reduce number of experiments. The Orthogonal array L_{25}, selected to perform experiments is shown in Table 5. In order to find the final output parameters, total 25 number of experiments were carried out. The results obtained by the experiments on varying engine operating parameters are shown in Table 6.

Grey Relational Analysis

In this analysis, firstly the experimental data obtained is normalized between 0 and 1. This is called grey relational generation. The next step was to calculate grey relational coefficient using the normalized data, which depicts the relation between actual and desired values. Further, the grey relation grade was determined by averaging the values of grey relational coefficient of each result. The final performance of the multiple response problems depends on final value of Grey relational grade. The higher grey relational grade shows that combination is very close to optimum value. Hence the mean response of grey relational grade and its grand mean helps to identify optimum combination. The optimum combination is also obtained by main effect plot of grey relational grade. This analysis helps in converting a multi response optimization problem into a single response optimization problem having overall grey relational grade as objective function. Thereafter the combination of optimum parameters is obtained at highest grey relational grade. Further by using Taguchi approach, optimum parametric setting was used to maximize overall grey relational grade.

The GRG generation for parameters having larger-the-better criterion can be determined by using the relation given in equation 1.

Table 5. Taguchi L_{25} orthogonal array

S. No.	Engine Parameters				
	Blend (A)	Load (B)	Speed (C)	IT (D)	IP (E)
1	1	1	1	1	1
2	1	2	2	2	2
3	1	3	3	3	3
4	1	4	4	4	4
5	1	5	5	5	5
6	2	1	2	3	4
7	2	2	3	4	5
8	2	3	4	5	1
9	2	4	5	1	2
10	2	5	1	2	3
11	3	1	3	5	2
12	3	2	4	1	3
13	3	3	5	2	4
14	3	4	1	3	5
15	3	5	2	4	1
16	4	1	4	2	5
17	4	2	5	3	1
18	4	3	1	4	2
19	4	4	2	5	3
20	4	5	3	1	4
21	5	1	5	4	3
22	5	2	1	5	4
23	5	3	2	1	5
24	5	4	3	2	1
25	5	5	4	3	2

$$x_i(l) = \frac{y_i(l) - \min y_i(l)}{\max y_i(l) - \min y_i(l)} \qquad (1)$$

The GRG generation for parameters having lower-the-better criterion can be determined using the relation given in equation 2.

Table 6. Experimental results of engine performance and emission characteristics

S. No.	Performance Parameters				Emission Parameters			
	P_{max} (bar)	BTE (%)	BSFC (kg/ kW-h)	EGT (⁰C)	Smoke (%vol.)	HC (ppm)	CO (%vol.)	NO (ppm)
1	58	15.25	0.556	119	1.6	19	0.07	68
2	57.9	20.71	0.409	162	1.2	4	0.04	343
3	59.5	23.92	0.354	210	3.3	11	0.05	158
4	59.2	28.97	0.292	267	1.0	9	0.03	218
5	57.5	26.48	0.320	354	24.6	5	0.08	402
6	55.4	15.34	0.575	129	1.1	11	0.06	128
7	59.5	20.15	0.438	174	1.8	8	0.05	255
8	60.5	25.55	0.346	223	4.4	10	0.02	317
9	40.1	24.00	0.367	377	5.0	15	0.07	175
10	59.2	29.33	0.301	267	17.9	7	0.03	154
11	60.4	16.58	0.739	140	1.2	10	0.04	245
12	50.3	22.52	0.435	202	2.8	6	0.07	109
13	47.3	26.02	0.412	296	5.6	9	0.05	221
14	59.4	31.51	0.271	232	6.5	6	0.04	166
15	64.5	28.80	0.324	282	8.5	6	0.03	270
16	54.3	15.51	0.622	165	1.4	10	0.05	80
17	53.3	21.29	0.452	222	3.8	6	0.06	192
18	60.1	25.36	0.380	192	2.6	9	0.03	216
19	63.7	26.51	0.364	250	2.2	5	0.03	342
20	48.9	25.74	0.374	360	5.2	9	0.05	201
21	53.8	15.75	0.641	191	1.2	13	0.06	165
22	59.4	19.83	0.509	157	1.8	15	0.09	200
23	53.5	24.94	0.405	220	3.7	12	0.07	77
24	56.4	30.01	0.336	272	1.6	8	0.05	196
25	59.5	32.79	0.308	349	3.1	5	0.04	412

$$x_i(l) = \frac{\max y_i(l) - y_i(l)}{\max y_i(l) - \min y_i(l)} \qquad (2)$$

where $x_i(l)$ is value the after the grey relational generation, $\min y_i(l)$ is the smallest value of $y_i(l)$ for the l_{th} response, and max $y_i(l)$ is the largest value of $y_i(l)$ for the l_{th} response. The normalized data after grey relational generation is shown in Table 5. An ideal sequence is $x_0(l)$ ($l = 1, 2, 3 \ldots, 25$) for the responses. The role of grey relational grade in grey relational analysis is to reveal the degree of relation between the 25 sequences [$x_0(l)$ and $x_i(l)$, $i = 1, 2, 3 \ldots$]. The grey relational coefficient $_i(l)$ can be calculated as:

$$\xi_i(l) = \frac{\Delta_{min} + \psi \Delta_{max}}{\Delta_{0i}(l) + \psi \Delta_{max}} \tag{3}$$

where $\Delta_{0i} = x_0(l) - x_i(l)$ = difference of absolute value $x_0(l)$ and $x_i(l)$; ψ is the distinguish coefficient $0 \le \psi \le 1$;

$$\Delta_{min}(l) = \forall j^{min} \; \epsilon \; i \, \forall l^{min} x_0(l) - xj(l)$$

shows the smallest value of Δ_{0i}; and $\Delta_{max} = \forall j^{max} \; \epsilon \; i \, \forall l^{max} x_0(l) - xj(l)$ shows the largest value of Δ_{0i}.

The grey relational coefficient can be determined by using the following relation:

$$\gamma_i = \frac{1}{n} \sum_{l=1}^{n} m_i \xi_i(l) \tag{4}$$

where n = number of response variables and m = weighing factor assigned to each grey relation coefficient of individual response variable. The higher Grey relational grade corresponds to intense relational degree between the reference sequence $x_0(l)$ and the given sequence $x_i(l)$. The reference sequence $x_0(l)$ represents most accurate sequence.

All the experimental data was first normalized which is also called the grey relational generation and is shown in Table 7.

These parameters were optimized by taking higher-the-better (or larger-the-better) and lower-the-better criterion. The criterion of larger-the-better was selected for P_{max}, BTE and EGT and was applied by using Equation 1. Similarly the criterion of lower-the-better was taken for brake specific fuel consumption, CO, HC, NO and Smoke opacity and was applied by using Equation 2. The Grey relational coefficient is the most suitable parameter to compare the effectiveness responses. Grey relation

Table 7. Normalized values of responses (grey relational generation)

S. No.	Pmax	BTE	BSFC	EGT	Smoke	HC	CO	NO
1	0.7336	0	0.3914	0	0.9746	0	0.2857	1
2	0.7295	0.3112	0.7046	0.1667	0.9915	1	0.7144	0.2005
3	0.7951	0.4947	0.8224	0.3527	0.9025	0.5333	0.571429	0.7383
4	0.7828	0.7822	0.9542	0.5736	1	0.6667	0.8571	0.5639
5	0.7131	0.6402	0.8953	0.9108	0	0.9333	0.1428	0.0290
6	0.6270	0.0056	0.3494	0.0387	0.9957	0.5333	0.4285	0.8255
7	0.7951	0.2797	0.6428	0.2132	0.9661	0.7333	0.5714	0.4563
8	0.8361	0.5875	0.8408	0.4031	0.8559	0.6	1	0.2761
9	0	0.4996	0.7933	1	0.8305	0.2666	0.2857	0.6889
10	0.7828	0.8032	0.9360	0.5736	0.2839	0.8	0.8571	0.75
11	0.8320	0.0763	0	0.0814	0.9915	0.6	0.7143	0.4854
12	0.4180	0.4148	0.6483	0.3217	0.9237	0.8666	0.2857	0.8808
13	0.2951	0.6145	0.6973	0.6860	0.8051	0.6667	0.5714	0.5552
14	0.7909	0.9272	1	0.4379	0.7669	0.8667	0.7142	0.7151
15	1	0.7726	0.8868	0.6317	0.6822	0.8666	0.8571	0.4127
16	0.5819	0.0147	0.2504	0.1782	0.9830	0.6	0.5714	0.9651
17	0.5409	0.3444	0.6114	0.3992	0.8813	0.8666	0.4285	0.6395
18	0.8196	0.5767	0.7669	0.2829	0.9322	0.6666	0.8571	0.5697
19	0.9672	0.6421	0.8021	0.5078	0.9491	0.9333	0.8571	0.2034
20	0.3606	0.5983	0.7789	0.9341	0.8220	0.6667	0.5714	0.6133
21	0.5614	0.0287	0.2081	0.2790	0.9915	0.4	0.4286	0.7180
22	0.7909	0.2612	0.4901	0.1473	0.9661	0.2666	0	0.6162
23	0.5491	0.5525	0.7134	0.3914	0.8856	0.4666	0.2857	0.9738
24	0.6680	0.8418	0.8598	0.5930	0.9746	0.7333	0.5714	0.6279
25	0.7951	1	0.9207	0.8914	0.9110	0.9333	0.7142	0

coefficient for each performance and emission parameters was computed using the Equation 3. The values of grey relational coefficients obtained are listed in Table 8.

These values of grey relation coefficients were further used to obtain grey relational grade which depicts the quality of each response variable.

Table 8. Grey relational coefficient for responses

S. No.	Pmax	BTE	BSFC	EGT	Smoke	HC	CO	NO
1	0.6524	0.3333	0.4510	0.3333	0.9516	0.3333	0.4117	1
2	0.6489	0.4205	0.6286	0.375	0.9833	1	0.6363	0.3847
3	0.7093	0.4973	0.7378	0.4358	0.8368	0.5172	0.5384	0.6564
4	0.6971	0.6966	0.9160	0.5397	1	0.6	0.7778	0.5341
5	0.6354	0.5815	0.8269	0.8486	0.3333	0.8823	0.3684	0.3399
6	0.5727	0.3345	0.4345	0.3421	0.9915	0.5172	0.4667	0.7413
7	0.7093	0.4097	0.5834	0.3885	0.9365	0.6521	0.5384	0.4791
8	0.7530	0.5479	0.7585	0.4558	0.7763	0.5556	1	0.4085
9	0.3333	0.4997	0.7075	1	0.7468	0.4054	0.4117	0.6164
10	0.6971	0.7175	0.8865	0.5397	0.4112	0.7142	0.7778	0.6667
11	0.7484	0.3512	0.3333	0.3524	0.9833	0.5556	0.6363	0.4928
12	0.4621	0.4607	0.5871	0.4243	0.8676	0.7894	0.4117	0.8075
13	0.4149	0.5646	0.6229	0.6142	0.7195	0.6	0.5384	0.5292
14	0.7052	0.8729	1	0.4708	0.6820	0.7894	0.6363	0.6370
15	1	0.6874	0.8154	0.5758	0.6114	0.7894	0.7778	0.4598
16	0.5446	0.3366	0.4001	0.3782	0.9672	0.5556	0.5384	0.9347
17	0.5213	0.4326	0.5627	0.4542	0.8082	0.7894	0.4666	0.5810
18	0.7349	0.5415	0.6820	0.4108	0.8806	0.6	0.7778	0.5375
19	0.9384	0.5828	0.7164	0.5039	0.9076	0.8823	0.7778	0.3856
20	0.4388	0.5545	0.6934	0.8835	0.7375	0.6	0.5384	0.5639
21	0.5327	0.3398	0.3870	0.4095	0.9833	0.4545	0.4667	0.6394
22	0.7052	0.4036	0.4951	0.3696	0.9365	0.4054	0.3333	0.5657
23	0.5258	0.5277	0.6356	0.4510	0.8137	0.4838	0.4117	0.9502
24	0.6009	0.7596	0.7810	0.5512	0.9516	0.6521	0.5384	0.5733
25	0.7093	1	0.8631	0.8216	0.8489	0.8823	0.6363	0.3333

Weighing Factor

The weighing factor is assigned on the basis of importance of individual response or by selecting an optimum range of experiments by hit and trial. In this analysis we have total eight responses including four performance and four emission parameters. Different weightage, out of 1 was assigned to each performance and emission parameters according to their importance shown in Table 9.

Table 9. Weighting factor assigned to each response variable

S. No.	Response Variables	Weighing Factor
1	P_{max}	0.2
2	BTE	0.2
3	BSFC	0.2
4	EGT	0.05
5	CO	0.1
6	HC	0.05
7	NO	0.1
8	Smoke	0.1

P_{max} is important for combustion point of view and BTE, brake specific fuel consumption have greater importance than EGT. Therefore, 0.2 weighing was assigned to Pmax, BTE, brake specific fuel consumption and 0.05 weighing was assigned to EGT. Similarly CO, NO and smoke emissions have greater impact on environment in case of biodiesel combustion. Therefore 0.1 weighing factor was assigned to CO, NO and smoke opacity. Remaining .05 was given to HC. The grey relational grade was determined by using the equation 4 and the values of GRG are shown in Table 10. Therefore, this multi-objective optimization problem was converted into a single objective problem. Hence this type of problems can be solved using Taguchi approach and grey relational analysis. Here the higher value of grey relational grade shows the value of individual parameter is close to the optimum value. The mean response table of overall grey relation grade is shown in Table 11.

ANOVA Analysis

ANOVA method is used to determine the individual effect parameters in terms of percentage contribution of responses. The results in terms of degree of freedom, sum of squares, mean of squares, P and F ratios from ANOVA analysis of overall grey relational grades are shown in Table 12. The F ratio represents the effect of parameters on response variables. Sum of squares (SS_p) and Degree of freedom (DF) was determined using the following equation number 6 and 7 respectively (Yuvarajan, Ravikumar, Babu, et al., 2016):

$$\left[SS_p = \sum_{i=1}^{5} N \left(\eta_i - \eta \right)^2 \right] \tag{6}$$

Table 10. Final Grey Relational Grade, S/N ratio and its order

S. No.	Grade	S/N Ratio	Order
1	0.0696	-23.1478	18
2	0.0761	-22.3723	11
3	0.0800	-21.9382	10
4	0.0938	-20.5559	4
5	0.0749	-22.5104	13
6	0.0664	-23.5566	24
7	0.0735	-22.6743	15
8	0.0851	-21.4014	8
9	0.0695	-23.1603	19
10	0.0886	-21.0513	6
11	0.0679	-23.3626	23
12	0.0714	-22.926	16
13	0.0700	-23.098	17
14	0.0968	-20.2825	2
15	0.0942	-20.519	3
16	0.0684	-23.2989	21
17	0.0689	-23.2356	20
18	0.0827	-21.6499	9
19	0.0905	-20.867	5
20	0.0744	-22.5685	14
21	0.0630	-24.0132	25
22	0.0679	-23.3626	22
23	0.0753	-22.4641	12
24	0.0869	-21.2196	7
25	0.0977	-20.2021	1

η_i = average over all grey relational grade of each parameter at ith level and η= mean of avg. overall grey relational grade of each parameter.

Error sum of square $(SS_e) = SS_T - \sum_1^5 SS$ for levels

Mean sum of square = MSS = (Individual sum of square/ Degree of Freedom),

Table 11. Overall Grey relational grade for each parameters

Parameters	Grey Relational Grade					
	Level 1	Level 2	Level 3	Level 4	Level 5	Delta
Blends	0.0789	0.0766	0.0801	0.0770	0.0782	0.0034
Load	0.0671	0.0716	0.0786	0.0875	0.0860	0.0204
Speed	0.0811	0.0805	0.0765	0.0833	0.0693	0.0140
IT	0.0720	0.0780	0.0820	0.0814	0.0773	0.0099
IP	0.0809	0.0788	0.0787	0.0745	0.0778	0.0064

Total mean Grey relational grade= 0.0751

Table 12. Analysis of variance for SN ratio

Source	DF	Sum of Squares (SS)	Mean of Squares (MS)	F	P	% Contribution
A	4	0.4423	0.1006	0.56	0.707	1.4077
B	4	19.1943	4.7486	26.36	0.004	61.0877
C	4	7.4639	1.8160	10.08	0.023	23.7546
D	4	3.4792	0.8298	4.61	0.084	11.0729
E	4	.7806	0.3444	1.91	0.273	2.4843
Error	4	.7806	0.1802			100
Total	24	32.1409				

$F = MSS/MSS_e,$ and percentage contribution $= (SS_p/SS_T) \times 100$

Degree of freedom = Number of levels – 1

Total mean grey relation grade is the average of all grey relational grades. Hence the optimal value for each input variable is represented by the higher grey relation grade for each individual parameter which can be analysed by the Figure 2. Therefore it is clear from the figure that the optimal combination of parameters for the current problem is *A3B4C4D3E1*.

Confirmatory Experiments

After finding the combination of optimal parameters for the selected problem, next goal is to predict and verify increment in the quality of responses with the help of optimum combination of parameters. The experiments were also performed on optimal parameter setting and the results are shown in table 13.

Figure 2. The main effect plots for the mean of S/N ratios

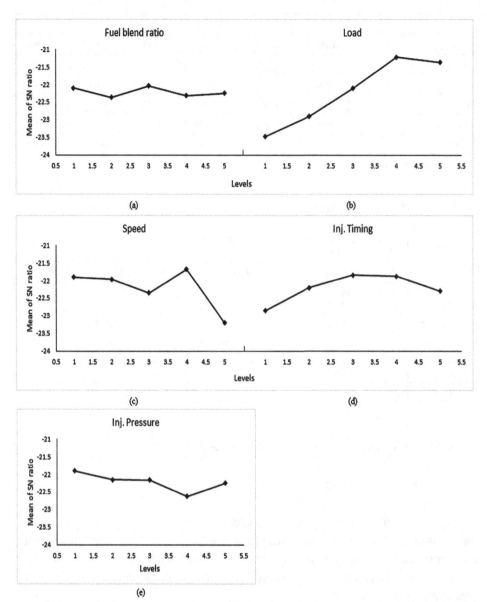

Table 13. Result of experiment at the optimal parameter setting

P_{max}	BTE	BSFC	EGT	Smoke	HC	CO	NO
59.3	33.568	.2979	310	2.8	7	.03	348

Grey relational grade $\hat{\gamma}$ using optimum levels of design parameters is calculated by using the relation:

$$\hat{\gamma} = \gamma_m + \sum_{i=1}^{l}\left(\overline{\gamma}_i - \gamma_m\right) \tag{6}$$

where γ_m represents the total mean grey relational grade, $\overline{\gamma}_i$ is the mean grey relational grade at the optimum level condition and l is the number design parameters that affect the performance and emission characteristics of the engine. Final results of confirmation test are shown in Table 14.

RESULTS AND DISCUSSION

Experiments were performed according to L_{25} orthogonal array to analyse the performance and emission from diesel engine. Taguchi method coupled with Grey Relational Analysis was used for multi objective optimization of engine operating parameters. The following results are obtained:

1. For the optimum parameters setting, Peak cylinder pressure was found 59.3 bar. Brake thermal efficiency and brake specific fuel consumption was 33.57% and 0.298 kg/kWh respectively. Exhaust gas temperature was 310^0C. Exhaust emissions form the engine exhaust were also found to be lower. The CO and HC emissions were 0.3% and 7 ppm respectively. Smoke also reduced up to 0.3% which is closer to minimum level. NO_x emission (348) also reduced for the optimum combination setting.
2. B50 was found to be optimum fuel blend ratio for the test engine at modified injection parameters. Optimum load was 80% of full load, hence engine gives

Table 14. Results of confirmation test

	Initial Parameter Setting	Optimum Parameters	
		Prediction	Experiment
Level	A5B5C4C3D2	A3B4C4D3E1	A3B4C4D3E1
S/N ratio	-20.2021	-19.8	-19.8878
GRG	0.0977	0.1132	.1013

Improvement in grey relational grade= 0.0036
Percentage improvement in GRG= 3.69

optimum performance and exhaust emission at higher loads with modified injection characteristics. At higher load temperature inside the combustion chamber was also high because of this higher temperature, fuel inside the combustion chamber burns completely and gives better combustion. Optimum speed was found 1900 rpm which shows engine performs better at higher speeds and higher loads. At the higher speeds better turbulence is achieved which leads to better mixing of fuel. Hence the better fuel-air mixture is available to ignite the fuel. Hence the fuel burns completely and gives better combustion, performance and emission characteristics of diesel engine.

3.   Advance injection timing 15.5^0 btdc was found optimum level for static injection timing. Due to higher density biodiesel has lower compressibility so pressure wave travels faster. Biodiesel also has longer penetration and shorter cone angle than those of diesel due to higher viscosity. Therefore by advancing the injection timing shorter ignition delay can be avoided. Hence for biodiesel and its blends, the better fuel ignition takes place. Brake thermal efficiency and brake specific fuel consumption were improved emission of CO, HC and smoke were reduced, NO_x emission was found to be higher. For the optimum combination, nozzle opening pressure 225 bar was found to be optimum at which better performance and emission characteristics were obtained.

CONCLUSION

Form the above discussion it can be inferred that peak cylinder pressure, brake specific fuel consumption, brake thermal efficiency and exhaust gas temperature of a diesel engine depend upon fuel blend ratio, load, speed, injection parameters. The optimum combination of engine operating parameters was found *A3B4C4D3E1*. The analysis reveals that the Taguchi method, with grey relational analysis, can be effectively used to optimize operating parameters of a CI engine. Results are well supported by confirmation test results. The grey relational grade for confirmation test is improved by 3.7%.

ACKNOWLEDGMENT

Author is greatly acknowledges the financial support from Ministry of Human Resources and Development, Govt. of India in the form of research scholarship to carry out this work.

REFERENCES

A., K., N., K., & M.M., H. (2011). Multi-Response Optimization of Diesel Engine Performance Parameters Using Thumba Biodiesel-Diesel Blendsby Applying the Taguchi Method and Grey Relational Analysis. *International Journal of Automotive Technology, 12*(4), 599–610.

Agarwal, A. K., Dhar, A., Srivastava, D. K., Maurya, R. K., & Singh, A. P. (2013). Effect of fuel injection pressure on diesel particulate size and number distribution in a CRDI single cylinder research engine. *Fuel, 107*, 84–89. doi:10.1016/j.fuel.2013.01.077

Amarnath, H. K., & Prabhakaran, P. (2012). A study on the thermal performance and emissions of a variable compression ratio diesel engine fuelled with karanja biodiesel and the optimization of parameters based on experimental data. *International Journal of Green Energy, 9*(8), 841–863. doi:10.1080/15435075.2011.647167

An, H., Yang, W. M., Chou, S. K., & Chua, K. J. (2012). Combustion and emissions characteristics of diesel engine fueled by biodiesel at partial load conditions. *Applied Energy, 99*, 363–371. doi:10.1016/j.apenergy.2012.05.049

An, H., Yang, W. M., Maghbouli, A., Li, J., Chou, S. K., & Chua, K. J. (2013). Performance, combustion and emission characteristics of biodiesel derived from waste cooking oils. *Applied Energy, 112*, 493–499. doi:10.1016/j.apenergy.2012.12.044

ASTM Standards. (2016). Standard Specification for Biodiesel Fuel Blend Stock (B100) for Middle Distillate. ASTM.

Atmanli, A., Yüksel, B., Ileri, E., & Deniz Karaoglan, A. (2015). Response surface methodology based optimization of diesel-n-butanol -cotton oil ternary blend ratios to improve engine performance and exhaust emission characteristics. *Energy Conversion and Management, 90*, 383–394. doi:10.1016/j.enconman.2014.11.029

Barnwal, B. K., & Sharma, M. P. (2005). Prospects of biodiesel production from vegetable oils in India. *Renewable & Sustainable Energy Reviews, 9*(4), 363–378. doi:10.1016/j.rser.2004.05.007

Betiku, E., Okunsolawo, S. S., Ajala, S. O., & Odedele, O. S. (2015). Performance evaluation of artificial neural network coupled with generic algorithm and response surface methodology in modeling and optimization of biodiesel production process parameters from shea tree (Vitellaria paradoxa) nut butter. *Renewable Energy, 76*, 408–417. doi:10.1016/j.renene.2014.11.049

Can, Ö. (2014). Combustion characteristics, performance and exhaust emissions of a diesel engine fueled with a waste cooking oil biodiesel mixture. *Energy Conversion and Management, 87*, 676–686. doi:10.1016/j.enconman.2014.07.066

Chamoli, S., Yu, P., & Kumar, A. (2016). Multi-response optimization of geometric and flow parameters in a heat exchanger tube with perforated disk inserts by Taguchi grey relational analysis. *Applied Thermal Engineering, 103*, 1339–1350. doi:10.1016/j.applthermaleng.2016.04.166

Dhar, A., & Agarwal, A. K. (2014). Performance, emissions and combustion characteristics of Karanja biodiesel in a transportation engine. *Fuel, 119*, 70–80. doi:10.1016/j.fuel.2013.11.002

Ganapathy, T., Gakkhar, R. P., & Murugesan, K. (2011). Influence of injection timing on performance, combustion and emission characteristics of Jatropha biodiesel engine. *Applied Energy, 88*(12), 4376–4386. doi:10.1016/j.apenergy.2011.05.016

Ganapathy, T., Murugesan, K., & Gakkhar, R. P. (2009). Performance optimization of Jatropha biodiesel engine model using Taguchi approach. *Applied Energy, 86*(11), 2476–2486. doi:10.1016/j.apenergy.2009.02.008

Ghobadian, B., Rahimi, H., Nikbakht, A. M., Najafi, G., & Yusaf, T. F. (2009). Diesel engine performance and exhaust emission analysis using waste cooking biodiesel fuel with an artificial neural network. *Renewable Energy, 34*(4), 976–982. doi:10.1016/j.renene.2008.08.008

Graboski, M. S., & McCormick, R. L. (1998). Combustion of fat and vegetable oil derived fuels in diesel engines. *Progress in Energy and Combustion Science, 24*(2), 125–164. doi:10.1016/S0360-1285(97)00034-8

Gumus, M. (2010). A comprehensive experimental investigation of combustion and heat release characteristics of a biodiesel (hazelnut kernel oil methyl ester) fueled direct injection compression ignition engine. *Fuel, 89*(10), 2802–2814. doi:10.1016/j.fuel.2010.01.035

Heywood, J. (1988). *Pollutant formation and control in internal combustion engine fundamentals*. New York: McGraw-Hill.

Hirkude, J. B., & Padalkar, A. S. (2014). Performance optimization of CI engine fuelled with waste fried oil methyl ester-diesel blend using response surface methodology. *Fuel, 119*, 266–273. doi:10.1016/j.fuel.2013.11.039

Huang, Z. H., Lu, H. B., Jiang, D. M., Zeng, K., Liu, B., Zhang, J. Q., & Wang, X. B. (2004). Combustion characteristics and heat release analysis of a compression ignition engine operating on a diesel/methanol blend. *Proceedings of the Institution of Mechanical Engineers. Part D, Journal of Automobile Engineering*, *218*(9), 1011–1024. doi:10.1243/0954407041856818

Hwang, J., Jung, Y., & Bae, C. (2015). Spray and combustion of waste cooking oil biodiesel in a compression-ignition engine. *International Journal of Engine Research*, *16*(5), 664–679. doi:10.1177/1468087415585282

Jadhav, S. D., & Tandale, M. S. (2016). Multi-objective Performance Optimization of Compression Ignition Engine Operated on Mangifera Indica Biodiesel by Applying Taguchi Grey Relational Analysis. *Waste and Biomass Valorization*, *7*(5), 1309–1325. doi:10.100712649-016-9504-6

Ju-long, D. (1982). Control problems of grey systems. *Systems & Control Letters*, *1*(5), 288–294. doi:10.1016/S0167-6911(82)80025-X

Julong, D. (1989). Introduction to Grey System Theory. *Journal of Grey System*, *1*(1), 1–24.

Karuppasamy, K., & Basha, C. A. (2012). The Effect of Biodiesel Blends on Single Cylinder DI Diesel Engine and Optimization using Response Surface Methodology. *European Journal of Scientific Research*, *84*(3), 365–376.

Kumar, N., & Chauhan, S. R. (2014). *Evaluation of the effects of engine parameters on performance and emissions of diesel engine operating with biodiesel blend.* Academic Press.

Kumar, N., Varun, & Chauhan, S. R. (2013). Performance and emission characteristics of biodiesel from different origins: A review. *Renewable & Sustainable Energy Reviews*, *21*, 633–658. doi:10.1016/j.rser.2013.01.006

Kumar, S. (2013). Influence of injection timings on performance and emissions of a biodiesel engine operated on blends of Honge methyl ester and prediction using artificial neural network. *Journal of Mechanical Engineering Research*, *5*(1), 5–20. doi:10.5897/JMER12.057

Lapuerta, M., Armas, O., & Rodríguez-Fernández, J. (2008). Effect of biodiesel fuels on diesel engine emissions. *Progress in Energy and Combustion Science*, *34*(2), 198–223. doi:10.1016/j.pecs.2007.07.001

Masood, M. I., Shah, A. N., Aslam, A., Gul, M., Naveed, A., & Usman, M. (2016). *Combustion and Emission Based Optimization of Turbocharged Diesel Engine Run on Biodiesel using Grey-Taguchi Method Combustion and Emission Based Optimization of Turbocharged Diesel Engine Run on Biodiesel using Grey-Taguchi Method.* Academic Press.

Moffat, R. J. (1988). *Describing the Uncertainties in Experimental Results.* Academic Press.

Mohamed Ismail, H., Ng, H. K., Queck, C. W., & Gan, S. (2012). Artificial neural networks modelling of engine-out responses for a light-duty diesel engine fuelled with biodiesel blends. *Applied Energy, 92,* 769–777. doi:10.1016/j.apenergy.2011.08.027

Muralidharan, K., Vasudevan, D., & Sheeba, K. N. (2011). Performance, emission and combustion characteristics of biodiesel fuelled variable compression ratio engine. *Energy, 36*(8), 5385–5393. doi:10.1016/j.energy.2011.06.050

Ozsezen, A. N., Canakci, M., Turkcan, A., & Sayin, C. (2009). Performance and combustion characteristics of a DI diesel engine fueled with waste palm oil and canola oil methyl esters. *Fuel, 88*(4), 629–636. doi:10.1016/j.fuel.2008.09.023

Pachbhai, J. S., Deshmukh, P. M. M., & Dhanfule, R. R. (2014). Application of ANN to Optimize The Performance of CI Engine Fuelled With Cotton Seed Oil. *IJETAE, 4*(6), 351–358.

Pali, H. S., Kumar, N., & Alhassan, Y. (2015). Performance and emission characteristics of an agricultural diesel engine fueled with blends of Sal methyl esters and diesel. *Energy Conversion and Management, 90,* 146–153. doi:10.1016/j.enconman.2014.10.064

Patle, D. S., Sharma, S., Ahmad, Z., & Rangaiah, G. P. (2014). Multi-objective optimization of two alkali catalyzed processes for biodiesel from waste cooking oil. *Energy Conversion and Management, 85,* 361–372. doi:10.1016/j.enconman.2014.05.034

Phan, A. N., & Phan, T. M. (2008). Biodiesel production from waste cooking oils. *Fuel, 87*(17–18), 3490–3496. doi:10.1016/j.fuel.2008.07.008

Pohit, G., & Misra, D. (2013). Optimization of Performance and Emission Characteristics of Diesel Engine with Biodiesel Using Grey-Taguchi Method. *Journal of Engineering, 2013,* 1–8. doi:10.1155/2013/915357

Qi, D., Leick, M., Liu, Y., & Lee, C. F. F. (2011). Effect of EGR and injection timing on combustion and emission characteristics of split injection strategy DI-diesel engine fueled with biodiesel. *Fuel, 90*(5), 1884–1891. doi:10.1016/j.fuel.2011.01.016

Raheman, H., & Ghadge, S. V. (2008). Performance of diesel engine with biodiesel at varying compression ratio and ignition timing. *Fuel, 87*(12), 2659–2666. doi:10.1016/j.fuel.2008.03.006

Rajasekar, E., Murugesan, A., Subramanian, R., & Nedunchezhian, N. (2010). Review of NO x reduction technologies in CI engines fuelled with oxygenated biomass fuels. *Renewable & Sustainable Energy Reviews, 14*(7), 2113–2121. doi:10.1016/j.rser.2010.03.005

Rakopoulos, C. D., Antonopoulos, K. A., & Rakopoulos, D. C. (2007). Experimental heat release analysis and emissions of a HSDI diesel engine fueled with ethanol-diesel fuel blends. *Energy, 32*(10), 1791–1808. doi:10.1016/j.energy.2007.03.005

Ross, P. J. (1988). *Taguchi Techniques for Quality Engineering*. New York: McGraw-Hill.

Sahoo, P. K., & Das, L. M. (2009a). Combustion analysis of Jatropha, Karanja and Polanga based biodiesel as fuel in a diesel engine. *Fuel, 88*(6), 994–999. doi:10.1016/j.fuel.2008.11.012

Sahoo, P. K., & Das, L. M. (2009b). Process optimization for biodiesel production from Jatropha, Karanja and Polanga oils. *Fuel, 88*(9), 1588–1594. doi:10.1016/j.fuel.2009.02.016

Saravanan, S., Nagarajan, G., Lakshmi Narayana Rao, G., & Sampath, S. (2014). Theoretical and experimental investigation on effect of injection timing on NOx emission of biodiesel blend. *Energy, 66*(x), 216–221. doi:10.1016/j.energy.2014.01.003

Sathish Kumar, R., Sureshkumar, K., & Velraj, R. (2015). Optimization of biodiesel production from Manilkara zapota (L.) seed oil using Taguchi method. *Fuel, 140*(x), 90–96. doi:10.1016/j.fuel.2014.09.103

Sayin, C., & Gumus, M. (2011). Impact of compression ratio and injection parameters on the performance and emissions of a DI diesel engine fueled with biodiesel-blended diesel fuel. *Applied Thermal Engineering, 31*(16), 3182–3188. doi:10.1016/j.applthermaleng.2011.05.044

Shivakumar, S. P., Srinivasa Pai, P., & Shrinivasa Rao, B. R. (2011). Artificial Neural Network based prediction of performance and emission characteristics of a variable compression ratio CI engine using WCO as a biodiesel at different injection timings. *Applied Energy*, *88*(7), 2344–2354. doi:10.1016/j.apenergy.2010.12.030

Sivasakthivel, T., Murugesan, K., & Thomas, H. R. (2014). Optimization of operating parameters of ground source heat pump system for space heating and cooling by Taguchi method and utility concept. *Applied Energy*, *116*, 76–85. doi:10.1016/j. apenergy.2013.10.065

Sun, J., Caton, J. A., & Jacobs, T. J. (2010). Oxides of nitrogen emissions from biodiesel-fuelled diesel engines. *Progress in Energy and Combustion Science*, *36*(6), 677–695. doi:10.1016/j.pecs.2010.02.004

Tesfa, B., Mishra, R., Gu, F., & Powles, N. (2010). Prediction models for density and viscosity of biodiesel and their effects on fuel supply system in CI engines. *Renewable Energy*, *35*(12), 2752–2760. doi:10.1016/j.renene.2010.04.026

Verma, V., & Murugesan, K. (2014). Optimization of solar assisted ground source heat pump system for space heating application by Taguchi method and utility concept. *Energy and Building*, *82*, 296–309. doi:10.1016/j.enbuild.2014.07.029

Win, Z., Gakkhar, R. P., Jain, S. C., & Bhattacharya, M. (2005). Investigation of diesel engine operating and injection system parameters for low noise, emissions, and fuel consumption using Taguchi methods. *Proceedings of the Institution of Mechanical Engineers. Part D, Journal of Automobile Engineering*, *219*(10), 1237–1250. doi:10.1243/095440705X34865

Ye, P., & Boehman, A. L. (2012). An investigation of the impact of injection strategy and biodiesel on engine NO x and particulate matter emissions with a common-rail turbocharged di diesel engine. *Fuel*, *97*(x), 476–488. doi:10.1016/j.fuel.2012.02.021

Yuvarajan, D., Ravikumar, J., & Babu, M. D. (2016). Analytical Methods Simultaneous optimization of smoke and NO x emissions in a stationary diesel engine fuelled with diesel – oxygenate blends using the grey relational analysis in the Taguchi method. *Analytical Methods*, *8*(x), 6222–6230. doi:10.1039/C6AY01696K

Yuvarajan, D., Ravikumar, J., Babu, M. D., Jadhav, S. D., Tandale, M. S., Gul, M., ... Masood, I. (2016). Multi-variable optimization of diesel engine fuelled with biodiesel using grey-Taguchi method. *Journal of the Brazilian Society of Mechanical Sciences and Engineering*, *38*(2), 621–632. doi:10.100740430-015-0312-x

APPENDIX

Table 15. Notation

B25 = Blend of 25% waste cooking oil methyl ester and 75% diesel (by vol.) B50 = Blend of 50% waste cooking oil methyl ester and 50% diesel (by vol.) B75 = Blend of 75% waste cooking oil methyl ester and 25% diesel (by vol.) B100 = Pure Biodiesel BSFC = Brake Specific Fuel Consumption BTDC = Before Top Dead Center BTE = Brake Thermal Efficiency CAD = Crank Angle Degree CI = Compression Ignition CO = Carbon Monoxide CO_2 = Carbon Dioxide CR = Compression Ratio EGT = Exhaust Gas Temperature	GRG = Grey Relational Grade HC = Unburned Hydrocarbons HRR = Heat Release Rate IP = Injection Pressure IT = Injection Timing NO = Nitric Oxide NO_x = Oxides of Nitrogen P_{max} = Peak Cylinder Pressure ppm = Parts Per Million ROPR = Rate of Pressure Rise S/N = Signal to Noise Ratio SOC = Start of Combustion SOI = Start of Injection TDC = Top Dead Center WCO = Waste Cooking Oil

Chapter 9
Land Cover Classification Using the Proposed Texture Model and Fuzzy k–NN Classifier

Jenicka S.
Sethu Institute of Technology, India

ABSTRACT

Texture feature is a decisive factor in pattern classification problems because texture features are not deduced from the intensity of current pixel but from the grey level intensity variations of current pixel with its neighbors. In this chapter, a new texture model called multivariate binary threshold pattern (MBTP) has been proposed with five discrete levels such as -9, -1, 0, 1, and 9 characterizing the grey level intensity variations of the center pixel with its neighbors in the local neighborhood of each band in a multispectral image. Texture-based classification has been performed with the proposed model using fuzzy k-nearest neighbor (fuzzy k-NN) algorithm on IRS-P6, LISS-IV data, and the results have been evaluated based on confusion matrix, classification accuracy, and Kappa statistics. From the experiments, it is found that the proposed model outperforms other chosen existing texture models.

INTRODUCTION

The term land cover refers to the biophysical attributes of the surface of the earth. Land cover classification involves classifying the remotely sensed image into various land cover types such as land, vegetation, and water. Texture is a measure of variation

DOI: 10.4018/978-1-5225-5091-4.ch009

in pixel intensities existing in the local neighborhood of a digital image. In this chapter, a new texture model called Multivariate Binary Threshold Pattern (MBTP) is proposed for land cover classification and the performance of the proposed texture model is evaluated through experiments conducted on IRS-P6, LISS-IV data.

BACKGROUND

Texture feature is a decisive factor in pattern classification problems because texture features are not deduced from the intensity of the current pixel but from the gray level intensity variations of current pixel with its neighbors. The proposed model uses five discrete levels such as -9,-1, 0, 1 and 9 for characterizing the gray level intensity variations of the center pixel with its neighbors in the local neighborhood of each band in a multispectral image. For land cover classification, the proposed model MBTP has been used along with fuzzy k-Nearest Neighbor (Fuzzy k-NN) classifier.

MAIN FOCUS OF THE CHAPTER

Related Work

A variety of texture models are found in literature. Local Binary Pattern (LBP) (Ojala *et al.* 2001), a texture model with discrete levels 0 and 1 was proposed for characterizing patterns in gray level images. The classification accuracies of LBP and its derivatives were found better in many applications. A multivariate extension of LBP texture model, Multivariate Local Binary Pattern (MLBP) (Lucieer *et al.* 2005) was proposed for remotely sensed images and it was suggested that the texture features of bands with their cross relations can register the pattern in the neighborhood. Xiaoyang et al. (2010) proposed Local Ternary Pattern with discrete levels 0, 1 and -1 for face recognition under difficult lighting conditions. Multivariate Local Texture Pattern (MLTP) (Suruliandi, 2009), an extension of Local Texture Pattern (Suruliandi and Ramar, 2008) with 0, 1 and 9 as discrete levels, was proposed for land cover classification of remotely sensed images. A computationally simple feature, the multilevel local pattern histogram (MLPH) (Dai *et al.* 2011) was proposed for synthetic aperture radar (SAR) image classification which produced better results than other commonly used features. In another work (Suruliandi and Jenicka, 2015), a comparative study of texture models was performed and it was found that MLTP texture model outperformed other models taken for study. In order to include directional information in conventional LBP, a new improved LBP (Yu et al., 2014) incorporating mean and standard deviation of the local absolute difference was proposed. It was shown that the new improved LBP produced better classification accuracy on texture and face datasets. A new texture model Multivariate Discrete Local Texture Pattern (MDLTP) (Jenicka and Suruliandi, 2014) was proposed with four discrete levels like -1, 0, -1 and 9 for land cover classification which yielded better results compared to the contemporary models considered for study. In MDLTP, the pattern labels are assigned uniquely for each combination of positive and negative sums of discrete levels to avoid collision. An unsupervised neural network (Sari et al., 2015) approach known as the topological map of Kohonen was applied to perform classification of satellite images and the method was evaluated to obtain optimal classes.

Linear regression has been useful in determining a linear relationship between the variables in dataset but better regression models that can model nonlinearly implied variables are needed in various applications. Therefore, nonlinear models like multivariate adaptive regression splines (MARS) (Friedman, 1991) and conic multivariate adaptive regression splines (CMARS) (Weber et al., 2012) were developed. A newly developed robust conic multivariate adaptive regression splines (RCMARS) (Özmen et al., 2011) had an advantage of coping with the noise in both input and output data and of obtaining more consistent optimization results than CMARS. The data sets which included both linearly and nonlinearly involved variables were modelled efficiently by a semiparametric model, conic generalized partial linear model (CGPLM) (Çavuşoğlu, 2010). Robust conic generalized partial linear model (RCGPLM) (Özmen et al., 2012) was introduced to decrease the complexity of RCMARS through reducing the number of variables by transferring the linear ones to logistic regression. CMARS was applied to build a model for the atmospheric correction of a MODerate-resolution Imaging Spectroradiometer (MODIS) image data-set (Kuter et al., 2015). Later they estimated snow-covered area using MARS (Kuter et al., 2016).

Optimization techniques (Vasant, 2013) like support vector machine were used to control mobile robot while procedures using hybrid linear search and genetic algorithms were formulated for simulated annealing for fuzzy nonlinear industrial production planning problems. Fuzzy logic based and stochastic approaches (Vasant 2015, Vasant et al. 2016) were applied in various applications where optimization was needed. Soft computing approaches (Vasant 2014, Vasant et al. 2012) were used for analysis, prediction of market data and for solving hard problems. Fuzzy random regression based modeling (Vasant and Voropai 2016) were applied for modelling uncertainty. Some real world problems were addressed using big data processing and data science approaches (Vasant and Kalaivanthan 2017).

The Fuzzy k-NN algorithm was proposed by Keller et al. (1985) and the classification accuracy obtained using fuzzy k-NN was better than k-NN algorithm.

A survey of various classification algorithms including pixel based, sub pixel based, parametric, non parametric, hard and soft classification algorithms was performed by Lu and Weng (2007). They summarize that the success of classification algorithm depends on the availability of high quality remotely sensed imagery, the design of classification procedure and analyst's skills.

Motivation for the Proposed Approach

It is observed from literature that texture models with increasing number of discrete levels can discriminate patterns better. But the drawback of increasing the number of discrete levels will be a proportionate increase in the number of bins required. The drawback can be overcome by finding the number of effective bins using a factor called uniformity measure. Motivated by this fact, a texture model with two thresholds and five discrete levels such as -1,-9, 0, 1and 9, is proposed. Justified by the inherent fuzziness of fuzzy k-NN algorithm, the proposed model is combined with fuzzy k-NN classifier in performing land cover classification. The main contribution of the paper lies in proposing the multivariate texture model, MBTP for land cover classification of remotely sensed images.

Organisation of the Chapter

The paper is organized as follows. The 'Study Area' section describes the study area and data for experimentation. The 'Method' section describes the proposed texture model and the classification procedure of multispectral image with the proposed model using fuzzy k-NN classification algorithm. The subsequent section describes the experiments conducted, results obtained and performance evaluation of the proposed model. The final section draws conclusion.

STUDY AREA

The remotely sensed source image was formed by combining bands 2, 3, and 4 of IRS P6, LISS-IV data (Green, red, and near IR). The source image has a spatial resolution of 5.8 m and it was taken in July 2007. It is a clear and cloud free image which is geometrically and radiometrically corrected. It was supplied by National Remote Sensing Centre (NRSC), Hyderabad, India. The source image covers the area in and around Tirunelveli city located in the state of Tamil Nadu, India. The source image is transected by the river, Thamirabarani. The image is defined by the following coordinates in the upper left and lower right corners: lat 8.79 lon 77.55 and lat 8.66 lon 77.7. The image is of size 1004x1158x3 and is shown in Figure 1.

Figure 1. IRS P6, LISS-IV Remotely sensed image

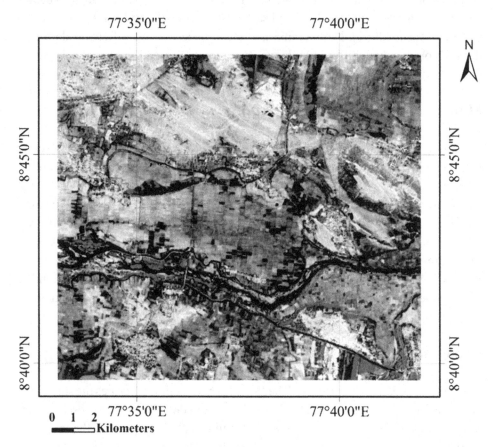

According to National Land Cover Database (NLCD 2006) [http://www.mrlc.gov/nlcd06_leg.php], the land cover classes have been divided into nine major classes. Following the guidelines and classification criteria specified in NLCD 2006, the area covered in the experimental data is divided into four major classes as shown in Figure 2. Among the four major classes, the 'Cultivated crops' class is further subdivided into three types of vegetation. So altogether six experimental classes of size 16x16 were extracted from source image in Figure.1 and are shown in Figure 2.

Among the six classes, the Soil class is dominated by barren land with soil, sand and rocks. The Vegetation -1 class is dominated by rice crop in its early phase. The vegetation-3 class predominantly refers to rice crop in the ripening phase. The Vegetation-2 class is dense and thick cultivated vegetation. Settlement class is dominated by residential buildings either thickly populated or sparsely populated. The water class refers to water in river and tanks.

Figure 2. Training samples and their descriptions

NLCD 2006 Class	NLCD 2006 class description	Class No	Actual Class	Samples	Description
82	Cultivated crops	Class1	Vegetation-1		Rice crops with tender sprouts
82	Cultivated crops	Class2	Vegetation-2		Thick cultivated vegetation
82	Cultivated crops	Class3	Vegetation-3		Ripe rice crops
2	Developed	Class4	Settlement		Residential area
11	Open water	Class5	Water		Water in river and tanks
31	Barren land	Class6	Soil		Barren land with sparsely and randomly scattered shrubs

METHOD

Proposed Global Feature: Multivariate Binary Threshold Pattern (MBTP) Histogram

Let us take a 3x3 neighborhood where the value of the center pixel is g_c and $g_0, g_1, \ldots g_7$ are the pixel values of its neighbors. The gray level intensity variation between the center pixel and one of its neighbor pixels is described as follows.

$$p(g_i, g_c) = \begin{cases} -9 & \text{if } g_i \leq (g_c - t2) \\ -1 & \text{if } (g_c - t2) < g_i \leq (g_c - t1) \\ 0 & \text{if } (g_c - t1) < g_i \leq (g_c + t1) \\ 1 & \text{if } (g_c + t1) < g_i < (g_c + t2) \\ 9 & \text{if } g_i \geq (g_c + t2) \end{cases} \tag{1}$$

where 't1' and 't2' are the thresholds (small positive integers) fixed to express the closeness of neighbor pixel with the center pixel. Of the two thresholds, t1 is the primary threshold and t2 is the secondary threshold. The thresholds are used for pattern based partitioning of pixels into regions on either sides of the center pixel as shown in Figure 3.

The primary threshold t1 is fixed to be less than the secondary threshold t2. The value $p(g_i, g_c)$ stands for the discrete level assigned to i^{th} pixel in the neighborhood. Apart from the discrete levels 0 and 1, 9 is chosen because it is the smallest number that does not overlap with the maximum sum of 8 obtained later when all eight neighbors are 1. So the discrete levels have been fixed to -9, -1, 0, 1 and 9. The purpose of using thresholds (or fuzzy values) is to address the issue of uncertainty in assigning the discrete levels. Concatenation of these levels in a neighborhood

Figure 3. Pictorial representation of thresholds and discrete levels

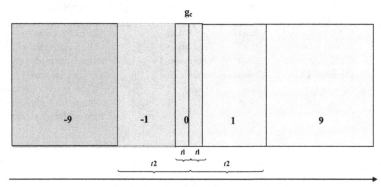

Gray levels of pixels in neighbourhood

gives us a pattern unit. The sample calculation of pattern unit for t1=1 and t2=4 is shown below.

$$
\begin{bmatrix} 195 & 50 & 220 \\ 230 & 197 & 198 \\ 215 & 210 & 200 \end{bmatrix} \rightarrow \begin{bmatrix} -1 & -9 & 9 \\ 9 & & 0 \\ 9 & 9 & 1 \end{bmatrix} \rightarrow
$$

$$
-1 \quad -9 \quad 9 \quad 0 \quad 1 \quad 9 \quad 9 \quad 9 \,(Pattern\ Unit)
$$

(2)

The total number of patterns considering all combinations of five discrete levels with eight pixels in the neighborhood will be 5^8. In order to reduce the number of possible patterns, a uniformity measure (U) is defined as in equation (4). It corresponds to the number of circular spatial transitions between discrete levels in the pattern unit. Patterns for which U value is less than or equal to two are considered uniform while others are considered non uniform. The gray scale Binary Threshold Pattern (BTP) for a 3x3 local region 'X' is derived as in equation (3). The value 'PS' stands for the sum of all positive discrete levels and 'NS' stands for the absolute value of the sum of all negative discrete levels in the pattern unit. To each pair of (NS, PS) values of uniform patterns, a unique BTP value is obtained from the lookup table 'L'. The value 286 is assigned for non uniform patterns.

$$
BTP(X) = \begin{cases} L(NS, PS) & U \leq 2 \\ 286 & Otherwise \end{cases}
$$

(3)

where

$$U = \left| s(g_7 - g_c) - s(g_0 - g_c) \right| + \sum_{k=1}^{7} \left| s(g_k - g_c) - s(g_{k-1} - g_c) \right| \tag{4}$$

where

$$s(x, y) = \begin{cases} 1 & if & |x - y| > 0 \\ 0 & if & otherwise \end{cases}$$

and

$$PS = \sum_{i=0}^{7} p(g_i, g_c) \quad if \quad s(p(g_i, g_c) \geq 0$$

$$NS = \left| \sum_{i=0}^{7} p(g_i, g_c) \quad if \quad s(p(g_i, g_c) < 0 \right|$$

The lookup table (L) of size (73x73) can be generated following the Pseudocode:1 while the BTP descriptor for a gray level image can be generated following the Pseudocode:2 and both are listed in appendix.

The proposed BTP operator for gray scale image is extended as Multivariate BTP (MBTP) for the multispectral images. Three most suitable multispectral bands for land cover classification are chosen and combined to form a RGB image. Nine BTP operators are calculated in the RGB image. Out of nine, three BTP operators describe the local texture in each of the three bands R, G and B individually (BTP^{RR}, BTP^{GG} and BTP^{BB}) and others are calculated from the cross relations of each band with other bands. The MBTP descriptor is calculated as in equation (5).

$$MBTP = BTP \begin{bmatrix} BTP^{RR} & BTP^{GR} & BTP^{BR} \\ BTP^{RG} & BTP^{GG} & BTP^{BG} \\ BTP^{RB} & BTP^{GB} & BTP^{BB} \end{bmatrix} \tag{5}$$

where

$$BTP^{RR} = BTP \begin{bmatrix} g_0^R & g_1^R & g_2^R \\ g_7^R & \rightarrow g_c^R & g_3^R \\ g_6^R & g_5^R & g_4^R \end{bmatrix} \text{ and}$$

$$BTP^{GR} = BTP \begin{bmatrix} g_0^G & g_1^G & g_2^G \\ g_7^G & g_c^R \downarrow & g_3^G \\ g_6^G & g_5^G & g_4^R \end{bmatrix} \qquad (6)$$

For example, the arrows in equation (6) denote how BTP^{GR} cross relation is found by replacing the center pixel of R band in place of the center pixel of G band. The MBTP descriptor describes the texture pattern over any local region. The global feature of an image is obtained by forming MBTP histogram. The MBTP histogram has 286 bins.

Land Cover Classification Procedure: MBTP With Fuzzy k-NN

The feature extraction and classification of a multispectral image is shown in Figure 4. The steps are as follows.

1.   In the training phase, assign the membership value of a training sample 'x' in class 'i' as given below.

Figure 4. (a) Feature extraction using the proposed model; (b) classification using fuzzy k-NN algorithm

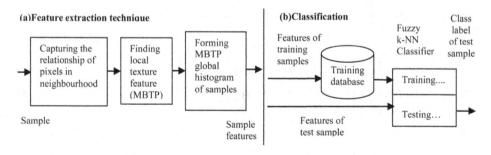

$$\mu_i(x) = \begin{cases} \left[.51 + \left(\dfrac{n_j}{k} \right) \right] \times .49 & if \ i = j \\[2em] \left(\dfrac{n_j}{k} \right) \times .49 & if \ i \neq j \end{cases} \tag{7}$$

where n_j is the number of neighbors within 'k' closest neighbors belonging to class 'j'. The fuzzy membership values are found based on two conditions. The condition i=j means that the classified land cover class is the same as the actual land cover class and i≠j means otherwise. The fuzzy membership values for the training samples can be obtained using the Pseudocode:3 listed in appendix.

2. In each training sample, for each 3x3 neighborhood, find MBTP texture descriptor.
3. Form MBTP histogram for global description of each training sample as shown in Figure. 4(a).
4. In the testing phase as shown in Figure. 4(b), store the MBTP histograms of training samples in database.
5. Extract a testing sample using a sliding window that runs from top left to bottom right in the remotely sensed image, form MBTP histogram and give the histogram as input to fuzzy k-NN classifier.
6. The classifier finds similarity between the test sample and each training sample to pick out 'k' closest training samples.
7. The classifier assigns the membership of the test sample by finding $\mu_i(x)$ as given below.

$$\mu_i(x) = \frac{\displaystyle\sum_{j=1}^{k} \mu_{ij} \left(\dfrac{1}{\left\| x - x_j \right\|^{\frac{2}{m-1}}} \right)}{\displaystyle\sum_{j=1}^{k} \dfrac{1}{\left\| x - x_j \right\|^{\frac{2}{m-1}}}} \tag{8}$$

where μ_{ij} is the membership of training sample of ith class to j[th] class, $\left\| x - x_j \right\|$ is the distance between the training sample x and x_j (j[th] nearest neighbor) and 'm' stands for weight attached to the distance $\left\| x - x_j \right\|$. The test sample 'x' is assigned to the class based on the expression value that goes as, $\max_{n}^{i=1} \mu_i(x)$ where 'n' is the number of classes.

8. Repeat steps from 5 to 7 till all the testing samples in the remotely sensed image are classified.

The Pseudocode: 4 listed in appendix gives the overall procedure for land cover classification of remotely sensed image.

Advantages and Disadvantages of the Proposed Approach

Feature extraction is the first part in any classification methodology. The effectiveness of features extracted determines the classification accuracy achieved through the application of the classification methodology. The main thrust of the book chapter lies in the texture model proposed. Its advantage will be quantitatively proved in the subsequent section through calculating classification accuracy. The disadvantage in the proposed texture model is that it requires 286 bins.

EXPERIMENT, RESULTS, AND PERFORMANCE EVALUATION

Experiment 1: Land Cover Classification of Remotely Sensed Image Using the Proposed Algorithm

It is essential to experiment and fix the neighborhood and window sizes but in the present case, it is understood that the land cover classes (texture classes) are micro textures which can be captured without being cut using a small neighborhood and window size. We know that the neighborhood size cannot be decreased further below (3x3) and a window size of (8x8) may be too small. So a neighborhood size of (3x3) and a window size of (16x16) were fixed in all experiments. The training samples and their fuzzy memberships (computed using equation (6)) are shown in Figure 5.

Thresholds t1 and t2 can be altered to adjust the level of fuzziness needed in describing texture. In all the experiments, the size of the testing sample was also fixed to 16x16. The thresholds t1 and t2 were set to 1 and 4 by experimentation to achieve optimal result. The value 'k' in fuzzy k-NN algorithm was set to 3. The classified image obtained using the proposed algorithm is shown in Figure 6.

The MBTP model discriminates well between the various land covers because it uses five discrete levels for describing texture in neighborhood. For ground truth verification, a set of stratified random samples comprising 2400 pixels were taken

Figure 5. Training samples, their fuzzy memberships, and descriptions

Class No	Actual class	Sample	Fuzzy memberships to samples						Description
			C1	C2	C3	C4	C5	C6	
C1	Vegetation-1		0.6733	0.1633	0.1633	0	0	0	Rice crop in initial phase
C2	Vegetation -2		0.1633	0.6733	0.1633	0	0	0	Thick cultivated vegetation
C3	Vegetation -3		0.1633	0	0.6733	0.1633	0	0	Rice crop in ripening phase
C4	Settlement		0.1633	0	0.1633	0.6733	0	0	Residential area
C5	Water		0.1633	0	0.1633	0	0.6733	0	Water
C6	Soil		0.1633	0	0.1633	0	0	0.6733	Barren land

Figure 6. Classified image using MBTP and Fuzzy k-NN

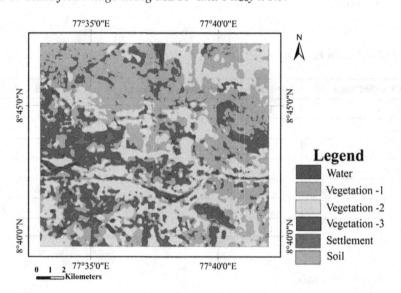

from the remotely sensed image and used for building confusion matrix. In the following way, an updated geological map (geo referenced) was used as a guide for ground truth study of the area covered in the image. The geo referenced topo sheets with features like roads, rivers, distributary, channels, gullies, settlement and water bodies incorporated with stratified random pixels from the source image were used for ground study information. On field visit, the Global Positioning System (GPS) receiver was used to locate the sample sites and the reference values (actual land cover classes) were recorded. The confusion matrix, overall classification accuracy and Kappa coefficient are the performance metrics for assessing the classified image.

For the classified image in Figure 6, the confusion matrix and accuracy totals are shown in Table 1 and Table 2 respectively.

The proposed algorithm achieves 96.2% classification accuracy.

Experiment 2: Land Cover Classification of Remotely Sensed Image Using MDLTP and Fuzzy k-NN

DLTP texture operator proposed by Jenicka and Suruliandi [2014] extracts local texture information from a 3x3 neighborhood of a gray level image. The MDLTP texture feature (Jenicka and Suruliandi 2014) is a multivariate extension of the basic DLTP operator. Considering the local and cross relations of each band with other bands as explained before in the 'Method' section (where the proposed MBTP descriptor was derived), DLTP is found using equation (9). The MDLTP histogram requires 166 bins.

Table 1. Confusion matrix

Classified Total	Vegetation-1	Vegetation-2	Settlement	Water	Soil	Row Total
Vegetation-1	100	1	4	0	0	0
Vegetation-2	0	264	19	0	0	0
Vegetation-3	1	2	615	4	0	29
Settlement	0	0	9	341	0	0
Water	0	0	2	0	252	0
Soil	0	0	20	0	0	737
Column total	101	267	669	345	252	766

Table 2. Accuracy totals

Class Name	Reference Total	Classified Total	Number Correct	Producer's Accuracy %	User's Accuracy %
Vegetation-1	105	99	100	95.24	99.01
Vegetation-2	283	266	264	93.29	98.88
Vegetation-3	651	671	615	94.47	91.93
Settlement	350	348	341	97.43	98.84
Water	254	249	252	99.21	100
Soil	757	764	737	97.36	96.21
Totals	2400	2400	2309		
Overall Accuracy =96.2%			Overall Kappa=0.9512		

$$MLTP = DLTP \begin{bmatrix} DLTP^{RR} & DLTP^{GR} & DLTP^{BR} \\ DLTP^{RG} & DLTP^{GG} & DLTP^{BG} \\ DLTP^{RB} & DLTP^{GB} & DLTP^{BB} \end{bmatrix} \tag{9}$$

The procedure for finding DLTP for a local neighborhood of a gray level image is given in Pseudocode: 5 listed in appendix. In the Pseudocode: 4 listed earlier, if function BTP is replaced with function DLTP (listed in Pseudocode: 5) and if we replace 286 bins with 166 bins, we can perform land cover classification using MDLTP and Fuzzy k-NN. The classified image obtained by applying the described procedure on Figure 1 is shown in Figure 7.

The MDLTP texture model gives a classification accuracy of 93% because it uses four discrete levels.

Experiment 3: Land Cover Classification of the Remotely Sensed Image Using MLTP and Fuzzy k-NN

LTP texture operator proposed by Suruliandi and Ramar [2008] extracts local texture information from a 3x3 neighborhood of a gray level image. The MLTP texture feature (Suruliandi 2009) is a multispectral extension of the basic LTP operator. Nine LTP operators were found (as described in the 'Method' section where the proposed MBTP operator was derived) and MLTP was found using equation (10). The MLTP histogram requires 46 bins.

Figure 7. Classified image obtained using MDLTP and Fuzzy k-NN

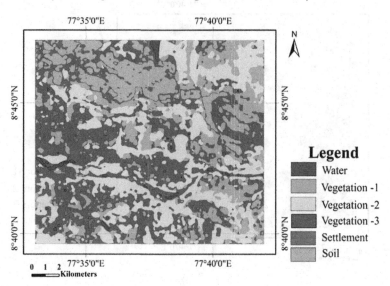

$$MLTP = LTP \begin{bmatrix} LTP^{RR} & LTP^{GR} & LTP^{BR} \\ LTP^{RG} & LTP^{GG} & LTP^{BG} \\ LTP^{RB} & LTP^{GB} & LTP^{BB} \end{bmatrix} \qquad (10)$$

The procedure for extracting LTP texture feature for the local neighborhood of a gray level image is given in Pseudocode: 6 listed in appendix. In Pseudocode: 4 listed earlier, if function BTP is replaced with function LTP (listed in pseudocode 6) and if we replace 286 bins with 46 bins, we can perform land cover classification using MLTP and Fuzzy k-NN. The classified image obtained by applying the described procedure on Figure 1 is shown in Figure 8.

The MLTP texture model gives a classification accuracy of 90.4% because it uses only three discrete levels.

Experiment 4: Land Cover Classification of Remotely Sensed Image Using MLBP and Fuzzy k-NN

The LBP texture operator proposed by Ojala et al. [2001] used for characterizing texture in a local neighborhood of a gray scale image can be derived as follows. Let the neighborhood be g_c, g_0. ... g_7 where g_c corresponds to the gray level value of the center pixel, g_i (i = 0,1, . . ., 7) corresponds to the gray level values of neighbors. The relationship between the center pixel and one of its neighbors is given below.

Figure 8. Classified image using MLTP and Fuzzy k-NN

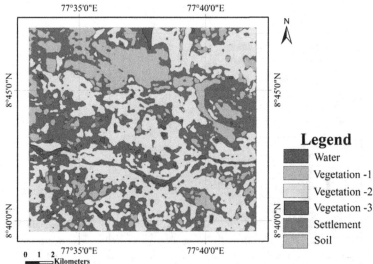

$$s(x) = \begin{cases} 1 & if\ x \geq 0 \\ 0 & if\ x < 0 \end{cases} \tag{11}$$

Then the conventional LBP is calculated as follows.

$$LBP = \sum_{i=0}^{7} s(g_i - g_c) 2^i \tag{12}$$

A sample calculation of conventional LBP for a 3x3 neighborhood is given in equation (13).

$$\begin{bmatrix} 123 & 110 & 113 \\ 117 & 120 & 135 \\ 130 & 125 & 128 \end{bmatrix} \rightarrow \begin{bmatrix} 1 & 0 & 0 \\ 0 & & 1 \\ 1 & 1 & 1 \end{bmatrix} \rightarrow \tag{13}$$
$$= 1*2^0 + 1*2^3 + 1*2^4 + 1*2^5 + 1*2^6 = 121$$

The LBP texture measure characterizes the pattern in the local region of a gray level image. To extend this for remotely sensed images with multiple bands, Lucieer et al. [2005] proposed the MLBP operator as defined in equation (18). Nine 3x3 matrices (with s(x) values) were formed from the local neighborhood of the remotely sensed image as described in the derivation of the proposed multivariate descriptor, MBTP. Out of nine, three describe the local texture (RR, GG and BB) while six more describe the cross relations of each band with other bands (RG, RB, GR, GB, BR and BG) where g_i^G stands for the gray level of ith neighbor pixel in the local neighborhood of G band.

$$MLBP = \sum_{i=0}^{7} \begin{matrix} s(g_i^R - g_c^R) + s(g_i^G - g_c^R) + s(g_i^B - g_c^R) + \\ s(g_i^R - g_c^G) + s(g_i^G - g_c^G) + s(g_i^B - g_c^G) + \\ s(g_i^R - g_c^B) + s(g_i^G - g_c^B) + s(g_i^B - g_c^B) + \end{matrix} \tag{14}$$

The MLBP histogram has 72 bins. The Pseudocode: 7 listed in appendix helps in finding conventional LBP. The procedure for land cover classification of remotely sensed image using MLBP and Fuzzy k-NN is given in Pseudocode: 8 listed in appendix. The classified image obtained following it is shown in Figure 9.

The MLBP texture model gives a classification accuracy of 88% because it uses only two discrete levels.

Figure 9. Classified image using MLBP and Fuzzy k-NN

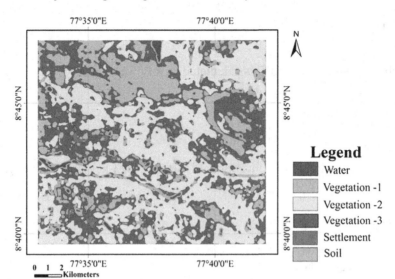

Discussion and Performance Evaluation of the Proposed Algorithm

For performance comparison of the proposed algorithm, texture-based classification was performed using MDLTP, MLTP and MLBP in combination with fuzzy k-NN classifier on the remotely sensed image shown in Figure.1. The classification results obtained are shown in Table 3. During the experiments, the threshold value for MLTP and MDLTP was fixed to 4. From the classified results, it is observed that Vegetation-1 class is seen minimally in Figure.9 and Figure.8 whereas it is nominally classified in Figure.7 but clearly classified only in Figure.6 (matching with the geological reference map) which is the reason why we get difference in classification accuracies. The Vegetation -1 and Vegetation -3 classes mark the initial and ripening phases of rice crop and are discriminated well in the classified

Table 3. Performance Comparison of proposed algorithm with existing methods

Name of the Algorithm	Number of Bins Used	Overall Classification Accuracy (in %)	Overall Kappa Coefficient
MBTP	286	96.2	0.9512
MDLTP	166	93.0	0.91
MLTP	46	90.4	0.8758
MLBP	73	88	0.852

image obtained using MBTP than others. From Table 3, it is understood that for discriminating the micro patterns (Vegetation-1 and Vegetation-3), more uniform patterns are needed which is possible only when the number of discrete levels used in the texture model is increased.

From the above table, it is inferred that the proposed model MBTP performs better than the chosen methods and gives 96.2% classification accuracy.

CONTRIBUTION OF THE CHAPTER

In the book chapter, a new texture model, MBTP has been proposed for land cover classification of remotely sensed images addressing the challenge of discriminating different types of vegetations. The performance of the new texture model was compared against the performances of a subset of chosen multivariate texture models and it is inferred that the proposed texture model yields high classification accuracy.

SOLUTIONS AND RECOMMENDATIONS

The challenges faced in land cover classification can be pointed as follows. The fact that the land covers have fuzzy pattern characteristics requires the issue of uncertainty to be addressed somewhere in the overall classification methodology. Improving classification accuracy is inevitable because a single pixel classification error in a remotely sensed image with a spatial resolution of 5.8m, covers an area of (5.8x5.8) sq.m. Another issue is related to the size and storage requirement of the remotely sensed images as they usually span across a huge area in ground. As these images are data intensive, when classification methodologies are developed, care should be taken to reduce the computational and runtime complexity. Finally for validating the classified results the authors must have a thorough knowledge of the area covered in the image and they must have geological reference maps and topo-sheets of the concerned area.

FUTURE RESEARCH DIRECTIONS

In future, the following research extensions can be performed on the proposed approach. The proposed algorithm can be extended to object-based image analysis. It may be applied on hyper spectral and synthetic aperture radar (SAR) images. It may also be extended to medical and biometric applications where high precision pattern discrimination is needed. The proposed algorithm can be extended for character and gesture recognition as well. The proposed algorithm will be useful in real world problems like early warning System, agriculture, tourism, meteorology, finance etc. where texture based techniques may be needed for prediction of missing or future data through modelling of variables in dataset.

CONCLUSION

A multivariate texture model (MBTP) is proposed for land cover classification of remotely sensed images. The proposed model extracts more uniform patterns than its predecessors such as MLBP, MLTP and MDLTP. The performance of the proposed model is proved with a high classification accuracy of 96.2%. Like conventional models, the proposed model can also be scaled to 5x5 and 7x7 neighborhoods as well. The benefits of the research work are as follows. In the proposed algorithm, high classification accuracy is achieved. Only minimum number of fuzzy training samples of size (16x16x3) was used. Furthermore, the uncertainty factor in assigning a land cover class label to a pixel is effectively handled by Fuzzy k-NN because it uses fuzzy membership values. The only limitation of the research work is that the proposed texture model, MBTP requires 286 bins.

ACKNOWLEDGMENT

The author is very grateful to the editor and the anonymous referees for the comments and suggestions, which led to the present improved version of the book chapter.

REFERENCES

Çavuşoğlu, Z. (2010). *Predicting Debt Crises in Emerging Markets Using Generalized Partial-linear Models. Term Project, Institute of Applied Mathematics*. Ankara, Turkey: Middle East Technical University.

Dai, D., Yang, W., & Sun, H. (2011). Multilevel local pattern histogram for SAR image classification. *IEEE Geoscience and Remote Sensing Letters, 8*(2), 225–229. doi:10.1109/LGRS.2010.2058997

Friedman, J. H. (1991). Multivariate adaptive regression splines. *Annals of Statistics, 19*(1), 1–67. doi:10.1214/aos/1176347963

Jenicka, S., & Suruliandi, A. (2014). A textural approach for land cover classification of remotely sensed image. *CSI transactions on ICT, 2*(1), 1-9.

Keller, J. M., Gray, M. R., & Givens, J. A. (1985). A fuzzy k-nearest neighbor algorithm. *IEEE Transactions on Systems, Man, and Cybernetics, SMC-15*(4), 580–585. doi:10.1109/TSMC.1985.6313426

Kuter, S., Akyürek, Z., & Weber, G. W. (2016). Estimation of subpixel snow-covered area by nonparametric regression splines. *The International Archives of the Photogrammetry, Remote Sensing and Spatial Information Sciences, 42.*

Kuter, S., Weber, G. W., Akyürek, Z., & Özmen, A. (2015). Inversion of top of atmospheric reflectance values by conic multivariate adaptive regression splines. *Inverse Problems in Science and Engineering, 23*(4), 651–669. doi:10.1080/1741 5977.2014.933828

Lu, D., & Weng, Q. (2007). A survey of image classification methods and techniques for improving classification performance. *International Journal of Remote Sensing, 28*(5), 823–870. doi:10.1080/01431160600746456

Lucieer, A., Stein, A., & Fisher, P. (2005). Multivariate texture-based segmentation of remotely sensed imagery for extraction of objects and their uncertainty. *International Journal of Remote Sensing, 26*(14), 2917–2936. doi:10.1080/01431160500057723

Ojala, T., Pietikäinen, M., & Mäenpää, T. (2001, March). A generalized local binary pattern operator for multiresolution gray scale and rotation invariant texture classification. In *International Conference on Advances in Pattern Recognition* (pp. 399-408). Springer Berlin Heidelberg. 10.1007/3-540-44732-6_41

Özmen, A., & Weber, G. W. (2012, November). Robust conic generalized partial linear models using RCMARS method-A robustification of CGPLM. In N. Barsoum, D. Faiman, & P. Vasant (Eds.), AIP Conference Proceedings: Vol. 1499. *No. 1* (pp. 337–343). AIP. doi:10.1063/1.4769011

Özmen, A., Weber, G. W., Batmaz, İ., & Kropat, E. (2011). RCMARS: Robustification of CMARS with different scenarios under polyhedral uncertainty set. *Communications in Nonlinear Science and Numerical Simulation, 16*(12), 4780–4787. doi:10.1016/j. cnsns.2011.04.001

Sari, K., Tighiouart, F., & Tighiouart, B. (2015). Using unsupervised neural network approach to improve classification of satellite images. *International Journal of Computer Applications in Technology, 51*(1), 3–8. doi:10.1504/IJCAT.2015.068393

Suruliandi, A. (2009). *Study on classification of remotely sensed multispectral mages-a textural approach.* Tamil Nadu, India: Manonmaniam Sundaranar University.

Suruliandi, A., & Jenicka, S. (2015). Texture-based classification of remotely sensed images. *International Journal of Signal and Imaging Systems Engineering*, *8*(4), 260–272. doi:10.1504/IJSISE.2015.070546

Suruliandi, A., & Ramar, K. (2008, December). Local texture patterns-a univariate texture model for classification of images. In *Advanced Computing and Communications, 2008. ADCOM 2008. 16th International Conference on* (pp. 32-39). IEEE. 10.1109/ADCOM.2008.4760424

Tan, X., & Triggs, B. (2010). Enhanced local texture feature sets for face recognition under difficult lighting conditions. *IEEE Transactions on Image Processing*, *19*(6), 1635–1650. doi:10.1109/TIP.2010.2042645 PMID:20172829

Vasant, P. (Ed.). (2011). *Innovation in Power, Control, and Optimization: Emerging Energy Technologies: Emerging Energy Technologies*. IGI Global.

Vasant, P. (2015). Handbook of Research on Artificial Intelligence Techniques and Algorithms (Vols. 1-2). IGI Global. doi:10.4018/978-1-4666-7258-1

Vasant, P. (Ed.). (2016). *Handbook of Research on Modern Optimization Algorithms and Applications in Engineering and Economics*. IGI Global. doi:10.4018/978-1-4666-9644-0

Vasant, P., & M., K. (2017). *Handbook of Research on Holistic Optimization Techniques in the Hospitality, Tourism, and Travel Industry*. IGI Global.

Vasant, P., & Voropai, N. (2016). *Sustaining Power Resources through Energy Optimization and Engineering*. IGI Global. doi:10.4018/978-1-4666-9755-3

Vasant, P. M. (Ed.). (2012). *Meta-heuristics optimization algorithms in engineering, business, economics, and finance*. IGI Global.

Vasant, P. M. (2014). *Handbook of Research on Novel Soft Computing Intelligent Algorithms: Theory and Practical Applications* (Vols. 1–2). IGI Global. doi:10.4018/978-1-4666-4450-2

Weber, G. W., Batmaz, İ., Köksal, G., Taylan, P., & Yerlikaya-Özkurt, F. (2012). CMARS: A new contribution to nonparametric regression with multivariate adaptive regression splines supported by continuous optimization. *Inverse Problems in Science and Engineering*, *20*(3), 371–400. doi:10.1080/17415977.2011.624770

Yu, W., Gan, L., Yang, S., Ding, Y., Jiang, P., Wang, J., & Li, S. (2014). An improved LBP algorithm for texture and face classification. *Signal, Image and Video Processing*, *8*(1), 155–161. doi:10.100711760-014-0652-5

APPENDIX

Pseudocode 1: Building Lookup Table

```
//Input        : 5⁸ possible pattern units
//Output       : Lookup table L(0:72,0:72)
L (0:72, 0:72) =0
b=0
for each pattern unit do
     Find uniformity measure (U)
        if U<=2
            Find NS and PS
              if (L (NS, PS) ==0)
                      L (NS, PS) =b
                      b=b+1
              end if
        end if
end for
end //end of Pseudocode
```

Pseudocode 2: Finding Binary Threshold Pattern

```
//Input         : p(1:3,1:3)holding the gray level intensity
values of 8 //neighbors in a 3x3 neighborhood and L(0:72, 0:72)
holding the //lookup table
//Output        : Binary Threshold Pattern value for the
center pixel of //the 3x3 neighborhood, BTP
//Let t1 and t2 be thresholds
t1=1;
t2=4;
// Let f(1:8) hold the gray level values of neighbor pixel
f(1:8)=0;
f(1)=p(1,1);
f(2)=p(1,2);
f(3)=p(1,3);
f(4)=p(2,3);
f(5)=p(3,3);
f(6)=p(3,2);
f(7)=p(3,1);
```

```
f(8)=p(2,1);
// Let gc hold the gray level value of the center pixel
gc=p(2,2);
// Finding discrete level of neighbor pixels in g(1:8)
for i=1:8
        if (f(i)<=(gc-t2))
            g(i)=-9;
        else if (f(i)<(gc-t1))
            g(i)=-1;
        else if (f(i)>=(gc-t1) && f(i)<=(gc+t1))
            g(i)=0;
        else if (f(i)<(gc+t2))
            g(i)=1;
        else
            g(i)=9;
        end if
 end for
//Finding uniformity measure U
 U=0;
 z=abs(g(8)-g(1));
 for(j=2:8)
          if(z==1 || z==8 || z==9 || z==10 ||z==2 || z==18)
                U=U+1;
               end if
       z=abs(g(j)- g(j-1));
 end for
// Finding BTP
 if (U<=2)
       NS=0;
       PS=0;
       for(i=1:8)
            if g(i)<0
                    NS=NS+abs(g(i));
            else
                    PS=PS+g(i);
            end if
       end for
       BTP=L(PS+1,NS+1);
else
```

```
        BTP=286;
end if
end //end of Pseudocode
```

Pseudocode 3:   Finding Fuzzy Membership Values for Fuzzy Training Samples Belonging to Six Land Cover Classes

```
Input: Six fuzzy training samples each of size (16x16x3)
Output: membership matrix me(1:6, 1:6)
// Read 6 fuzzy training samples in p{1:6}
for (i=1:6)
            p{i}= Read fuzzy training sample
end for
// Find MBTP descriptor
for (i=1:6)
            q{i}= Find MBTP descriptor for each 3x3
neighborhood of p{i}
end for
// Find MBTP histogram of the fuzzy training samples
c=16;
c1(1:286)=0;
for (j=1:6)
        temp1=q{j};
                for (u=1:c)
                    for (v=1:c)
                        c1(temp1(u,v))=c1(temp1(u,v))+1;
                    end for
                end for
w{j}=c1(1:286);
c1(1:286)=0;
end for
// Assign actual classes of fuzzy training samples in m2
m2= [1 2 3 4 5 6];
// In fuzzy k-NN, set k=3
k=3;
like(1:6)=0;
s(1:k)=0;
// Find distances of each fuzzy training sample with others,
sort and                       // choose 'k' nearest neighbors
with minimum distances. Find count            //
```

```
s(1:k) of each land cover class in 'k' nearest neighbors.
Apply                          // Keller's formula for finding
membership matrix.
for(i=1:6)
        temp2=w{i};
              for (j=1:6)
                like(j)=Find log likelihood distance between
temp2 and                          w{j}
        end for
[b1,b2] = SORT like(1:6) in ascending order
              t3(i,1:k)=[m2(b2(1)) m2(b2(2)) m2(b2(3))];
        for (l=1:k)
                  s(t3(i,l))=s(t3(i,l))+1;
        end for
            for (o=1:6)
                if (o == m2(i))
                        me(i,o)=.51+((s(o)/3)*.49);
                  else
                        me(i,o)=.49*(s(o)/3);
                  end if
          end for
              s(1:k)=0;
end for
```

Pseudocode 4: Land Cover Classification Algorithm Using MBTP and Fuzzy k-NN

Input: Read RGB bands of the remotely sensed image in p{1,1:3} and
RGB bands of six fuzzy training samples in p{2:7,1:3}.
Let the size of each band in the remotely sensed image be (mxn).
Let the size of each fuzzy training sample be (16x16x3).
Let me(1:6,1:6) hold membership matrix.
Let BTP be the function that reads a 3x3 matrix and returns its BTP value
Output: a classified result matrix rs(1:m,1:n)
// Find MBTP of each 3x3 nighbourhood of fuzzy training samples and   // remotely sensed image
c=16;

```
r=p{1,1};
g=p{1,2};
b=p{1,3};
for(i=2:7)
        for (j=1:3)
                o(i,j,1:c,1:c)=p{i,j};
        end for
end for
for (i=1:7)
    if(i>1)
                r=0;g=0;b=0;
                f1=0;f2=0;f3=0;f4=0;f5=0;f6=0;f7=0;f8=0;f9=0;
                r(1:c,1:c)=o(i,1,:,:);
                g(1:c,1:c)=o(i,2,:,:);
                b(1:c,1:c)=o(i,3,:,:);
    end if
    f1(:,:)= Find BTP for each 3x3 neighborhood of r;
    f2(:,:)= Find BTP for each 3x3 neighborhood of g;
    f3(:,:)= Find BTP for each 3x3 neighborhood of b;
    n1(:,:)= Find centerpixel of each 3x3 neighborhood of g;
    f4(:,:)= Find BTP for each 3x3 neighborhood of r using n1;
    f5(:,:)= Find BTP for each 3x3 neighborhood of b using n1;
    n1(:,:)= Find centerpixel of each 3x3 neighborhood of b;
    f6(:,:)= Find BTP for each 3x3 neighborhood of r using n1;
    f7(:,:)= Find BTP for each 3x3 neighborhood of g using n1;
    n1(:,:)= Find centerpixel of each 3x3 neighborhood of r;
    f8(:,:)= Find BTP for each 3x3 neighborhood of g using n1;
    f9(:,:)= Find BTP for each 3x3 neighborhood of b using n1;
//In order to find MBTP, the 'arrayfun' takes 9 pixels (one
from each                      //matrix) from the nine matrices
f1,f2,f3,f4,f5,f6,f7,f8 and f9 //obtained and forms a 3x3
matrix to find BTP.
    if(i>1)
                f10(i,1:c,1:c)=arrayfun(@BTP,f1,f2,f3,f4,f5,f6,
f7,f8,f9);
    else
            f11(1:m,1:n)=arrayfun(@BTP,f1,f2,f3,f4,f5,f6,f7,f8
,f9);
    end if
```

```
end for
// Find MBTP histogram of fuzzy training samples
c1(1:286)=0;
for i=2:7
        temp1(1:c,1:c)=f10(i,1:c,1:c);
        for (u=1:c)
            for (v=1:c)
                c1(temp1(u,v))=c1(temp1(u,v))+1;
            end for
        end for
        w{i}=c1(1:286);
c1(1:286)=0;
end for
// Call CLASSIFY subroutine to return land cover class values.
for (u=1:m)
            for (v=1:n)
h{u,v}= Read 16x16 window of values from f11 with the help of a
sliding window that moves from top left to bottom right padding
zeros wherever necessary.
                rs=call sub CLASSIFY(h{u,v},w,c)
            end for
end for
end //end of pseudocode
subroutine p=CLASSIFY(g,w,c)
// Find MBTP histogram of h
c1(1:286)=0;
for (u=1:c)
    for (v=1:c)
        c1(g(u,v))=c1(g(u,v))+1;
    end for
end for
// Call f_knn built-in function with relevant parameters
m1=cat(1,w{2}, w{3}, w{4}, w{5},w{6},w{7});
m3=c1(1:286);
m4=3;
[y,p]=f_knn(m1,me,m3,m4);
end sub
```

Pseudocode 5: Finding DLTP for a 3x3 Neighborhood of a Gray Level Image

```
//Input: The array p(1:3,1:3) holding the gray levels of pixels
in a // 3x3 neighborhood
//Output: The Discrete Local texture pattern value of the 3x3
//neighborhood in DLTP
// Let f(1:8) hold the gray level intensity values of 8
neighbors in a //3x3 neighborhood.
f(1)=p(1,1);
f(2)=p(1,2);
f(3)=p(1,3);
f(4)=p(2,3);
f(5)=p(3,3);
f(6)=p(3,2);
f(7)=p(3,1);
f(8)=p(2,1);
// Let L(0:72,0:8) array hold the lookup table
```

L=[1	2	3	4	5	6	7	8	9
10	11	12	13	14	15	16	17	0
18	19	20	21	22	23	24	0	0
25	26	27	28	29	30	0	0	0
31	32	33	34	35	0	0	0	0
36	37	38	39	0	0	0	0	0
40	41	42	0	0	0	0	0	0
43	44	0	0	0	0	0	0	0
45	0	0	0	0	0	0	0	0
46	47	48	49	50	51	52	53	0
54	55	56	57	58	59	60	0	0
61	62	63	64	65	66	0	0	0
67	68	69	70	71	0	0	0	0
72	73	74	75	0	0	0	0	0
76	77	78	0	0	0	0	0	0
79	80	0	0	0	0	0	0	0
81	0	0	0	0	0	0	0	0
0	0	0	0	0	0	0	0	0
82	83	84	85	86	87	88	0	0
89	90	91	92	93	94	0	0	0
95	96	97	98	99	0	0	0	0
100	101	102	103	0	0	0	0	0

104	105	106	0	0	0	0	0	0
107	108	0	0	0	0	0	0	0
109	0	0	0	0	0	0	0	0
0	0	0	0	0	0	0	0	0
0	0	0	0	0	0	0	0	0
110	111	112	113	114	115	0	0	0
116	117	118	119	120	0	0	0	0
121	122	123	124	0	0	0	0	0
125	126	127	0	0	0	0	0	0
128	129	0	0	0	0	0	0	0
130	0	0	0	0	0	0	0	0
0	0	0	0	0	0	0	0	0
0	0	0	0	0	0	0	0	0
0	0	0	0	0	0	0	0	0
131	132	133	134	135	0	0	0	0
136	137	138	139	0	0	0	0	0
140	141	142	0	0	0	0	0	0
143	144	0	0	0	0	0	0	0
145	0	0	0	0	0	0	0	0
0	0	0	0	0	0	0	0	0
0	0	0	0	0	0	0	0	0
0	0	0	0	0	0	0	0	0
0	0	0	0	0	0	0	0	0
146	147	148	149	0	0	0	0	0
150	151	152	0	0	0	0	0	0
153	154	0	0	0	0	0	0	0
155	0	0	0	0	0	0	0	0
0	0	0	0	0	0	0	0	0
0	0	0	0	0	0	0	0	0
0	0	0	0	0	0	0	0	0
0	0	0	0	0	0	0	0	0
0	0	0	0	0	0	0	0	0
156	157	158	0	0	0	0	0	0
159	160	0	0	0	0	0	0	0
161	0	0	0	0	0	0	0	0
0	0	0	0	0	0	0	0	0
0	0	0	0	0	0	0	0	0
0	0	0	0	0	0	0	0	0
0	0	0	0	0	0	0	0	0
0	0	0	0	0	0	0	0	0

0	0	0	0	0	0	0	0	0
162	163	0	0	0	0	0	0	0
164	0	0	0	0	0	0	0	0
0	0	0	0	0	0	0	0	0
0	0	0	0	0	0	0	0	0
0	0	0	0	0	0	0	0	0
0	0	0	0	0	0	0	0	0
0	0	0	0	0	0	0	0	0
0	0	0	0	0	0	0	0	0
0	0	0	0	0	0	0	0	0
165	0	0	0	0	0	0	0	0

```
];
//Let d hold the small threshold
d=4;
// Let gc hold the gray level intensity of the center pixel in
the                // neighborhood
gc=p(2,2);
p=1;
// Finding discrete level of neighbor pixels in s(1:8)
s(1:8)=0;
for(i=1:8)
        if (f(i)<(gc-d))
            s(i)=-1;
        else if (f(i)<=gc)
            s(i)=0;
        else if (f(i)<=(gc+d))
            s(i)=1;
        else if (f(i)>(gc+d))
            s(i)=9;
        end if
end for
// Finding uniformity measure U
U=0;
z=abs(s(8)-s(1));
    for(j=2:8)
        if(z==1 || z==8 || z==9 || z==10 ||z==2)
            U=U+1;
        end if
        z=abs(s(j)- s(j-1));
    end for
```

```
          if (U<=3)
              NS=0;
              PS=0;
                for(i=1:8)
                    if s(i)<0
                        NS = NS +abs(s(i));
                    else
                        PS = PS +s(i);
                    end if
                end for
              DLTP=L(PS +1, NS +1);
          else
              DLTP=166;
          end if
end //end of pseudocode
```

Pseudocode 6: Finding LTP for a 3x3 Neighborhood of a Gray Level Image

```
//Input: Let the gray levels of pixels in a 3x3 neighborhood be
in    // p(1:3,1:3)
//Output: Local texture pattern value of the 3x3 neighborhood
in LTP
// Let f(1:8) hold the gray level intensity values of 8
neighbors in a // 3x3 neighborhood.
f(1)=p(1,1);
f(2)=p(1,2);
f(3)=p(1,3);
f(4)=p(2,3);
f(5)=p(3,3);
f(6)=p(3,2);
f(7)=p(3,1);
f(8)=p(2,1);
// Let L(0:72) hold the lookup table
L=[1 2 3 4 5 6 7 8 9 10 11 12 13 14 15 16 17 0 18 19 20 21 22
23 24 0 0 25 26 27 28 29 30 0 0 0 31 32 33 34 35 0 0 0 0 36 37
38 39 0 0 0 0 0 40 41 42 0 0 0 0 0 0 43 44 0 0 0 0 0 0 0 45];
// Let gc hold the gray level intensity of the center pixel in
the                // neighborhood
gc=p(2,2);
```

```
//Let d hold the small threshold
d=4;
s(1:8)=0;
// Assigning discrete levels 0,1 and 9 to neighbor pixels
for(i=1:8)
if (f(i)<(gc-d))
s(i)=0;
else if ((gc-d)<=f(i) && f(i)<=(gc+d))
s(i)=1;
else if (f(i)>(gc+d))
s(i)=9;
end if
end for
// Finding uniformity measure U
U=0;
z1=abs(s(8)-s(1));
for(j=2:8)
if(z1==1 || z1==8 || z1==9)
U=U+1;
end if
z1=abs(s(j)- s(j-1));
end for
// Assigning pattern labels based on U
if (U<=3)
x=sum(s(:))+1;
LTP=L(x);
else
x=46;
LTP=x;
end if
end //end of pseudocode
```

Pseudocode 7: Finding Conventional LBP for a 3x3 Neighborhood in a Gray Level Image

```
//Input: p(1:3,1:3)holding the gray levels of pixels in a 3x3
// neighborhood
//Output: Local binary pattern value of the center pixel in the
3x3 //neighborhood stored in LBP
// Let f(1:8) hold the gray level intensity values of 8
```

```
neighbors in a // 3x3 neighborhood
f(1)=p(1,1);
f(2)=p(1,2);
f(3)=p(1,3);
f(4)=p(2,3);
f(5)=p(3,3);
f(6)=p(3,2);
f(7)=p(3,1);
f(8)=p(2,1);
// Let gc hold the gray level intensity of the center pixel in
the                // neighborhood
gc=p(2,2);
s(1:8)=0;
// Assigning discrete levels 0 and 1 to neighbor pixels
for(i=1:8)
if (f(i)< gc)
s(i)=0;
else
s(i)=1;
end if
end for
// the built-in function 'bi2de' performs binary to decimal
conversion        // considering left most bit as the most
significant bit.
LBP=bi2de(s,'left-msb');
end     //end of pseudocode
```

Pseudocode 8: Land Cover Classification Procedure Using MLBP and Fuzzy k-NN

```
// Input: Let the RGB bands of the remotely sensed image be in
p{1,1:3} and
// the RGB bands of six training samples be in p{2:7,1:3}.
// Output: a classified result matrix in rs(1:m,1:n)
// Let the size of each band in the remotely sensed image be
(mxn).
// Let the size of each training sample be (16x16x3).
// Let LBP be the function that reads a 3x3 matrix and returns
its LBP //value.
// Find MLBP descriptor of each 3x3 neighborhood of training
```

```
samples // and test samples extracted from the remotely sensed
image.
c=16;
r=p{1,1};
g=p{1,2};
b=p{1,3};
for(i=2:7)
        for (j=1:3)
                o(i,j,1:c,1:c)=p{i,j};
        end for
end for
for (i=1:7)
    if(i>1)
                r=0;g=0;b=0;
                 f1=0;f2=0;f3=0;f4=0;f5=0;f6=0;f7=0;f8=0;f9=0;
                r(1:c,1:c)=o(i,1,:,:);
                g(1:c,1:c)=o(i,2,:,:);
                b(1:c,1:c)=o(i,3,:,:);
    end if
//For computing f1 up to f9 and n1, consider 3x3 neighborhood
//extracted with the help of a sliding window that moves from
top //left to bottom right in the matrix padding zeros wherever
//necessary.
```

// Evaluating LBP^{RR}
```
    f1(:,:)= Find LBP for each 3x3 neighborhood of r;
```
// Evaluating LBP^{GG}
```
    f2(:,:)= Find LBP for each 3x3 neighborhood of g;
```
// Evaluating LBP^{BB}
```
    f3(:,:)= Find LBP for each 3x3 neighborhood of b;
    n1(:,:)= Find center pixel of each 3x3 neighborhood of g;
```
 // Evaluating LBP^{RG}
```
    f4(:,:)= Find LBP for each 3x3 neighborhood of r using n1;
```
// Evaluating LBP^{BG}

```
    f5(:,:)= Find LBP for each 3x3 neighborhood of b using n1;
    n1(:,:)= Find center pixel of each 3x3 neighborhood of b;
```
// Evaluating LBP^{RB}
```
    f6(:,:)= Find LBP for each 3x3 neighborhood of r using n1;
```
// Evaluating LBP^{GB}

```
    f7(:,:)= Find LBP for each 3x3 neighborhood of g using n1;
    n1(:,:)= Find center pixel of each 3x3 neighborhood of r;
        // Evaluating  LBP^GR
    f8(:,:)= Find LBP for each 3x3 neighborhood of g using n1;
// Evaluating  LBP^BR
    f9(:,:)= Find LBP for each 3x3 neighborhood of b using n1;
//In order to find MLBP, the 'arrayfun' takes 9 pixel values
(one //from each matrix) from the nine matrices
f1,f2,f3,f4,f5,f6,f7,f8 //and f9 obtained and sends them as
arguments to 'combine' //subroutine.
    if(i>1)
                f10(i,1:c,1:c)=arrayfun(@combine,f1,f2,f3,f4,f5,
f6,f7,f8,f9);
    else
                    f11(1:m,1:n)=arrayfun(@combine,f1,f2,f3,f4
,f5,f6,f7,f8,f9);
    end if
end for
// Find MLBP histogram of fuzzy training samples which has 73
bins.
c1(0:72)=0;
for i=2:7
        temp1(1:c,1:c)=f10(i,1:c,1:c);
        for (u=1:c)
            for (v=1:c)
                c1(temp1(u,v))=c1(temp1(u,v))+1;
            end for
          end for
        w{i}=c1(0:72);
c1(0:72)=0;
end for
// Call CLASSIFY subroutine to return land cover class values.
for (u=1:m)
            for (v=1:n)
h{u,v}= Read 16x16 window of values from f11 with the help of a
sliding window that moves from top left to bottom right padding
zeros wherever necessary.
                rs=call sub CLASSIFY(h{u,v},w,c)
```

```
            end for
end for
end //end of pseudocode
subroutine l=combine(f1,f2,f3,f4,f5,f6,f7,f8,f9)
s=[f1 f2 f3 f4 f5 f6 f7 f8 f9];
// the built-in function 'de2bi' performs decimal to binary
conversion        // considering left most bit as the most
significant bit.
x=de2bi(s,8,'left-msb');
l=sum(x(:));
end sub
subroutine p=CLASSIFY(g,w,c)
// Find MBTP histogram of h
c1(1:286)=0;
for (u=1:c)
    for (v=1:c)
        c1(g(u,v))=c1(g(u,v))+1;
    end for
end for
// Call f_knn built-in function with relevant parameters
m1=cat(1,w{2}, w{3}, w{4}, w{5},w{6},w{7});
m3=c1(1:286);
m4=3;
[y,p]=f_knn(m1,me,m3,m4);
end sub
```

Chapter 10

Supply Chain Network Design in Uncertain Environment:
A Review and Classification of Related Models

Gholam Reza Nasiri
Amirkabir University of Technology, Iran & Institute for Trade Studies and Research, Iran

Fariborz Jolai
University of Tehran, Iran

ABSTRACT

Dynamic environment imposes such conditions that make it necessary for companies to consider sources of uncertainty in designing core business processes and optimizing supply chain operations. Efficient management of a supply system requires an integrated approach towards various operational functions and related source of uncertainties. Uncertain conditions in supply network design problem such as market demands, delivery time, and facility capacity are considered and incorporated by many studies at the mathematical programming formulations as well. In this chapter, extensive review of existing SCND literature, brief overview and classification on uncertainty sources, useful strategies to deal uncertainties, model formulation with uncertain/stochastic parameters, efficient developed solution methodologies, and improvement adjustment mechanisms are discussed. Lastly, some directions for further research in this area are suggested.

DOI: 10.4018/978-1-5225-5091-4.ch010

INTRODUCTION

Supply Chain Management (SCM) includes all activities related to transportation, warehousing, work-in-process, finished products, financial, and information management flow from the origin point to the consumption/customers locations. The SCM involves integrating key business processes such as procurement, production, inventory holding, vehicle routing, pricing, and distribution strategies. In other words, Supply Chain (SC) is defined as an integrated system performing the functions of materials procurement, materials transformation into the intermediate and finished products, and furthermore, collaborative distribution processes to delivery finished products to the customers and consumers.

Nowadays, effective materials management, goods transportation, and product distribution's issues play an important role in successful organization competitiveness. In fact, the aforementioned issues have an enormous impact on improving productivity and flexibility, optimizing distribution cost and inventory amounts, resource utilization, and especially, better dealing with uncertainty (Turan et al., 2017).

Therefore, SCM deserves much more attention of researchers due to several reasons such as market globalization, growing competition among different SCs, information and communication technology development, more differentiation and uncertainties in marker needs and demands, and also shorter product life cycle time (Nasiri, 2009).

There are several major and important decision areas in SCM namely SC planning, SC Network Designing (SCND), network configuration, manufacturing strategy, inventory policies, and transportation (distribution) designing, as each one involves strategic, tactical, and operational decisions. Basically, while these areas were already considered separately, recent studies have attempted to investigate them simultaneously (Acar and Atadeniz, 2015; Glock and Kim, 2015).

This book chapter aims to explain integrated approaches to formulate SCND problem in uncertain environment. Moreover, it presents comprehensive overview on optimization models for distribution network design (DND), considering real world assumptions such as the effect of uncertainty on customer's demand, flexible inventory control policy, total network costs, and roles.

This book chapter will be organized as follows: in Section 2, the related literature review on SCND problem and categories of problem concepts, and features are presented. In Section 3, sources of uncertainty and well-known SCND strategies to deal uncertainty are defined more precisely. Section 4 presented the typical mathematical formulation of the DND problem. Furthermore, several proposed solution methodologies and solving mechanisms are explained in Section 5. Finally, in Section 6, concluding remarks are provided.

SCND LITERATURE REVIEW

The SCND is one of the strategic issues that required to be optimized in the SCM. This problem consists of selecting best sites for establishing and operating physical facilities (e.g., plants, warehouses, and distribution centers), assigning customers to the opened facilities, and interconnecting facilities via flow assignment decisions. The facility location problem (FLP) consists of choosing the best locations of desired facilities in such a way that all clients or partial of them can be served, at least by one operating facility to obtain pre-defined goals (minimizing total costs or maximizing total revenues). On the other hand, reverse logistics (also called recovery chain) planning for moving and flow of surplus or unwanted materials, and returned products to reuse or rework is also a well-known area in the SCND.

However, the dynamic facility location problem (DFLP) which is a specific version of the FLP considers the location of facilities and assignment pattern of customer during a planning horizon. According to fluctuation in pre-existed conditions in each period of the planning horizon, the location of facilities and assignment of each client are not fixed and may be changed.

Features of SCND mathematical formulation can be categorized into five stages (Figure1): problem definition and assumptions, objective function (contains the metrics that should be optimized), solution approach to solve the formulated model, and expected model's outputs.

Review of previous studies (e.g., Nasiri et al., 2010a; Mangiaracina et al., 2015; Govindan et al., 2017) indicated that important problem definitions and assumption include (Figure2): considered planning level (strategic, tactical, and operational, or all of them), SC products (single commodity or multi-commodity), facility location (single facility location or multi-facility location), nature of planning horizon (continuous or discrete), and finally type of planning period (single or multi-period planning). If the decisions have been made for a multi-period situation, one of the strategic decisions at the beginning of each planning period is location selection of the opened facilities; this type of SCND called location-relocation problem. On the other hand, considering the manufacturing sites location and the other operations features such as production volume at each sites and overtime production restrictions, makes

Figure 1. Components of SCND formulation

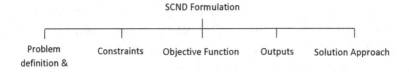

the formulated model more complex, which usually called production-distribution problem (Fahimnia et al., 2013; Nasiri et al., 2014; Olhager et al., 2015).

In fact, large investment on establishing and operating required infrastructure facilities at the supply network such as manufacturing sites, warehouses, distribution centers, etc., make this objective as a strategic decision at SCM (Mousavi et al., 2013). Therefore, prior researchers investigated cost minimization at their formulate model, which includes: investment cost for opening and operating facilities, transportation costs (unit cost of supplying raw materials from the suppliers to the manufacturing sites, unit cost of distributing finished product to the distribution centers and customers, and finally, transportation of returned goods), and inventory holding costs (Nasiri et al., 2010a; Yu and Lin, 2015). Figure3 illustrates the popular objective functions at the SCND. As seen in the Figure3, these objectives (e.g., maximizing revenues, minimizing delivery time, and minimizing expenses), in essence, are inconsistent/ conflicted with each other, which are considered as a multi-objective programming in the prior articles (Nasiri and Davoudpour, 2012; Salehi et al., 2015; Bilir et al., 2017).

Besides the economic goals that consider profit and sales maximization or cost minimization (e.g. facility location costs, operating costs, inventory system costs, logistics and transportation costs, processing/manufacturing costs, and so on), many researchers analyze other important objectives such as robustness, environmental impacts, service and responsiveness measures, and social responsibility in the SCND area (Govindan et al., 2017).

Constraint of the network entities is the other feature of the SCND mathematical programming model (Figure4). Capacity restriction of the facilities such as production capacity, storage capacity, transportation/vehicle capacity, and so on, make the

Figure 2. Classification of SCND problems

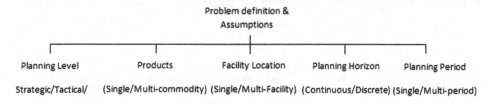

Figure 3. Classification of SCND objectives

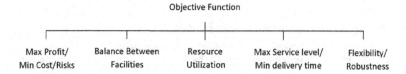

Figure 4. Classification of SCND constraints

model as a Capacitated Facility Location Problem (CFLP). Total customers' demand satisfaction, coverage restriction, pre-defined service level, single source supply, and the number of opened facilities are the other considered constraints on the SCND literature.

Since the FLPs are categorized as mixed-integer linear or non-linear programming models, powerful solution approaches are required to solve these complex problems in real world scales and sizes. Moreover, incorporating pricing strategy, inventory control policy, facility's capacities, and other network/logistics restrictions make these models more complex (Kaya and Urek, 2016). Therefore, the SCND model belongs to the NP-hard class of problems, developing heuristics and meta-heuristics algorithms have attracted the attention of many researchers during recent years (Melo, et al., 2009; Farahani et al., 2015). However, uncertain parameters such as customer's demands and unstable market make nature of SCND as a mixed-integer non-linear programming model. The review of SCND literature indicated that Lagrangian Relaxation (LR), Bender's decomposition, simulation, and population-based meta-heuristics are widespread algorithms applied to this type of strategic problems (Sourirajan et al., 2009; Sadjady and Davoudpour, 2012; Diabat et al., 2015 and 2017; Karaoglan and Altiparmak, 2015; Pereira et al., 2015, Zhang et al., 2016). The other approaches and outputs of the SCND are shown in Figures 5 and 6.

Figure 5. Classification of SCND solution approaches

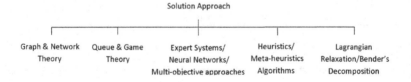

Figure 6. Classification of SCND outputs

At the end of this section the SCND problems are classified based on main aspects of SC including modeling approach, number of facilities, capacity restriction, and planning horizon nature (Figure 7). In the planar (or two-dimensional approach) the site location is calculated by longitude and latitude; therefore, three distance calculation methods are utilized. On the other hand, candidate points or notes to opening and operating facilities are considered in the network approach.

In the next Section, the well-known sources of uncertainty in SCND are presented and discussed.

SOURCES OF UNCERTAINTY

Review the literature of SCM indicated that uncertainty is defined based on characterize the nature of some conditions and situations which has three major indicators include volatility, complexity, and ambiguity that cause future prediction difficult or impossible.

Nowadays, globalization has significant impact on uncertainty, complexity, and high fluctuation in the business environment. In fact, free trade between countries causes to increasing global economic growth and wealth. But on the other hand, increasing market demands changing and decreasing goods life cycle time, face operations management of companies with more complexity.

Figure 7. Classification of SCND problem

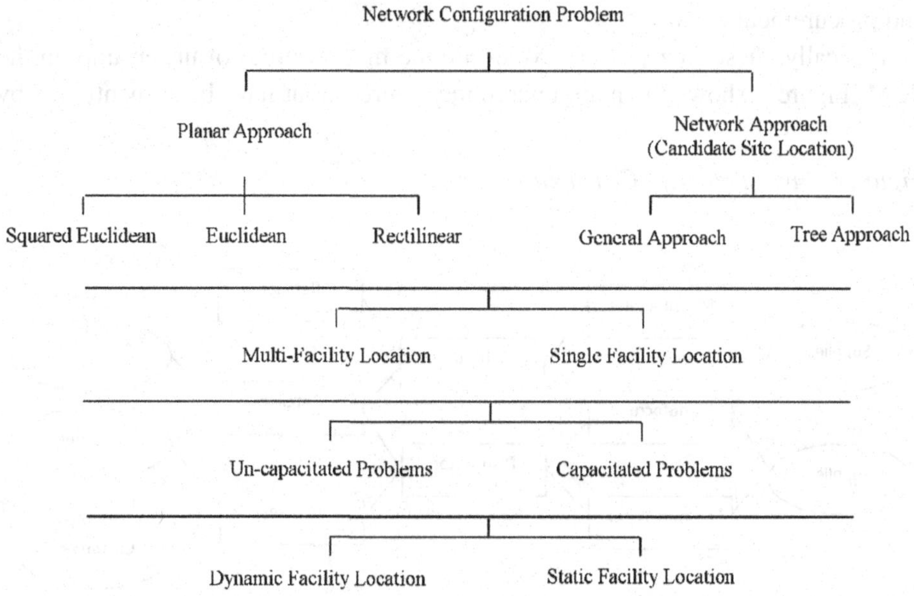

In this regard, dynamic environment imposes such conditions that make it necessary for companies to consider sources of risk/uncertainty in designing process of the SC. In order to use the most proper strategic decisions in a SC, decision makers should focus on the identification and management of the sources of uncertainties in the key SC processes toward better risk management and improve SC efficiency.

In this environment, occurrence of defect in one part of the SC, will affect to total performance of the whole chain. On the other hand, in several researches, uncertainties in supply, processes, and market's demands are recognized to have a major impact on the manufacturing functions. Davis (1993) mentions that the real problem in managing and controlling complex networks is "the uncertainty management". Uncertainty spreads throughout the whole chain and motivates the inefficient processes and non-value adding tasks. This uncertainty is expressed the questions such as: What customers now expect? How many goods we should store at the warehouses (finished products and raw materials)? Finally, according to the order specifications, when the suppliers will deliver the requested goods? Will they fulfill their commitments on time?

The presence of uncertainty stimulates the decision maker to create safety buffers in resources to prevent low SC performance; therefore it will cause higher supply costs and lower resources utilization.

In this section, these risk factors and main sources of them in the SCND problem, and parameter evolution over the planning horizon are considered. The well-known five- stage SC structure is shown in Figure 8.

Generally, all SC core processes within these five stages can be classified at four process cycles: customer order cycle, replenishment cycle, manufacturing cycle, and procurement cycle.

Basically, these four process cycles are the main sources of uncertainty in the SCM. Figure 9 shows the main uncertainty sources that have been mentioned by

Figure 8. Five stages of SC structure

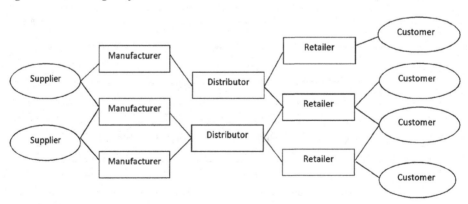

Figure 9. Classification of uncertainty sources

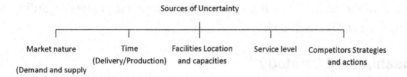

several studies (Song et al., 2017; Vahdani et al., 2013; Van der Vorst and Beulens, 2002). At the strategic level, these factors could be divided in two categories: microeconomics (dependent of internal nature of SC business) and macroeconomics (dependent on the external and the general nature of business).

Another classification of the logical foundation for uncertainty is:

- Inherent characteristics that influence predictable fluctuation in demand and supply;
- Potential properties that cause defective performance in SCM such as unflexible capacities, rigid network configuration, risk on information sharing, and so on.

Some major sources of uncertainty mentioned by previous studies can be summarized as follows:

- Unstable target markets situation through new players (companies and brands) and market share changing;
- Market demand's fluctuations base on high inflation rate on prices and costs;
- Actions of the other competitors through pricing strategies, promotions, and offered trade discounts to the customers that have significant influence on the market's demands and requirements;
- Complexity on demand prediction because of market nature such as correlated customers' demands, time dependent product's demands, and product's demands correlation, price dependent demands, and technology development.

Another relevant source of uncertainty is service level, which plays an important role at competitive SC planning. Service level includes several parameters such as: response time, product variety, product availability, previous customer's experience, order visibility, and return ability. In customers' point of view, these items must be maintained at the highest level by suppliers; therefore, this issue may impose additional costs of goods distribution at the SC.

Three helpful strategies to deal uncertainty and reduce supply risks that widely considered in the SCND literature are: transshipment, Multi-period planning, and

Multi-capacity facility location, which are cited in the model formulation and structure. In the next sub-sections, these three important issues regarding SCND problem are briefly discussed.

Transshipment Strategy

Literature review of transshipment cases indicated that this issue typically has two separate manners: preventive and emergency transshipment (Nasiri et al., 2015). The preventive transshipment referred to a situation that goods movement could be used in different facility locations at the same echelon of the SC before an inventory stock out happens at any DCs before demand's submission by any customers.

On the other hand, emergency transshipment demonstrated a situation that goods may be supply by any main distribution center to inventory stock out elimination at regular distribution branch after demand's submission by any customers.

Considering the supply lead time of finished product from central distribution center (CDC) to the warehouses/DCs, two types of DC have been defined in the SC: main and regular DCs. Due to flexibility aspects on product's lead time and reducing product stock out, each regular DCs may receive a part of its requested demands from the allocated main DC, instead of direct supply by the manufacturing plant or CDC (Figure 10). Therefore, the main DCs maybe play the role of secondary supplier of the regular DCs to cover the inventory at the delivery time. In this strategy, decision makers assumed that product shipment from assigned main warehouse are adequately fast to supply the DC which is facing product stock out.

Figure 10. Structure of SC with transshipment

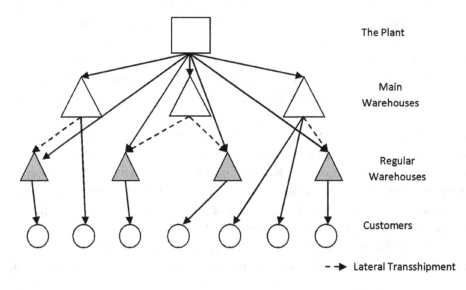

Multi-Period Planning Horizon

In real world, the single period SCND problem could not handle uncertainties in strategic decision making properly; therefore, these conditions could not guarantee appropriate efficiency of the designed SC. Due to the large investment on facility establishment, in dynamic location/relocation problem it is assumed that facilities can be located/opened, closed, and relocated frequently over the planning horizon (Nasiri et al., 2010b). Therefore, reviewing market conditions and considered business environment can help decision makers to update the data and develop adjusted strategies to the last SC situation.

Van der Vorst and Beulens (2002), suggest several strategies for decreasing uncertainty effects in SCM. They propose SC redesign strategies to focus on SC performance improvement. Furthermore, relocation of the located facilities is one of the most important strategies for controlling uncertainties in SCM (Nasiri et al., 2010b). Since establishment and setup a new facility is typically a costly and time-sensitive function, before facility establishment, best locations to access customers and facility capacity should be determined and sufficient amounts of investment budget must be allocated. Since the objectives of the facility location are dependent on the firm or government policy, the high cost associated with this process make almost any location decision as a long-term investment. During the facility's life time, changing trends in market demands and environmental transformation can turning today's optimal location into investment blunder at future. Thus, determining proper facility location is an important strategic challenge for each SC.

Based on the Correia and Melo (2017) study, many researches address the dynamic facility location in a multi-commodity, multi-echelon SC network up to now.

When the objective is cost minimization, a wide variety of models have been mentioned total network costs. On the other hand, some researchers propose another objective function category that maximized profit in SC and developed the branch and bound, LR, and heuristics algorithms for solving the multi-period facility location problem (Canel and Das, 1999; Hinojosa et al., 2000). Melo et al. (2005) propose a mathematical modeling framework that captures many practical aspects of network design problems simultaneously. These aspects include: dynamic planning horizon, generic SC network structure, external supply of materials, inventory levels of goods, distribution of commodities, facility configuration, capital availability for investment, and storage capacity restrictions. In this regard, Dias et al. (2007) formulate dynamic location problem with opening, closing, reopening of facilities, and propose an efficient primal-dual heuristic that computes both upper and lower limits to the optimal solutions. Tanh et al. (2008) consider a multi-echelon, multi-commodity production-distribution network with deterministic demands. The purpose of their paper is to help decision makers for strategic and tactical decisions such as opening, closing or enlargement of facilities, supplier selection, and flows along the SC.

The final strategy that is called multi-capacitated FLP is discussed in the next section.

Multi-Capacitated FLP

One major drawback in most previous articles in the context of SCND is that they limit CFLP by a pre-known specific capacity at just one level (Amiri, 2006; Nasiri et al., 2010b). However, at the real case problems may be there are multiple capacity levels available for each facility; therefore, decision makers could select the best position between two situations: higher investment to establishing bigger and less DCs in contrast with installing smaller but more DCs to satisfy allocated customer's demand. Multi-capacitated FLP allows several levels to the opened facilities; thus, this strategy makes the SCND problem more adjusted with the future uncertain conditions, but on the other hand, formulated model is more complex to be solved.

Equation (1) is the total cost function of DCs' location j ($\forall j=1, ..., J$) at capacity level h ($\forall h=1, ...,H$):

$$\min \sum_{j=1}^{J} \sum_{h=1}^{H} F_{jh} \cdot X_{jh} \tag{1}$$

where F_{jh} is the fixed cost of locating and operating DC_j ($j=1, ..., J$) at capacity levels h ($h=1, ...,H$), and X_{jh} is the zero-one variable. It takes 1, if a DC with capacity level h is opened on candidate location j, and 0 otherwise. Capacity constraint (2) ensures that each DC will be opened at only one capacity level:

$$\sum_{h=1}^{H} X_{jh} \leq 1, \forall j = 1,...,J \tag{2}$$

Mathematical formulation of SCND problem and useful measurement metrics are presented in the next section.

MATHEMATICAL FORMULATION OF SCND PROBLEM

Cost-based measurement metrics have a widespread use in the literature of SCND. Minimizing total cost of supply network such as investment of facility location, goods transportation, ordering, and holding inventory costs are considered in many articles. Furthermore, improvement of customer's service level and resource utilization are notified also. The well-known mathematical formulation characteristic of SCND problem is present in the next sub-sections.

Objective Functions

As it is mentioned in previous section, minimizing total investment costs in opening and operating facilities is a useful function that is formulated as follows:

$$\min Z_1 = \sum_{j=1}^{J} F_j \cdot X_j \forall i \tag{3}$$

where F_j is the fixed cost of locating and operating DC_j $(j=1, ..., J)$ and X_j is the zero-one variable.

For multi-capacity FLP additional summation on available capacities is needed (see Equation1).

The next function is transportation cost between pre-known and fixed plant location to the opened DCs, which is given by:

$$\min Z_2 = \sum_{j=1}^{J} \sum_{l=1}^{L} TC_{jl} \cdot D_{jl} \tag{4}$$

where TC_{jl} is the unit cost of transportation product l to DC_j from the plant and D_{jl} is the shipment/demand quantity of product l per time unit at DC_j.

Transportation costs of product l between the opened DCs and customers, which should be minimized is as follows:

$$\min Z_3 = \sum_{i=1}^{I} \sum_{j=1}^{J} \sum_{l=1}^{L} tc_{ijl} \cdot d_{il} \cdot Y_{ijl} \tag{5}$$

where tc_{ijl} is the unit cost of transportation product l from DC_j to customer i; d_{il} is the demand of customer i per time unit of product l, and Y_{ijl} is the allocation variable. It takes 1, if the DC_j supplies the product l of customer i, and 0 otherwise.

By incorporating inventory control policy into the FLP, joint location-inventory problem is introduced; therefore, additional costs such as ordering and inventory holding cost are mentioned in the objective function:

$$\min Z_4 = \sum_{j=1}^{J} \sum_{l=1}^{L} \sqrt{2 \cdot HC_{jl} \cdot OC_{jl}} \cdot \sqrt{D_{jl}} \qquad (6)$$

where HC_{jl} and OC_{jl} are holding and ordering cost per time unit of product l at DC_j to the plant, respectively.

If customer's demand is considered as an uncertain parameter and is assumed that market has stochastic (with Standard Normal Distribution) demand, in which d_{il} and v_{il} denote mean and variance customer i for product l, then the inventory safety stock that must be hold at each DC_j is shows by the following function (Nasiri et al., 2010a):

$$\min Z_5 = \sum_{j=1}^{J} \sum_{l=1}^{L} HC_{jl} \cdot Z_{1-\alpha} \cdot \sqrt{DELt_{jl}} \cdot \sqrt{V_{jl}} \qquad (7)$$

where $Z_{1-\alpha}$ is the value of the Standard Normal distribution, which accumulates a probability of $1 - \alpha$; $DELt_{jl}$ is delivery time of supply each product l from the plant to the DC_j, and V_{jl} is the variance of the demand per time unit of product l to be assigned to DC_j.

Penalty cost of inventory stock out (due to backorder) can be added in the objective function (see Miranda and Garrido, 2009):

$$\min Z_6 = Bc \left[\frac{1}{\sqrt{2\pi}} e^{\frac{-1}{2} z_\delta^2} - Z_\delta (1-\delta) \right] \sum \sum \sqrt{\frac{HC_{jl} DELt_{jl} D_{jl} V_{jl}}{2OC_{jl}}} \qquad (8)$$

where Bc is the backorder cost for each unit of unsatisfied demand and Z_δ is the Normal distribution value of the system service level δ.

For situation that delivery time also assumed as a stochastic parameter by mean $E(LT_{jl})$ and variance $\sigma^2_{LT_{jl}}$, the safety stock holding cost can be written by:

$$\min Z_7 = \sum_{j=1}^{J} \sum_{l=1}^{L} HC_{jl} \cdot Z_{1-\alpha} \cdot \sqrt{(E[D_{jl}])^2 \sigma^2_{LT_{jl}}} \cdot \sqrt{E(LT_{jl})V_{jl}} \qquad (9)$$

Minimizing total delivery time is the other objective function that is considered by the researchers (Nasiri and Davoudpour, 2012):

$$\min Z_8 = \sum_{i=1}^{I} \sum_{j=1}^{J} \sum_{l=1}^{L} (DELt_{jl} + delt_{ijl}) \cdot d_{il} \cdot Y_{ijl} \qquad (10)$$

where $delt_{ijl}$ is delivery time of supply each product l from DC_j to customer i.

The last objective function that is mentioned in this sub-section is DC utilization storage capacity, which can be determined by:

$$\max Z_9 = \sum_{j=1}^{J} \frac{\sum_{l=1}^{L} s_l \cdot D_{jl}}{cap_j \cdot X_j} \Bigg/ \sum_{j=1}^{J} X_j \qquad (11)$$

where s_l is the space requirement of product l storage at any DC and cap_j is the capacity limitation of DC_j.

In the literature, all above objectives have been considered, but more attention is paid to the cost minimization, and fewer cases take into account the profit maximization and multi-objective environments (Mangiaracina et al., 2015).

Based on the considered study situation and environment including healthcare SC, disaster, agriculture, FMCG[1], green SC, and so on, researchers formulate two or more goals at multi-objective cases.

Model Constraints

Two familiar constraints named single sourcing and DC's capacity restrictions are given by Equations (12) and (13):

$$\sum_{j=1}^{J} Y_{ijl} = 1 \forall i = 1,...,I, \forall l = 1,...,L \qquad (12)$$

which assure that each customer exactly is supplied for each requested product by one and only one DC.

$$\sum_{i=1}^{I}\sum_{l=1}^{L} d_{il} \cdot s_l \cdot Y_{ijl} \leq \sum_{h=1}^{H} cap_{jh} \cdot X_{jh} \, \forall j = 1,...,J \tag{13}$$

where cap_{jh} is the capacity limitation of DC$_j$ at level h.

Determination of solution methodologies to find optimal or near optimal mathematical model outputs are discussed in the subsequent section.

SCND SOLUTION METHODOLOGIES AND SOLVING MECHANISMS

The related literature presents different and various approaches to solve the SCND problems. For example, Amiri (2006) and Nasiri et al., (2010a and 2014) apply LR and sub-gradient search method in addition to the basic imbedded heuristics to obtain feasible solutions at each iteration. In these heuristics algorithms the main problem have been divided into two or more sub-models. Therefore, commercial optimization software (such as GAMS, LINGO, or CPLEX), or heuristics/meta-heuristics algorithms could be used to solve the generated sub-models.

Some papers solved the SCND through Branch and Bound considering the dual problem of a set of linear relaxations (Farahani et al., 2015). In addition, to evaluate the performance of the proposed algorithm in the large scale competitive SCs, the lower bound LP relaxation method is provided to show the quality of the model results(Nasiri et al., 2010a).

To solve multi-objective SCND problems many researchers used Multi-Criteria Decision Making (MCDM) techniques, Multi-Attribute Decision Making (MADM) methods, Analytical Hierarchy Process (AHP), and Goal Programming (GP) for assess the viability of the configuration of supply networks to aid the management for formulating the more efficient and effective business strategies (Nasiri and Davoudpour, 2012). Recently some authors utilized Non-dominated Ranking Genetic Algorithm (NRGA) and Non-dominated Sorting Genetic Algorithm (NSGA) to solve the formulated bi-objective deterministic/stochastic mixed-integer programming model of the SCND problem (Pasandideh et al., 2015). They reported that the results show the applicability of the proposed solution approach.

Furthermore, well-known meta-heuristics such as Genetic Algorithm (GA), Simulated Annealing (SA), Memetic Algorithm (MA), Artificial Immune Algorithm (AIA), Variable Neighborhood Search (VNS), and hybrid meta-heuristics are developed to solve the industrial real-size SCND models. Review of the SCND articles illustrated that population-based meta-heuristics such as MA, GA, and SA provided high quality results to the SCND problems. Furthermore, other solution approaches such as ε-constraint method, column generation, and L-shaped algorithm have been applied to solve SCND problem (Farahani et al., 2014).

CONCLUSION

In this book chapter, appropriate modeling structures that have been applied for SCND under uncertainty were notified carefully and the partly comprehensive review of FLP is presented. Characteristics of mathematical formulation were discussed in terms of general modeling attributes including problem definition and assumptions, objective functions, solution methodologies, and expected model's outputs. Common FLP objective functions such as investment on facility location, goods transportation, ordering, and holding inventory costs, improvement of customer's service level, and network resource utilization are discussed.

The SC risk factors and main sources of uncertainty in the SCND problem is considered and classified into six general categories which is defined as nature of marker demands and requirements, un-flexible capacities, rigid network configuration and location, risk on information sharing, service level, and competitors strategies and actions. Furthermore, three well-known strategies to deal to modeling DND with uncertain parameters are presented.

The first direction for further research is payment term, account settlement, and their important implications on goods price. Although pricing issue recently is incorporated in the SCND problem, but also considering the other marketing strategies on different sales & distribution channels and their effect on the market's demand is the other interesting research area to future studies. In this regard, analyzing competition factors to maximum income is necessary.

ACKNOWLEDGMENT

The authors would like to thank Dr. Mahyar Zaman for her valuable and constructive support, which improved the content essentially.

Additionally, the first author would like to acknowledge the financially support of the Institute for Trade Studies and Research under grant number 9606.

REFERENCES

Acar, Y., & Atadeniz, S. N. (2015). Comparison of integrated and local planning approaches for the supply network of a globally-dispersed enterprise. *International Journal of Production Economics, 167*, 204–219. doi:10.1016/j.ijpe.2015.05.028

Amiri, A. (2006). Designing a distribution network in a supply chain system: Formulation and efficient solution procedure. *European Journal of Operational Research, 171*(2), 567–576. doi:10.1016/j.ejor.2004.09.018

Bilir, C., Ekici, S. O., & Ulengin, F. (2017). An integrated multi-objective supply chain network and competitive facility location model. *Computers & Industrial Engineering, 108*, 136–148. doi:10.1016/j.cie.2017.04.020

Canel, C., & Das, S. R. (1999). The uncapacitated multi-period facilities location problem with profit maximization. *International Journal of Physical Distribution & Logistics Management, 29*(6), 409–433. doi:10.1108/09600039910283640

Correia, I., & Melo, T. (2017). A multi-period facility location problem with modular capacity adjustments and flexible demand fulfillment. *Computers & Industrial Engineering, 110*, 307–321. doi:10.1016/j.cie.2017.06.003

Davis, T. (1993). Effective Supply Chain Management. *Sloan Management Review*, 35–46.

Diabat, A., Battaia, O., & Nazzal, D. (2015). An improved Lagrangian relaxation-based heuristic for a joint location-inventory problem. *Computers & Operations Research, 61*, 170–178. doi:10.1016/j.cor.2014.03.006

Diabat, A., Dehghani, E., & Jabarzadeh, A. (2017). Incorporating location and inventory decisions into a supply chain design problem with uncertain demands and lead times. *Journal of Manufacturing Systems, 43*(1), 139–149. doi:10.1016/j.jmsy.2017.02.010

Dias, J., Captivo, M. E., & Climaco, J. (2007). Efficient primal-dual heuristic for a dynamic location problem. *Computers & Operations Research, 34*(6), 1800–1823. doi:10.1016/j.cor.2005.07.005

Fahimnia, B., Farahani, R. Z., Marian, R., & Luong, L. (2013). A review and critique on integrated production-distribution planning models and techniques. *Journal of Manufacturing Systems, 32*(1), 1–19. doi:10.1016/j.jmsy.2012.07.005

Farahani, R. Z., Bajgan, H. R., Fahimnia, B., & Kaviani, M. (2015). Location-inventory problem in supply chains: A modeling review. *International Journal of Production Research, 53*(12), 3769–3788. doi:10.1080/00207543.2014.988889

Farahani, R. Z., Rezapour, S., Drezner, T., & Fallah, S. (2014). Competitive supply chain network design: An overview of classifications, models, solution techniques and applications. *Omega, 45,* 92–118. doi:10.1016/j.omega.2013.08.006

Glock, C. H., & Kim, T. (2015). The effect of forward integration on a single-vendor-multi-retailer supply chain under retailer competition. *International Journal of Production Economics, 164,* 179–192. doi:10.1016/j.ijpe.2015.03.009

Govindan, K., Fattahi, M., & Keyvanshokooh, E. (2017). Supply chain network design under uncertainty: A comprehensive review and future research directions. *European Journal of Operational Research, 263*(1), 108–141. doi:10.1016/j.ejor.2017.04.009

Hinojosa, Y., Puerto, J., & Fernandez, F. R. (2000). A multi-period two-echelon multi-commodity capacitated plant location problem. *European Journal of Operational Research, 123*(2), 271–291. doi:10.1016/S0377-2217(99)00256-8

Karaoglan, I., & Altiparmak, F. (2015). A memetic algorithm for the capacitated location-routing problem with mixed backhauls. *Computers & Operations Research, 55,* 200–216. doi:10.1016/j.cor.2014.06.009

Kaya, O., & Urek, B. (2016). A mixed integer nonlinear programming model and heuristic solutions for location, inventory and pricing decisions in a closed loop supply chain. *Computers & Operations Research, 65,* 93–103. doi:10.1016/j.cor.2015.07.005

Mangiaracina, R., Song, G., & Perego, A. (2015). Distribution network design: A literature review and a research agenda. *International Journal of Physical Distribution & Logistics Management, 45*(5), 506–531. doi:10.1108/IJPDLM-02-2014-0035

Melo, M. T., Nickel, S., & Gama, F. S. (2005). Dynamic multi-commodity capacitated facility location: A mathematical framework for strategic supply chain planning. *Computers & Operations Research, 33*(1), 181–208. doi:10.1016/j.cor.2004.07.005

Melo, M. T., Nickel, S., & Gama, F. S. (2009). Facility location and supply chain management- A review. *European Journal of Operational Research, 196*(2), 401–412. doi:10.1016/j.ejor.2008.05.007

Miranda, P., & Garrido, R. (2009). Inventory service-level optimization within distribution network design problem. *International Journal of Production Economics, 122*(1), 276–285. doi:10.1016/j.ijpe.2009.06.010

Mousavi, S. M., Tavakkoli-Moghaddam, R., & Jolai, F. (2013). A possibilistic programming approach for the location problem of multiple cross-docks and vehicle routing scheduling under uncertainty. *Engineering Optimization*, *45*(10), 1223–1249. doi:10.1080/0305215X.2012.729053

Nasiri, G. R. (2009). *Multi-echelon, Multi-Commodity supply chain designing in an uncertain environment* (Ph.D. Thesis). Amirkabir University of Technology, Tehran, Iran.

Nasiri, G. R., & Davoudpour, H. (2012). Coordinated location, distribution and inventory decisions in supply chain network design: A multi-objective approach. *South African Journal of Industrial Engineering*, *23*(2), 159–175.

Nasiri, G. R., Davoudpour, H., & Karimi, B. (2010a). The Impact of Integrated Analysis on Supply chain Management: A Coordinated Approach for Inventory Control Policy, Supply Chain Management. *International Journal (Toronto, Ont.)*, *15*(4), 277–289.

Nasiri, G. R., Davoudpour, H., & Movahedi, Y. (2010b). A Genetic Algorithm Approach for the Multi-commodity, Multi-period Distribution Planning in a Supply Chain Network Design, SEMCCO 2010. *LNCS*, *6466*, 494–505.

Nasiri, G. R., Nasim, G., & Davoudpour, H. (2015). Location-inventory and shipment decisions in an integrated distribution system: An efficient heuristics solution. *European Journal of Industrial Engineering*, *9*(5), 613–637. doi:10.1504/EJIE.2015.071779

Nasiri, G. R., Roholla, Z., & Davoudpour, H. (2014). An integrated supply chain production-distribution planning with stochastic demands. *Computers & Industrial Engineering*, *77*, 35–45. doi:10.1016/j.cie.2014.08.005

Olhager, J., Pashaei, S., & Sternberg, H. (2015). Dessign of global production and distribution networks: A literature review and research agenda. *International Journal of Physical Distribution & Logistics Management*, *45*(1/2), 138–158. doi:10.1108/IJPDLM-05-2013-0131

Pasandideh, S. H. R., Akhavan Niaki, S. T., & Asadi, K. (2015). Bi-objective optimization of a multi-product multi-period three-echelon supply chain problem under uncertain environments: NSGA-II and NRGA. *Information Sciences*, *292*, 57–74. doi:10.1016/j.ins.2014.08.068

Pereira, M. A., Coelho, L. C., Lorena, L. A. N., & Souza, L. C. (2015). A hybrid method for the probabilistic maximal covering location-allocation problem. *Computers & Operations Research*, *57*, 51–59. doi:10.1016/j.cor.2014.12.001

Sadjady, H., & Davoudpour, H. (2012). Two-echelon multi commodity supply chain network design with mode selection, lead- times and inventory costs. *Computers & Operations Research, 39*(7), 1345–1354. doi:10.1016/j.cor.2011.08.003

Salehi, H., Moghaddam, R. T., & Nasiri, G. (2015). A multi-objective location-allocation problem with lateral transshipment between distribution centers. *International Journal of Logistics Systems and Management, 22*(4), 464–482. doi:10.1504/IJLSM.2015.072749

Song, W., Ming, X., & Liu, H-C. (2017). Identifying critical risk factors of sustainable supply chain management: A rough strength-relation analysis method. *Journal of Cleaner Production, 143*, 100-115.

Sourirajan, K., Ozsen, L., & Uzsoy, U. (2009). A genetic algorithm for a single product network design model with lead time and safety stock considerations. *European Journal of Operational Research, 197*(2), 599–608. doi:10.1016/j.ejor.2008.07.038

Tanh, P. N., Bostel, N., & Peton, O. (2008). A dynamic model for facility location in the design of complex supply chains. *International Journal of Production Economics, 113*(2), 678–693. doi:10.1016/j.ijpe.2007.10.017

Turan, B., Minner, S., & Hartl, R. F. (2017). A VNS approach to multi-location inventory redistribution with vehicle routing. *Computers & Operations Research, 78*, 526–536. doi:10.1016/j.cor.2016.02.018

Vahdani, B., Tavakoli-Moghaddam, R., & Jolai, F. (2013). Reliable design of a logistics network under uncertainty: A fuzzy possibilistic queuing model. *Applied Mathematical Modelling, 37*(5), 3254–3268. doi:10.1016/j.apm.2012.07.021

Van der Vorst, J. G. A. J., & Beulens, A. J. M. (2002). Identifying sources of uncertainty to generate supply chain redesign strategies. *International Journal of Physical Distribution & Logistics Management, 32*(6), 409–430. doi:10.1108/09600030210437951

Yu, V. F., & Lin, S.-Y. (2015). A simulated annealing heuristic for the open location-routing problem. *Computers & Operations Research, 62*, 184–196. doi:10.1016/j.cor.2014.10.009

Zhang, Y., Snyder, L. V., Ralphs, T. K., & Xue, Z. (2016). The competitive facility location problem under disruption risks. *Transportation Research Part E, Logistics and Transportation Review, 93*, 453–473. doi:10.1016/j.tre.2016.07.002

KEY TERMS AND DEFINITIONS

Facility Location Problem: Involves determining the best sites to establishing service facilities location at the considered network and the best strategy for connecting demand nodes to the located service nodes.

Supply Chain Management: Includes all activities related to transportation, warehousing, work-in-process, finished products, financial, and information management flow from the origin point to the consumption/customers locations, mutually.

Transshipment Strategy: Referred to a situation that goods movement could be used between different facility locations at the same echelon of the supply chain for customer service improvement.

Uncertainty: A situations which has three major indicators including volatility, complexity, and ambiguity that cause future prediction difficult or impossible.

ENDNOTE

[1]   Fast moving consumer goods.

Compilation of References

A., K., N., K., & M.M., H. (2011). Multi-Response Optimization of Diesel Engine Performance Parameters Using Thumba Biodiesel-Diesel Blendsby Applying the Taguchi Method and Grey Relational Analysis. *International Journal of Automotive Technology, 12*(4), 599–610.

Acar, Y., & Atadeniz, S. N. (2015). Comparison of integrated and local planning approaches for the supply network of a globally-dispersed enterprise. *International Journal of Production Economics, 167*, 204–219. doi:10.1016/j.ijpe.2015.05.028

Agarwal, A. K., Dhar, A., Srivastava, D. K., Maurya, R. K., & Singh, A. P. (2013). Effect of fuel injection pressure on diesel particulate size and number distribution in a CRDI single cylinder research engine. *Fuel, 107*, 84–89. doi:10.1016/j.fuel.2013.01.077

Amarnath, H. K., & Prabhakaran, P. (2012). A study on the thermal performance and emissions of a variable compression ratio diesel engine fuelled with karanja biodiesel and the optimization of parameters based on experimental data. *International Journal of Green Energy, 9*(8), 841–863. doi:10.1080/15435075.2011.647167

Amiri, A. (2006). Designing a distribution network in a supply chain system: Formulation and efficient solution procedure. *European Journal of Operational Research, 171*(2), 567–576. doi:10.1016/j.ejor.2004.09.018

Ando, N., & Taniguchi, E. (2006). Travel time reliability in vehicle routing and scheduling with time windows. *Networks and Spatial Economics, 6*(3-4), 293–311. doi:10.100711067-006-9285-8

An, H., Yang, W. M., Chou, S. K., & Chua, K. J. (2012). Combustion and emissions characteristics of diesel engine fueled by biodiesel at partial load conditions. *Applied Energy, 99*, 363–371. doi:10.1016/j.apenergy.2012.05.049

An, H., Yang, W. M., Maghbouli, A., Li, J., Chou, S. K., & Chua, K. J. (2013). Performance, combustion and emission characteristics of biodiesel derived from waste cooking oils. *Applied Energy, 112*, 493–499. doi:10.1016/j.apenergy.2012.12.044

ASTM Standards. (2016). Standard Specification for Biodiesel Fuel Blend Stock (B100) for Middle Distillate. ASTM.

Astolfi, A. (2006). *Optimization- An Introduction.* Retrieved from www3.imperial.ac.uk/pls/portallive/docs/1/7288263.pdf

Atmanli, A., Yüksel, B., Ileri, E., & Deniz Karaoglan, A. (2015). Response surface methodology based optimization of diesel-n-butanol -cotton oil ternary blend ratios to improve engine performance and exhaust emission characteristics. *Energy Conversion and Management, 90,* 383–394. doi:10.1016/j.enconman.2014.11.029

Babonneau, F., Vial, J.-P., & Apparigliato, R. (2010). Robust optimization for environmental and energy planning. In *Uncertainty and Environmental Decision Making* (pp. 79–126). Springer.

Bahrami, S., Hooshmand, R.-A., & Parastegari, M. (2014). Short term electric load forecasting by wavelet transform and grey model improved by PSO (particle swarm optimization) algorithm. *Energy, 72,* 434–442. doi:10.1016/j.energy.2014.05.065

Bajalinov, E. B. (2001). *Linear-Fractional Programming: Theory, Methods, Applications and Software.* Kluwer Academic Publishers.

Bandi, C., & Bertsimas, D. (2012). Tractable stochastic analysis in high dimensions via robust optimization. *Mathematical Programming, 134*(1), 23–70. doi:10.100710107-012-0567-2

Barnwal, B. K., & Sharma, M. P. (2005). Prospects of biodiesel production from vegetable oils in India. *Renewable & Sustainable Energy Reviews, 9*(4), 363–378. doi:10.1016/j.rser.2004.05.007

Bean, J. C. (1994). Genetic algorithms and random keys for sequencing and optimization. *ORSA Journal on Computing, 6*(2), 154–160. doi:10.1287/ijoc.6.2.154

Bellman, R. (2010). Dynamic Programming. In First Princeton Landmarks in Mathematics. Princeton University Press.

Bellman, R. E. (1954). Dynamic Programming and a new formalism in the calculus of variations. *Proceedings of the National Academy of Sciences of the United States of America, 40*(4), 231–235. doi:10.1073/pnas.40.4.231 PMID:16589462

Bellman, R. E., & Zadeh, L. A. (1970). Decision making in fuzzy environment. *Management Science, 17*(4), 141–146. doi:10.1287/mnsc.17.4.B141

Ben-Tal, A., den Hertog, D., De Waegenaere, A. M. B., Melenberg, B., & Rennen, G. R. (2013). Robust solutions of optimization problems affected by uncertain probabilities. *Management Science, 59*(2), 341–357. doi:10.1287/mnsc.1120.1641

Ben-Tal, A., den Hertog, D., & Vial, J.-P. (2015). Deriving robust counterparts of nonlinear uncertain inequalities. *Mathematical Programming, 149*(1-2), 265–299. doi:10.100710107-014-0750-8

Ben-Tal, A., El Ghaoui, L., & Nemirovski, A. (2009). *Robust Optimization. Princeton Series in Applied Mathematics.* Princeton University Press.

Ben-Tal, A., El Ghaoui, L., & Nemirovski, A. (2009). *Robust Optimization.* Princeton University Press.

Ben-Tal, A., Golany, B., Nemirovski, A., & Vial, J.-P. (2005). Retailer-supplier flexible commitments contracts: A robust optimization approach. *Manufacturing & Service Operations Management: M & SOM, 7*(3), 248–271. doi:10.1287/msom.1050.0081

Ben-Tal, A., & Nemirovski, A. (2000). Robust solutions of linear programming problems contaminated with uncertain data. *Mathematical Programming, 88*(3), 411–424. doi:10.1007/PL00011380

Ben-Tal, A., & Nemirovski, A. (2002a). Robust optimization–methodology and applications. *Mathematical Programming, 92*(3), 453–480. doi:10.1007101070100286

Bertsimas, D., Brown, D., & Caramanis, C. (2011). Theory and applications of robust optimization. *SIAM Review, 53*(3), 464–501. doi:10.1137/080734510

Bertsimas, D., & Caramanis, C. (2007). Adaptability via sampling. *46th IEEE Conference on Decision and Control,* 4717–4722.

Bertsimas, D., Dunning, I., & Lubin, M. (2016). Reformulations versus cutting planes for robust optimization: A computational and machine learning perspective. *Computational Management Science, 13*(2), 195–217. doi:10.100710287-015-0236-z

Bertsimas, D., & Georghiou, A. (2014). Binary decision rules for multistage adaptive mixed-integer optimization. *Mathematical Programming,* 1–39.

Bertsimas, D., Iancu, D. A., & Parrilo, P. A. (2010). Optimality of affine policies in multistage robust optimization. *Mathematics of Operations Research, 35*(2), 363–394. doi:10.1287/moor.1100.0444

Bertsimas, D., Litvinov, E., Sun, X. A., Zhao, J., & Zheng, T. (2013). Adaptive robust optimization for the security constrained unit commitment problem. *IEEE Transactions on Power Systems, 28*(1), 52–63. doi:10.1109/TPWRS.2012.2205021

Bertsimas, D., & Sim, M. (2004). The price of robustness. *Operations Research, 52*(1), 35–53. doi:10.1287/opre.1030.0065

Bertsimas, D., & Thiele, A. (2006). A robust optimization approach to inventory theory. *Operations Research, 54*(1), 150–168. doi:10.1287/opre.1050.0238

Betiku, E., Okunsolawo, S. S., Ajala, S. O., & Odedele, O. S. (2015). Performance evaluation of artificial neural network coupled with generic algorithm and response surface methodology in modeling and optimization of biodiesel production process parameters from shea tree (Vitellaria paradoxa) nut butter. *Renewable Energy, 76,* 408–417. doi:10.1016/j.renene.2014.11.049

Beyer, H.-G., & Sendhoff, B. (2007). Robust optimization – a comprehensive survey. *Computer Methods in Applied Mechanics and Engineering, 196*(33–34), 3190–3218. doi:10.1016/j.cma.2007.03.003

Bhatia, N., & Kumar, A. (2012). Mehar's method for solving fuzzy sensitivity analysis with LR flat fuzzy numbers. *Applied Mathematical Modelling, 36*(9), 4087–4095. doi:10.1016/j.apm.2011.11.038

Bienstock, D., & Ozbay, N. (2008). Computing robust basestock levels. *Discrete Optimization*, *5*(2), 389–414. doi:10.1016/j.disopt.2006.12.002

Bilegan, I., Faye, R. M., Cosenza, A. C. N., & Mora-Camino, F. (2003). A Dynamic Booking Model Revenue for Airline Management. *Journal of Decision Systems*, *12*(3-4), 417–428. doi:10.3166/jds.12.417-428

Bilir, C., Ekici, S. O., & Ulengin, F. (2017). An integrated multi-objective supply chain network and competitive facility location model. *Computers & Industrial Engineering*, *108*, 136–148. doi:10.1016/j.cie.2017.04.020

Birge, J. R., & Louveaux, F. V. (2011). *Introduction to Stochastic Programming*. Springer. doi:10.1007/978-1-4614-0237-4

Braekers, K., Caris, A., & Janssens, G. K. (2011). A deterministic annealing algorithm for a bi-objective full-truckload vehicle routing problem in drayage operations. *Procedia: Social and Behavioral Sciences*, *20*, 344–353. doi:10.1016/j.sbspro.2011.08.040

Braekers, K., Ramaekers, K., & Van Nieuwenhuyse, I. (2016). The vehicle routing problem: State of the art classification and review. *Computers & Industrial Engineering*, *99*, 300–313. doi:10.1016/j.cie.2015.12.007

Calafiore, G., & Campi, M. C. (2005). Uncertain convex programs: Randomized solutions and confidence levels. *Mathematical Programming*, *102*(1), 25–46. doi:10.100710107-003-0499-y

Campi, M. C., & Garatti, S. (2008). The exact feasibility of randomized solutions of uncertain convex programs. *SIAM Journal on Optimization*, *19*(3), 1211–1230. doi:10.1137/07069821X

Canel, C., & Das, S. R. (1999). The uncapacitated multi-period facilities location problem with profit maximization. *International Journal of Physical Distribution & Logistics Management*, *29*(6), 409–433. doi:10.1108/09600039910283640

Can, Ö. (2014). Combustion characteristics, performance and exhaust emissions of a diesel engine fueled with a waste cooking oil biodiesel mixture. *Energy Conversion and Management*, *87*, 676–686. doi:10.1016/j.enconman.2014.07.066

Capitanul, E. M. (2016). *Airport Strategic Planning under Uncertainty: Fuzzy dual dynamic programming approach* (PhD Thesis). Toulouse University-ENAC.

Capitanul-Conea, E., Krykhtine, F., Alfazari, H., Cosenza, C. A. N., & Mora-Camino, F. (2016). *Airport Planning using Fuzzy Dual Dynamic Programming*. Brazil: XV SITRAER, São Luis do Maranhão.

Capitanul, E. M., Cosenza, C. A. N., El Moudani, W., & Mora-Camino, F. (2014). Airport Investment Risk Assessment under Uncertainty. *International Journal of Mathematical, Computational, Physical, Electrical and Computer Engineering*, *8*(9), 1202–1206.

Çavuşoğlu, Z. (2010). *Predicting Debt Crises in Emerging Markets Using Generalized Partial-linear Models. Term Project, Institute of Applied Mathematics.* Ankara, Turkey: Middle East Technical University.

Chakraborty, C., & Chakraborty, D. (2006). A theoretical development on a fuzzy distance measure for fuzzy numbers. *Mathematical and Computer Modelling, 43*(3-4), 254–261. doi:10.1016/j.mcm.2005.09.025

Chamoli, S., Yu, P., & Kumar, A. (2016). Multi-response optimization of geometric and flow parameters in a heat exchanger tube with perforated disk inserts by Taguchi grey relational analysis. *Applied Thermal Engineering, 103*, 1339–1350. doi:10.1016/j.applthermaleng.2016.04.166

Chanas, S., & Zielinski, P. (2002). The computational complexity of the criticality problems in a network with interval activity times. *European Journal of Operational Research, 136*(3), 541–550. doi:10.1016/S0377-2217(01)00048-0

Charnes, A., & Cooper, W. W. (1959). Chance-constrained programming. *Management Science, 6*(1), 73–79. doi:10.1287/mnsc.6.1.73

Charnes, A., & Cooper, W. W. (1962). Programming with linear fractional functions. *Naval Research Logistics Quarterly, 9*(3-4), 181–186. doi:10.1002/nav.3800090303

Cheng, C. H. (1998). A new approach for ranking fuzzy numbers by distance method. *Fuzzy Sets and Systems, 95*(3), 307–317. doi:10.1016/S0165-0114(96)00272-2

Chen, M. J., & Huang, G. H. (1999). A derivative algorithm for inexact quadratic program – application to environmental decision-making under uncertainty. *European Journal of Operational Research, 128*(3), 570–586. doi:10.1016/S0377-2217(99)00374-4

Chen, X., Sim, M., Sun, P., & Zhang, J. (2006). A tractable approximation of stochastic programming via robust optimization. *Operations Research*.

Chiang, J., Yao, J.-S., & Lee, H.-M. (2005). Fuzzy inventory with backorder defuzzification by signed distance method. *Journal of Information Science and Engineering, 21*, 673–694.

Correia, I., & Melo, T. (2017). A multi-period facility location problem with modular capacity adjustments and flexible demand fulfillment. *Computers & Industrial Engineering, 110*, 307–321. doi:10.1016/j.cie.2017.06.003

Cosenza, K., El Moudani, & Mora-Camino. (2016). Introduction to Fuzzy Dual Mathematical Programming. In *Fuzzy Systems and Data Mining, Proceedings of FSDM 2016*. IOS Press.

Cosenza, C. A. N., & Mora-Camino, F. (2016). *Fuzzy Dual Numbers: Theory and Applications.* COPPE/UFRJ.

Craven, B. D. (1988). Fractional Programming. *Sigma Series in Applied Mathematics, 4*, 145.

Craven, B. D., & Mond, B. (1975). On fractional programming and equivalence. *Naval Research Logistics Quarterly*, 2(2), 405–410. doi:10.1002/nav.3800220216

Dai, D., Yang, W., & Sun, H. (2011). Multilevel local pattern histogram for SAR image classification. *IEEE Geoscience and Remote Sensing Letters*, 8(2), 225–229. doi:10.1109/LGRS.2010.2058997

Dantzig, G. B. (1947). Maximization of a linear function of variables subject to linear equalities. In Activity analysis of production and allocation. New York: Wiley.

Davis, T. (1993). Effective Supply Chain Management. *Sloan Management Review*, 35–46.

De Campos Ibanez, L. M., & Gonzalez Munoz, A. (1989). A subjective approach for ranking fuzzy numbers. *Fuzzy Sets and Systems*, 29(2), 145–153. doi:10.1016/0165-0114(89)90188-7

De, P. K., & Deb, M. (2015). Solution of fuzzy multi-objective linear fractional programming problems by Taylor series approach. *International Conference on Man and Machine Interfacing, IEEE- MAMI*, 1-5.

Deb, M., & De, P.K. (2014). Study of possibility programming in stochastic fuzzy multi-objective linear fractional programming problems by possibility programming. *8th IEEE Intelligent Systems and Control (ISCO)*, 331-337.

Deb, M., Das, D., & De, P. K. (2017). An approach to study the optimal solution of linear fractional programming problems under Intutionistic fuzzy setting. *Far East Journal of Mathematical Sciences*, 101(11), 24212443.

Deb, M., & De, P. K. (2015). Optimal solution of a fully fuzzy linear fractional programming problem by using graded mean integration representation method. *Applications and Applied Mathematics*, 10(1), 571–587.

Delage, E., & Ye, Y. (2010). Distributionally robust optimization under moment uncertainty with application to data-driven problems. *Operations Research*, 58(3), 595–612. doi:10.1287/opre.1090.0741

Delgado, M., Verdegay, J. L., & Vila, M. A. (1987). Imprecise Costs in Mathematical Programming Problems. *Control and Cybernetics*, 16, 114–121.

De, P. K., & Deb, M. (2013). Solving fuzzy linear fractional programming problem using signed distance ranking. *3rd IEEE International Advance Computing Conference*, 806-812. 10.1109/IAdCC.2013.6514330

Dhar, A., & Agarwal, A. K. (2014). Performance, emissions and combustion characteristics of Karanja biodiesel in a transportation engine. *Fuel*, 119, 70–80. doi:10.1016/j.fuel.2013.11.002

Diabat, A., Battaia, O., & Nazzal, D. (2015). An improved Lagrangian relaxation-based heuristic for a joint location-inventory problem. *Computers & Operations Research*, 61, 170–178. doi:10.1016/j.cor.2014.03.006

Diabat, A., Dehghani, E., & Jabarzadeh, A. (2017). Incorporating location and inventory decisions into a supply chain design problem with uncertain demands and lead times. *Journal of Manufacturing Systems, 43*(1), 139–149. doi:10.1016/j.jmsy.2017.02.010

Dias, J., Captivo, M. E., & Climaco, J. (2007). Efficient primal-dual heuristic for a dynamic location problem. *Computers & Operations Research, 34*(6), 1800–1823. doi:10.1016/j.cor.2005.07.005

Dorigo, M., Birattari, M., & Stutzle, T. (2006). Ant colony optimization. *IEEE Computational Intelligence Magazine, 1*(4), 28–39. doi:10.1109/MCI.2006.329691

Drexl, M. (2012). Rich vehicle routing in theory and practice. *Logistics Research, 5*(1-2), 47–63. doi:10.100712159-012-0080-2

Dubois, D., & Prade, H. (1979). Fuzzy real algebra: Some results. *Fuzzy Sets and Systems, 2*(4), 327–348. doi:10.1016/0165-0114(79)90005-8

Dubois, D., & Prade, H. (1980). *Fuzzy Sets and Systems: Theory and Applications*. London: Academic Press.

Durkota, K. (2011). *Implementation of a discrete firefly algorithm for the QAP problem within the sage framework* (BSc thesis). Czech Technical University.

Dutta, D., Rao, J. R., & Tiwari, R. N. (1992). Sensitivity analysis in fuzzy linear fractional programming problem. *Fuzzy Sets and Systems, 48*(2), 211–216. doi:10.1016/0165-0114(92)90335-2

Ebrahimnejad, A. (2011). Sensitivity analysis in fuzzy number linear programming problems. *Mathematical and Computer Modelling, 53*(9-10), 1878–1888. doi:10.1016/j.mcm.2011.01.013

El Moudani, W., & Mora-Camino, F. (2000). A dynamic approach for aircraft assignment and maintenance scheduling by airlines. *Journal of Air Transport Management, 6*(4), 233–237. doi:10.1016/S0969-6997(00)00011-9

Erera, A. L., Morales, J. C., & Savelsbergh, M. (2010). The vehicle routing problem with stochastic demand and duration constraints. *Transportation Science, 44*(4), 474–492. doi:10.1287/trsc.1100.0324

Esfahani, P. M., & Kuhn, D. (2015). *Data-driven distributionally robust optimization using the Wasserstein metric: Performance guarantees and tractable reformulations*. arXiv preprint arXiv:1505.05116

Esogbue & Bellman. (n.d.). Fuzzy Dynamic Programming and its Extensions. *TIMS/Studies in the Management Sciences, 20*, 147-167.

Fahimnia, B., Farahani, R. Z., Marian, R., & Luong, L. (2013). A review and critique on integrated production-distribution planning models and techniques. *Journal of Manufacturing Systems, 32*(1), 1–19. doi:10.1016/j.jmsy.2012.07.005

Fama, E. F., & French, K. R. (1993). Common risk factors in the returns on stocks and bonds. *Journal of Financial Economics*, *33*(1), 3–56. doi:10.1016/0304-405X(93)90023-5

Farahani, R. Z., Bajgan, H. R., Fahimnia, B., & Kaviani, M. (2015). Location-inventory problem in supply chains: A modeling review. *International Journal of Production Research*, *53*(12), 3769–3788. doi:10.1080/00207543.2014.988889

Farahani, R. Z., Rezapour, S., Drezner, T., & Fallah, S. (2014). Competitive supply chain network design: An overview of classifications, models, solution techniques and applications. *Omega*, *45*, 92–118. doi:10.1016/j.omega.2013.08.006

Farhadinia, B. (2014). Pontryagin's Minimum Principle for Fuzzy Optimal Control Problems. *Iranian Journal of Fuzzy Sets*, *11*(2), 27–43.

Farhadinia, B. (2014). Sensitivity analysis in interval-valued trapezoidal fuzzy number linear programming problems. *Applied Mathematical Modelling*, *38*(1), 50–62. doi:10.1016/j.apm.2013.05.033

Faye, R. M., Sawadogo, S., Lishou, C., & Mora-Camino, F. (2003). Long-term Fuzzy Management of Water Resource Systems. *J. of Applied Mathematics and Computation*, *137*(2-3), 459–475. doi:10.1016/S0096-3003(02)00151-0

Faye, R. M., Sawadogo, S., & Mora-Camino, F. (2002). Logique floue Appliquée à la Gestion à Long-terme des Resources en Eau. *Revue des Sciences de l'Eau*, *15*(3), 579–596. doi:10.7202/705470ar

Fisher, I. S. (1999). *Dual-Number Methods in Kinematics, Statics and Dynamics*. CRC Press.

Fredriksson, A., Forsgren, A., & H°ardemark, B. (2011). Minimax optimization for handling range and setup uncertainties in proton therapy. *Medical Physics*, *38*(3), 1672–1684. doi:10.1118/1.3556559 PMID:21520880

Friedman, J. H. (1991). Multivariate adaptive regression splines. *Annals of Statistics*, *19*(1), 1–67. doi:10.1214/aos/1176347963

Gabrel, V., Murat, C., & Thiele, A. (2014). Recent advances in robust optimization: An overview. *European Journal of Operational Research*, *235*(3), 471–483. doi:10.1016/j.ejor.2013.09.036

Gal, T., & Greenbers, H. J. (Eds.). (1997). *Advances in Sensitivity Analysis and Parametric Programming*. Kluwer Academic Publishers. doi:10.1007/978-1-4615-6103-3

Ganapathy, T., Gakkhar, R. P., & Murugesan, K. (2011). Influence of injection timing on performance, combustion and emission characteristics of Jatropha biodiesel engine. *Applied Energy*, *88*(12), 4376–4386. doi:10.1016/j.apenergy.2011.05.016

Ganapathy, T., Murugesan, K., & Gakkhar, R. P. (2009). Performance optimization of Jatropha biodiesel engine model using Taguchi approach. *Applied Energy*, *86*(11), 2476–2486. doi:10.1016/j.apenergy.2009.02.008

Gani, A. N., & Assarudeen, S. N. M. (2012). A new operation on triangular fuzzy number for solving fuzzy linear programming problem. *Applied Mathematical Sciences, 6*(11), 525–532.

Gani, A. N., Duraisamy, C., & Veeramani, C. (2009). A note on fuzzy linear programming problem using LR-fuzzy number. *International Journal of Algorithms, Computing and Mathematics, 2*(3), 93–106.

Gendreau, M., Laporte, G., & Séguin, R. (1995). An exact algorithm for the vehicle routing problem with stochastic demands and customers. *Transportation Science, 29*(2), 143–155. doi:10.1287/trsc.29.2.143

Gendreau, M., Laporte, G., & Séguin, R. (1996). A tabu search heuristic for the vehicle routing problem with stochastic demands and customers. *Operations Research, 44*(3), 469–477. doi:10.1287/opre.44.3.469

Georghiou, A., Wiesemann, W., & Kuhn, D. (2015). Generalized decision rule approximations for stochastic programming via liftings. *Mathematical Programming, 152*(1-2), 301–338. doi:10.100710107-014-0789-6

Gerla, G., & Volpe, R. (1986). The definition of distance and diameter in fuzzy set theory, *Studia Univ. Babes-Bolyai Ser. Math., 31*, 21–26.

Ghobadian, B., Rahimi, H., Nikbakht, A. M., Najafi, G., & Yusaf, T. F. (2009). Diesel engine performance and exhaust emission analysis using waste cooking biodiesel fuel with an artificial neural network. *Renewable Energy, 34*(4), 976–982. doi:10.1016/j.renene.2008.08.008

Glock, C. H., & Kim, T. (2015). The effect of forward integration on a single-vendor-multi-retailer supply chain under retailer competition. *International Journal of Production Economics, 164*, 179–192. doi:10.1016/j.ijpe.2015.03.009

Goel, L., Jain, N., & Srivastava, S. (2017). A novel PSO based algorithm to find initial seeds for the k-means clustering algorithm. *Proceedings of the International Conference on Communication and Computing Systems (ICCCS 2016).*

Goh & Sim. (2010). Distributionally robust optimization and its tractable approximations. *Operations Research, 58*(4-part-1), 902–917.

Gorissen, B. L., Yanıkoğlu, İ., & den Hertog, D. (2015). A practical guide to robust optimization. *Omega, 53*, 124–137. doi:10.1016/j.omega.2014.12.006

Govindan, K., Fattahi, M., & Keyvanshokooh, E. (2017). Supply chain network design under uncertainty: A comprehensive review and future research directions. *European Journal of Operational Research, 263*(1), 108–141. doi:10.1016/j.ejor.2017.04.009

Graboski, M. S., & McCormick, R. L. (1998). Combustion of fat and vegetable oil derived fuels in diesel engines. *Progress in Energy and Combustion Science, 24*(2), 125–164. doi:10.1016/S0360-1285(97)00034-8

Gumus, M. (2010). A comprehensive experimental investigation of combustion and heat release characteristics of a biodiesel (hazelnut kernel oil methyl ester) fueled direct injection compression ignition engine. *Fuel*, *89*(10), 2802–2814. doi:10.1016/j.fuel.2010.01.035

Gupta, P. K. (1987). *Linear Programming and Theory of Games* (1st ed.). Khanna Publishers.

Gupta, P., & Bhatia, D. (2001). Sensitivity analysis in fuzzy multi-objective linear fractional programming problem. *Fuzzy Sets and Systems*, *122*(2), 229–236. doi:10.1016/S0165-0114(99)00164-5

Hagelauer, P., & Mora-Camino, F. (1998). A Soft Dynamic Programming Approach for On-line Aircraft 4D-trajectory Optimization. *European Journal of Operational Research*, *107*(1), 87–95. doi:10.1016/S0377-2217(97)00221-X

Hamacher, H., Leberling, H., & Zimmermann, H.-J. (1978). Sensitivity analysis in fuzzy linear programming problem. *Fuzzy Sets and Systems*, *1*(4), 269–281. doi:10.1016/0165-0114(78)90018-0

Hamadneh, N. (2013). *Logic Programming in Radial Basis Function Neural Networks*. Universiti Sains Malaysia.

Hamadneh, N., Khan, W. A., Sathasivam, S., & Ong, H. C. (2013). Design optimization of pin fin geometry using particle swarm optimization algorithm. *PLoS One*, *8*(5).

Hamadneh, N., Sathasivam, S., Tilahun, S. L., & Choon, O. H. (2012). Learning Logic Programming in Radial Basis Function Network via Genetic Algorithm. *Journal of Applied Sciences (Faisalabad)*, *12*(9), 840–847. doi:10.3923/jas.2012.840.847

Hamadneh, N., Tilahun, S. L., Sathasivam, S., & Choon, O. H. (2013). Prey-Predator Algorithm as a New Optimization Technique Using in Radial Basis Function Neural Networks. *Research Journal of Applied Sciences*, *8*(7), 383–387.

Hartl, R. F., Hasle, G., & Janssens, G. K. (2006). Editorial to the Special Issue on Rich Vehicle Routing Problems. *Central European Journal of Operations Research*, *14*(2), 103–104. doi:10.100710100-006-0162-9

Haughton, M. A. (1998). The performance of route modification and demand stabilization strategies in stochastic vehicle routing. *Transportation Research Part B: Methodological*, *32*(8), 551–566. doi:10.1016/S0191-2615(98)00017-4

Heilpern, S. (1997). Representation and application of fuzzy numbers. *Fuzzy Sets and Systems*, *91*(2), 259–268. doi:10.1016/S0165-0114(97)00146-2

Heywood, J. (1988). *Pollutant formation and control in internal combustion engine fundamentals*. New York: McGraw-Hill.

Hinojosa, Y., Puerto, J., & Fernandez, F. R. (2000). A multi-period two-echelon multi-commodity capacitated plant location problem. *European Journal of Operational Research*, *123*(2), 271–291. doi:10.1016/S0377-2217(99)00256-8

Hirkude, J. B., & Padalkar, A. S. (2014). Performance optimization of CI engine fuelled with waste fried oil methyl ester-diesel blend using response surface methodology. *Fuel, 119,* 266–273. doi:10.1016/j.fuel.2013.11.039

Huang, G. H. (1994). *Grey mathematical programming and its application to municipal solid waste management planning.* McMaster University.

Huang, G. H. (1994). *Grey mathematical programming and its application to municipal waste management planning* (Ph.D. Dissertation). McMaster University, Hamilton, Canada.

Huang, G. H., Baetz, B. W., & Patry, G. G. (1995). Grey Quadratic Programming and Its Application to Municipal Solid Waste Management Planning Under Uncertainty. *Engineering Optimization, 23*(3), 201–223. doi:10.1080/03052159508941354

Huang, G., Baetz, B. W., & Patry, G. G. (1992). A Grey Linear Programming Approach for Municipal Solid Waste Management Planning Under Uncertainty. *Civil Engineering Systems, 9*(4), 319–335. doi:10.1080/02630259208970657

Huang, G., & Dan Moore, R. (1993). Grey linear programming, its solving approach, and its application. *International Journal of Systems Science, 24*(1), 159–172. doi:10.1080/00207729308949477

Huang, G.-H., & Loucks, D. P. (2000). An inexact two-stage stochastic programming model for water resources management under uncertainty. *Civil Engineering Systems, 17*(2), 95–118. doi:10.1080/02630250008970277

Huang, Z. H., Lu, H. B., Jiang, D. M., Zeng, K., Liu, B., Zhang, J. Q., & Wang, X. B. (2004). Combustion characteristics and heat release analysis of a compression ignition engine operating on a diesel/methanol blend. *Proceedings of the Institution of Mechanical Engineers. Part D, Journal of Automobile Engineering, 218*(9), 1011–1024. doi:10.1243/0954407041856818

Hwang, J., Jung, Y., & Bae, C. (2015). Spray and combustion of waste cooking oil biodiesel in a compression-ignition engine. *International Journal of Engine Research, 16*(5), 664–679. doi:10.1177/1468087415585282

Iancu, D., & Trichakis, N. (2013). Pareto efficiency in robust optimization. *Management Science, 60*(1), 130–147. doi:10.1287/mnsc.2013.1753

Ishibuchi, H., & Tanaka, H. (1990). Multiobjective programming in optimization of the interval objective function. *European Journal of Operational Research, 48*(2), 219–225. doi:10.1016/0377-2217(90)90375-L

Jadhav, S. D., & Tandale, M. S. (2016). Multi-objective Performance Optimization of Compression Ignition Engine Operated on Mangifera Indica Biodiesel by Applying Taguchi Grey Relational Analysis. *Waste and Biomass Valorization, 7*(5), 1309–1325. doi:10.100712649-016-9504-6

Jain, R. (1976). Decision making in the presence of fuzzy variable. *IEEE Transactions on Systems, Man, and Cybernetics, 6,* 698–703.

Jenicka, S., & Suruliandi, A. (2014). A textural approach for land cover classification of remotely sensed image. *CSI transactions on ICT, 2*(1), 1-9.

Jershan, C., Yao, J.-S., & Lee, H.-M. (2005). Fuzzy inventory with backorder. *Journal of Information Science and Engineering, 21*, 673–694.

Jin, Hu, & Chan. (2013). *A Genetic-Algorithms-Based Approach for Programming Linear and Quadratic Optimization Problems with Uncertainty.* Hindawi Publishing Corporation Mathematical Problems in Engineering.

Jin. (2005). *A Genetic Algorithms Framework for Grey Non-Linear Programming Problems.* Saskatoon: IEEE CCECE/CCGEI.

Jin, W. H., Hu, Z. Y., & Chan, C. (2017). An Innovative Genetic Algorithms-Based Inexact Non-Linear Programming Problem Solving Method. *Journal of Environmental Protection, 8*(03), 231–249. doi:10.4236/jep.2017.83018

Joshi, R. (2013). Optimization Techniques for Transportation Problems of Three Variables. *IOSR Journal of Mathematics, 9*(1), 46–50. doi:10.9790/5728-0914650

Julong, D. (1982). Control problems of Grey Systems, systems and Control Letters,(1) 5,288-94.

Ju-long, D. (1982). Control problems of grey systems. *Systems & Control Letters, 1*(5), 288–294. doi:10.1016/S0167-6911(82)80025-X

Julong, D. (1989). Introduction to grey system theory. *Journal of Grey System, 1*(1), 1–24.

Julong, D. (1989). Introduction to Grey System Theory. *Journal of Grey System, 1*(1), 1–24.

Kacprzyk, J. (1983). *Multistage Decision Making under Fuzziness. Verlag TÜV.*

Kacprzyk, J., & Esogbue, A. O. (1996). Fuzzy Dynamic Programming: Main Developments and Applications. *Fuzzy Sets and Systems, 81*(1), 31–45. doi:10.1016/0165-0114(95)00239-1

Kaleva, O., & Seikkala, S. (1984). On fuzzy metric spaces. *Fuzzy Sets and Systems, 12*(3), 215–229. doi:10.1016/0165-0114(84)90069-1

Kantorrovich, L. V. (1940). A new method of solving some classes of extremal problems. *Doklady Akad Science, 28*, 211–214.

Karaoglan, I., & Altiparmak, F. (2015). A memetic algorithm for the capacitated location-routing problem with mixed backhauls. *Computers & Operations Research, 55*, 200–216. doi:10.1016/j.cor.2014.06.009

Karuppasamy, K., & Basha, C. A. (2012). The Effect of Biodiesel Blends on Single Cylinder DI Diesel Engine and Optimization using Response Surface Methodology. *European Journal of Scientific Research, 84*(3), 365–376.

Kaufmann, A., & Gupta, M. M. (1991). *Introduction to Fuzzy Arithmetic, Theory and Applications.* New York: Van Nostrand Reinhold.

Kayacan, E., Ulutas, B., & Kaynak, O. (2010). Grey system theory-based models in time series prediction. *Expert Systems with Applications*, *37*(2), 1784–1789. doi:10.1016/j.eswa.2009.07.064

Kaya, O., & Urek, B. (2016). A mixed integer nonlinear programming model and heuristic solutions for location, inventory and pricing decisions in a closed loop supply chain. *Computers & Operations Research*, *65*, 93–103. doi:10.1016/j.cor.2015.07.005

Keller, J. M., Gray, M. R., & Givens, J. A. (1985). A fuzzy k-nearest neighbor algorithm. *IEEE Transactions on Systems, Man, and Cybernetics*, *SMC-15*(4), 580–585. doi:10.1109/TSMC.1985.6313426

Kennedy, J., & Eberhart, R. (1995). *Particle swarm optimization.* Paper presented at the International Conference on Neural Networks IV, Perth, Australia. 10.1109/ICNN.1995.488968

Khan, W. A., Hamadneh, N. N., Tilahun, S. L., & Ngnotchouye, J. M. T. (2016). A Review and Comparative Study of Firefly Algorithm and its Modified Versions. In O. Baskan (Ed.), Optimization Algorithms- Methods and Applications. Rijeka: InTech. doi:10.5772/62472

Khan, W. S., Hamadneh, N. N., & Khan, W. A. (2017). Prediction of thermal conductivity of polyvinylpyrrolidone (PVP) electrospun nanocomposite fibers using artificial neural network and prey-predator algorithm. *PLoS One*, *12*(9), e0183920. doi:10.1371/journal.pone.0183920 PMID:28934220

Kheirfam, B. (2010). Multi-parametric sensitivity analysis of the constraint matrix in piecewise linear fractional programming problem. *Journal of Industrial and Management Optimization*, *6*(2), 347–361. doi:10.3934/jimo.2010.6.347

Kheirfam, B., & Hasani, F. (2010). Sensitivity analysis for fuzzy linear programming problems with fuzzy variables. *Advanced Modelling and Optimization*, *12*, 257–272.

Kosinsky, W. (2006). On Fuzzy Number Calculus. *International Journal of Applied Mathematics and Computer Science*, *16*(1), 51–57.

Kuhn, D., Wiesemann, W., & Georghiou, A. (2011). Primal and dual linear decision rules in stochastic and robust optimization. *Mathematical Programming*, *130*(1), 177–209. doi:10.100710107-009-0331-4

Kumar, N., & Chauhan, S. R. (2014). *Evaluation of the effects of engine parameters on performance and emissions of diesel engine operating with biodiesel blend.* Academic Press.

Kumar, V. (2016). *Modified Grey Wolf Algorithm for optimization problems.* Paper presented at the International Conference on Inventive Computation Technologies (ICICT), India.

Kumar, A., & Bhatia, N. (2011). A new method for solving sensitivity analysis for fuzzy linear programming problems. *International Journal of Applied Science and Engineering*, *9*(3), 169–176.

Kumar, N., Varun, & Chauhan, S. R. (2013). Performance and emission characteristics of biodiesel from different origins: A review. *Renewable & Sustainable Energy Reviews*, *21*, 633–658. doi:10.1016/j.rser.2013.01.006

Kumar, S. (2013). Influence of injection timings on performance and emissions of a biodiesel engine operated on blends of Honge methyl ester and prediction using artificial neural network. *Journal of Mechanical Engineering Research*, *5*(1), 5–20. doi:10.5897/JMER12.057

Kuter, S., Akyürek, Z., & Weber, G. W. (2016). Estimation of subpixel snow-covered area by nonparametric regression splines. *The International Archives of the Photogrammetry, Remote Sensing and Spatial Information Sciences*, 42.

Kuter, S., Weber, G. W., Akyürek, Z., & Özmen, A. (2015). Inversion of top of atmospheric reflectance values by conic multivariate adaptive regression splines. *Inverse Problems in Science and Engineering*, *23*(4), 651–669. doi:10.1080/17415977.2014.933828

Laporte, G., Louveaux, F., & Mercure, H. (1992). The vehicle routing problem with stochastic travel times. *Transportation Science*, *26*(3), 161–170. doi:10.1287/trsc.26.3.161

Lapuerta, M., Armas, O., & Rodríguez-Fernández, J. (2008). Effect of biodiesel fuels on diesel engine emissions. *Progress in Energy and Combustion Science*, *34*(2), 198–223. doi:10.1016/j.pecs.2007.07.001

Lee, K. H. (2005). First Course on Fuzzy Set Theory and Applications. Springer.

Li, H.-w., Liu, Q.-y., & Mao, W.-j. (2010). *An Optimized GM(1,1) Model Based on the Modified Construction Method of Background Value.* Paper presented at the Computational and Information Sciences (ICCIS), Chengdu, China. 10.1109/ICCIS.2010.17

Li, K., Liu, L., Zhai, J., Khoshgoftaar, T. M., & Li, T. (2016). The improved grey model based on particle swarm optimization algorithm for time series prediction. *Engineering Applications of Artificial Intelligence*, *55*, 285–291. doi:10.1016/j.engappai.2016.07.005

Lim, S. (2013). A joint optimal pricing and order quantity model under parameter uncertainty and its practical implementation. *Omega*, *41*(6), 998–1007. doi:10.1016/j.omega.2012.12.003

Liu, S., & Forrest, J. Y. L. (2010). *Grey systems: theory and applications.* Springer. doi:10.1007/978-3-642-13938-3

Liu, S., & Lin, Y. (2010). *Grey systems Theory and Applications.* Berlin: Springer.

Liu, S., Yang, Y., & Forrest, J. (2017). *Grey Numbers and Their Operations. In Grey Data Analysis* (pp. 29–43). Springer. doi:10.1007/978-981-10-1841-1_3

Li, X., Tian, P., & Leung, S. (2010). Vehicle routing problems with time windows and stochastic travel and service times: Models and algorithms. *International Journal of Production Economics*, *125*(1), 137–145. doi:10.1016/j.ijpe.2010.01.013

Lobo, M. S. (2000). *Robust and convex optimization with applications in finance* (PhD thesis). Stanford University. Retrieved from http://sousalobo.com/thesis/thesis.pdf

Lotfi, F. H., Jondabeh, M. A., & Faizrahnemoon, M. (2010). Sensitivity analysis in fuzzy environment. *Applied Mathematical Sciences*, *4*, 1635–1646.

Lucieer, A., Stein, A., & Fisher, P. (2005). Multivariate texture-based segmentation of remotely sensed imagery for extraction of objects and their uncertainty. *International Journal of Remote Sensing, 26*(14), 2917–2936. doi:10.1080/01431160500057723

Lu, D., & Weng, Q. (2007). A survey of image classification methods and techniques for improving classification performance. *International Journal of Remote Sensing, 28*(5), 823–870. doi:10.1080/01431160600746456

Madhi, M. H., & Mohamed, N. (2017). A Modified Grey Model Gm (1, 1) Based on Reconstruction of Background Value. *Far East Journal of Mathematical Sciences, 101*(1), 189–199. doi:10.17654/MS101010189

Madhi, M., & Mohamed, N. (2017). An Initial Condition Optimization Approach for Improving the Prediction Precision of a GM (1, 1) Model. *Mathematical and Computational Applications, 22*(1), 21. doi:10.3390/mca22010021

Maleki, H. R., Tata, M., & Mashinchi, M. (2000). Linear programming with fuzzy variables. *Fuzzy Sets and Systems, 109*(1), 21–33. doi:10.1016/S0165-0114(98)00066-9

Mangiaracina, R., Song, G., & Perego, A. (2015). Distribution network design: A literature review and a research agenda. *International Journal of Physical Distribution & Logistics Management, 45*(5), 506–531. doi:10.1108/IJPDLM-02-2014-0035

Manisri, T., Mungwattana, A., & Janssens, G. K. (2011). Minimax optimization approach for the robust vehicle routing problem with time windows and uncertain travel times. *International Journal of Logistics Systems and Management, 10*(4), 461–477. doi:10.1504/IJLSM.2011.043105

Maqsood, I., Huang, G. H., & Zeng, G. (2004). An inexact two-stage mixed integer linear programming model for waste management under uncertainty. *Civil Engineering and Environmental Systems, 21*(3), 187–206. doi:10.1080/10286600410001730698

Martos, B. (1960). Hyperbolic programming by simplex method. Deuxieme Congress Mathematique Hongrois, 2, 44-48.

Martos, B. (1960). Hyperbolic programming. *Publications of the Research Institute for Mathematical Sciences, 5*(B), 386-40.

Masood, M. I., Shah, A. N., Aslam, A., Gul, M., Naveed, A., & Usman, M. (2016). *Combustion and Emission Based Optimization of Turbocharged Diesel Engine Run on Biodiesel using Grey-Taguchi Method Combustion and Emission Based Optimization of Turbocharged Diesel Engine Run on Biodiesel using Grey-Taguchi Method.* Academic Press.

Melo, M. T., Nickel, S., & Gama, F. S. (2005). Dynamic multi-commodity capacitated facility location: A mathematical framework for strategic supply chain planning. *Computers & Operations Research, 33*(1), 181–208. doi:10.1016/j.cor.2004.07.005

Melo, M. T., Nickel, S., & Gama, F. S. (2009). Facility location and supply chain management-A review. *European Journal of Operational Research, 196*(2), 401–412. doi:10.1016/j.ejor.2008.05.007

Messelmi, F. (2013). *Analysis of Dual Functions*, Annual Review of Chaos Theory. *Bifurcations and Dynamical Systems*, *4*, 37–54.

Miranda, P., & Garrido, R. (2009). Inventory service-level optimization within distribution network design problem. *International Journal of Production Economics*, *122*(1), 276–285. doi:10.1016/j.ijpe.2009.06.010

Mirjalili, S., Mirjalili, S. M., & Lewis, A. (2014). Grey wolf optimizer. *Advances in Engineering Software*, *69*, 46–61. doi:10.1016/j.advengsoft.2013.12.007

Moffat, R. J. (1988). *Describing the Uncertainties in Experimental Results*. Academic Press.

Moghaddam, B. F., Ruiz, R., & Sadjadi, S. J. (2012). Vehicle routing with uncertain demands: An advanced particle swarm algorithm. *Computers & Industrial Engineering*, *62*(1), 306–317. doi:10.1016/j.cie.2011.10.001

Mohamed Ismail, H., Ng, H. K., Queck, C. W., & Gan, S. (2012). Artificial neural networks modelling of engine-out responses for a light-duty diesel engine fuelled with biodiesel blends. *Applied Energy*, *92*, 769–777. doi:10.1016/j.apenergy.2011.08.027

Mora-Camino, F., & Faye, R. M. (2017). Commande optimale: Approche Variationnelle. Harmattan.

Mora-Camino, F., & Nunes Cosenza, C. A. (2017). Fuzzy Dual Numbers, Theory and Applications. In Studies in Fuzziness and Soft Computing. Springer.

Mousavi, S. M., Tavakkoli-Moghaddam, R., & Jolai, F. (2013). A possibilistic programming approach for the location problem of multiple cross-docks and vehicle routing scheduling under uncertainty. *Engineering Optimization*, *45*(10), 1223–1249. doi:10.1080/0305215X.2012.729053

Muralidharan, K., Vasudevan, D., & Sheeba, K. N. (2011). Performance, emission and combustion characteristics of biodiesel fuelled variable compression ratio engine. *Energy*, *36*(8), 5385–5393. doi:10.1016/j.energy.2011.06.050

Nasiri, G. R. (2009). *Multi-echelon, Multi-Commodity supply chain designing in an uncertain environment* (Ph.D. Thesis). Amirkabir University of Technology, Tehran, Iran.

Nasiri, G. R., & Davoudpour, H. (2012). Coordinated location, distribution and inventory decisions in supply chain network design: A multi-objective approach. *South African Journal of Industrial Engineering*, *23*(2), 159–175.

Nasiri, G. R., Davoudpour, H., & Karimi, B. (2010a). The Impact of Integrated Analysis on Supply chain Management: A Coordinated Approach for Inventory Control Policy, Supply Chain Management. *International Journal (Toronto, Ont.)*, *15*(4), 277–289.

Nasiri, G. R., Davoudpour, H., & Movahedi, Y. (2010b). A Genetic Algorithm Approach for the Multi-commodity, Multi-period Distribution Planning in a Supply Chain Network Design, SEMCCO 2010. *LNCS*, *6466*, 494–505.

Nasiri, G. R., Nasim, G., & Davoudpour, H. (2015). Location-inventory and shipment decisions in an integrated distribution system: An efficient heuristics solution. *European Journal of Industrial Engineering, 9*(5), 613–637. doi:10.1504/EJIE.2015.071779

Nasiri, G. R., Roholla, Z., & Davoudpour, H. (2014). An integrated supply chain production-distribution planning with stochastic demands. *Computers & Industrial Engineering, 77,* 35–45. doi:10.1016/j.cie.2014.08.005

Nasseri, H. (2006), Fuzzy Numbers: Positive and Nonnegative. *International Mathematical Forum, 3,* 1777-1780.

Nasseri, S. H., Ardil, E., Yazdani, A., & Zaefarian, R. (2005). Simplex method for solving fuzzy variable linear programming problems. *World Academy of Science, Engineering and Technology, 10,* 284–288.

Nemirovski, A. (2012). On safe tractable approximations of chance constraints. *European Journal of Operational Research, 219*(3), 707–718. doi:10.1016/j.ejor.2011.11.006

Niu, D.-x., Zhao, L., Zhang, B., & Wang, H.-f. (2007). The application of particle swarm optimization based grey model to power load forecasting. *Chinese Journal of Management Science, 1,* 12.

Ojala, T., Pietikäinen, M., & Mäenpää, T. (2001, March). A generalized local binary pattern operator for multiresolution gray scale and rotation invariant texture classification. In *International Conference on Advances in Pattern Recognition* (pp. 399-408). Springer Berlin Heidelberg. 10.1007/3-540-44732-6_41

Olhager, J., Pashaei, S., & Sternberg, H. (2015). Dessign of global production and distribution networks: A literature review and research agenda. *International Journal of Physical Distribution & Logistics Management, 45*(1/2), 138–158. doi:10.1108/IJPDLM-05-2013-0131

Ong, H. C., Tilahun, S. L., Lee, W. S., & Ngnotchouye, J. M. T. (2017). Comparative Study of Prey-Predator Algorithm and Firefly Algorithm. *Intelligent Automation & Soft Computing,* 1-8.

Özmen, A., & Weber, G. W. (2012, November). Robust conic generalized partial linear models using RCMARS method-A robustification of CGPLM. In N. Barsoum, D. Faiman, & P. Vasant (Eds.), AIP Conference Proceedings: Vol. 1499. *No. 1* (pp. 337–343). AIP. doi:10.1063/1.4769011

Özmen, A., Weber, G. W., Batmaz, İ., & Kropat, E. (2011). RCMARS: Robustification of CMARS with different scenarios under polyhedral uncertainty set. *Communications in Nonlinear Science and Numerical Simulation, 16*(12), 4780–4787. doi:10.1016/j.cnsns.2011.04.001

Ozsezen, A. N., Canakci, M., Turkcan, A., & Sayin, C. (2009). Performance and combustion characteristics of a DI diesel engine fueled with waste palm oil and canola oil methyl esters. *Fuel, 88*(4), 629–636. doi:10.1016/j.fuel.2008.09.023

Pachbhai, J. S., Deshmukh, P. M. M., & Dhanfule, R. R. (2014). Application of ANN to Optimize The Performance of CI Engine Fuelled With Cotton Seed Oil. *IJETAE, 4*(6), 351–358.

Pali, H. S., Kumar, N., & Alhassan, Y. (2015). Performance and emission characteristics of an agricultural diesel engine fueled with blends of Sal methyl esters and diesel. *Energy Conversion and Management, 90,* 146–153. doi:10.1016/j.enconman.2014.10.064

Pardo, L. (2005). *Statistical inference based on divergence measures.* CRC Press. doi:10.1201/9781420034813

Parida. (2013). Fuzzy Dynamic System Approach to Multistage Decision Making Problems. *Ultra Scientist, 25*(2), 350-360.

Pasandideh, S. H. R., Akhavan Niaki, S. T., & Asadi, K. (2015). Bi-objective optimization of a multi-product multi-period three-echelon supply chain problem under uncertain environments: NSGA-II and NRGA. *Information Sciences, 292,* 57–74. doi:10.1016/j.ins.2014.08.068

Patle, D. S., Sharma, S., Ahmad, Z., & Rangaiah, G. P. (2014). Multi-objective optimization of two alkali catalyzed processes for biodiesel from waste cooking oil. *Energy Conversion and Management, 85,* 361–372. doi:10.1016/j.enconman.2014.05.034

Pattnaik, M. (2013). Fuzzy multi-objective linear programming problems: Sensitivity analysis. *Journal of Mathematics and Computer Science, 7,* 131–137.

Peng. (1992). Stochastic Hamilton-Jacobi-Bellman Equation. *SIAM J. Control Optim., 30*(2), 284–304.

Pereira, M. A., Coelho, L. C., Lorena, L. A. N., & Souza, L. C. (2015). A hybrid method for the probabilistic maximal covering location-allocation problem. *Computers & Operations Research, 57,* 51–59. doi:10.1016/j.cor.2014.12.001

Phan, A. N., & Phan, T. M. (2008). Biodiesel production from waste cooking oils. *Fuel, 87*(17–18), 3490–3496. doi:10.1016/j.fuel.2008.07.008

Pohit, G., & Misra, D. (2013). Optimization of Performance and Emission Characteristics of Diesel Engine with Biodiesel Using Grey-Taguchi Method. *Journal of Engineering, 2013,* 1–8. doi:10.1155/2013/915357

Pontryagin, L. S. (1986). *The Mathematical Theory of Optimal Processes.* Gordon and Breach Science Publishers.

Prékopa, A. (1995). *Stochastic Programming.* Kluwer Academic Publishers. doi:10.1007/978-94-017-3087-7

Pu, P. M., & Liu, Y. M. (1980). Fuzzy topology 1, neighbourhood structure of a fuzzy point and moore-smith convergence. *Journal of Mathematical Analysis and Applications, 76*(2), 571–599. doi:10.1016/0022-247X(80)90048-7

Qi, D., Leick, M., Liu, Y., & Lee, C. F. F. (2011). Effect of EGR and injection timing on combustion and emission characteristics of split injection strategy DI-diesel engine fueled with biodiesel. *Fuel, 90*(5), 1884–1891. doi:10.1016/j.fuel.2011.01.016

Raheman, H., & Ghadge, S. V. (2008). Performance of diesel engine with biodiesel at varying compression ratio and ignition timing. *Fuel, 87*(12), 2659–2666. doi:10.1016/j.fuel.2008.03.006

Rajasekar, E., Murugesan, A., Subramanian, R., & Nedunchezhian, N. (2010). Review of NO x reduction technologies in CI engines fuelled with oxygenated biomass fuels. *Renewable & Sustainable Energy Reviews, 14*(7), 2113–2121. doi:10.1016/j.rser.2010.03.005

Rakopoulos, C. D., Antonopoulos, K. A., & Rakopoulos, D. C. (2007). Experimental heat release analysis and emissions of a HSDI diesel engine fueled with ethanol-diesel fuel blends. *Energy, 32*(10), 1791–1808. doi:10.1016/j.energy.2007.03.005

Razi, F. F., & Shahabi, V. (2016). Forming the stock optimized portfolio using model Grey based on C5 and the Shuffled frog leap algorithm. *Journal of Statistics and Management Systems, 19*(3), 397–421. doi:10.1080/09720510.2015.1086165

Rosenberg, D. E. (2009). Shades of Grey: A critical review of grey number optimization. *Engineering Optimization, 41*(6), 573–592. doi:10.1080/03052150902718125

Ross, T. J. (2005). *Fuzzy Logic with Engineering Applications* (2nd ed.). Singapore: John Wiley and Sons Private Limited.

Ross, P. J. (1988). *Taguchi Techniques for Quality Engineering*. New York: McGraw-Hill.

Russell, R. A., & Urban, T. L. (2008). Vehicle routing with soft time windows and Erlang travel times. *The Journal of the Operational Research Society, 59*(9), 1220–1228. doi:10.1057/palgrave. jors.2602465

Ruszczynski, A., & Shapiro, A. (2003). Stochastic Programming. *Handbooks in Operations Research and Management Science, 10*.

Sadjady, H., & Davoudpour, H. (2012). Two-echelon multi commodity supply chain network design with mode selection, lead- times and inventory costs. *Computers & Operations Research, 39*(7), 1345–1354. doi:10.1016/j.cor.2011.08.003

Sahoo, P. K., & Das, L. M. (2009a). Combustion analysis of Jatropha, Karanja and Polanga based biodiesel as fuel in a diesel engine. *Fuel, 88*(6), 994–999. doi:10.1016/j.fuel.2008.11.012

Sahoo, P. K., & Das, L. M. (2009b). Process optimization for biodiesel production from Jatropha, Karanja and Polanga oils. *Fuel, 88*(9), 1588–1594. doi:10.1016/j.fuel.2009.02.016

Sakawa, M., & Yano, H. (1988). An interactive fuzzy satisficing method for multi-objective linear fractional programming problems. *Fuzzy Sets and Systems, 28*(2), 129–144. doi:10.1016/0165-0114(88)90195-9

Salehi, H., Moghaddam, R. T., & Nasiri, G. (2015). A multi-objective location-allocation problem with lateral transshipment between distribution centers. *International Journal of Logistics Systems and Management, 22*(4), 464–482. doi:10.1504/IJLSM.2015.072749

Saravanan, S., Nagarajan, G., Lakshmi Narayana Rao, G., & Sampath, S. (2014). Theoretical and experimental investigation on effect of injection timing on NOx emission of biodiesel blend. *Energy*, *66*(x), 216–221. doi:10.1016/j.energy.2014.01.003

Sari, K., Tighiouart, F., & Tighiouart, B. (2015). Using unsupervised neural network approach to improve classification of satellite images. *International Journal of Computer Applications in Technology*, *51*(1), 3–8. doi:10.1504/IJCAT.2015.068393

Sathish Kumar, R., Sureshkumar, K., & Velraj, R. (2015). Optimization of biodiesel production from Manilkara zapota (L.) seed oil using Taguchi method. *Fuel*, *140*(x), 90–96. doi:10.1016/j.fuel.2014.09.103

Sayin, C., & Gumus, M. (2011). Impact of compression ratio and injection parameters on the performance and emissions of a DI diesel engine fueled with biodiesel-blended diesel fuel. *Applied Thermal Engineering*, *31*(16), 3182–3188. doi:10.1016/j.applthermaleng.2011.05.044

Shivakumar, S. P., Srinivasa Pai, P., & Shrinivasa Rao, B. R. (2011). Artificial Neural Network based prediction of performance and emission characteristics of a variable compression ratio CI engine using WCO as a biodiesel at different injection timings. *Applied Energy*, *88*(7), 2344–2354. doi:10.1016/j.apenergy.2010.12.030

Sifeng, L. J. F. Y. Y. (2012). A brief introduction to grey systems theory", Grey Systems. *Theory and Application*, *2*(2), 89–104.

Sivasakthivel, T., Murugesan, K., & Thomas, H. R. (2014). Optimization of operating parameters of ground source heat pump system for space heating and cooling by Taguchi method and utility concept. *Applied Energy*, *116*, 76–85. doi:10.1016/j.apenergy.2013.10.065

Song, W., Ming, X., & Liu, H-C. (2017). Identifying critical risk factors of sustainable supply chain management: A rough strength-relation analysis method. *Journal of Cleaner Production*, *143*, 100-115.

Sörensen, K., & Sevaux, M. (2009). A practical approach for robust and flexible vehicle routing using metaheuristics and Monte Carlo sampling. *Journal of Mathematical Modelling and Algorithms*, *8*(4), 387–407. doi:10.100710852-009-9113-5

Sourirajan, K., Ozsen, L., & Uzsoy, U. (2009). A genetic algorithm for a single product network design model with lead time and safety stock considerations. *European Journal of Operational Research*, *197*(2), 599–608. doi:10.1016/j.ejor.2008.07.038

Stanujkic, D., Magdalinovic, N., Jovanovic, R., & Stojanovic, S. (2012). An objective multi-criteria approach to optimization using MOORA method and interval grey numbers. *Technological and Economic Development of Economy*, *18*(2), 331–363. doi:10.3846/20294913.2012.676996

Stengel, R. (1993). *Optimal Control and Estimation*. New York: Dover publications.

Sungur, F., Ordonez, F., & Dessouky, M. M. (2008). A robust optimization approach for the capacitated vehicle routing problem with demand uncertainty. *IIE Transactions*, *40*(5), 509–523. doi:10.1080/07408170701745378

Sun, J., Caton, J. A., & Jacobs, T. J. (2010). Oxides of nitrogen emissions from biodiesel-fuelled diesel engines. *Progress in Energy and Combustion Science*, *36*(6), 677–695. doi:10.1016/j. pecs.2010.02.004

Suruliandi, A., & Ramar, K. (2008, December). Local texture patterns-a univariate texture model for classification of images. In *Advanced Computing and Communications, 2008. ADCOM 2008. 16th International Conference on* (pp. 32-39). IEEE. 10.1109/ADCOM.2008.4760424

Suruliandi, A. (2009). *Study on classification of remotely sensed multispectral mages-a textural approach*. Tamil Nadu, India: Manonmaniam Sundaranar University.

Suruliandi, A., & Jenicka, S. (2015). Texture-based classification of remotely sensed images. *International Journal of Signal and Imaging Systems Engineering*, *8*(4), 260–272. doi:10.1504/ IJSISE.2015.070546

Swarup, K., Gupta, P. K., & Mohan, M. (1997). *Operations Research* (8th ed.). S.Chand and Publishers.

Szmidt, E., & Kacprzyk, S. (2000). Distances between intuitionistic fuzzy sets. *Fuzzy Sets and Systems*, *114*(3), 505–518. doi:10.1016/S0165-0114(98)00244-9

Taha, H. M. (n.d.). *Operations Research- An Introduction with AMPL, Solver, Excel and Tora Implementations* (8th ed.). Prentice Hall.

Tanaka, H., Ichihashi, H., & Asai, K. (1974). On Fuzzy Mathematical Programming. *Journal of Cybernetics*, *3*(4), 37–46. doi:10.1080/01969727308545912

Tanaka, H., Ichihashi, H., & Asai, K. (1986). A value of information in FLP problems via sensitivity analysis. *Fuzzy Sets and Systems*, *18*(2), 119–129. doi:10.1016/0165-0114(86)90015-1

Tanh, P. N., Bostel, N., & Peton, O. (2008). A dynamic model for facility location in the design of complex supply chains. *International Journal of Production Economics*, *113*(2), 678–693. doi:10.1016/j.ijpe.2007.10.017

Tan, X., & Triggs, B. (2010). Enhanced local texture feature sets for face recognition under difficult lighting conditions. *IEEE Transactions on Image Processing*, *19*(6), 1635–1650. doi:10.1109/ TIP.2010.2042645 PMID:20172829

Tesfa, B., Mishra, R., Gu, F., & Powles, N. (2010). Prediction models for density and viscosity of biodiesel and their effects on fuel supply system in CI engines. *Renewable Energy*, *35*(12), 2752–2760. doi:10.1016/j.renene.2010.04.026

Thissen, U., Pepers, M., Üstün, B., Melssen, W., & Buydens, L. (2004). Comparing support vector machines to PLS for spectral regression applications. *Chemometrics and Intelligent Laboratory Systems*, *73*(2), 169–179. doi:10.1016/j.chemolab.2004.01.002

Tilahun, S. L., & Ong, H. C. (2013). Prey-predator algorithm: A new metaheuristic algorithm for optimization problems. *International Journal of Information Technology & Decision Making*, 1–22.

Tilahun, S. L., Kassa, S. M., & Ong, H. C. (2012). *A new algorithm for multilevel optimization problems using evolutionary strategy, inspired by natural adaptation. In PRICAI 2012: Trends in Artificial Intelligence* (pp. 577–588). Springer.

Tilahun, S. L., Ngnotchouye, J. M. T., & Hamadneh, N. N. (2017). Continuous versions of firefly algorithm: A review. *Artificial Intelligence Review*, 1–48.

Tilahun, S. L., & Ong, H. C. (2014). Comparison between genetic algorithm and prey-predator algorithm. *Malaysian Journal of Fundamental and Applied Sciences*, 9(4). doi:10.11113/mjfas.v9n4.104

Tran, L., & Duckstein, L. (2002). Comparison of fuzzy numbers using a fuzzy distance measure. *Fuzzy Sets and Systems*, 130(3), 331–341. doi:10.1016/S0165-0114(01)00195-6

Turan, B., Minner, S., & Hartl, R. F. (2017). A VNS approach to multi-location inventory redistribution with vehicle routing. *Computers & Operations Research*, 78, 526–536. doi:10.1016/j.cor.2016.02.018

Vahdani, B., Tavakoli-Moghaddam, R., & Jolai, F. (2013). Reliable design of a logistics network under uncertainty: A fuzzy possibilistic queuing model. *Applied Mathematical Modelling*, 37(5), 3254–3268. doi:10.1016/j.apm.2012.07.021

Van der Vorst, J. G. A. J., & Beulens, A. J. M. (2002). Identifying sources of uncertainty to generate supply chain redesign strategies. *International Journal of Physical Distribution & Logistics Management*, 32(6), 409–430. doi:10.1108/09600030210437951

Van Woensel, T., Kerbache, L., Peremans, H., & Vandaele, N. (2008). Vehicle routing with dynamic travel times: A queueing approach. *European Journal of Operational Research*, 186(3), 990–1007. doi:10.1016/j.ejor.2007.03.012

Vasant, P. (2015). Handbook of Research on Artificial Intelligence Techniques and Algorithms (Vols. 1-2). IGI Global. doi:10.4018/978-1-4666-7258-1

Vasant, P., & M., K. (2017). *Handbook of Research on Holistic Optimization Techniques in the Hospitality, Tourism, and Travel Industry*. IGI Global.

Vasant, P. (Ed.). (2011). *Innovation in Power, Control, and Optimization: Emerging Energy Technologies: Emerging Energy Technologies*. IGI Global.

Vasant, P. (Ed.). (2016). *Handbook of Research on Modern Optimization Algorithms and Applications in Engineering and Economics*. IGI Global. doi:10.4018/978-1-4666-9644-0

Vasant, P. M. (2014). *Handbook of Research on Novel Soft Computing Intelligent Algorithms: Theory and Practical Applications* (Vols. 1–2). IGI Global. doi:10.4018/978-1-4666-4450-2

Vasant, P. M. (Ed.). (2012). *Meta-heuristics optimization algorithms in engineering, business, economics, and finance*. IGI Global.

Vasant, P., & Voropai, N. (2016). *Sustaining Power Resources through Energy Optimization and Engineering*. IGI Global. doi:10.4018/978-1-4666-9755-3

Vayanos, P., Kuhn, D., & Rustem, B. Decision rules for information discovery in multi-stage stochastic programming. In *Decision and Control and European Control Conference (CDC-ECC), 2011 50th IEEE Conference on* (pp. 7368–7373). IEEE. 10.1109/CDC.2011.6161382

Verma, V., & Murugesan, K. (2014). Optimization of solar assisted ground source heat pump system for space heating application by Taguchi method and utility concept. *Energy and Building*, *82*, 296–309. doi:10.1016/j.enbuild.2014.07.029

Voxman, W. (1998). Some remarks on distances between fuzzy numbers. *Fuzzy Sets and Systems*, *100*(1-3), 353–365. doi:10.1016/S0165-0114(97)00090-0

Wang, X., & Curry, D. J. (2012). A robust approach to the share-of-choice product design problem. *Omega*, *40*(6), 818–826. doi:10.1016/j.omega.2012.01.004

Wang, Y., Wei, F., Sun, C., & Li, Q. (2016). The Research of Improved Grey GM (1, 1) model to predict the postprandial glucose in Type 2 diabetes. *BioMed Research International*. PMID:27314034

Weber, G. W., Batmaz, İ., Köksal, G., Taylan, P., & Yerlikaya-Özkurt, F. (2012). CMARS: A new contribution to nonparametric regression with multivariate adaptive regression splines supported by continuous optimization. *Inverse Problems in Science and Engineering*, *20*(3), 371–400. doi:10.1080/17415977.2011.624770

What is Fuzzy Number? (n.d.). Retrieved from http://whatis.techtarget.com/definition/fuzzy-number

Wiesemann, W., Kuhn, D., & Sim, M. (2014). Distributionally robust convex optimization. *Operations Research*, *62*(6), 1358–1376. doi:10.1287/opre.2014.1314

Win, Z., Gakkhar, R. P., Jain, S. C., & Bhattacharya, M. (2005). Investigation of diesel engine operating and injection system parameters for low noise, emissions, and fuel consumption using Taguchi methods. *Proceedings of the Institution of Mechanical Engineers. Part D, Journal of Automobile Engineering*, *219*(10), 1237–1250. doi:10.1243/095440705X34865

Xie, N., & Liu, S. (2009). Discrete grey forecasting model and its optimization. *Applied Mathematical Modelling*, *33*(2), 1173–1186. doi:10.1016/j.apm.2008.01.011

Yang, Y. (2010). Extended Grey Numbers. *Advances in Grey Systems Research*, 73-85.

Yang, X.-S. (2010). *Nature-inspired metaheuristic algorithms*. Luniver press.

Yang, X.-S. (2011). Review of meta-heuristics and generalised evolutionary walk algorithm. *International Journal of Bio-inspired Computation*, *3*(2), 77–84. doi:10.1504/IJBIC.2011.039907

Yang, X.-S. (2013). Multiobjective firefly algorithm for continuous optimization. *Engineering with Computers*, *29*(2), 175–184. doi:10.100700366-012-0254-1

Yanıkoğlu, Gorissen, & den Hertog. (2017). *Adjustable Robust Optimization – A Survey and Tutorial.* Available online at ResearchGate.

Yanıkoğlu, İ., & den Hertog, D. (2013). Safe approximations of ambiguous chance constraints using historical data. *INFORMS Journal on Computing, 25*(4), 666–681. doi:10.1287/ijoc.1120.0529

Yanıkoğlu, İ., & Kuhn, D. (2017). Decision rule bounds for two-stage stochastic bilevel programs. *SIAM Journal on Optimization.* (in press)

Yan, S., & Tang, C.-H. (2009). Inter-city bus scheduling under variable market share and uncertain market demands. *Omega, 37*(1), 178–192. doi:10.1016/j.omega.2006.11.008

Yao, J.-S., & Wu, K. (2000). Ranking fuzzy numbers based on decomposition principle and signed distance. *Fuzzy Sets and Systems, 116*(2), 275–288. doi:10.1016/S0165-0114(98)00122-5

Ye, P., & Boehman, A. L. (2012). An investigation of the impact of injection strategy and biodiesel on engine NO x and particulate matter emissions with a common-rail turbocharged di diesel engine. *Fuel, 97*(x), 476–488. doi:10.1016/j.fuel.2012.02.021

Ying, H. (2000). *Fuzzy Control and Modelling: Analytical Foundations and Applications.* Wiley-IEEE Press. doi:10.1109/9780470544730

Yu, V. F., & Lin, S.-Y. (2015). A simulated annealing heuristic for the open location-routing problem. *Computers & Operations Research, 62,* 184–196. doi:10.1016/j.cor.2014.10.009

Yuvarajan, D., Ravikumar, J., & Babu, M. D. (2016). Analytical Methods Simultaneous optimization of smoke and NO x emissions in a stationary diesel engine fuelled with diesel – oxygenate blends using the grey relational analysis in the Taguchi method. *Analytical Methods, 8*(x), 6222–6230. doi:10.1039/C6AY01696K

Yuvarajan, D., Ravikumar, J., Babu, M. D., Jadhav, S. D., Tandale, M. S., Gul, M., ... Masood, I. (2016). Multi-variable optimization of diesel engine fuelled with biodiesel using grey-Taguchi method. *Journal of the Brazilian Society of Mechanical Sciences and Engineering, 38*(2), 621–632. doi:10.100740430-015-0312-x

Yu, W., Gan, L., Yang, S., Ding, Y., Jiang, P., Wang, J., & Li, S. (2014). An improved LBP algorithm for texture and face classification. *Signal, Image and Video Processing, 8*(1), 155–161. doi:10.100711760-014-0652-5

Zadeh, L. A. (1965). Fuzzy sets. *Information and Control, 8*(3), 338–353. doi:10.1016/S0019-9958(65)90241-X

Zavadskas, E. K., Kaklauskas, A., Turskis, Z., & Tamošaitienė, J. (2009). Multi-attribute decision-making model by applying grey numbers. *Informatica, 20*(2), 305–320.

Zhang, Y., Snyder, L. V., Ralphs, T. K., & Xue, Z. (2016). The competitive facility location problem under disruption risks. *Transportation Research Part E, Logistics and Transportation Review, 93,* 453–473. doi:10.1016/j.tre.2016.07.002

Zhou, J., Ren, J., & Yao, C. (2017). Multi-objective optimization of multi-axis ball-end milling Inconel 718 via grey relational analysis coupled with RBF neural network and PSO algorithm. *Measurement*, *102*, 271–285. doi:10.1016/j.measurement.2017.01.057

Zimmermann, H. J. (1986). Fuzzy Sets Theory and Mathematical Programming. In A. Jones & ... (Eds.), *Fuzzy Sets Theory and Applications* (pp. 99–114). D.Reidel Publishing Company. doi:10.1007/978-94-009-4682-8_7

Zimmermann, H.-J. (1978). Fuzzy programming and linear programming with several objective functions. *Fuzzy Sets and Systems*, *1*(1), 45–55. doi:10.1016/0165-0114(78)90031-3

Zimmermann, H.-J. (1983). Fuzzy mathematical programming. *Computers & Operations Research*, *10*(4), 291–298. doi:10.1016/0305-0548(83)90004-7

Zimmermann, H.-J. (2001). *Fuzzy Set Theory and Its Applications*. Boston: Kluwer Academic Publishers. doi:10.1007/978-94-010-0646-0

About the Contributors

Hakim Bouadi graduated in Electrical Engineering with MSc from Algiers University, he obtained PhD in Flight Control from Toulouse University and ENAC. Currently he is Head of Guidance & Navigation Laboratory at Ecole Militaire Polytechnique in Algiers, Algeria.

Kris Braekers is an assistant professor in the research group Logistics of Hasselt University, Belgium. He got his doctoral degree in Business Economics on the topic Optimisation of Empty Container Movements in Intermodal Transport in 2012 from the Faculty of Business Economics, Hasselt University. Currently he is focusing on solving complex combinatorial optimization problems in the context of transport and logistics, mainly using meta-heuristic solution approaches. Topics of interest include rich vehicle routing problems, train load planning in intermodal transportation, operational planning problems in warehouses, and emergency department modelling.

Elena Capitanul Conea graduated from Polytechnic Institute in Bucharest with MSc and PhD from Toulouse University and ENAC.

Carlos Alberto Nunes Cosenza, MSc from UFRJ in Rio de Janeiro and PhD from UFSC in Florianopolis, Brazil, Research Fellow at Cambridge University, LAAS du CNRS and ENAC in Toulouse, founder of Labfuzzy at COPPE, Professor Emeritus.

Moumita Deb completed her B.Sc. (Mathematics) from G.C.College, Silchar in 1996, Masters degree in Mathematics from Assam University, Silchar in 1999. In 2001, she has received B.Ed. degree from Teachers' Training College, Silchar which is affiliated from Assam University, Silchar. She has awarded Ph.D. degree in Mathematics from Department of Mathematics, National Institute of Technology Silchar in May'2016. Her research interests include linear fractional programming problem and multi-objective linear fractional prosgramming problem, Stochastic programming under fuzzy set theory. Currently she is working as a Faculty of Mathematics in Karimganj Polytechnic, Maizgram, Karimganj, Assam, India.

Roger Marcelin Faye graduated in Electrical Engineering from Ecole Supérieure Polytechnique of Senegal with PhD in Control from Toulouse University and LAAS du CNRS. He was a full professor at Cheikh Anta Diop University and currently he is Director of the UFR of Engineering Sciences and Techniques at Amadou Mahtar Mbow newly created university.

R. P. Gakkhar is Professor (retired), Department of Mechanical & Industrial Engineering, IIT Roorkee. He is PhD from University of Roorkee. He is working on biofuels, I C engines, Combustion and Optimization techniques.

Nawaf N. Hamadneh received his bachelor's and Master's degree in Mathematics from Jordan Universities, and his PhD in Applied Mathematics/ artificial intelligence from Universiti Sains Malaysia, Malaysia. He is a researcher in artificial neural networks, mathematical optimization, clustering, and decision making. Currently, he is an assistant professor in Saudi Electronic university- Medina branch, Saudi Arabia.

Gerrit K. Janssens received a Ph.D. in Computer Science from the Free University of Brussels (VUB), Belgium. After some years of work at General Motors Continental, Antwerp, he joined the University of Antwerp (Faculty of Business Administration) until the year 2000. From then, he was Professor of Operations Management and Logistics at the Hasselt University within the Faculty of Business Economics. He also holds the CPIM certificate of the American Production and Inventory Control Society (APICS). During the last twenty years he has been several times visiting faculty in universities in Thailand, Vietnam, Philippines, Cambodia, South-Africa and Zimbabwe, mostly within the framework of development cooperation. Since October 2016 he is emeritus Professor. His main research interests include the development and application of operations research models in production and distribution logistics.

Fariborz Jolai has graduated from Polytechnique of Tehran, Tehran, Iran (BS, 1988 and M.Sc. of Industrial Engineering, 1991) and from Institute National Polytechnique de Grenoble, Grenoble, France (DEA Diploma 1995 and Ph.D in Industrial Engineering 1998). He is head of school of Industrial Engineering, College of Engineering, University of Tehran, His current research interests are modelling and solving optimizations problems such as supply chains networks, production and scheduling problems with uncertainty.

Fabio Krykhtine is PhD from COPPE, Federal University of Rio de Janeiro. He is currently the manager of Klam company devoted to development of decision making tools for industry and commerce.

Rajesh Kumar is a PhD research scholar. He completed his ME from university of Delhi, India. He has two years teaching experience. He is working on combustion, biofuels, I C engines, optimization.

Pu Li received the M.Eng. degree from Zhejiang University, Hangzhou, China, in 1989, and the Ph.D. degree from the Technical University of Berlin, Berlin, Germany, in 1998. He was a Senior Researcher with the Technical University of Berlin, Berlin, Germany, from 1998 to 2005. Since 2005, he has been a Full Professor with the Ilmenau University of Technology, Ilmenau, Germany. His research interest is process systems engineering, i.e., modeling, simulation, optimization, and control of industrial processes.

Felix Mora-Camino graduated in Aeronautical Engineering from ENSICA, MSc and D.Ing. from Applied Science Institute INSA and D.Sc. from Paul Sabatier University, all in Toulouse, France. He has been successively professor at Federal University of Rio de Janeiro, Marrocco Royal Air Force Academy and French Civil Aviation Institute ENAC in Toulouse. He is currently adjunct staff at the rank of Professor with the Systems Science Institute of Durban University of Technology-DUT.

Walid Moudani graduated from the University of Lebanon, with MSc and PhD from Toulouse University in France. Professor Walid Moudani currently works at the Doctorate School of Science and Technology, Lebanese University. Walid does research in Data Mining, Computing in Mathematics, Natural Science, Engineering and Medicine and Algorithms.

G. Reza Nasiri received his M.S. and Ph.D. from The Amirkabir University of Technology in Industrial and Operations Research. His research interests include supply chain and distribution planning, inventory systems analysis and operations research applications in FMCG industries. He has published his research in supply chain management: an international journal, lecture notes on computer sciences, Computers & Industrial Engineering, etc.

Adem Guluma Negewo earned his Bachelors and Masters degrees in Mathematics from Haramaya University and Addis Ababa University respectively. He is now working for Addis Ababa Science and Technology University as a Lecturer of Mathematics.

Jenicka S. (Associate Professor, Sethu Institute of Technology, Pulloor, Kariapatti Taluk, Virudhunagar District) completed her under graduation in Computer Science and Engineering at Thyagarajar College of Engineering, Madurai, Tamil Nadu in

1994. Later she finished her post graduation in the same discipline in 2009 from Manonmaniam Sundaranar University, Tirunelveli. She was awarded Ph.D in the same discipline in 2014. Her interests include Satellite image processing and texture segmentation. She has several notable online publications with citation indices.

İhsan Yanıkoğlu is an Assistant Professor of Industrial Engineering at Özyeğin University, İstanbul, Turkey. He obtained his Ph.D. in Econometrics and Operations Research at Tilburg University in 2014. His research focuses on developing robust optimization methodologies and their applications in real-life problems. His research has been published in journals such as SIAM Journal on Optimization, INFORMS Journal on Computing, IISE Transactions, and OMEGA.

Lunlong Zhong graduated in Engineering in China with MSC from CAUC and PhD from Toulouse University and the French Civil Aviation Institute -ENAC at Toulouse. Currently he is part of the Tianjin Key Laboratory for Advanced Signal Processing at CAUC.

Index

Stay Current on the Latest Emerging Research Developments

Become an IGI Global Reviewer for Authored Book Projects

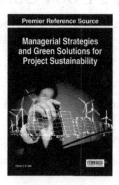

The overall success of an authored book project is dependent on quality and timely reviews.

In this competitive age of scholarly publishing, constructive and timely feedback significantly decreases the turnaround time of manuscripts from submission to acceptance, allowing the publication and discovery of progressive research at a much more expeditious rate. Several IGI Global authored book projects are currently seeking highly qualified experts in the field to fill vacancies on their respective editorial review boards:

Applications may be sent to:
development@igi-global.com

Applicants must have a doctorate (or an equivalent degree) as well as publishing and reviewing experience. Reviewers are asked to write reviews in a timely, collegial, and constructive manner. All reviewers will begin their role on an ad-hoc basis for a period of one year, and upon successful completion of this term can be considered for full editorial review board status, with the potential for a subsequent promotion to Associate Editor.

If you have a colleague that may be interested in this opportunity,
we encourage you to share this information with them.

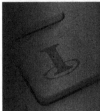